A SPIRITUAL GUIDE TO HEAL YOUR CHRONIC PAIN:
Backaches, Headaches, Shoulder Pain, Arthritis and Fibromyalgia

Compelled by his teenage daughter's disability, the author immersed himself into discovering the roadblocks leading to ever persisting psychophysiological stress, the pure outcome of our modern lifestyle of convenience.

A SPIRITUAL GUIDE TO HEAL YOUR CHRONIC PAIN:

Backaches, Headaches, Shoulder Pain, Arthritis and Fibromyalgia

DR. GREG FORS
Founder of Fenix Recovery Enterprises

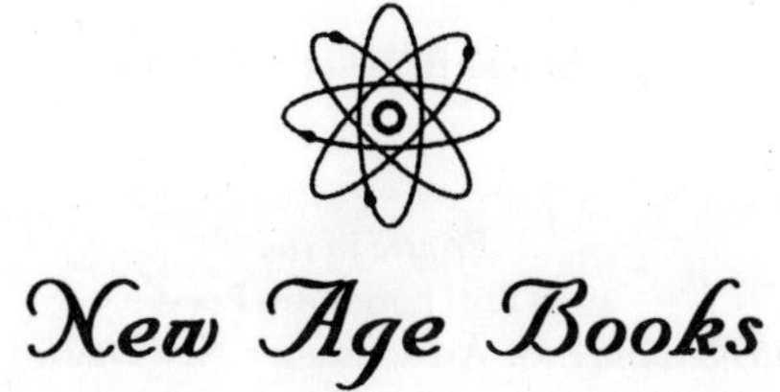

A SPIRITUAL GUIDE TO HEAL YOUR CHRONIC PAIN

ISBN: 978-81-7822-356-8

First Indian Edition: Delhi, 2011
First Edition: 2007

Published by Llewellyn Publications
Woodbury, MN 55125-2989, USA
www.llewellyn.com

Disclaimer

The author, publisher, and/or their respective directors, shareholders, officers, employees, agents, trainers, contractors, representatives, and successors do not guarantee or warrant the quality, accuracy, completeness, timeliness, appropriateness, or suitabilility of the information in this or any product or service referenced by this book. All information in this book is provided on an "as is" basis, and the author and publisher make no representations or warranties of any kind with respect to this information.

Published by
NEW AGE BOOKS
A-44 Naraina Industrial Area, Phase-I
New Delhi (India)-110 028
Email: nab@vsnl.in
Website: www.newagebooksindia.com

For Sale in South Asia Only

Printed in India
at Shri Jainendra Press
A-45 Naraina Indl. Area, Phase-I, New Delhi-110 028

This book is dedicated
to my daughter, Phoenix,
who courageously arose
out of the ashes
of her chronic pain.

Contents

SECTION 2
Roadblocks to Healing, 44

Book Two

THE TRIANGLE OF HEALING: PHYSICAL/BIOCHEMICAL/SPIRITUAL, III

SECTION 3
Physically Healing Your Pain, 112

11: SOLVING THE MYSTERY OF YOUR CHRONIC SHOULDER AND ARM PAIN 161

13: OVERCOMING UPPER BACK, NECK, AND CHRONIC HEAD PAIN 205

SECTION 4
Biochemically Healing Your Pain, 228

SECTION 5
Spiritually Healing Your Pain, 326

Disclaimer

This book provides general wellness management, in an informational and educational manner only. The information provided is general in nature and is not specific to you, the reader. The information provided is intended only to assist you and others in your wellness efforts. Reliance on any information provided by this book, the publisher, author, or others appearing within these informational materials or in conjunction with these educational materials is solely at your own risk.

Nothing in this book should be construed as personal advice, diagnosis, or treatment for any disease, disorder, or ailment and must not be used in this manner. Never disregard professional medical advice or delay in seeking medical attention because of something you have read in this book. Always seek a proper diagnosis and treatment from a qualified health-care provider before you begin any home-care or self-care program. If you think you may have a medical emergency, call your doctor or 911 immediately.

The information provided about conditions is general in nature only. The information in this book must not be considered complete and does not purport to cover the diagnosis or treatment of any disease, disorder, or ailment. The purpose of this book is to compliment, amplify, and supplement other sources of information. You are urged to pursue all available materials and professional opinions to learn as much as possible about your muscle and joint pain (called myofascial pain in this book), and tailor the information to your own individual needs.

Because aches and pains can be caused by underlying pathological processes and diseases, such as but not limited to fractures, tumors, and infections, you must consult a physician before beginning any home-care program for any myofascial pain. This book cannot and must not be used in place of a visit to a competent health-care professional. You should consult a health-care provider before adopting any suggestions in this book on myofascial pain or before drawing any inferences from the information provided herein. If a doctor or therapist is presently treating you for your myofascial pain, it is highly recommended that you share with them knowledge gained from this book. Show him or her what you are doing for home care of your myofascial pain.

Acknowledgments

I am very grateful to my daughter, Phoenix, whose challenges with fibromyalgia and courageous fight to recover were the primary inspirations for this book. Additionally, her help in putting the manuscript together and her patient ability to transform my sketches into discernable graphics helped to make this book possible. Moreover, her willingness to serve as my lovely model for the photographs is deeply appreciated.

In addition, I want to extend a heartfelt thanks to my other wonderful children, Odin and April, for all their moral support during this project. Furthermore, I extend my deep gratitude to my dear friend and mother of my children, Carolyn Heyneker Fors, for her support and encouragement throughout the entire process. Our discussions and her patient editing of the manuscript helped to make this book possible.

I also want to thank my dear friend Lowell Nelson for his editing as well as the insights that he brought to this work.

A special thanks goes out to all of the Llewellyn staff who worked on this book. A strong sense of gratitude extends to Carrie Obry for believing in the importance of this book and my ability to communicate it. Our many discussions and her constant support made this book possible. Rebecca Zins has been a wonderful editor and a real pleasure to work with; I greatly appreciate her enthusiasm and her attention to detail.

Finally, a special thank-you goes out to my many mentors, named and unnamed: Dr. Jeffrey Bland for his inspirational instruction in human nutrition, Dr. Thomas Bergmann for his expert training in the care of the human frame, and many more, who must remain unnamed for the sake of brevity, but who are not forgotten.

Introduction

If you are one of the millions of "walking wounded" who suffer with pain in your back, neck, or extremities, or the all-over ache of fibromyalgia, this comprehensive self-care manual was written specifically for you. Perhaps the title caught your eye because someone you love suffers with chronic pain or you are a health-care provider that must face chronic pain disorders in your practice every day. Either way, this book will be a valuable reference guide to help you heal your pain or assist others in healing theirs.

Pain is something most of us fear and try to avoid, yet chronic physical and emotional pain is something that is all too common in our society today. Pain is the most common reason anyone seeks the advice of a health-care provider. The good news is that there is hope to have the life you may now only dream of; you *can* heal your pain! To accomplish this, though, the primary question to ask is not "How do I get out of pain?" The question to ask is "What good will I bring to life when I heal my pain?" When we begin by imagining all the goodness we can bring to others—to the earth itself—with our newfound freedom from pain and suffering, it is *then* that we begin to really heal.

As a doctor of chiropractic and a board-certified neurologist who specializes in chronic myofascial pain disorders, I will show you the paths to healing your pain in this book. In addition, I will uncover for you practical and effective ways to accomplish this. However, to fully find freedom from suffering and become truly healthy, we must compassionately connect with something greater than our physical and emotional self; this subject is covered in detail in section 5.

The word *freedom* gives us our first clue to the path we must follow, for it comes from the ancient root *freon*, meaning "to love," and the suffix *-dom,* meaning "the state, domain, or condition of." Therefore, if we want freedom from our suffering, we must do so by entering the domain or condition of loving. With this always in mind, what you do to heal—eating a healthier diet, becoming more active, exercising, whatever it is—is done out of love for one's true self, for this earth, and for those around us. With this, each act of healing is connected to a greater purpose in life, and *this* is where real, sustainable health begins. Look around you: in a world that holds so much potential for beauty and grace, why is it filled with so much pain and suffering? Where does one even begin? We can only begin with our self to build a more peaceful world within us and around us, a process I explore step-by-step in the second half of the book, The Triangle of Healing: Physical / Biochemical / Spiritual.

Chronic Pain: Ignored and Misunderstood

If you suffer from chronic pain, it is easy to feel isolated, but you are not alone. Chronic nonpathological pain is actually very common. It is now estimated that as many as 105 million Americans have some element of chronic pain in their lives, and about 50 million Americans are partially or totally disabled due to their chronic pain. As we shall discover, problems involving the myofascial tissues of the musculoskeletal system are the most common causes of chronic pain. The American College of Rheumatology reports that more than 75 million adults in the United States at any given time are affected by pain and stiffness of their musculoskeletal system. Chronic pain disorders of the muscles and joints are the leading cause of work-related disability among men and women aged 16 to 72 years. Furthermore, chronic back pain is now the most common cause of disability in Americans younger than 45 years old. It is estimated that as many as 10 million individuals currently struggle with the disabling pain and fatigue of fibromyalgia, and the number of diagnosed cases is increasing.

Chronic Pain Statistics

- 105 million Americans suffer with chronic pain.
- 50 million Americans are partially or totally disabled by their chronic pain.
- 75 million adults are affected by pain and stiffness.
- Chronic muscle / joint pain is the leading cause of work disability.
- Back pain is the leading cause of disability in those younger than 45 years old.
- 10 million are now diagnosed with fibromyalgia.

Yet chronic myofascial pain disorders do not get the proper attention that they deserve, even though they are extremely common and can make life unbearable. When you are one of the millions of the "walking wounded" suffering with the *unwellness* of chronic pain and fatigue, chances are there is no diagnosable pathology. This can make it very difficult for you to find a clinician who takes a serious comprehensive and integrative approach to your chronic pain. All too often it is dismissed as being "all in your head," adding insult to injury when your life has already been turned upside-down by chronic pain. In fact, the leading prescriptions for individuals with chronic myofascial pain disorders are NSAIDs (nonsteroidal anti-inflammatory drugs) and antidepressants. As we shall see, this medical approach leaves the underlying causes untreated and can cause further metabolic injury to you.

This book has been written with the express purpose of:

1. Empowering you with a comprehensive and practical guide that allows you to help yourself.
2. Providing you with the knowledge to ask the hard questions and find quality health care that can help you on your journey to healing your pain.
3. Or, if you are a health-care provider, providing you an ideal reference guide for treating individuals with chronic myofascial pain disorders; with well over 200 references, it brings you the most up-to-date information for your practice.

Finding the Way on Your Journey Toward Healing Your Pain

To assist you on your journey, this guide includes a comprehensive table of contents and index, and is divided into two books and five sections:

Book One, The Story of Chronic Pain: How We Got Here

Section 1: Misconceptions in Our Modern Healing, chapters 1 to 3

Section 2: Roadblocks to Healing, chapters 4 to 8

Book Two, The Triangle of Healing: Physical / Biochemical / Spiritual

Section 3: Physically Healing Your Pain, chapters 9 to 13

Section 4: Biochemically Healing Your Pain, chapters 14 to 18

Section 5: Spiritually Healing Your Pain, chapters 19 to 21

See below for descriptions of each section.

This detailed table of contents and division into five sections with chapters and subchapters will allow you to easily navigate through the material to locate and relocate information most relevant to you. For example, if you wish to get right into physically relieving your low-back pain, you may want to go directly to the chapter in section 3: Physically Healing Your Pain that relates to your region of chronic pain, e.g., chapter 10 for chronic low-back pain. You then can explore that particular chapter to find out how to self-treat the muscle knots specifically causing your chronic back pain. However, to assist this abbreviated process, I highly recommend that you also go to chapter 14: Eating Your Way out of Pain and into Wellness, and follow my simple "baby steps" program to help jumpstart your pain-healing program by addressing the basic metabolic dysfunction of your pain.

Book One: The Story of Chronic Pain

However, I have found that those individuals who actually take the time to understand why they are hurting have a much better chance of healing their pain and becoming healthier and happier individuals. Therefore, I highly recommend that you fully explore section 1 to find out why it is so important to avoid relying on drugs for quick pain relief. Then go on to investigate section 2: Roadblocks to Healing, to fully understand what it is about our modern diet, lifestyle, and environmental exposures that set us up for chronic pain and disease. Section 2 will also help you understand why you may need to change your diet and take certain supplements to fully conquer your pain and create real wellness. And for a complete holistic approach, section 5 explores the body/mind connection and the role of spirituality in healing your pain.

This book was written as a comprehensive guide that will provide a broad audience with useful information not for quick pain relief, but to heal their pain—and, as we shall see, there is a vast difference. Therefore, you may find that you utilize this book more as a reference guide, picking and choosing information useful to where you are on your path to recovery. But, with that said, this book was written in a way that tells a story, a comprehensive interconnected narrative, from the first to the last page, and it is best read that way.

As with most things important, we usually take our health for granted—that is, until it is taken away from us, often due to our own negligence. A problem today is that we want everything in simplistic, quick sound bites, whether it concerns politics or health care. These simplistic answers to our lives, as well as ignoring the real underlying causes, may be hastening us toward more complex health disorders and degenerative diseases. As a society, we constantly talk about quality, but genuine quality does not appear to be our real concern in our frantic race to get somewhere in life. To recognize this, all one needs to do is examine what we feed ourselves and our loved ones in the form of fast foods and convenience foods. Presently, American families eat more than half their meals outside the home, primarily at fast-food places instead of quality "slow meals" at home.

Section 1 of this comprehensive narrative explores the vital importance of taking charge of your own healing and not blindly surrendering to our modern model of health care focused on disease, not wellness. It goes on to examine the fallacy of any quick pain relief, whether prescription, over-the-counter, natural, or alternative in nature. Throughout my years of clinical experience, I have found that when individuals seek quick pain-relief instead of healing their pain, they generally end up eroding their health further.

As explained in section 1, the drugs we take to relieve our pain actually inhibit or block vital biochemical pathways. The problem with this approach, as we will examine in detail, is that there are no unnecessary metabolic pathways in your body. When you take a drug to relieve your pain, that drug actually inhibits important pathways, which over time will damage vital tissues in your body. The commonly used nonsteroidal anti-inflammatory drugs (NSAIDs), such as ibuprofen, can inhibit the biochemistry that keeps your liver, kidneys, and gastrointestinal tissues healthy.[1] In fact, nearly 17,000 people die from gastrointestinal bleeding each year from prescription NSAIDs.[2]

In section 2, you will discover that to overcome the challenge of your chronic pain, whether simple back pain or fibromyalgia syndrome, it is vital to heed the warnings of your biochemical individuality. This is achieved by dancing eloquently with our personal genetics through proper diet and lifestyle choices. Our Standard American Diet (SAD for short) and our modern lifestyle promote lives of overconsumption and undernutrition, causing us a painful unwellness that undermines our health and happiness. Also, since World War II, more than 80,000 different chemicals have been introduced into our environment. The EPA National Human Adipose Tissue Survey has found that the five most toxic chemicals known to man are now found in 100 percent of all tissue samples taken.[3] (More on this in chapter 7: Our Injured Earth, Your Injured Self.)

---

1 P. E. Lipsky, P. Brooks, and L. J. Crofford, et al., "Unresolved issues in the role of cyclooxygenase-2 in normal physiologic processes and disease," *Arch Intern Med* 160 (2000): 913–20.

2 *NEJM* 340 (June 17, 1999): 1888–9.

3 http://cfpub.epa.gov/ncea/cfm/recordisplay.cfm?deid=55204.

SAD equals . . .

Standard American Diet

This painful unwellness caused by dietary, environmental, and lifestyle exposures does not affect every individual the same, due to personal genetics and subsequent biochemical individuality. Therefore, from the same dietary, environmental, and lifestyle exposures, some individuals may develop full-blown fibromyalgia syndrome while others only have occasional stiffness and pain. It is vital to realize that our body first signals our unwellness as recurring pain and/or fatigue. And as you will uncover in section 2, the underlying metabolic factors of this recurrent pain and fatigue are the very same factors that can lead to degenerative diseases. These are the chronic disorders that plague our modern society and are the leading causes of death and disability: heart disease, cancer, diabetes, and neurodegenerative diseases (Alzheimer's, Parkinson's, dementia, etc.). Section 4 of this book fully illustrates how you can heal your pain through properly addressing these underlying metabolic causes, thereby helping to prevent the development of degenerative disease later in your life.

Book Two: The Triangle of Healing

In sections 3 through 5, you will explore the triangle of health and the importance of addressing all three aspects of healing physically, biochemically, and spiritually. Section 3 provides you with a powerful toolkit on how to physically remove myofascial trigger points anywhere on your body, a primary factor in any chronic pain syndrome. It starts out in chapter 9: Self-Care 101 for Myofascial Pain Syndromes, with the basics on physically self-treating your pain-causing muscle knots. Then chapters 10 through 13 bring you through the entire body, showing you how to treat the specific muscle groups that commonly cause you pain in the back, neck, or extremities.

Section 4 starts out with chapter 14: Eating Your Way Out of Pain and Into Wellness, which provides you with specific dietary changes to help heal your pain. This chapter contains my special "baby steps" program, helping you to make small, easy modifications that will dynamically transform your health and ease your pain. In chapter 15: Spice Up Your Healing, we examine ways to utilize standardized extracts of specific herbs to naturally heal your pain. You'll be pleasantly surprised to find that these herbs do not have side effects but provide you with side *benefits* promoting greater wellness overall. In chapters 16 and 17, we look at specific ways that we poison the healthy functioning of our body, inside and out. These chapters then go on to tell you what exactly you and your family can do to help improve your detoxification capacities. In chapter 18: From CRPs to Fibromyalgia Syndrome, we tackle the difficult subject of what exactly fibromyalgia syndrome is, how it develops, and what you can do to conquer it.

Section 5 of this comprehensive self-care manual is an important exploration of the body / mind / spirit connection to healing your pain. In this fifth section, we come to fully understand why it is so important to not fear our pain but instead embolden ourselves with a warrior's spirit of self-discovery that can lead to real healing. Pain is an integral part of life, and it is actually vital for your survival. If you ask, the ideal world for many would be one without pain. But if you were to neurologically remove the possibility of pain, you would make it impossible to experience pleasure as well. The same nerve endings and nerve tracts that elicit and carry the message of pain to the brain are also the very same that respond to pleasurable touch.[4]

As inseparable as pain and pleasure are in your body, so is it in your life. Imagine the loss of something or someone in your life that would cause you pain; it—he or she—is probably of great importance to you. In life, that which brings you your greatest pleasure can bring your greatest pain. Pain and pleasure are intertwined in a continuous dance that can bring you from delight to despair in a moment. Therefore, life also contains the possibility of pain leading to delight, and in section 5 we discover how our chronic pain can spiritually become our doorway to a healthier, more purpose-driven life!

In section 5, I borrow from the perennial wisdom of the Axial Age to create a five-step program to assist the spiritual healing of your pain and suffering. With this approach, you can begin to create a life in which the impact of physical and emotional pain is greatly lessened, and you will live in greater harmony and peace with yourself and your world.

Through my own painful ordeals and through my clinical practice, I have come to realize the necessity of having a knowledgeable guide to assist you in your journey of healing. This is my purpose in creating this comprehensive manual of wellness for

4 J. G. Kepecs, M. Robin, and C. Munro, "Tickle: The Organization of a Patterned Response," *Arch Gen Psychiatry* 5 (September 1961): 237–45.

healing chronic pain disorders: to act as your personal guide on this journey. But even the best guide is meaningless without the courage and discipline of a warrior's spirit to apply the knowledge gained. I know that healing your pain is possible, for throughout my clinical and teaching years I have seen thousands of patients who regained their health naturally to live lives without pain.

I also know this to be true from my own personal experience; I was once so severely disabled with chronic low-back pain that I had to leave clinical practice for a period of time. Even though I had access to some of the best resources in natural and conventional medicine, I spent much of my time in agony, flat on my back. I eventually realized that it was up to me to discover the underlying cause of my own chronic pain. This further became evident and poignant when my daughter was overcome with the pain and fatigue of fibromyalgia. I witnessed the courage of a true warrior when I saw my own daughter apply this knowledge and fight back to conquer her fibromyalgia. At one point, the pain in her legs and back became so severe that she had to crawl up the stairs to her bedroom. Watching her suffer drove me back into academia to begin a three-year program to become a board-certified neurologist. Building upon my years of clinical experience, this process of intense study revealed to me the underlying causes of chronic pain and its effective treatment. It also inspired me to create the FENIX Rehab System, a self-care product that allowed her to effectively remove her pain-causing muscle knots.

Through all this, I was able to effect dramatic changes in my own experience with chronic pain. Additionally, my daughter was able to heal her pain, and she is now a vibrant, active young woman, working and going to college. You will meet her in this book because she graciously consented to model the self-care section, chapters 9 through 13. Her story is told in greater detail later in the book, along with case histories of others who were able to heal their pain naturally. Through this very personal journey with chronic pain disorders, I have come to a deeper appreciation of the suffering it causes and the importance of effective natural treatment strategies to properly address its various causes. These efforts all culminated in my founding of FENIX Recovery Enterprises and my seminars for doctors and the public, along with this book.

How to Use This Book

The trigger point illustrations included in this book indicate where the points are, as well as areas of common referral pain. The myofascial trigger point on these charts is indicated by a ✱, and its referral pain is indicated by a shaded area. Just remember that the locations of the ✱ for the trigger spots and shaded-in areas for the referral pain are only the typical locations. Your own precise location for each myofascial trigger spot may vary slightly, so search around in the muscle. In addition, the referral area of pain can vary widely from the diagrams, which are only examples of a typical distribution.

Book One

THE STORY OF CHRONIC PAIN: HOW WE GOT HERE

For most individuals, their chronic back pain is an unfathomable mystery and even more confounding when it is disabling fibromyalgia. The problem is that for many health-care providers, the cause and cure for these chronic myofascial pain disorders remain elusive. Book One contains the map that can bring you to the source of your chronic myofascial pain, and then, in Book Two, you are provided with the way out.

It takes a warrior's spirit to face pain and ill health, discover your road to recovery, and then have the personal discipline to walk the path before you. I commend you on your courage and wish you good health and happiness in the near future.

Section I

Misconceptions in Our Modern Healing

The difficulty in beginning any journey is always in taking the first step. It is therefore helpful to have something that motivates us to move on down the road. Many times, inspiration is found when we truly examine where we are and how we got there. Insanity is said to be doing the same thing repeatedly and expecting a different result. For many in our society, the tendency is to keep taking medications even though they are not bringing us the health and happiness we seek.

Sometimes what we take for scientific *evidence* is only *belief* driven by prejudice, greed, ignorance, or ego. It is therefore helpful to bring our generally accepted beliefs into the bright sunlight of real scrutiny. We might find that the best way to heal our pain and bring about true wellness does not come through swallowing multiple medications.

It may be that the only way to change our life is *to change our life*! However, real dietary and lifestyle changes are not as easy as swallowing drugs. Therefore, in this section we examine a prevalent modern belief that there is always "better living through chemistry."

To take hold of something better, you have to let go of what you are grasping; in this section, we will examine some of the dangers in just going along with generally accepted practices of our modern disease-care model. We then examine where real wellness comes from and what factors can keep us from the health and happiness we desire.

1

An Uncomfortable Reality

Questions to Consider:

1. Is our modern approach to health care really the best model to follow for achieving real health and preventing disease?
2. If not, how can I turn my health concerns into an opportunity for true wellness?

With your chronic pain, do you sometimes feel like you have fallen down the rabbit hole of Alice's Wonderland? Are you caught in the web of modern medicine, handed one drug after another, never receiving the answer to your most basic question: "Why is this happening to me?" Perhaps it does seem a little like Alice's Wonderland, where nothing is what it appears to be: concerned doctors who have only a few minutes for your appointment, health-maintenance organizations that aren't maintaining your health, and the pharmaceutical industry—driven by record profits—always ready with another drug to treat the symptoms caused by the last drug. Possibly you have felt like you are in the middle of a mad tea party, not knowing which door to take to escape the madness.

At this juncture, the most important question you must answer is "Who do I rely on for help?" The usual response is to rely on the health "expertise" of modern medicine. But, as you will see, the model of modern medicine is one of heroic intervention for disease and trauma, but not of wellness care. With this approach, modern medicine can cause you *more* problems, especially when you have chronic pain related to dysfunction and not related to pathology, or an aggressive disease process. It may be best to realize that when it comes to healing, *you* are your own best friend and must take responsibility for your own well-being. The inconvenient truth of our present paradigm of "health care" can be an uncomfortable reality; however, it has been said that the truth can set you free. It is the aim of this book to set you free from the pain and fatigue that keeps you from being all that you want to be.

Science-Based Alternative Answers

As a chiropractic neurologist, I have dedicated myself to assisting individuals in escaping this upside-down "Wonderland" and finding their way back to a life that works for them. Having worked with thousands of patients who suffered with chronic pain, having been disabled with chronic back pain myself, and having watched my daughter suffer with fibromyalgia, I have made understanding chronic pain and overcoming it a very personal quest. This quest was intensified by facing patients every day asking the same difficult questions: "Why do I hurt? What's wrong with me? How can I feel better again?" Usually these patients had been through the medical mill of conventional medicine and were now looking for alternative answers. Most end up being treated as if they had an ibuprofen and antidepressant "deficiency."

Modern medicine of the twentieth century had its greatest success in overcoming infectious diseases. In this model of health care, the doctor identifies the single vector cause—in other words, the microbe causing the infection. The clinician then finds the proper antibiotic to reduce the number of infecting microbes so the body's immune system can finish the job. This seeming victory of modern medicine over death caused by infectious diseases has led to countless saved lives and a specific approach to healing. In today's world, though, the vast majority of suffering and death is caused by preventable degenerative diseases related to our diet and lifestyle choices and not to an infectious single agent.

The problem with modern medicine is that it is still looking for that single cause and that miraculous life-saving drug to counteract it. But there is so much more to the ecology of your unique biology than can be addressed by a single drug designed to attack a supposed single cause; it is a reality that does not exist. Wellness is maintained by multiple interconnected weblike components, and the loss of your health over time is from a combination of many different factors in the ecology of your well-being. Because of the time constraints of an office visit, I have longed for a book that would not only answer all my patients' vital questions but also give them an appreciation of the interconnected wonder of their lives. Your health is the most blessed treasure you will ever possess; to reclaim it and maintain it, you need comprehensive answers based on sound science. Therefore, this is *not* a "100 Health-Care Secrets Your Medical Doctor Does Not Want You to Know" book. It is a serious work distilled from hundreds of peer-reviewed research studies to help guide you through the confusing issues of health care today and empower you to find your own path to heal your pain.

Best Medicine in the World?

If you suffer with chronic or recurrent pain, you may at times feel as if you have slipped through the cracks of modern medicine. The uncomfortable reality is that our modern paradigm of health care may be failing all of us. Every westernized nation provides at least some basic health-care coverage to all its citizens. And yet, even with the largest health-care expenditures in the world, the United States has nearly 47 million uninsured as of 2005, and the number continues to grow.[5] We want to believe that we have the very best health care, probably because it is by far the costliest system in the world. But this logic doesn't bear up to scrutiny.

By 2005, the United States was spending over $2 trillion on health care annually, rising twice the rate of inflation; it is expected to reach nearly $3 trillion by 2009.[6] This amount is more than double, in the terms of percent of GNP, than any other industrial nation spends on health care. In spite of this massive spending, we are ranked twenty-fourth out of thirty-nine developed countries in infant mortality, and twenty-second out of the top twenty-three industrialized countries in healthy life expectancy.[7]

Utilizing the sixteen primary indicators of a healthy population, the United States is ranked twelfth out of the thirteen industrialized nations of the world—this, despite the fact that we outspend all of them on health care. In fact, the United States is twenty-seventh in life expectancy, just edging out Cuba in the twenty-eighth position.[8] Among the English-speaking countries of Canada, the UK, Australia, and New Zealand, the United States has the highest rate of serious medical errors.[9] This alarming statistic is in spite of the fact that the United States spends 2½ times more than the United Kingdom,

---

5 C. Borger, et al., "Health spending projections through 2015: changes on the horizon," Health Affairs Web Exclusive (22 Feb 2006), http://content.healthaffairs.org/cgi/content/abstract/hlthaff.25.w61.

6 Ibid.

7 B. Starfield, "Is U.S. health really the best in the world?" *JAMA* 284, 4 (2000): 483–85.

8 Ibid., and B. Starfield, "Deficiencies in U.S. medical care," *JAMA* 284, 17 (2000): 2184–85.

9 J. Lazarou, B. H. Pomeranz, and P. N. Corey, "Incidence of adverse drug reactions in hospitalized patients: a meta-analysis of prospective studies," *JAMA* 279, 15 (1998): 1200–5.

with its socialized health-care system.[10] A study published in the *Journal of the American Medical Association* in 2003 determined that deaths in hospitals attributed to medical injuries, mishaps, errors, and negligence is estimated to be anywhere from the first to the third leading cause of death in hospitalized patients in the United States.[11] The most recent estimate of deaths from medical mistakes in American hospitals found the number is now estimated to be 195,000 yearly.[12] That is twice as many deaths estimated by the Institute of Medical Study, published in 1999. The present number of deaths from medical mishaps in hospitals is now equivalent to crashing a fully loaded Boeing 747 every day of the year with no survivors! The cost of these preventable medical errors is now pushing $30 billion yearly.[13]

An even more troubling study involved the safety of our children in U.S. hospitals, reported in the prestigious journal *Pediatrics* in June 2004. The data presented in this study was a near census of all pediatric hospitals in the year 2000. Among pediatric patients in this study who experienced a "safety event" (an adverse health event in the hospital) that year, it is estimated that more than 4,483 pediatric deaths occurred. The authors point out, however, that their methods of analysis could detect only a small portion of patient safety events that actually happened in the hospitals. They conclude that it is likely there are substantially greater numbers of pediatric deaths from safety events in U.S. hospitals.[14]

Drugs: Not the Safest Way to Achieve Health

A widely reported study from the *Journal of the American Medical Association* published in 1998 found that in one year's time, 2.23 million hospitalized patients suffered serious adverse drug reactions (ADRs) causing serious injury, permanent disability, or death. Of these 2.23 million serious ADRs, 106,000 patients died in hospitals from medication reactions. This study counted only those drug deaths caused by medications that were properly prescribed and properly administered. If the study had included medication deaths from the wrong drug being administered, medication overdose, drug abuse, or

---

10 K. Davis and B. S. Cooper, "American Health Care: Why So Costly?" Invited testimony before the Senate Appropriations Committee, Subcommittee on Labor, Health, and Human Services, Education and Related Agencies; Hearing on Health Care Access and Affordability; Cost Containment Strategies (June 11, 2003).

11 C. Zhan and M. Miller, "Excess Length of Stay, Charges, and Mortality Attributable to Medical Injuries During Hospitalization," *JAMA* 291 (2003): 1868–74.

12 Healthgrades, "Patient safety in American hospitals" (July 2004).

13 Ibid. For more details, see www.americansmadandangry.org.

14 M. Miller and C. Zhan, "Pediatric patient safety in hospitals: a national picture in 2000," *Pediatrics* 113, no. 6 (June 6, 2004): 1741–46.

therapeutic failures, the number of medication deaths would be even more staggering. This study concluded that hospital deaths from properly prescribed medications represent between the fourth to sixth leading cause of death in the United States, depending on which ADR death statistics are utilized.[15]

However, injuries and deaths from drugs should not be your only concern. Because of your biological uniqueness, the drugs marketed to you do not always do what they're supposed to do. In a news article on December 11, 2003, the worldwide vice president of genetics at GlaxoSmithKline, Allen Roses, said that "the vast majority of drugs—more than 90%—only work in 30 to 50% of the people."[16] In other words, the executive of a major drug company is admitting that 9 out of 10 drugs taken do not work in up to 50% of people who take them, due to each individual's genetic uniqueness.

U.S. Health-Care Statistics

- 49 million uninsured as of 2007.
- United States is ranked 12 out of the 13 industrialized nations of the world.
- Deaths in hospitals attributed to medical injuries, errors, and negligence are estimated to be the first to the third leading cause of death in hospitalized patients, depending on statistics utilized.
- Hospital mishaps and errors are estimated to cost our health-care system well over $30 billion a year.
- 2.23 million hospitalized patients suffered serious adverse drug reactions (ADRs) causing serious injury, permanent disability, or death in 1994.[17]
- 106,000 patients died in hospitals from medication reactions in 1994.[18]
- The vast majority of drugs—more than 90%—only work in 30–50% of people because of genetic variability.

15 Lazarou, Pomeranz, and Corey, "Incidence," 1998.

16 S. Connor, "Glaxo chief: our drugs do not work on most patients," accessed online December 11, 2003, at http://news.independent.co.uk.

17 Lazarou, Pomeranz, and Corey, "Incidence," 1998.

18 Ibid.

The Adequacy of Musculoskeletal Care in the United States

As alarming as these health-care statistics are, you may wonder what this means to you as an individual with chronic musculoskeletal pain. Because pain is the primary reason that you or any individual seeks health care in the United States, and the vast majority of this pain occurs in the musculoskeletal system, it would seem essential that medical school graduates have an in-depth grasp of the subject. The ability of your doctor to quickly rule out any possible dangerous or pathological causes for the pain, and then with great accuracy find the underlying causes of your musculoskeletal pain, seems a necessity in today's health care. If a treating doctor does not have this ability, they may fall back upon the accepted standard of care for chronic muscle and joint pain problems by handing out prescriptions for NSAIDs, antidepressants, and possibly a sleep aid as well. However, as this book attempts to prove, this does not get to the real underlying causes of your chronic myofascial pain.

In 1998, a study was completed to examine the competency of recent medical school graduates in musculoskeletal medicine.[19] This examination was validated by 124 orthopedic program directors that established a passing grade of 73.1%. Based on this test, 82% of the recent medical graduates could not show competency in musculoskeletal medicine: they failed the exam! Surprisingly, the poorest grades on the test were in the ability to treat musculoskeletal spinal conditions. This finding is very disconcerting, considering 8 out of 10 people experience low-back pain some time in their life. The study went on to report that the average time spent in medical education at orthopedics was only 2.1 weeks, or less than 2% of the entire curriculum. Even more surprising, the study found that one-third of all medical school graduates had no orthopedic education.

Because this study's findings were so shocking, the researchers had the study repeated in 2002.[20] This time, the exam was validated by 417 program directors of internal medicine departments in the United States. Possibly, it was thought that this might be a more accurate evaluation than using specialists in orthopedics. These directors of internal medicine set a passing score of 70%. With this standard, 78% of the recent

---

19 K. B. Freedman and J. Bernstein, "The adequacy of medical school education in musculoskeletal medicine," *J Bone Joint Surg Am* 80, no. 10 (October 1998): 1421–27.

20 K. B. Freedman and J. Bernstein, "Educational deficiencies in musculoskeletal medicine." *J Bone Joint Surg Am* 84-A, 4 (April 2002): 604–8.

medical graduates failed to demonstrate basic competency in musculoskeletal medicine. The authors of the study concluded: "It is therefore reasonable to conclude that medical school preparation in musculoskeletal medicine is inadequate."

There are possibly many reasons why this is happening, but what it means to the individual with some form of chronic musculoskeletal pain is overwhelming. It means that it can be very difficult to find a physician who truly understands the complexity of your musculoskeletal problem. The result of this is obvious: when an ache or pain is found to be not threatening to a patient's life, it is written off with a prescription of NSAIDs and possibly an antidepressant or sleep medication.

However, what you will find in reading this book is that there are underlying metabolic problems that relate to your musculoskeletal pain, systemic inflammation, oxidative stress, and insulin resistance that must be addressed by diet and lifestyle. You will also learn that these same metabolic problems are at the source of the many degenerative diseases that plague our modern world: heart disease, cancers, and diabetes, to name a few. Therefore, this book will teach you how to heal your pain, promote wellness, and prevent degenerative disease. Aware of all the information presented in this chapter, you might begin to realize why it is so important for you to become involved in your own health care; in fact, you may want to get into the driver's seat. Why not? It is your life!

Why Not Rely on Yourself? You're in the Driver's Seat

Perhaps, though, upon deeper examination, we may find that it is *we* who are failing ourselves. As challenging as this thought can be, it is the awareness of our own folly that can be most empowering to create real change in our lives. It is now estimated that more than 125 million Americans suffer with diet- and lifestyle-related degenerative diseases, and about 105 million Americans have some type of chronic pain affecting their lives. More than 70% of all health-care issues faced by doctors in the United States today are chronic and degenerative in nature, and they consume 78% of all U.S. health-care dollars, according to Halstead Holman, MD, of Stanford Medical School.[21] Research has well established that multiple nongenetic factors you control, such as diet, activity, and environmental exposures (e.g., smoking), account for more than 80

21 H. Holman, "Chronic disease: the need for a new clinical education," *JAMA* 292, 9 (2004): 1057–59.

to 90% of your risk for developing these chronic degenerative diseases or a chronic pain disorder. This means that your genetics account for less than 20% of your risk for generating these dreadful disorders.[22] The uncomfortable reality is that we cannot hide behind our genes; it is more about how we choose to live.

These chronic and degenerative diseases are the primary cause of suffering, disability, and death in our society today—disorders such as heart disease, strokes, cancers, diabetes, autoimmune disorders, mental illness, and neurodegenerative diseases. A primary example of their growth is that one out of two Americans has now or will develop insulin resistance, a precursor to diabetes and heart disease. And one out of three babies born at the turn of this century will eventually develop type 2 diabetes, according to the U.S. Centers for Disease Control, June 15, 2003. Type 2 diabetes is now known to be caused almost entirely by improper diet and lifestyle. The greatest threats to your health and happiness in our modern world may come from the way you choose to live and eat, and what you expose yourself to. As we will explore throughout this book, subjecting yourself to the hazards of fast foods,[23] along with stressful and sedentary life patterns, greatly increases your risk for chronic pain and disease.[24] Also examined in this work is how environmental exposures from outdoor and indoor air pollution, water pollution, and pesticide and herbicide exposure through foods all contribute greatly to your development of chronic pain and disease.[25]

Turning Crisis into Opportunity

The rewards from changing your diet and lifestyle patterns can be tremendous, but the quest will challenge even the most courageous and disciplined individual. I have found in my years as a clinician that this quest for personal change requires the spirit of a warrior because you face your greatest adversary: your fearful and grasping self. To learn the necessary skills to heal your pain and have the courage to implement

22 "For most diseases contributing importantly to mortality in Western populations, epidemiologists have long known that non-genetic factors have high attributable risks, often in at least 80 or 90%, even when the specific etiologic factors are not clear." W. C. Willett, "Balancing life-style and genomics research for disease prevention," *Science* 296 (2002): 695–97.

23 J. H. Weisburger, "Hazards of fast food," *Environ Health Perspect* 112, no. 6 (2004): 336.

24 J. E. Manson, P. J. Skerrett, P. Greenland, and T. B. VanItallie, "The escalating pandemics of obesity and sedentary lifestyle: a call to action for clinicians," *Arch Intern Med* 164, no. 3 (2004): 249–58.

25 D. Briggs, "Environmental pollution and the global burden of disease," *Br Med Bull* 68 (2003): 1–24.

them, you must pledge your first allegiance to the heart of your True Self. For you to succeed in healing your physical and mental pain, it is vital to stop playing small with your existence and begin to play large. To paraphrase a great modern sage from India, Nisargadatta Maharaj, "it is not that you desire too much, it is that you desire too little. You crave for the small things that glitter and do not last. Your failure is that you do not desire for that which is most precious and is divine." This vital aspect of healing your pain will be the focus of the third section of this book where I examine the body/mind/spirit connection. In that section, I provide you with a five-step program to help heal this vital connection. However, I have found that it is often easier for individuals to face healing at this level *after* they have made some dietary and lifestyle changes to reduce their pain and suffering.

Change is never easy; however, life is nothing but change. Our bodies and our lives are in constant flux, and it is our resistance to this change that can bring us our greatest mental and physical discomfort. If you have come to trust in a certain worldview and paradigm of what health care is, it can be very difficult to turn your world right-side up. Nevertheless, all the previously referenced statistics are found in peer-reviewed journals and are available for your review. These revelations, along with your chronic pain, can be a little overwhelming, but together they can serve as a wake-up call for you to re-examine how you live your life. If the ways you are living and eating are not bringing you the health and happiness you desire, it may be time to change your life and heal. As a doctor, I have seen miraculous changes in people's health and lives when they apply the strategies presented in this book.

Also, as a clinician, I have noticed that the most motivated people are those faced with a life challenged by chronic pain. Whether you suffer with chronic headaches, a constant sore neck, disabling low-back pain, crippling arthritis, or the all-over pain of fibromyalgia, you can turn this crisis into an opportunity for a better life. Interestingly, the word or ideogram in Chinese for a *crisis* also refers to the meaning of *opportunity*. Our English word for *crisis* comes from an ancient Greek root that meant "to discern, separate out, or sift through." This book will guide you in your effort to sift through and discern the path you must take to reclaim your life from pain.

Running Toward the Wrong Goal

The preceding analysis of modern health care is not to say that the twentieth century has not seen tremendous strides when it comes to treating trauma and life-threatening illness. Novel technological advances never cease to amaze us—everything from reattachment of severed limbs to organ transplants and advanced life-support systems. Probably you have seen futuristic sci-fi films in which sophisticated scanners of some sort instantly tell the doctor everything, and "parts" are built, regenerated, or cloned and replaced. We seem to dream of a future in which we can live indefinitely without pain or disease. It may be, though, that we have blinded ourselves with our quest for better living through chemistry. But no matter how advanced our life becomes through technology, if we disconnect from nature and live and eat in a way that no longer truly nourishes us, we will fail to thrive physically, mentally, and emotionally.

No matter how advanced our health care becomes, if it is aimed in the wrong direction it will not bring about a healthy or a happy society. It is as if in the game of wellness, your health-care team, playing against degeneration and disease, is running toward the wrong goal. If your team is racking up points against itself, it doesn't matter how many coaches, pundits, or experts weigh in on how to get your team faster to the goal—you only end up going backwards faster! Our modern concept of wellness and prevention tends toward earlier detection of the disease and not real, substantial changes in diet and lifestyle to prevent the dysfunction of the body that leads to the disease in the first place.

For example, "prevention," in our society, is x-raying the breast so we can cut out the diseased tissue as early as possible. Yet there is a great body of well-researched science on dietary and lifestyle changes that a woman can make to actually prevent the development of breast cancer. Or our concept of prevention is monitoring blood pressure until an individual needs multiple drugs to control their hypertension. Our health-care industry could attack the underlying diet and lifestyle causes of hypertension and could work more diligently to change these factors in our society.

The most common reason individuals seek health care is because their bodies are sending signals of pain, indicating that tissues are not functioning properly. Instead of ascertaining the source of their dysfunction and giving them dietary and lifestyle changes to normalize function, most doctors prescribe anti-inflammatory drugs that inhibit the healing and tissue regeneration process. As you will see in chapter 2, NSAIDs (nonsteroidal anti-inflammatory drugs), the number-one prescribed drug for chronic pain, can cause tremendous damage to your tissues.

The Menagerie of Holistic Medicine

At the other end of the spectrum from allopathic or "modern" medicine is alternative or holistic medicine, much of which tries to take a more integrative approach. But the journey through this menagerie of options many times ends up being a rather hodgepodge approach to your health care. Studies have shown that alternative health care is almost entirely self-referred; this means individuals are finding their own ways to various practitioners of different biases and different levels of training. Frequently, individuals pursuing holistic or alternative care are still seeking a "quick fix," but this time through some form of magic from nature. Often an individual will start to take some supplements of questionable quality, try a little chiropractic, dabble with herbs, get an occasional massage, and maybe even try a little acupuncture, in a rather hodgepodge attempt to find relief.

The problem is that there is no integrative approach addressing the causes of their dysfunction and pain—the underlying causes directly related to how we eat, live, and think. To properly address these fundamental issues in a fully integrative approach can be a daunting task. Again, it takes the spirit of a warrior to seek out the knowledge, and then the discipline of a champion to apply the methods. Do not sell yourself short: if you take on this journey and challenge the "conventional" wisdom, you truly are one in a million.

Along the way, though, it is helpful to find knowledgeable guides rooted in a rational approach that can assist you on your journey. This book has been written to serve as that guide. It emphasizes a more scientific, functional approach to your health care that attempts to integrate the physical, biochemical, and spiritual aspects of overcoming the challenge of chronic pain. It is *scientific* because the information supplied here is garnered from hundreds of peer-review studies. It is *functional* because the approach is to uncover the root of your dysfunction or imbalance and restore it to proper function before it becomes a degenerative disease. And it is *integrative* because you are looked upon as an integral whole in which every tissue and organ relies on and affects every other tissue and organ in your body. To accomplish this, let us look to the entire tapestry of your well-being and introduce you to effective strategies that can naturally heal your pain.

The Beautiful Tapestry of You

Your body and its ongoing health maintenance is an interconnected, weblike reality. Yet we treat it like some two-dimensional novel or action film. In this simplistic story, the "good guy" (medication) must destroy the evil "bad guy" (disease) to make the world (body) well again. But life is much more complex than this, and so is your health. With my patients I like to use the image of their health being more like an intricate woven tapestry.

The wall-hanging tapestries of the Middle Ages were able to tell an entire story using complex allegories. This complex story was made from the simple weavings of many different brightly colored yarns of various sizes. These yarns of silk or wool were expertly dyed by artisans; for example, red yarn was achieved through the use of pomegranates. Wool fibers and plant dyes, along with intelligence and a great deal of energy, were the basic elements woven into a beautiful story.

This is not unlike your health and life—a complex, beautiful story, intricately woven from basic earthly elements of food, water, and air. This interwoven web is an interconnected whole, and like those medieval tapestries it can only be understood by viewing it in its entirety. The medieval tapestry reveals its entire story to the viewer, who is able to take in the whole picture. An observer could not understand the story by just looking at one part of the tapestry. If viewers examine only the corner or even the center, they cannot see what the story reveals. The proper functioning of your body/mind is the same way. If you examine just one part of the story, without taking in the interconnected, weblike functions of your whole body, the wisdom is lost, and you cannot heal your pain.

When we attempt the simplistic, quick approach to our health care in which every symptom deserves its own drug, we create an ever-deepening health crisis. For example, drugs for acid reflux and ulcers, such as Nexium and Prilosec, are among the top-used drugs today. The primary reason for the astronomical increase in the use of these drugs is because of the increased use of nonsteroidal anti-inflammatory drugs, or NSAIDs. These NSAIDs, such as any ibuprofen or aspirin, can cause severe damage to your gastrointestinal lining. Of course, the number-one reason someone is prescribed or takes over-the-counter NSAIDs is because of muscle and joint pain problems. Research has now shown that NSAID drugs taken for chronic pain cause many side effects. It is conservatively estimated that 16,500 individuals die annually due to gastrointestinal bleeding from prescription NSAIDs.[26] This is an excellent example of a single-cause/single-drug model that leads to greater health problems and not to wellness. In this journey, it is vital to step back and take in the entire tapestry of your health if you want to heal your pain and live the life you deserve. This may seem daunting at first, but with some diligence on your part and guidance on mine, you will be able to see the whole magnificent story.

Disease-Care vs. Wellness Care

You might be wondering why you cannot rely on your own doctor to take this approach with your health. The answer lies in the fact that people can see only what they look for. When your doctor is trained within a system in which everything is reduced to its part and every part has a specialty, there is little hope for the interconnected whole to be seen. Furthermore, our health-care system is based on a business model in which the more individuals you get through the door in the shortest amount of time, the more money the health organization can make. It is an assembly-line approach to health care without any real efficiency. Do not be deceived; the health-care industry is really about profit! Health care is presently more than *2 trillion dollar* industry, and it is projected to grow to a 4 trillion dollar industry by 2015.[27] The bulk of the profit is not going into the hands of the health-care providers, but rather into the pockets of health-care organizations and corporations. With this type of profit to be made, one wonders if it can transform itself into a health-care system that looks to the real answers to health. Real answers to our present health challenges are generally low- tech and involve diet and lifestyle changes that are inexpensive to provide, therefore with little profit to be made. But our society tends to gravitate toward the expensive, high-tech, shiny gadgets to provide us health!

It's interesting to contrast this Western symptomatic disease-care model with ancient traditional Chinese medicine. In traditional Chinese medicine, the practitioner would look at all signs and symptoms to determine the patient's present state of health. The traditional Chinese doctor would examine his patients within a mosaic of weblike connections: their relationship to their families, work, emotions, seasons, weather, diet,

---

26 *NEJM* 340 (1999): 1888–9.

27 C. Borger, et al., "Health spending projections through 2015: changes on the horizon," Health Affairs Web Exclusive (22 Feb 2006), http://content.healthaffairs.org/cgi/content/abstract/hlthaff.25.w61.

and so on. Patients were then given specific directions on what they should eat, exercises to do, herbs to take, and treatments they should receive. His approach was to keep his patients healthy and optimize their lives. In this health-care system, the patients paid the doctor only when he kept them well. But, when a patient got sick, even though he or she was following the physician's advice, the traditional doctor then paid the patient until he or she returned to wellness. This gave the traditional physician a great deal of incentive to maintain wellness in a system already oriented toward real health care.

Actually, our modern health-care system is not about health care at all; rather, it is a model predicated on disease care. How many times have you heard from your doctor, "It's nothing serious, why don't we just watch it for now?" In other words, "I treat disease, and you are only manifesting the 'walking wounded' syndrome of poor health. Why don't you wait until you have a pathology I can identify? Then I can give you a diagnosis, and with a diagnosis I can give you a drug to treat your pathology." We in the West have grown accustomed to this and even look forward to receiving our diagnosis and the newest drug on the market.

A patient I treated years ago exemplified this attitude. Diane (not her real name) came in with some chronic muscle and joint pains, gastrointestinal upset, and fatigue. But her main concern was a persistent rash. In her first consultation after a complete history and workup, I began to explain the relationship of her skin condition to her overall health and her various other complaints. Soon after this visit, some test results came back and I began to discuss with her how these different conditions were linked together. But soon after that visit, she came in for an appointment with me and was very excited. She had just seen her medical doctor, who knew exactly what was "wrong" with her skin, and she now had a new drug to treat it.

I asked her what the doctor had said was wrong with her. She proudly proclaimed that she had "dermatitis" and showed me her new cortisone pills. I did not have the heart to tell her that she had gone to her MD complaining of a rash or "skin irritation" and he had just said the same thing back to her in Latin: *derma* means "skin" and *-itis* "irritation" or "inflammation." Therefore, she really knew nothing more than when she first went in to get her question answered: "What's wrong with me?" As for her drug, cortisone, it would suppress her immune system and therefore stop the rash for a while. It would not fix the actual cause of her rash, however. If continued, the cortisone would eventually have a harmful effect on her overall health. In unraveling her case, I found that her complaints of rash and pain were related to her GI upset. Her "upset tummy" was, in actuality, IBS or irritable bowel syndrome, caused by dysbiosis or unwanted microbes growing in her intestines, releasing toxins and causing her systemic symptoms, including her rash. We will examine this subject matter in greater detail throughout the book.

Diagnosis?

derma = skin

-itis = irritation

dermatitis = skin irritation

You may find yourself at a point in life where you are on multiple drugs from multiple doctors just because you simply were not feeling good and you hurt. The most commonly prescribed drugs for the symptoms of this "walking wounded" syndrome are NSAIDs (nonsteroidal anti-inflammatory drugs) and antidepressants. However, your recurrent pain and fatigue, signaling distress and dysfunction in your body, will continue to progress until it becomes the pain of degenerative disease. An eventual medical diagnosis of a degenerative disease represents a broken strand in the interconnected web of your well-being. These broken strands are not the cause of your problem but rather the effects of the underlying physical, biochemical, and emotional distress that have not been properly addressed for years. Your underlying problem was not a heart problem or a problem with diabetes but rather the imbalance created by years of poor diet and lifestyle choices that broke the strands. Because of our societal view on health and our compartmentalized modern health-care system, no one sees or treats the underlying causes; there is no one to take an integrative approach to healing your pain but you. This book is the source for the code to unlock the story of your personal tapestry of health.

What Does This Mean for Me?

- Our present health-care model is focused on disease care; therefore, I need to find my own road to real wellness. After all, I am in the driver's seat!
- The first step on this journey is to turn my crisis into an opportunity and respect the entire interconnected tapestry of my being by not seeking quick fixes to my pain.

monthat
than th
you ca
expecte
that, as
Because
dromes
utilized

2

The Problem with Pain

Questions to Consider:

1. Could my recurring back pain (neck pain, shoulder pain, tension headaches, fibromyalgia, etc.) be a signal of things to come if I don't change my ways?
2. Is it prudent to take drugs for my everyday aches and pains?
3. What is chronic benign pain, and what forms can it take?

Chronic pain is very common today, therefore many of us have already fallen down the rabbit hole of Alice's Wonderland, where all is perplexing and nothing is as it seems. Chronic pain is defined as any pain that lasts longer than six months, but other experts have shortened that time frame to any pain lasting longer than three months, the definition that I adhere to. Since no established definition exists, you can designate your pain as chronic pain if it has lasted longer than a reasonable expected healing time. Chronic pain syndromes are a confusing collection of disorders that, as we have seen, usually do not respond well to our medical model of health care. Because of their lack of response to modern medicine, patients with chronic pain syndromes are often dismissed as having psychological disorders. Leading the list of drugs utilized for treating chronic pain syndromes are antidepressants and nonsteroidal anti-inflammatory drugs, or NSAIDs. As we shall continue to examine, the ever-popular NSAIDs and antidepressants may not be the best approach to your chronic pain.

Chronic Pain and Chronic Disease: Same Source

Recurrent pain disorders are often referred to in medicine as chronic benign pain syndromes—*benign* because the source of the pain is neither life threatening nor arises from a disease or pathological process. The benign, painful disorder may be disabling to you or make your life miserable, but it will not kill you, at least not in the near future. As we begin to unpack these chronic benign pain syndromes, we will see that the underlying mechanisms that cause your recurrent pain are also the mechanisms of chronic degenerative diseases such as cardiovascular disease, cancer, and diabetes, which are the primary killers today. Therefore, the ability to see this story held within the tapestry of your health will allow you not only to find your way out of pain now but also to prevent suffering in the future. On this journey of healing, you will not only conquer your pain but also implement the changes necessary in order to live a happy, healthy, and vibrant life.

Chronic pain can be ugly—not only figuratively but literally. The underlying mechanisms that can cause chronic inflammation and pain are the same metabolic factors that can cause you to prematurely age. Also, if you develop chronic pain, it is hard to look good when you are hurting. Not only that, the metabolic factors that help to create chronic pain—free radicals, "silent" inflammation, insulin resistance, and chemical toxin exposure—can cause you to wrinkle more quickly and take the luster out of your hair and the bounce out of your step; pain can make you look and feel older before your time. The primary problem with pain is not that it hurts, but that it also signals that things are not working in your body as they should.

Looking for a Quick Fix

Imagine, if you will, that you are about to undertake a journey in your automobile. Generally, you take the time to get your car ready for the trip. You check the oil, the belts, maybe even get a tune-up. When you are on the road, you will no doubt regularly check the dashboard of your car for vital information: your speed, the temperature of your engine, and the oil pressure. Pain is like the check-engine light on the dashboard of your car. When the warning light comes on in your car, it is usually nothing severe—only a service requirement eventually needing attention. But if it is not tended to, it can cause you severe problems in the future. The check-engine light can be annoying, and we are often just too hurried to take the time to care for it immediately. But would you go so far as to have your car-care provider disconnect the wires of your check-engine light for a quick fix, instead of taking care of the problem? Or, if you went to a car-care specialist whose recommendation of repair was to "surgically" remove the wires, would you follow through on your specialist's advice?

More importantly, if the oil-warning light flares bright red on your dashboard during the journey, would you ignore it? Of course not—you have taken enough interest in your car to realize that the oil-warning light on your dashboard signals to you that the engine oil pressure is low, and you cannot run your car low on oil. You can run your car out of fuel, then just fill the tank and go again. But you understand that if you run your engine low on oil, you will quickly ruin it completely. As annoying as it is to stop, find oil, and add it to your car's engine, you would not chance a ruined engine by ignoring this vital signal. Even more unthinkable is the concept of going to a car-care specialist to have the wires to the oil-warning light "surgically" disconnected so that it no longer bothers you as you continue on your way.

Yet as a culture and as individuals, we seem to have no problem disconnecting or inhibiting the warning signals of pain in our body while on our journey of life. Generally we can get away with it, because more than nine out of ten times the pain is signaling dysfunction and not a life-threatening pathology. This is much like the check-engine light on our car signaling the need for maintenance service. When we ignore our check-engine light of pain long enough, we will develop more challenging health problems that may eventually threaten our lives. If you ignore warnings of service requirements in your car, the vehicle will perform more poorly. The same thing is true in your life. If you block pain messages and ignore the dietary and lifestyle changes they indicate, it will cause you to feel lousy, lower your performance, and eventually lead to disease.

Everyday Pain and NSAIDs

In our modern society, we tend to turn to drugs for quick relief from our physical pain as well as mental anguish. As a society, we have become very sensitive to individuals suffering with pain. It seems unnecessary for people to suffer when we have so many wonderful drugs now to combat pain. There are many different types of pain, however.

There is the acute, short-term pain of trauma or the intractable chronic pain of an untreatable pathology such as cancer that must be managed or even blocked. Then there is the non-life-threatening "everyday" pain of headaches, back pain, or arthritis; the signals that tell us we need to make some adjustments to how we live and eat.

No one is advocating that people should just grin and bear it, that they should suffer with pain. But it might be time to take a look at the direction we, both as individuals and as a society, are headed in our treatment of recurring or chronic nonpathological pain. A June 2004 study in the medical journal *Pain* found that since 1980, prescriptions for muscle and joint pain have increased greatly, and the primary prescriptions are for nonsteroidal anti-inflammatory drugs, or NSAIDs.[28] This study does not take into account the incredible 30 billion tablets of NSAIDs sold annually over-the-counter in the United States, so it reveals only a portion of the actual increase in NSAID usage. These NSAIDs are the common drugs everyone is familiar with: aspirin, ibuprofen (Advil, Nuprin, and Motrin), ketoprofen (Orudis), and naproxen (Aleve).

Common NSAIDs

- Aspirin
- Ibuprofen (Advil, Nuprin, Motrin)
- Ketoprofen (Orudis)
- Naproxen (Aleve)

But to be fair to our health, let's for a moment examine what the NSAIDs actually do in our tissues. These medications do not get in special little "boats" and float in the bloodstream until arriving at your sore low back, stiff neck, or inflamed shoulder. These NSAIDs (and all other drugs) are delivered to *all* the tissues of your body, therefore affecting the biochemistry of your entire body. These NSAIDs work by inhibiting a specific enzyme called cyclooxygenase, which comes in two different forms in our cells: COX-1 and COX-2. Sometimes you will hear NSAIDs referred to as COX enzyme-inhibiting drugs. However, there is a problem! The COX enzyme, in both its forms

28 M. A. Caudill-Slosberg, et al., "Office visits and analgesic prescriptions for musculoskeletal pain in the U.S.: 1980 vs. 2000," *Pain* 109, 3 (2004): 514–19.

1 and 2, are vital to the health of your body.[29] These COX enzymes in your tissues take fatty acids from your cell membranes to make very important hormonelike cell messengers called prostaglandins. NSAIDs inhibit or block the formation of these all-important prostaglandins. The family of prostaglandins plays a vital role in the health of your body.

Throughout your body, complex and dynamic functions are continually being performed every single second. Nevertheless, no matter how complex the function, at the final steps the body usually utilizes simple on and off switches. This is similar to your computer, which performs very complex functions using a simple binary code of 0s and 1s acting like on and off switches. At the end of many complex cellular functions, your body utilizes a simple biologic code. For example, the simple influx of calcium into a specific cell acts as a biological switch that turns on a complex cellular function. The COX-1 and COX-2 enzymes are used by your cells to make various prostaglandins that also act as simple off and on switches for many important functions that maintain your overall health and well-being.

Inflammation: Not the Bad Guy

All healing in your body begins with the much-feared, maligned inflammatory response. Your tissues utilize specific prostaglandins to enhance inflammation in order to fight off infections, defeat cancerous cells, or heal a sprain/strain of your muscles and joints. Certain prostaglandins also moderate or inhibit this inflammation response so it does not get out of hand. As it turns out, the prostaglandins that turn on the inflammatory healing response—yes, inflammation is vital for health and healing—also stimulate pain in your body.

This, of course, makes logical sense. If you have stressed or injured tissue that needs to be protected and healed from either trauma or infection, you would want to consciously know about it. This signal to your conscious brain, or sensory cortex, is what we call *pain*! Generally, the greater the tissue stress or injury present, the greater the signal to your brain. However, do not be fooled; you can maintain a level of chronic pain after the tissue is all healed or even develop severe chronic pain without any tissue injury in the first place. This is a very important concept for you to understand if you wish to overcome the challenge of your chronic pain. If you keep treating your chronic

29 Lipsky, Brooks, and Crofford, et al., "Unresolved issues," 913–20.

pain like an acute inflammatory response after it has evolved into a chronic condition, you are setting yourself up for more pain and more health problems.

Therefore, when you take NSAIDs or COX-inhibiting drugs, you are not blocking pain; you are inhibiting the inflammatory or healing response of your immune system throughout your body. When you take these drugs, you are inhibiting enzymes, COX-1 and/or COX-2, that are vital to keeping your digestive, cardiovascular, and central nervous system, as well as kidney and liver tissue, healthy. Multiple studies have shown that use of NSAIDs, whether over-the-counter or prescription, can cause harm to these vital tissues. The harm caused by NSAIDs to these tissues takes place with each dose taken; the amount of damage caused is dependent upon your rate of removal of the drug from your system and your rate of tissue repair. Taking NSAIDs over time increases your risk for GI bleeding, perforation of your gastrointestinal tract, and also acute liver and kidney injury, as well as heart failure.

Our Misguided War on Inflammation

As previously mentioned, a recent study in the *New England Journal of Medicine* estimated conservatively that there were 16,500 NSAID-related deaths per year from gastrointestinal bleeding. This would make it the fifteenth-most-common cause of death in the United States—*and these mortality statistics do not include the deaths from the use of over-the-counter NSAIDs.*[30] The detrimental effect of NSAIDs on the gastrointestinal system is again one of the leading reasons individuals have to take over-the-counter antacids or receive anti-ulcer prescription medications. This is an excellent example of how the taking of one drug can lead to individuals needing to take another drug to deal with symptoms of the first drug. This vicious cycle leads to a health-care system based more on polypharmacy, or multiple drug use, instead of multiple lifestyle changes, primarily through diet and exercise.

The devastating effect that NSAIDs have on the gastrointestinal health of individuals pushed research to find a "safer" drug. Recent research discovered that COX-1 is an enzyme that maintains the health of the gastrointestinal tract and kidney blood flow, whereas COX-2 is more involved in the inflammatory healing response from triggers such as trauma and infection.

---

30 *NEJM* 340 (June 17, 1999): 1888–99.

Since our society typically divides issues up into a simplistic "good" and "bad" reality, COX-1 became the "good enzyme" while COX-2 was seen as the "bad enzyme." Since aspirin and ibuprofen NSAIDs inhibited both COX-1 and COX-2 enzymes, researchers realized they would inhibit the maintenance of vital tissues and organs as well as inflammation.

The discovery of the COX-2 enzyme brought forth the first selective COX-2 inhibiting drug in 1998 and the second in 1999. They were immediately promoted as safe and effective alternatives to help individuals with chronic pain problems because they were targeting the "bad guys." These new drugs quickly became the top-selling drugs in the world, generating more than $3 billion in annual sales. The problem was that the promise of the COX-2 inhibitors never truly was fulfilled. As it turns out, COX-2 enzymes are also responsible for maintaining the health of many tissues in the body, especially of the cardiovascular system, central nervous system, and the kidneys.[31] Therefore, inhibition of this vital COX-2 enzyme will have a detrimental effect on your overall health and well-being.

Our misguided war against inflammation with ever more powerful drugs, such as the COX-2 inhibitors, began to reveal a shadow side to our technological quick "fixes" of pain. Besides costing 10 to 20 times more than the old NSAIDs, research has never shown these newer COX-2 inhibitors to be any better at relieving pain and inflammation. Furthermore, these COX-2 inhibiting drugs were found to have widespread and catastrophic negative effects on the cardiovascular system.[32] According to a 1998 study published in the *American Journal of Medicine*, prior to the introduction of the COX-2 inhibiting drugs, prescribed NSAIDs were killing at least 16,500 patients per year.[33] This all changed with the introduction of the COX-2 inhibiting NSAIDs. According to a 2005 study published in *Archives of Internal Medicine*, the selective COX-2 NSAID Vioxx may have caused conservatively as many as 88,000 to 140,000 heart attacks, strokes, and other serious complications before being taken off the market.[34]

---

31 Lipsky, Brooks, and Crofford, et al., "Unresolved issues," 913–20.

32 A. Bertolini, A. Ottani, and M. Sandrini, "Selective COX-2 inhibitors and dual acting anti-inflammatory drugs: critical remarks," *Frontiers in Medicinal Chemistry* 1, no. 1 (2004): 85–95.

33 Singh Gurkirpal, "Recent consideration in nonsteroidal anti-inflammatory drug gastropathy," *Amer J Med* (27 July 1998): 315.

34 C. Dai, R. Stafford, and G. C. Alexander, "National trends in cyclooxygenase-2 inhibitor use since market release," *Arch Int Med* (24 January 2005): 171–77.

These overwhelming statistics can act as motivation for you to find safer and more effective answers to the underlying causes of your chronic pain. Through understanding the causes of your pain and applying the strategies outlined in the middle section of this book, you will not only conquer your pain but also possibly prevent the onset of chronic disease. Through your own efforts, you can avoid becoming just another number in these alarming statistics. To accomplish this, it is vital for you to develop a rudimentary understanding of the actual underlying physical and metabolic causes of your chronic pain instead of relying on quick fixes. Once these causative factors are understood, it then becomes easier to find your bearing for your journey to real wellness.

The Many Faces of Chronic Benign Pain

In modern medicine, chronic benign pain syndromes are generally divided up between pain disorders of the neuromusculoskeletal, gastrointestinal, urological, and reproductive systems. Recent research is now showing, however, that there are common underlying mechanisms to these various disorders, such as free radicals and systemic inflammation. The vast majority of all diagnosed chronic pain disorders fall into the muscle and joint category, which is the leading cause of work-related disability in men and women.[35] Because of this, the neuromusculoskeletal system will be the primary focus of this book, but the healing strategies presented do generally apply to all chronic benign pain disorders and the promotion of genuine wellness.

In the neuromusculoskeletal category, you can receive one or more of many different diagnoses of chronic disorders. One or more of the following conditions may sound familiar: myofascial pain syndrome, myofascitis, fibromyalgia syndrome, repetitive strain injury, tendonitis, bursitis, muscle-tension headaches, migraines, atypical fascial pain, trigeminal neuralgia, neurovascular entrapment, multiple tendonitis and bursitis syndrome, osteoarthritis, spondylosis, rheumatoid arthritis, mechanical low-back pain syndrome, or any one of many more possibilities. Sound familiar? Notice a lot of *-itis* endings; this suffix means "inflammation." When the tendon is inflamed, it is tendonitis, and when an arthroidial joint is inflamed, it is arthritis.

---

35 R. C. Lawrence, et al., "Estimates of the prevalence of arthritis and selected musculoskeletal disorders in the UW," *Arthritis & Rheumatism* 41, no. 5 (May 1998): 778–99.

The Role of "Silent" Inflammation in Chronic Pain and Disease

In many disorders, it is easy to recognize the signs of acute inflammation, such as redness, swelling, and heat. In most chronic pain disorders of the neuromusculoskeletal system, such as myofascial pain syndrome, osteoarthritis, or fibromyalgia, you cannot find these cardinal signs of inflammation. It has long been thought that these disorders did not involve inflammation, and therefore they are still sometimes called noninflammatory disorders. But recent research has shown that chronic low-grade systemic inflammation (sometimes referred to as a "silent" inflammation) is involved in these disorders. As we will explore, based on numerous recent studies, this silent inflammation is involved in all chronic pain and degenerative disease disorders.

Because of its huge importance in healing your pain, later in the book we will spend more time exploring the topic of low-grade chronic inflammation and how it is directly tied to how we eat and live. New research is being published almost daily in journals demonstrating the strong connection between this silent inflammation and degenerative diseases such as cardiovascular disease, certain cancers, insulin resistance, diabetes, and neurodegenerative disorders such as Alzheimer's and Parkinson's disease. So, if you begin to understand how to manage this chronic silent inflammatory process through improved diet and lifestyle, you will improve your ability to overcome chronic pain *and* you will also be preventing the possible development of degenerative diseases later in life!

It is also important to point out here that as this research becomes more popular, drug companies will begin to aggressively market anti-inflammatory drugs as preventative medicines. The problem with this model of health care is the inability to realize that chronic systemic inflammation is not acute inflammation and it cannot be treated as such. Recent studies have shown that the use of these NSAIDs may show a decreased risk in one disease while actually increasing the risk of death from other diseases. This was well illustrated in a study on COX-2 inhibitory NSAID use to prevent colon cancer, which eventually led to an increase in cardiovascular deaths.[36] Chronic systemic silent inflammation can best be treated through diet and lifestyle changes, as fully described in chapter 5.

---

36 R. S. Bresalier, R. S. Sandler, and H. Quan, et al., "Cardiovascular events associated with Rofecoxib in colorectal adenoma chemoprevention trial," *New England J Med* 352, no. 11 (17 Mar 2005): 1092–1102.

What Does This Mean for Me?

- The underlying metabolic factors of chronic benign pain disorders (e.g., oxidative stress, chronic inflammation, toxic exposures, as discussed) are the same factors that promote degenerative diseases.
- Inflammation is the beginning of any healing response; therefore, I do *not* want to block it with a drug but instead learn to properly manage it!
- Furthermore, to promote real wellness in my life and prevent the development of degenerative disease (heart disease, diabetes, Alzheimer's, etc.), I want to heal my pain by properly addressing these underlying metabolic factors.

3

The Fallacy of Pain Relief

Questions to Consider:

1. If real health does not come from swallowing pills, what is its source?
2. Is there any connection between the health of the earth and my health?
3. Is there a connection between what I eat and absorb and how I feel?
4. What role do toxins play in my pain and in my overall health?

Have you ever wondered why individuals working the same job will react differently to the body mechanics of their labor? For example, two individuals work the same assembly job, and one develops chronic tendonitis while the other individual has no aches or pains at all. In an office full of workers sitting at computers doing data entry, some develop disabling neck and shoulder problems while others are barely bothered. Some might say that it is because their genetics differ. But how true is that really?

Dancing with Our Genes

Except for a few genetically determined diseases, genes are not as deterministic as we tend to view them in our modern world. What we really inherit in our genes are multiple genetic tendencies. Our genes tend to code for various strengths and weaknesses that give rise to resistance or susceptibility to health problems. Our genes are genetic cards we have been dealt; some of us are given a better hand than others, but research is showing us that for most of us it comes down to how we play our cards. If we play well with the cards we are dealt, through diet and lifestyle, we can experience better health and a longer life. If we play badly, even with an excellent hand of genetic cards, we can lose and suffer with chronic pain and disease!

One way that genes can code for an increased susceptibility to chronic myofascial pain disorders, or degenerative disease in some individuals, is by establishing a higher need for a certain micronutrient in their bodies. The work of Bruce Ames, as reported in the *American Journal of Clinical Nutrition* in 2002, found that your genetic uniqueness could increase your need of a particular micronutrient, such as a specific vitamin or mineral, by more than 100 times that of a family member or your neighbor.[37]

But genetic tendencies are not a predetermined destiny. In a recent study reported in the *New England Journal of Medicine* in 2002, investigators in Sweden's Karolinska Institute studied 44,788 pairs of identical twins. They found that the twins did not experience cancer at the same rate. A conclusion of their study was that inherited genetic factors make only a minor contribution to the susceptibility to most cancers. Their findings indicated that the environment and diet play major roles in the cause of sporadic cancer.[38] In other words, disease is more of an outcome of how we dance with our given genetics or "play our genetic hand."

You Have Control!

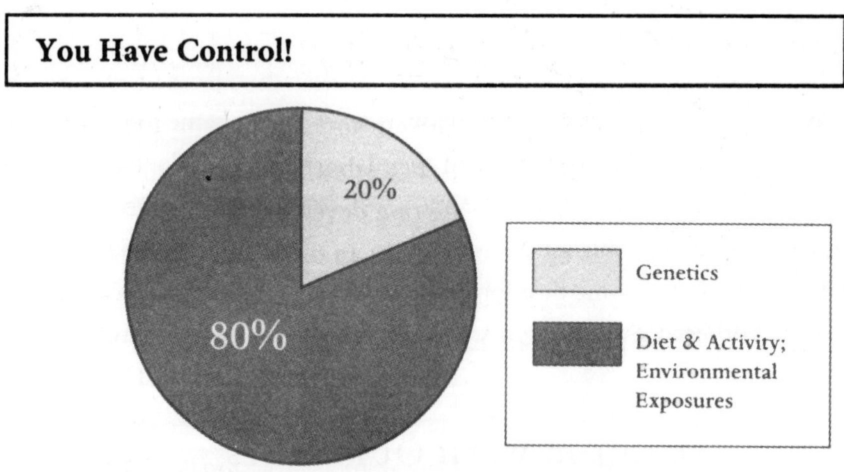

37 B. N. Ames, I. Elson-Schwab, and E. A. Silver, "High-dose vitamin therapy stimulates variant enzymes with decreased coenzyme binding affinity (increased km): relevance to genetic disease and polymorphism," *AM J Clin Nutr* 75 (2002): 616–58.

38 P. Lichtenstein, N. V. Holm, et al., "Environmental and inheritable factors in the causation of cancer; analysis of cohorts of twins from Sweden, Denmark and Finland," *NEJM* 343, no. 2 (2000): 78–85.

Where Most Chronic Pain and Disease Come From

If the development of chronic muscle and joint pain disorders is not primarily caused by our genetic makeup or the work we do, then maybe we have to look to other factors, such as diet, lifestyle, and environment. In our society today, we tend to avoid connecting our aches and pains to what we eat or to the health of our environment. Recent research, however, now shows a very direct connection between how we feel, what we eat, and even the health of our environment. No matter how skeptical you may be of this fact, all you need to do to test it is perform a little experiment. For just a month, try changing your diet, reducing chemical exposure in your immediate environment, and add some specific nutritional supplements (strategies fully described later in this book); then just see what happens. What do you have to lose but your pain and stiffness?

Many of us have heard the statement "you are what you eat," but how many of us live our lives by this fundamental truth? This truth was well illustrated by a thorough examination the U.S. Department of Health and Human Services completed and published in 1988 called the *Surgeon General's Report on Nutrition and Health.* This report found that heart disease, cancer, and strokes account for as much as 75% of all deaths in the United States and that these diseases are diet related. In other words, what we eat, digest, and absorb are directly related to the "big three" killers in the Western world. The surgeon general's report went on to state that "one personal choice seems to influence long-term health prospects more than any other: *what we eat*" (my emphasis).

However, the ecology of our health is deeper than the choices of the food we eat. Our modern society has forgotten the link between what we eat and how we feel, as well as the ecological bond between ourselves and our earth. This bond is most intimately maintained through our food and drink, substances that come directly from the earth itself. To fully understand this vital bond, we must first understand what food actually is. When we live an unexamined life controlled by sound bites and commercialism, food need only be something to overcome our hunger cravings and taste good. When we live at the surface of life, food becomes nothing more than a substance that slides past our tongue with delight and fills us up. This may have worked for millennia when human existence was sustained by natural and whole foods, but modern processed foods of commerce are no longer the wholesome, natural products humanity once consumed.

What Food Is and Its Connection to Pain and Disease

Food is sustenance composed of macro- and micronutrients. Macronutrients are those elements of food needed in large quantities by the body. These macronutrients—carbohydrates, proteins, and fats, as well as oxygen we breathe in—provide us with the basic building blocks with which we construct and maintain ourselves. They also provide the basic fuel for the energy to create, build, and maintain our tissues and organs, as well as energy for movement. Within our Standard American Diet (SAD for short), there is an overabundance of calories, or macronutrients. This overabundance of macronutrients is usually consumed in the form of simple sugars and fats, but also protein. Excessive animal protein can put on fat, damage the kidneys, and cause osteoporosis; as always, there can be too much of a good thing. Sweets and fats are the macronutrients that quickly fill us up and taste good to our tongue. We can utilize these caloric concentrated foods to make energy, but when we intake more than we need, they will cause all sorts of health issues besides the dreaded stored fat.

On the other hand, our foods are also composed of micronutrients, or nutrients that we need in smaller amounts. These micronutrients are generally familiar to us: vitamins, minerals, and plant phytonutrients. Our cells utilize these micronutrients to properly process macronutrients into needed structure and energy. Without adequate amounts of these micronutrients to properly process proteins, carbohydrates, and fats, healthy tissues do not get built and adequate usable energy does not get generated. In that case, we tend to feel lousy—we ache and feel tired, the two most common complaints reported to health-care providers today.

Also, when we do not consume adequate micronutrients to properly process these calories, all the body can do is store it as fat. Our SAD diet tends to be one of overconsumption and undernutrition, which leads to many health disorders.[39] Common deficiencies in micronutrients involve vitamins B_{12}, folic acid, B_6, niacin, C, and E, as well as iron and zinc. Bruce Ames reported in 2001 in the medical journal *Mutation Research* that half the population may be deficient in at least one or more of these micronutri-

39 A. K. Kant, "Consumption of energy-dense, nutrient-poor foods by adult Americans: nutritional and health implications; the third national health and nutrition examination survey 1988–1994," *Am J Clin Nutr* 72 (2000): 929–36.

ents, and 80% of children and adolescents and 68% of adults in America do not even eat five portions of fruit and vegetables a day.[40]

For an in-depth understanding of the ecology of health, we need to appreciate where our macro- and micronutrients come from. Carbohydrates, proteins, fats, and vitamins are made from the elements of our earth: for example, hydrogen, carbon, nitrogen, oxygen, phosphorus, and sulfur. When you take in proper levels of these macro- and micronutrients built from these basic elements and add in the minerals of the earth—calcium, phosphorus, magnesium, potassium, sodium, iron, zinc, copper, manganese, chromium, selenium, and other trace minerals—you can build and maintain a healthy body. These are the basic building blocks of life, which are actual elements of this earth and its atmosphere. We utilize these macro- and micronutrients to create a life of either health or disease, similar to the way a weaver can take the basic elements of plant and animal fibers and different dyes to create a magnificent tapestry that tells an entire story.

Hierarchy of Health (from the Earth Up)

- Healthy mind/body/spirit
- Organ systems
- Tissues
- Cells
- Carbohydrates, proteins, fats, and vitamins
- Hydrogen, carbon, nitrogen, oxygen, phosphorus, and sulfur
- Calcium, magnesium, potassium, sodium, iron, zinc, copper, manganese, chromium, selenium, and trace minerals
- Earth and its atmosphere

40 B. N. Ames, "DNA damage from micronutrient deficiencies is likely to be a major cause of cancer," *Mutat Res* 475 (2001): 7–20.

Our Health and the Health of the Earth Are One

This wisdom was not lost to our ancient ancestors. The origin of our word *human* comes from two ancient roots: *humus,* meaning "of the earth," and *mannus,* meaning "to think." The ancient origin for human, *humanus,* literally meant a "thinking being of earth." It is as if our ancient ancestors understood that to maintain their bodies of clay, they must replenish their earthly elements through food and drink. This food and drink is created out of an intimacy between the sun, the rain, and the earth itself, and out of this communion, we and all of life are created and sustained.

It seems easy enough for anyone to comprehend that if you stop the intake of macro- and micronutrients from the earth into your body through starvation, you will soon cease to exist. However, it seems very difficult for us to fully appreciate the next level of understanding: degrade the source of these nutrients we take in on a daily basis, and we will end up slowly poisoning our health. By no longer eating whole, natural foods, we easily become deficient in the micronutrients necessary for life. When we degrade the source of these nutrients by overprocessing our foods and add the burden of chemical toxins to the air, food, and water we take in, we pollute our bodies.

How bad is it? The U.S. Food and Drug Administration has approved nearly 4,000 different chemical food additives that are now found in our foods in various combinations. The problem is that many of these additives have been proven detrimental to human health and are actually banned in other countries. Furthermore, these 4,000 chemicals are not tested in combination, the way they are consumed and enter into our tissues. The average American will consume about five pounds a year of these chemical food additives: artificial colorings, flavorings, and preservatives. Another example of food additives is sweeteners; between 1970 and 1990, the United States consumption of high-fructose corn syrup exploded by over 1,000%. The extreme intake of this additive has helped to fuel the obesity epidemic in the United States.[41] The average American today is a guinea pig in a historic experimentation with human nutrition, one that may be causing the pandemic of chronic pain and chronic degenerative disease we are now witnessing.

41 G. A. Bray, S. J. Nielsen, and B. M. Popkin, "Consumption of high-fructose corn syrup in beverages may play a role in the epidemic of obesity," *Am J Clin Nutr* 79, no. 4 (2004): 537–43.

Our modern society has also created over 4 million synthetic compounds, many of which find their way into our environment and eventually our bodies. In 1999 alone, over one billion pounds of pesticides were applied in the United States, and over 5.6 billion pounds were spread on crops throughout the world.[42] The U.S. Environmental Protection Agency (EPA) announced in 2006 that all rivers and lakes in the United States now have measurable levels of herbicides and pesticides. Unbeknownst to the general public, from 1970 to 1989 the EPA measured the levels of chemical toxins stored in human fat tissues, through analyzing the fat from cadavers and elective surgeries. This National Human Adipose Tissue Survey (NHATS) found the five most toxic chemicals in 100% of the human tissue samples analyzed[43] (see chapter 7). There are also toxic heavy metals present in our environment: mercury, lead, cadmium, arsenic, nickel, and aluminum. Recent studies have found that at least 25% of humans currently store heavy metals in their tissues.

Your Food: The Great Modern Experiment!

- 4 million synthetic compounds manufactured
- 4,000 different chemical food additives
  - per person, we consume 5 pounds a year of chemical food additives: e.g., artificial colorings, flavorings, preservatives, and sweeteners
  - 1970 to 1990: high-fructose corn syrup consumption increased 1000%
- 80,000 industrial and agricultural chemicals
  - 5.6 billion pounds of pesticides are put on crops throughout the world
  - 5 most toxic chemicals are now found in 100% of human tissues sampled

42 *Annual Review of Public Health* 25 (2004): 155–97.

43 http://cfpub.epa.gov/ncea/cfm/recordisplay.cfm?deid=55204.

The deleterious role these synthetic compounds and heavy metals play in chronic pain and chronic disease will be covered in greater detail in chapter 7. For now, it is only important to recognize that these chemical toxins have a tremendous impact upon the ecological health of our earth and therefore on us. To finally arrive at real healing that leads to a life where pain no longer rules your life, it is vital to take a more ecological view of your health. We have seen that there is no real separation between ourselves and the earth; we are the *humanus*, "the thinking being of earth." If you stop the influx of earthly elements through your body via food and drink, you stop the possibility of life altogether. The more challenging realization for most of us is the awareness that if we pollute the earth, degrading the quality of our air, water, and food, we pollute our body/mind. It is just that simple! Ultimately, then, it is vital for us to begin to heal our earth to truly heal ourselves. In the interim, though, there are specific things you can do to protect yourself from unnecessary exposure to toxic chemicals and begin to remove them from your tissues. These issues will be discussed in greater detail in later chapters and will be a major focus of this book.

The Dance of Earth and Sun That Is You

To better understand the ecology of healing your pain, it will be helpful to take a short journey through the workings of your body. The journey begins at your nose and mouth with the intake of vital air, food, and water. It is at this juncture that massive amounts of this earth enter into you to become you. It is estimated that you will take in more then 1,538 pounds of earthly materials each year. This adds up to a whopping 30 to 60 tons of food that you will consume and process throughout your lifetime. The destination for a small portion of this annual 1,538 pounds of earthly bounty is to momentarily become bits and pieces of the entity that you call you. I say momentarily because you are constantly rebuilding yourself. For example, you create an entire new stomach lining each and every day.

You also take a small portion of these 1,538 pounds of the earth to produce the energy necessary to build, maintain, and move this "thinking being of earth." You utilize the influx of these earthly elements in the form of calories and micronutrients to convert these calories into usable energy in a molecule called ATP. When you break down ATP molecules in your cells, you release the energy you need to perform all the work you do inside your body as well as the work you do with your body. ATP is your currency of energy; if there is any inner process or outer work to be done, you buy it with ATP. This energy is so in demand and vital to your existence that you produce your weight in ATP each and every day, but of course you burn it up every day with activity.

It is important to note here your connection to the primal fires of the sun. The energy within your ATP molecules ultimately came from the sun, solar radiation converted into usable energy by plants. Therefore, whatever you do—whether hugging a loved one, dancing for joy, or sitting in thought—these activities are the very energy of the sun coming through you from the food you eat. You are the earth and sun momentarily existing as you in the miraculous dance we call life!

Appreciating Your Health from the Inside

To begin the process of making a small portion of this daily 4 to 5 pounds of earthly elements into you, you must properly digest and adequately absorb the needed macro- and micronutrients. If you were to unfold and stretch out your entire digestive tract from your mouth to anus, it would cover an area equal in size to a double's tennis court. This gives you a large surface area with which to digest and absorb your food, but also a large area to maintain and keep healthy. Today in the United States, over 100 million individuals suffer from painful digestive disorders. This phenomenon has given rise to more than 200 over-the-counter drugs for digestive complaints. However, many of these drugs only serve to create other digestive and general health problems.

These disorders of the gastrointestinal tract tend to show up as several common digestive diseases, such as gastroesophageal reflux disease (GERD), gastritis, peptic ulcer, irritable bowel syndrome (IBS), inflammatory bowel disease (IBD), and colitis, to name a few. Common underlying factors in these disorders are: inadequate stomach acid (or HCL), poor digestive enzyme function, and the overgrowth of bad bacteria and yeasts in your intestines. Research has linked these same underlying factors, which lead to typical digestive diseases, to common chronic pain disorders and diseases outside the gastrointestinal tract, such as chronic muscle and joint pain, arthritis, headaches, fibromyalgia, chronic fatigue, autism, asthma, allergies, eczema, and many more. Often, these different digestive disorders begin with poor food choices of overly processed, devitalized foods. This is made worse by not properly beginning the digestive process by eating slowly and chewing thoroughly, something few individuals are inclined to do in our hurried modern life.

The Hard Work of Digestion

Digestion is the slow, steady process of mechanically and chemically breaking down larger molecules of food into ever-smaller units so they can be properly absorbed and turned into you. To efficiently accomplish this, it has been said that you should "drink your food and eat your drink." In other words, it is important to completely masticate the foods you eat, mixing them thoroughly with the digestive secretions of your mouth. Nor should you gulp down your drinks. This is vital because the process of thoroughly chewing and slowly drinking begins the process of digestion; it readies the stomach to secrete adequate amounts of digestive enzymes. Your saliva also contains anti-infective agents that prevent "bad bugs" or unwanted microbes from entering your lower gastrointestinal (GI) tract and causing dysbiosis. Dysbiosis is the growth of bad bacteria in your lower GI tract, which recent research has linked to chronic pain and chronic diseases. A great deal more will be discussed later in this book pertaining to dysbiosis and its role in the development of your chronic pain and health disorders, as well as its treatment.

Connecting your mouth to your stomach is the muscular tube called the esophagus, well known to many individuals who suffer with the pain of GERD. Your stomach receives the food and stores it while mixing it with hydrochloric acid and other digestive enzymes. These digestive enzymes continue the work that was started by your mouth. At this point, vital proteins are broken down by the all-important hydrochloric acid, or HCL. The full acidification of your food in your stomach helps to properly stimulate your pancreas to secrete its all-important digestive enzymes.

Today, it is common for millions to view hydrochloric acid as the enemy and take drugs to turn off this vital digestive enzyme. The problem is that this makes it very difficult to digest and absorb the macro- and micronutrients from the food you eat. Not only does HCL help you to digest your food, it helps to destroy many unwanted microorganisms that come in through your mouth. Therefore, adequate levels of HCL lower your risk of bad "bugs" setting up housekeeping in your lower GI tract.

It turns out that the production of HCL is one of the most energy-consuming things you do, so your stomach need lots of ATP to produce adequate amounts of HCL to digest your food. When you become sick or have low energy, often your ability to produce HCL is reduced. When this happens, you may notice symptoms of nausea, bloating, belching, burning, gas, and other signs of indigestion. One interesting symptom of low HCL is heartburn.

After your stomach has thoroughly mixed and acidified your food, it passes on to the small intestine. Here your pancreas dumps major digestive enzymes to complete the breakdown of proteins, carbohydrates, and fats into small enough units so they can be absorbed and become you. Bile is also added at this point from your gallbladder to help improve the digestion of the fats in your diet. Low levels of pancreatic digestive enzymes, or bile, from the gallbladder can lead to maldigestion and poor absorption. Maldigestion from low levels of pancreatic digestive enzymes can lead to symptoms of abdominal pain, gas, bloating, constipation, or diarrhea. With poor digestion, food allergies become more prevalent, which are also associated with chronic pain disorders. Also, as previously stated, poor digestion and absorption are associated with chronic pain disorders and chronic diseases including but not limited to muscle pain, arthritis, allergies, autism, anxiety, depression, fatigue, and neurological disorders. Often, just by improving your digestion and absorption through the supplementation of HCL and pancreatic digestive enzymes, you can rid yourself of these chronic disorders.

Case Study

One of my first patients in clinical practice, Tom, a 35-year-old high school teacher, came to me with symptoms of heartburn, bloating, belching, and gas after meals, along with other signs of indigestion. However, his primary complaint was chronic muscle and joint pain in multiple areas. Because of his symptom profile, the first thing I did for him was to prescribe HCL supplements, in capsule form, to be taken at mealtime. In a short time, his heartburn and other symptoms of indigestion went away, and so did Tom's musculoskeletal pain!

This illustrates how important digestion of macro- and micronutrients is to your overall health and cnronic pain states. The mechanism for his recovery no doubt had to do with helping to normalize his digestion, absorption, and gut flora, and to reduce his food allergy potential from partially digested proteins. Later, we will examine in detail the vital connection between your digestive tract and healing your pain.

The Benefits of Bacteria

Frequently in our busy lives, we quickly look at issues, health or otherwise, promptly identify the "bad guy," and then declare war. Previously we saw this with inflammation and the major problems that can develop when we block this vital immune system function instead of properly managing it. Our modern society does the same thing when it comes to bacteria. We may be creating more problems by our all-out war on bacteria and our overuse of antibiotics and antibacterial soaps.

For instance, in your small and large intestines, beneficial bacteria grow that are necessary for the maintenance of your good health. In fact, our survival would be impossible without these bacteria. These microbes perform many vital functions: they maintain the health of the GI tract, fight off bad microbes, aid your immune system, produce certain vitamins, and influence your metabolic activities. These beneficial bacteria far outnumber your own human cells and collectively weigh about six pounds, making them one of the largest "organs" in your body. These bacteria in your intestines are like the microbes that live around the roots of plants and trees, allowing them to take in vital nutrients not otherwise available. Our intestines are the roots of our health, for it is here that we take in the world and begin the process of making it us.

When you do not have enough beneficial bacteria or you have an overgrowth of unwanted microbes such as pathogenic bacteria and yeasts, you have developed altered gut flora, a common condition known as dysbiosis. Recent research has shown a high correlation between dysbiosis and the common problems of irritable bowel syndrome and inflammatory bowel disease. In a recent study, dysbiosis of the small intestine was found to be present in 80% of irritable bowel syndrome patients.[44] It is now recognized that dysbiosis and irritable bowel syndrome are associated with many painful disorders such as fibromyalgia, interstitial cystitis of the bladder, and chronic fatigue syndrome. In another study, it was found that 100% of individuals with fibromyalgia had dysbiosis or "bad bugs" growing in their small intestine.[45]

---

44 M. Pimentel, E. J. Chow, and H. C. Lin, "Eradication of small intestinal bacterial overgrowth reduces symptoms of irritable bowel syndrome," *Am J Gastro* 95, no. 12 (Dec. 2000): 3503–6.

45 M. Pimentel, E. J. Chow, and D. Hallegua, et al., "Small intestinal bacterial overgrowth: a possible association with fibromyalgia," *J Musculoskeletal Pain* 9 (2001): 103–13.

Lacking 6 Pounds of Beneficial Bacteria = Dysbiosis

- Present in 80% of irritable bowel syndrome patients
- 100% of individuals with fibromyalgia also have dysbiosis
- Associated with interstitial cystitis and chronic fatigue

Case Study

Susie, a 21-year-old college student, had developed severe fibromyalgia at an early age. It is somewhat unusual for young individuals to develop this malady, but it made total sense in Susie's case. As a young adolescent, she had traveled outside the country with her parents. She was unaware that she had picked up a few "bad bugs" that began to set up housekeeping in her small bowel. When she came to my clinic, she had symptoms classic to fibromyalgia and some very mild indications of possible dysbiosis. Upon testing for specific urinary organic acids in her urine, I found that she had severely elevated metabolites present in her urine from the growth of bad bacteria in her small intestine. A course of therapeutic action (as described in chapter 16) helped her to overcome the dysbiosis and her fibromyalgia.

You may now begin to see how real healing of chronic pain involves a larger ecological approach to pain relief. By honoring your ecological connection to the earth by eating nutritious, natural whole foods and by maintaining a healthy inner ecology of your gastrointestinal tract, you can begin to promote real wellness in your life. This provides a solid basis from which you are able to build healthy tissues and adequate levels of ATP, giving you a chance to live a joyous and pain-free life. However, that's not the end of this journey, for it is here in the small intestine that critical decisions are made on which elements of this earth come into you to become you and what is to be rejected. Technically speaking, inside your gastrointestinal tract is still outside of your body. In the gastrointestinal tract, primarily in the small intestine, the body attempts to allow only health-promoting nutrients in while keeping potentially damaging chemicals and microbes out. Because of this, it's not that surprising to find that most of our immune system is housed in the gastrointestinal tract.

Your Liver and the Importance of Detoxification

From the gastrointestinal tract, anything absorbed into your bloodstream will be monitored by your liver. In fact, three-fourths of the blood received by the liver comes directly from the gastrointestinal tract. This is why a healthy liver is so vital to the body's detoxification ability. Today it has become extremely popular to talk about detoxification programs, but unfortunately a great deal of misinformation abounds. The actual process that the liver uses to detoxify chemicals in your body is extremely energy- and nutrient-demanding. Therefore, if you fast to "detoxify," you are cutting off the macronutrients for energy production and the micronutrients your liver uses in its detoxification process.

Your liver detoxifies chemicals that you inhale, ingest, absorb through skin, or produce in your body. If your liver is not up to the task of removing these chemical toxins, they will circulate through your body, doing damage and increasing pain. The work of I. R. Bell, reported in the *American Journal of Medicine* in 1998, found that even low levels of environmental chemicals in your tissues could cause chronic muscle and joint pain problems, along with fatigue.[46]

It is interesting to note that we all detoxify at different rates and abilities, and we all react differently to various chemical toxins. Various studies have shown as much as a 700% difference in the ability of the liver to detoxify from one individual to another. In other words, biochemically we are individuals with our own strengths and weaknesses when it comes to handling drugs, toxins, pollutants, and other substances deleterious to our health. It is exactly this genetic variability in our detoxification pathways that makes some of us more susceptible to pain and disease from smoking, drinking, drugs, and pollution.

The importance of proper detoxification, as well as strategies for proper detoxification, will be discussed in greater detail in chapter 17: Strategies to Enhance Detoxification and Energy Production. The point now is to realize that quick pain relief is a fallacy. By ignoring the ecology of your life—by disregarding all of the factors involved in your developing recurrent pain—you only deepen the dysfunction until it manifests as a disease process that becomes life threatening or disabling.

---

46 I. R. Bell, C. M. Baldwin, and G. E. Schwartz, "Illness from low levels of environmental chemicals: relevance to chronic fatigue syndrome and fibromyalgia," *Am J Med* 105, no. 3A (1998): 74S–82S.

Case Study

Sandy came into my office with severe muscle and joint pain with fatigue. She was in her late forties and was the wife of a farmer. Her symptoms began soon after she had been exposed to the aerial spraying of a pesticide for woolly caterpillar infestation on her farm. When the crop duster flew over, the windows to her house were open. Due to the wind direction and the close proximity of her house to the soybean fields, her home became enveloped with the toxic spray. Her adolescent daughter was also exposed to an equal amount of the pesticide at the same time. Because of her youth and vibrant health, she did not develop symptoms at that time. By working on improving Sandy's overall health and supporting her body's ability to detoxify these pesticides, I'm happy to say that Sandy returned to a more normal life. Her treatment program can be found in chapter 17.

What Does This Mean for Me?

- What I eat, digest, and absorb becomes me and therefore determines my physical and mental well-being; therefore, I want to maximize my life by improving my diet and digestion.
- Degrading this earth ultimately means I am polluting my own body; therefore, the earth must be healed so I may truly heal.
- I can also pollute my body from the inside; therefore, I need to promote good bowel and liver function.

SECTION 2
Roadblocks to Healing

On any journey, there are difficulties, challenges, and sometimes even roadblocks that must be overcome to reach a destination; so it is with your healing process. In this section, you will come to understand the challenges that lay before you as we explore the healing of the body's myofascial tissues.

You will find that because of dietary and lifestyle choices, physiological abnormalities take place in the myofascial tissues. These biochemical changes cause you pain and make health and happiness difficult to achieve. These physiological roadblocks to healing—oxidative stress, systemic inflammation, insulin resistance, and low-level toxic chemical exposure—require your understanding so you may find your way to a pain-free life.

In addition, there is a side benefit to understanding this. The roadblocks to healing your chronic pain are the same metabolic factors that can set you up for chronic and degenerative diseases: cardiovascular disease, cancer, diabetes, and neurodegenerative disorders. Therefore, comprehending these metabolic factors of chronic pain will allow you to create a life of real health and longevity.

4

Our Fantastic Fascia

Questions to Consider:

1. What is the actual source of most chronic pain?
2. Why is chronic muscle and joint pain also referred to as myofascial pain syndrome?
3. What is fascia, and what function does it perform?
4. What are nociceptors, and what's so special about them?

It is impossible to separate any one part of the body as being the most important, because the body is an interdependent whole. When it comes to enjoying your life, though, the most important system is probably the musculoskeletal system, even though we tend to think of the cardiovascular system as the primary structure of the body. No doubt this relates to the fact that when the heart stops beating, it's all over for us. This little fact does make the cardiovascular system rather central to our life. As logical as this is, on another level your primary system is the humble musculoskeletal system. Why? Because movement is life.

Movement Is Life

What makes movement possible? A healthy neuromusculoskeletal system makes smooth, pain-free movement possible, and in a sense all other body systems are designed to feed and maintain it. As previously discussed, your digestive system digests and absorbs nutrients into your bloodstream to be utilized by your body. Your liver then cleans the blood and removes the toxic substances from internal and external sources. This purified, nutrient-rich blood is then pumped from your heart to your lungs, where it picks up another vital nutrient: oxygen. This oxygenated, nutrient-rich blood returns to the heart to be pumped out to every cell in your body. The vast majority of this blood is delivered to your 400 muscles that normally constitute 50% of a healthy body weight. So energy demanding are these skeletal muscles that it is estimated they use up to 70% of the available energy-rich blood glucose to produce the necessary ATP to move you about through life. What is central to our discussion here is that if the neuromusculoskeletal system is not kept healthy, it becomes the major source of chronic or recurrent pain. Chronic neuromusculoskeletal pain is the leading cause of disability in our society and around the world.

Here's a simple example of how this all works. Let's say you enjoy life by playing golf or tennis, or just taking a walk with friends. To accomplish this, your nervous system (the *neuro* part) must tell some of your muscles (the *musculo* part) to shorten or contract and others to relax. In other words, you flex and extend your joints (the *skeletal* part) to create movement. With this, you move about the golf course, tennis court or down a walking path with your friends, enjoying your life. As with most things in life, this ability to move about pain-free in any way we wish is generally taken for granted until it is taken away through pain and/or disability.

There are so many other vital things your muscles do for you besides motion that it's hard to acknowledge them all. Besides movement, the neuromusculoskeletal system is constantly in action to maintain your body in a stable, upright position, whether sitting, standing, walking, or running. This part of the neuromusculoskeletal system involves the dynamic postural nervous system and muscles, and as we will see, postural strain can lead to a great deal of chronic pain in your life. Also, as your skeletal muscles perform work, they produce heat that allows you to maintain your normal body temperature. Muscles will generate as much as 85% of your body heat. This means that the colder it is, the more you have to move around to stay warm, which is why we shiver when our body temperature drops. Another type of muscle called smooth muscle moves materials through your body; for example, through your digestive tract, reproductive system, and urinary system. These smooth muscles also can be a primary source of chronic pain when things go wrong with those systems. A third type of specialized muscle is cardiac muscle (the heart, in other words), which of course acts to pump blood to all the cells of your body. Collectively, these muscles create the movement of your life.

Primary Source of Chronic Pain: Muscles and Fascia

Simply stated, wherever there is movement, there is potential for dysfunction to develop. In animals, this dysfunction is signaled by the experience of pain, and if this dysfunction becomes chronic, so will the pain signals. The primary movers, your muscles and the connective tissue that envelops them, are the primary contributors to pain in your body, for many reasons. First and foremost, your 400 muscles comprise the largest organ system in your body, so there's more to hurt. Secondarily, your musculoskeletal system is held together and functions through connective tissue called fascia, which collectively has one of the highest concentrations of pain receptors in your body, called nociceptors. Throughout the rest of this book, our focus will be primarily on this myofascial tissue, *myo-* for the muscle cells that can contract or shorten and *fascial* for all the connective tissue that holds it together.

Here's how it works: your muscle cells are basically proteins that can contract or shorten, held in connective tissue bags of fascia. These connective tissue bags of fascia enveloping the muscle cells come together to form the ropelike structures at the two ends of the muscle, called tendons. These connective tissue tendons then connect the muscle to the bone it moves. When your muscle cells shorten within a muscle, they pull on the tendons, moving the bones closer together. This connective tissue fascia of your tendons is therefore connected with the fascial coverings of your bones, called the periosteum, which literally means "around the bone." The fascia of your tendons and the periosteum is then continuous with the connective tissue that makes up the ligaments of your joints. Ligaments are the extremely tough fibrous fascia that hold one bone to another to form a joint. Because of the extremely high number of sensitive pain receptors laced throughout this fascia and the fact that it is under constant physical and chemical stress, this neuromyofascial tissue is the primary source of most chronic pain disorders.

What Fascia Is Made Of

This fascia throughout your body is made up of three primary materials. The first component is called collagen, fibers that thread through your fascia and are stronger than steel by weight. These fibers occur in linear parallel bundles, forming cablelike structures, which gives them their incredible strength. This is important because when you injure a joint or muscle, many times the collagen of the muscle or joint fascia heals in a haphazard format instead of linear parallel bundles. When this takes place after an injury, your muscles and joints don't have the same strength and flexibility they once had. Appropriate rehabilitative exercises are important in promoting the collagen to heal properly.

Your collagen fibers appropriately are made from a protein called collagen, which comprises one-fourth of the total protein in your body. This structural protein is very susceptible to damage from free radicals and chronic inflammation, and in fact the fascia are the primary arena where the process of chronic inflammation occurs. Therefore, when you feel pain due to acute or chronic inflammation, it undoubtedly involves the fascia of your body. Furthermore, dysfunctional changes in your fascia (e.g., stiffness and soreness) tend to be a harbinger of future chronic degenerative disease. So if you have healthy, pain-free, flexible fascia, it is an indication of overall good health. This is an important factor to consider in restoring your health and healing your chronic pain.

The second component of fascia is a network of smaller-diameter elastin fibers within this connective tissue. These elastin fibers provide strength, but their greatest attribute is their ability to be stretched and then reclaim their original position. Your elastin fibers can be stretched one and a half times their resting length without breaking. It is the elastin fibers in the connective tissue of your skin that allow it to return to its normal smooth contour after being stretched by facial expressions. This is particularly visible in a youthful face, with its normally high content of healthy elastin fibers. However, as we age, this connective tissue becomes damaged, especially by free radicals and silent inflammation (see chapter 5). This is quite noticeable in smokers, even at a relatively young age. The problem is that this free-radical damage affects not just your good looks but the connective tissue throughout your body. We wrinkle, so to speak, all over—inside and out. To get an idea of how healthy your connective tissues are, grab the skin of your cheek and gently pull and release it in front of a mirror. Feel how rubbery it is, and see how long it takes to snap fully back to its smooth contour.

The third component of your connective tissue is known as the ground substance in which the collagen and elastin fibers are embedded. To visualize this, imagine a sheet of gelatin with linear bundles of braided yarn (collagen fibers) and a network of elastic rubber bands (elastin fibers) embedded throughout it. This ground substance plays a major role in the health of your fascia and in the formation of chronic pain-causing muscle knots. Ground substance binds together and supports the cells it surrounds, making it of primary importance in the health of that tissue. Ground substance provides the medium through which nutrients flow from your blood into the cells that build and maintain healthy collagen and elastin fibers. It is also the medium which allows waste products to flow out to the blood vessels and be removed from your tissues. The connective tissue of your body holds about one-fourth of all body fluids. In chapter 9: Self-Care 101 for Myofascial Pain Syndromes, I will show how physically changing the consistency of this fascial ground substance can help you release your pain-causing muscle knots.

Components of Healthy Fascia

- Collagen: fibers stronger than steel
- Elastin: fibers that allow tissues to stretch
- Ground substance: the nurturing medium of fascia

The Interwoven Tapestry of Your Fascia

What is important to realize here is that all the fascia of your body is a continuous tapestry of interconnected connective tissue running from the top of your skull continuously down to the tip of your toes. This continuous woven tapestry of connective tissue ranges from thick, steel-like bands forming ligaments and tendons to lace-like fascial sheets separating and enveloping muscles, and these connective tissues are collectively called the myofascial tissues. This fascia interconnects your entire body; from muscles to tendons to the periosteum to ligaments, it is one continuous sheath. This same connective tissue fascia wraps around every nerve in your body, and these nerve coverings connect with the coverings of your spinal cord and your brain. This special tissue also flows through your pelvic, abdominal, and chest cavity, helping to hold all your vital organs in place. And of course, the fascia of your nervous system and organs also connects with the fascia of your muscle and joints.

This continuous fascial tapestry ties your entire body into one unit, into a whole being. Therefore, if you distort, twist, or deform the fascia by injury or other stress, through its interconnectedness it will affect other parts of your body. This interconnectedness of your body has already been well illustrated by the digestive tract and how problems there can, in fact, affect the entire body. It is similar also to the weblike interconnected metabolism of your body we discussed earlier, in which a deficiency in just one biochemical pathway will affect many different tissues in your body. On the other hand, as we saw, if we block a pathway with a drug, such as an NSAID like ibuprofen for inflammation, we can create damage in many different tissues of our bodies. In our modern health care, we tend to separate out parts of the body for treatment and even have specialists to address those areas. Nevertheless, I cannot stress enough that the interconnectedness of this fascinating body must be seen as and treated as a whole tapestry.

An Interconnected Whole

This idea of the body being an interconnected whole was brought to an even deeper understanding in 1997 by the British biophysicist Mae-Wan Ho. He developed a fascinating theory that describes the human being as a vibrant, conscious whole. Central to Ho's theory is the idea that this connective tissue fascia is actually a liquid crystalline matrix enabling instantaneous intercommunication and energy flow throughout the entire human organism. The important point to note here is the "instantaneous intercommunication," because this would indicate that there is no part of your body/mind separate from any other aspect of your body/mind.[47]

47 For more information, please see Mae-Wan Ho, "Quantum coherence and conscious experience," *Kybernetes* 6 (1997): 265–76.

Nociceptors: How We Hurt

As previously mentioned, the fascia that envelops your muscles and forms your tendons and ligaments is laced throughout with pain sensors, or free nerve endings, called nociceptors. The word *nociceptors* is Latin for "injury receptor," and these free nerve endings constantly monitor your tissues for stress, damage, or inflammation—in other words, for potential or actual injury. The stimulation of these nociceptors causes signals to be sent to your spinal cord and then on to your brain. When these signals reach all the way to the outer sensory cortex of your brain, only then do you consciously perceive the sensation of pain. These nociceptors have some very special qualities that are quite different from other nerve receptors, and understanding these characteristics can help you to overcome the chronic muscle and joint pain they create.

Nociceptors are located in nearly every tissue of your body, except for some very special locations. At the end of your bones where they meet to form a joint, you have a connective tissue called articular (joint) cartilage. There are no pain receptors in articular cartilage, which makes complete sense. If you had nociceptors in your joint cartilage, it would be extremely painful to walk, run, use your hands, or put any pressure on your joints. Therefore, joint pain does not come from inside the joint, the bones, or the cartilage. When you develop achy joints, arthritis, or sprains, the pain actually comes from the numerous nociceptors contained in the surrounding muscles, fascial tissues, and ligaments that make up the involved joint complex.

Your articular cartilage, like other connective tissue, is composed of a dense network of the same collagen and elastin fibers previously discussed. These fibers are embedded in a special rubbery ground substance called chondroitin sulfate. This material may sound familiar to you because it is now available in the form of a nutritional supplement. When you are young, this articular cartilage has the consistency of smooth ice against smooth ice. This allows free joint movement. As we age, though, this cartilage can break down, prematurely leading to the development of degenerative joint disease (DJD), commonly called osteoarthritis. This degeneration of the cartilage can become so severe that you end up with bone-on-bone joints. This can be prevented if you remove any existing muscle knots affecting joint function and improve the nutrition to your joints. If proper treatment is started early enough, you can overcome the pain and dysfunction of osteoarthritis. See section 3 to learn how to remove your pain-causing muscle knots and improve joint nutrition.

Another area of your body where we do not find nociceptors and therefore do not experience pain is inside the discs of your spine. You may have heard of these spinal discs because you or someone you know has had a herniated disc or even spinal disc surgery. These cushions between your vertebrae can be compared to a donut with jelly in the center. This jelly is called the nucleus pulposus, which is what leaks out when your disc degenerates and you develop a disc herniation. This jelly cushion of your spinal discs and the inside disc fibers immediately enveloping it do not contain nociceptors. Of course, not having pain receptors inside the cushions between your vertebrae also makes complete sense. If your spinal discs did contain nociceptors, it would be extremely painful to place any load on your spine or even to sit. However, the fascial connective tissue that makes up the outer third of your discs does contain pain receptors and can be a source of back pain.

For the sake of this discussion, it is only important to point out that the spinal discs and the cartilage of your spinal joints, called facets, do not contain nociceptors. They are not a source of pain until they begin to degenerate and make movement abnormal, leading to pain being generated in the muscles and fascia of your back. In addition, the discs can directly irritate a nerve root, causing pain when they herniate. Your spinal joints can also directly irritate a nerve root through the formation of bone spurs from arthritis. However, the primary source of this epidemic of disabling back pain, especially in those forty-five years old and younger, is the muscles and fascia of the back. In chapter 10, we will more fully discuss the spine and its role in chronic back and neck pain and how you can overcome it.

The Specialness of Nociceptors and Chronic Pain

The nociceptors located throughout your myofascial tissues have some very special characteristics that make you more susceptible to chronic pain. First, these sensory nerve endings *do not adapt*. To understand the importance of this, imagine walking into a room where a bad smell is present. At first this odor irritates you, but after a short while you no longer notice the smell. This is because the sensory nerve receptors in your nose will adapt to accommodate the smell. The same thing applies to the sensory pressure receptors in your buttocks that are stimulated when you first sit down. At first you notice the pressure and feel the chair, but after the receptors adapt, you no longer notice the pressure. However, your nociceptors do not adapt. If you were sitting on tacks, for example, the sensation of pain will continue until you remove all the tacks. If you leave in one or more tacks, the pain will become chronic. Furthermore, the longer these remaining tacks stimulate the nociceptors, the less stimulation it takes to cause pain in this area.

This is the second thing about pain receptors in your myofascial tissues: they can develop lowered thresholds. Imagine somebody patting you on the back; your nociceptors would not fire because this was only a firm, friendly pat, not a painful contact. Now, imagine that the tissue has been sunburned recently, making this innocent pat a painful experience. Because of the injury to the tissues from sun damage, the cutaneous nociceptors and nervous system are now much more sensitive. The threshold of stimulation necessary to cause the pain fibers (nociceptors) on your sunburned back to fire has been lowered.

This is exactly is what happens in the condition known as fibromyalgia, which affects nearly 10 million individuals in the United States. In fibromyalgia, the threshold of the nociceptors throughout the body, beginning first in the deep myofascial tissues, has been lowered. This condition of more sensitized nociceptors in the myofascial tissues is called peripheral sensitization. This book will specifically address how to overcome the condition of peripheral sensitization through comprehensive physical and nutritional strategies.

Your nerve endings fire and create the sensation of pain through the presence of certain chemical mediators produced in your tissues because of physical, chemical, or thermal stress. The chemicals produced in your tissues that stimulate your myofascial nociceptors are the same chemicals that drive systemic, or "silent," inflammation in your body. This means that any chronic low-grade inflammation can serve to sensitize your tissues, setting you up to more readily develop a chronic myofascial pain disorder in that region. Connected to this chronic inflammation in your tissues is always the presence of free radicals, which is why antioxidants can be beneficial in treating myofascial pain.

In the next chapter, we discuss in detail chronic inflammation and free radical tissue injury. You will also learn how dietary and lifestyle choices can either increase or decrease the presence of inflammatory chemicals and free radicals in your tissues. The increased presence of chronic inflammatory chemicals and free radicals in your tissues is not only connected to chronic pain but also to all the degenerative diseases present in modern society. This brings us back to the central theme of this book: when you properly address the underlying causes of your chronic pain, you are also optimizing your health and helping to prevent future degenerative disease.

What Does This Mean for Me?

- Life is movement made possible through my myofascial tissues.
- Fascia is a special single sheet of tissue that connects me from the top of my head to the tip of my toes.
- My myofascial tissues are highly susceptible to physical, chemical, and emotional distress.
- Fascia is a special single sheet of tissue that interconnects me from the top of my head to the tip of my toes.
- Nociceptors located throughout my myofascial tissues have special characteristics that keep me from harm and improve my chances of survival.
- My nociceptors are able to protect me because they do not adapt and their thresholds can be lowered.
- However, this can go too far and cause me chronic pain, even without tissue damage.
- Because the cartilage of joints does not contain nociceptors, the primary source of chronic pain are the myofascial tissues: muscles, fascia, tendons, and ligaments.

5

The Smoldering Fire of Chronic Inflammation

Questions to Consider:

1. What activates nociceptors?
2. What is inflammation, and is it good or bad?
3. What causes inflammation to become chronic and develop in myofascial tissues?
4. What role do free radicals play in all of this?

To overcome the challenge of chronic or recurrent pain and promote real wellness, it is vital to have some understanding of the process that causes the pain receptors to fire: inflammation. Inflammation is a biological process that everyone has experienced. If you have pulled a muscle, sprained an ankle, or had a fever from an infection, you have felt its effects. Generally, inflammation is something we try to eliminate by swallowing drugs; over 30 billion tablets of NSAIDs are sold over the counter each year for this purpose. But in reality, very few of us understand and appreciate inflammation for what it really is: a biological process that makes our very survival possible.

Inflammation: The Healing Response

Everyone has experienced red, warm, and swollen tissues from an acute inflammatory process caused by a sprained joint or an infected cut. It is easy to think of this red, angry tissue as an enemy that must be defeated. We spend tens of billions of dollars each year to wage war on this biological process, but the inflammatory process is more accurately understood as a healing response. This healing response, or inflammation, is called into action whenever a tissue in your body is stressed. This could be physical stress (e.g., trauma), microbial stress (e.g., infectious agents), or chemical stress (e.g., toxins from external or internal sources).

Inflammation Is Called Into Action By:

- Trauma
- Infection
- Toxins

This inflammatory response serves to protect, defend, and repair your tissues. It will protect and defend tissue by destroying, diluting, or walling off injurious stimulus, such as a microbe or a toxin. This inflammatory response prepares the site for repair and initiates the healing process. Therefore, if you take drugs to inhibit the inflammatory healing response, such as NSAIDs and other anti-inflammatory drugs, *you are actually inhibiting the healing process.* The short-term gain from NSAIDs can cost you dearly in the long run by inhibiting processes that maintain the health of your tissues.

When the inflammatory response is stimulated in any stressed tissues, three important things happen. First, there is an increase in blood flow to the stressed tissues; more blood in the tissue for healing is one reason for the increased warmth, redness, and swelling. The second vital step in the inflammatory process takes place within one hour, when special white blood cells are brought in to assist the healing process. Within forty-eight hours, the third step of the inflammatory healing response begins: the initiation of tissue repair and remodeling.

A proper understanding of this inflammatory process would make any reasonable person wonder who would ever want to inhibit or block it. Yet, NSAIDs and other anti-inflammatory drugs are the most frequently used drugs in the Western world, primarily for non-life-threatening chronic musculoskeletal conditions. Wouldn't it make more sense to find out what is stressing your myofascial tissues and causing the inflammatory process, remove it, and to then manage the healing process? Research has revealed that our modern diet, lifestyle, and chemical exposure are the underlying mechanisms of today's epidemic of chronic inflammation. If this is correct, wouldn't it be prudent to make dietary and lifestyle choices that would assist in managing inflammation and return the body to a more balanced and healthy state?

Chronic Inflammation and Our Nociceptors

The three previously described steps of inflammation describe an ideal acute inflammatory process, a necessary and healthy response in any distressed tissue. It has a beginning, a middle, and an end that leaves behind non-painful, healthy tissue. The final repair phase starts within forty-eight hours and is usually completed within six weeks, in most tissues. The exceptions are the tendons of muscles and the ligaments of your joints, which are not very vascular and thus do not normally receive a great deal of blood flow. Less blood means a slower healing process. In fact, it can take an inflamed joint ligament an entire year to totally heal and regain most of its strength in normal, healthy conditions! In an unhealthy individual prone to chronic inflammation and oxidative stress, the joint complex may never properly heal, becoming a source of chronic myofascial pain and dysfunction.

Inflammatory Response = The Healing Process

1. Increase in blood flow to the stressed tissues
2. Within 1 hour, white blood cells enter to assist healing
3. By 48 hours, final repair and remodeling begins
4. Completed within 6 weeks in most tissues (tendons and ligaments may heal more slowly)
5. Low-grade inflammatory response with recurrent pain for 3 months = chronic myofascial pain syndrome

The fact that muscles and their tendons normally make up more than 50% of body weight is one reason why chronic pain of the neuromusculoskeletal system is the most prevalent chronic pain disorder. If the inflammatory healing response of your musculoskeletal system has gone beyond the usual six weeks and has caused recurrent pain for over three months, you have a chronic myofascial pain syndrome. With this, the normal acute inflammatory healing response has now become an abnormal chronic inflammatory disorder. Chronic inflammation can smolder in the tissues of your body for years without causing any obvious disease or even conscious pain. This is vital to our discussion of pain, because the cellular chemicals that drive the chronic inflammatory process are the same chemicals that stimulate your nociceptors.

As previously discussed, your nociceptors have special characteristics that keep you safe from injury and damage.

Unlike Other Sensory Receptors, Nociceptors:

1. Do not adapt: they continue to register the stimuli (pain) until the stimulation stops.
2. Can become sensitized: it takes less and less stimulation to create pain.

Because of this:

- Chronically stimulated nociceptors do not adapt and eventually become sensitized, a process known as peripheral sensitization.
- If there is a greater presence of inflammatory chemicals in your tissues from the condition known as chronic system inflammation, your nociceptors may become chronically stimulated, creating this peripheral sensitization.
- It is called *peripheral* because it's taking place out in your muscles and joints and *sensitization* because your nociceptors are becoming more sensitive, creating chronic muscle and joint pain disorders.

Through the process of peripheral sensitization, chronic inflammation in your tissues from poor diet and lifestyle choices can make its presence known through nagging or reoccurring regional musculoskeletal pain of the back, neck, or extremities. The region that becomes problematic for you frequently relates to old injuries, present repetitive motions, or a stress position held for long periods, such as sitting or standing throughout the day. Chronic inflammation is also one of the causative factors in the development of multi-regional pain syndromes and even fibromyalgia syndrome.

To better comprehend what is actually taking place, it may be helpful to use an analogy. Imagine that your home is equipped with multiple high-sensitivity smoke detectors. One night, the fire alarms in your home go off. A search does not reveal any flames or obvious smoke in your house. Presently, you cannot find a reason for the alarms to have been tripped, yet they continue to ring loudly. It's late at night, and you want to go back to sleep. How many of us would go to the basement, disconnect the wiring to the alarm system, and then, without a second thought, calmly tuck our children back snug into their beds and soundly return to sleep ourselves? We would be treating the alarm as the problem and ignoring the underlying smoldering fire that could wreak havoc on our home and family. What is the difference between this and swallowing anti-inflammatory drugs to disconnect the alarm bells of our chronic inflammation showing itself as reoccurring muscle and joint pain problems?

Chronic Inflammation and Degenerative Disease

Our twenty-first-century epidemic of chronic degenerative diseases, as well as allergic and autoimmune disorders, is directly linked to this systemic "silent" inflammation (again, it is called *silent* because it causes no immediate outward signs, unlike the redness, warmth, and swelling of acute inflammation). This silent inflammation may be one reason many seemingly healthy individuals suddenly drop dead from a heart attack. People are more than two times as likely have a heart attack when they have higher levels of systemic "silent" inflammation. There are inexpensive blood tests that will help you monitor your levels of chronic inflammation. One blood test that is highly predictive and helpful in monitoring chronic inflammation is high-sensitivity C-reactive protein, or hsCRP. Ask your doctor about running this lab test for you.

Silent systemic inflammation can be caused by chronic exposure to foods that are extremely prevalent in our modern diet. The presence of refined sugars, high-fructose corn syrup, saturated fat, and trans-fatty acids in our diet, along with our sedentary lifestyles, are the primary factors in the cause of chronic inflammation. Another major factor is that our modern diet is deficient in antioxidants, micronutrients, and fiber. Research has established that the Standard American Diet (SAD), high in sugar and saturated fats, is inherently pro-inflammatory and is associated with the high incidence of chronic muscle and joint pain disorders epidemic in our modern life.[48]

Recent studies have shown that diets high in sugars and single carbohydrates, such as the Standard American Diet, will raise levels of chronic inflammation in the body. An excellent study in the *American Journal of Clinical Nutrition* found that diets with a high amount of sugar and simple carbohydrates actually raised hsCRP, that all-important marker of chronic silent inflammation.[49] This means that our sweet tooth and love of white-flour products are causing us a great deal of chronic pain and degenerative disease, because elevated hsCRP can be connected to both. How big a problem are sweets in our diet today? In the United States, our consumption of sugar now averages more than an unbelievable 154 pounds per person per year.[50] Between 1970 and 1990, the annual consumption of high-fructose corn syrup increased more than 10,000% in the United States, from one-half pound to over 72 pounds per person.[51] This consumption of high-fructose corn syrup comes primarily through soft drinks and processed foods and not through the family sugar bowl.

Another pro-inflammatory constituent of our SAD diet is the presence of trans-fatty acids. These types of fatty acids are generally not found in nature; they have been added to the food chain through man's manipulation. Trans-fatty acids are created when vegetable oils are hydrogenated to make them more solid in order to resemble saturated animal fat and reduce rancidity to extend shelf life. Trans-fatty acids are common in snack foods, commercial baked goods, deep-fried foods, fast foods, margarine, and vegetable shortening, to name just a few. Consumption of these trans-fatty acids has been shown to raise important indicators of chronic silent inflammation.[52] More importantly, the elimination of trans-fatty acids from your diet can help lower chronic inflammation in your tissues, thereby potentially lessening your chronic pain response.

48 A. Aljada, P. Mohanty, H. Ghanim, et al., "Increase in intranuclear nuclear factor KappaB and decrease in inhibitor KappaB in mononuclear cells after a mixed meal: evidence for a pro inflammatory effect," *Am J Clin Nutr* 79, no. 4 (2004): 682–89.

49 S. Liu, J. E. Manson, J. E. Buring, et al., "Relationship between a diet with a high glycemic load and plasma concentrations of high-sensitivity C-reactive protein in middle-aged women," *Am J Clin Nutr* 75, no. 3 (2002): 492–98.

50 "Food consumption, Prices, and Expenditures, 1970–1997," Economic Research Service, USDA. Statistical Bulletin No. 965. April 1999. http://www.ers.usda.gov/publications/sb565/

51 Bray, Nielsen, and Popkin, "Consumption," 537–43.

52 E. Lopez-Garcia, M. B. Schulze, J. B. Meigs, et al., "Consumption of trans-fatty acids is related to plasma biomarkers of inflammation and endothelial dysfunction," *J Nutr* 135, no. 3 (2005): 562–66.

Just look on your food labels for the words *trans-fatty acids*, *trans fats*, *hydrogenated oils*, and *partially hydrogenated oils* to identify these culprits.

If the threat of silent inflammation causing chronic muscle and joint pain is not enough to make you stop eating trans-fatty acids, perhaps a heart attack is. Research has established that trans-fatty acids significantly raise your "bad" cholesterol (LDL-C) and lower your "good" cholesterol (HDL-C) twice as much as saturated fat. Not only that, trans-fatty acids in your diet raise plasma lipoprotein(a), one of the most deadly fatty acids when it comes to heart attacks.[53] Additionally, trans-fatty acids have been shown to increase the risk of colon and breast cancer[54] and Alzheimer's disease,[55] and have been linked to the fast-growing rate of allergies in children.[56]

From Inflammation to Free Radicals and Chronic Pain

A major factor in the formation of systemic silent inflammation in your tissues is the presence of free radicals in greater abundance than your ability to remove them. This imbalanced condition is known as oxidative stress. The presence of oxidative stress in your myofascial tissues can easily generate an inflammatory response in your muscles and joints. This inflammatory response will cause the release of more free radicals in the effected tissues, creating a greater oxidative stress and causing an increased inflammatory response. As you can see, this forms a vicious cycle—but worse yet, this cycle can accelerate, creating what is known as a feed-forward cycle.

Here is the crucial fact to understand about your chronic muscle and joint pain problems: they develop primarily from improperly managed inflammation and oxidative stress in your tissues caused by diet and lifestyle choices. Probably the biggest mistake that can lead to the mismanagement of inflammation is the chronic use of NSAIDs. In chronic muscle and joint disorders, the presence of chronic inflammation and oxidative stress in your tissues is as inseparable as love and marriage; you cannot have one without the other. Therefore, to correctly heal chronic muscle and joint problems, you must learn how to manage the metabolic factors of chronic inflammation and

53 M. Katan, P. L. Zock, and R. P. Mensink, "Trans-fatty acids and their effects on lipoprotein in humans," *Annual Review of Nutrition* 15 (1995): 473–93.

54 N. Bakke, P. van't Veer, and P. L. Zock, "Adipose fatty acids and cancers of the breast, prostate and colon: an ecological study," EURAMIC Study Group, *Int J Cancer* 72, no. 4 (1997): 587–91.

55 M. C. Morris, D. A. Evans, J. L. Bienias, et al., "Dietary fats and the rise of incident Alzheimer disease," *Arch Neurol* 60, no. 2 (2003): 194–200.

56 S. Stender and J. Dyerberg, "Influence of trans-fatty acids on health," *Ann Nut Metab* 48 (2004): 61–66.

oxidative stress. Luckily, there are herbal and nutritional supplements that can assist you in naturally managing these metabolic factors of chronic pain and disease.

The Painful Cycle of Free Radicals and Inflammation

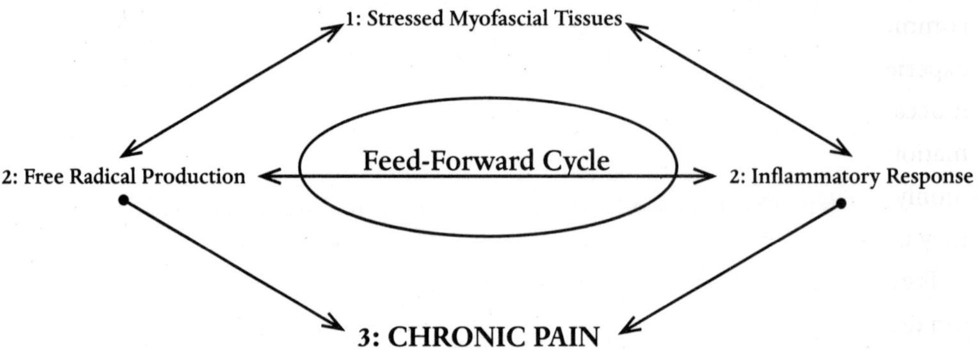

Today, almost everyone is aware of antioxidant supplements such as vitamins A, C, and E, beta-carotenes, and bioflavonoids, as well as other lesser-known phytonutrients. Also, certain dietary minerals such as selenium and zinc are utilized by your cells to produce their own antioxidants. But, even though many individuals take antioxidants, many don't realize exactly why they are taking them. Antioxidant supplementation is helpful in neutralizing free radicals in your tissues. Free radicals are unstable rogue molecules in your cells that have gone as far as joining the other side in your struggle for optimal health.

The Nature of Free Radicals and Oxidative Stress

Like bandits that enter your home, free radicals are rogue molecules that have the ability to harass and even destroy other molecules in your cells by stealing electrons from innocent molecules. This robbery then leaves these molecules unstable, causing them to become free radicals themselves, disrupting other molecules in the vicinity. In this way, free radicals can start a chain reaction in the body's tissues, causing damage that can destroy the structure and function of cells in your tissues. This revolution of unmanaged free radicals in your tissues is known as oxidative stress. Antioxidants produced in your cells or taken in through the foods you eat are used by your cells to keep these free radicals in check. Research has shown that if you allow these free radicals to get out of hand and cause oxidative stress, they will stimulate nociceptors and cause you aches and pains. Oxidative stress has also been established to be a major contributor to the development of degenerative diseases, such as heart disease, cancer, diabetes, and arthritis, just to name a few.

The most common free radicals are molecules in your cells containing oxygen, thus giving this process the name *oxidation*. These free radicals containing oxygen are commonly referred to as reactive oxygen species, or ROS for short. You have probably experienced reactive oxygen species unknowingly when you left out butter or oil and it became rancid. The rancidity of a fatty acid in your butter or cooking oil is the formation of free radicals when foods are exposed to air. Free radicals in your body commonly do their damage by disrupting the fatty acids in your cell membranes; in a way, they cause your fat to become "rancid."

Free radicals also like to damage or take apart other molecules in your cells. They can destroy the integrity of your cells by breaking apart the proteins of your cell membranes. Some of the most commonly damaged (oxidized) proteins in your cells are the enzymes. Enzymes are proteins made by your cells that make necessary biochemical reactions happen more easily and efficiently. If free radicals damage enzymes in your cells, they no longer can function as they should. If enough damage is produced in cell membranes and enzymes, and if this damage is left unchecked, then over time it will create premature aging and eventually a nasty degenerative disease.

Another molecule in your cells very commonly damaged by free radicals is the nucleic acids of the precious DNA in your genes. DNA is the code used to build various proteins that either become active enzymes or the physical building blocks in your cells. If free radicals in your cells cause severe enough damage to your DNA, mutations will occur. If this DNA damage, or mutations from free radicals, is not prevented or repaired in time, it can lead to real problems. This is probably the way that free radical pathology is connected to many degenerative diseases and even cancer.

An excellent example of a free radical is household bleach, and we all know what that can do when we accidentally get it on our colorful clothes. Also, free radical oxidation is what happens in an apple when it gets bumped and bruised; in a short time, its injured cells exposed to oxygen will begin to turn brown. This browning process is from disrupted cell membranes and the release of free radicals into the injured tissue, causing the oxidative process. Imagine this same process taking place over time in the cells of your body from physical or chemical injury. When these free radicals are not properly managed by our cells, they build up, causing oxidative stress. Oxidative stress can happen in specific tissues, or it can take place throughout your body. This oxidative stress can damage tissues locally, causing a diseased organ, or globally, causing a generalized response throughout your body's tissues.

Our modern life provides us with many opportunities to damage our tissues through oxidative stress: cigarette smoke, air pollution, water pollution, petrochemicals, pesticides, herbicides, charbroiled foods, micronutrient-deficient diets, and excessive calories. Two very common free radical-producing activities are smoking and consuming a diet high in calories and low in micronutrients. Additionally, herbicides and pesticides act as (or create) potent free radicals. This is one way that consuming foods containing these chemical toxins is detrimental to the health of your tissues. Dysbiosis, which is unhealthy microbes growing in your gut, can also become a reservoir for toxins that can act as (or create) potent free radicals. One can easily see that our modern lifestyle and diet allow us many opportunities to damage our tissues through the absorption and/or self-production of free radicals. It's not surprising, then, that the symptoms of oxidative stress read like a laundry list of the most common complaints individuals report to their doctors.

Primary Symptoms of Untreated Oxidative Stress	Untreated Chronic Oxidative Stress Can Lead to Degenerative Disease
muscle and joint pains, fatigue, poor mental function, irritability, depression, anxiety, digestive problems, headaches, chronic infections, and allergies	cardiovascular disease, cancer, diabetes, asthma, osteoarthritis, fibromyalgia, chronic fatigue syndrome, neurodegenerative disorders (Alzheimer's disease, Parkinson's disease, and multiple sclerosis)

Oxidative Stress, Aging, and Your Mitochondria

If chronic pain and degenerative diseases are not enough to make you want to change your diet and lifestyle to reduce free radicals in your body, possibly the fact that they make you look and feel older before your time will! The oxidative damage from smoking can cause some individuals to wrinkle fifteen times faster than normal; smokers in their forties often have as many wrinkles as nonsmokers in their sixties.[57] This is primarily because of free radical damage to the underlying connective tissue of the face.

In 1956, Dr. Denham Harman developed the free radical theory of aging. He proposed that the accumulative damage of oxidative stress in tissues throughout the body

57 I. Jaffe, "Cigarette smoking and fascial wrinkling," (letter) *Annals of Internal Medicine* (1991) 115:659.

creates the effects of aging, such as muscle/joint stiffness and pain, poor cognitive function, loss of memory, and the development of degenerative diseases.[58] Recent research by Dr. Bruce Ames and his associates has shown that premature aging is primarily created by free radical damage to your mitochondria, vital organelles (little organs) in each cell.[59]

Why would this part of your cell be so important? The mitochondria are the powerhouses of each and every cell in your body; they convert the calories in your food to usable energy by producing the energy molecule ATP. The more healthy and resilient your mitochondria are, the more vitality you have at the cellular level. There are several hundred of these little mitochondria within every cell of your body. Your mitochondria, however, carry a "memory" of the many injuries they experience over time, such as that from free radicals. This can eventually lead to a decline in the many vital functions of our cellular mitochondria. This leads to the inability to keep the cell vital, leading to dysfunction and finally cell death. If this dysfunction takes place in enough cells in certain vulnerable tissues or even throughout your body, you will lose your vitality through decreased ATP production and become susceptible to degenerative disease. In regard to chronic pain, without healthy mitochondria you will not have adequate energy to repair and maintain healthy myofascial tissues in response to stress in all its forms, thus leading to muscle and joint problems.

Mitochondria have intrigued me since my first biology class in high school, and through the years that fascination has only increased. A mitochondrion is one of the most primitive parts of your cells; molecular paleontologists have dated its origins back some 1.6 billion years to a primitive bacterium. This primitive bacterium 1.6 billion years ago was very efficient at utilizing the high level of corrosive oxygen available in the atmosphere to produce high amounts of energy—or, to be specific, ATP.[60] Somewhere along the way, about 1.4 billion years ago, one of these primitive bacteria entered a larger cell with a nucleus (eukaryotic cell) and a mutually beneficial or symbiotic relationship was developed. With its ability to produce high levels of energy, this symbiotic relationship allowed the new cells in this ancient environment a competitive edge over other organisms. This symbiotic relationship was so successful, it

58 D. Harman, "Aging: A theory based on free radical and radiation chemistry," *J Gerontol* 11 (1956): 298–300. K. B. Beckman and B. N. Ames, "The free radical theory of aging matures," *Physiol Rev* 78 (1998): 547–81.

59 M. K. Shigenaga, T. M. Hagen, and B. N. Ames, "Oxidative damage and mitochondrial decay in aging," *Proc Natl Acad Sci USA* 91 (1994): 1771–78.

60 I. Margulis, M. F. Dolan, and R. Guerrero, "The chimeric eukaryote: origins of the nucleus from the karyomastigont in amitochondriate protests," *Proc Natl Acad Sci USA* 97, no. 13 (2000): 6954–9.

has continued to evolve right up to our own human cells in their use of the efficient energy-producing mitochondria.[61]

Your Magnificent Mitochondria

- One of the most primitive parts of your cells
- Originated from a primitive bacterium 1.6 billion years ago
- Efficient at utilizing the corrosive oxygen available in the ancient atmosphere
- Able to produce high amounts of energy (ATP)
- 1.4 billion years ago, entered larger nucleated eukaryotic cell to form a mutually beneficial relationship
- Ability to produce high levels of energy gave new cells edge over other organisms
- Continued to evolve over eons of time right up to our own human cells
- We enjoy the many benefits of these efficient energy-producing bacteria as the powerhouses of our cells
- Our mitochondria function best when we eat whole foods that provide proper macro- and micronutrients (see chapter 14 for details)

Actually, the structure of mitochondria, with its own circular DNA, is still very similar to the bacteria of today. This brings a very interesting question to mind that has been asked by clinicians and well-respected medical researchers: if mitochondrial DNA and bacterial DNA are so similar, is it possible that some antibiotics that target the DNA of bacteria are causing damage to our mitochondria? If so, then repeated exposures over time may cause an energy-deficient condition in tissues affected by these antibiotics in certain susceptible individuals.

61 M. W. Gray, B. F. Lang, and G. Burger, "Mitochondria of protests," *Annu Rev of Genet* 38 (2004): 477–524.

How Mitochondria Are Vulnerable to Damage

No energy system is 100% efficient. For example, the energy-efficient furnace in your basement is around 94% efficient. Therefore, it cannot capture 100% of all the energy released by the burning of fuel. The same thing happens with the burning or oxidizing of calories in your cells to produce ATP. As energy efficient as these bacteria were, and your mitochondria are now, even in the healthy, slow oxidative fire of energy production (yes, oxidation can be beneficial), your mitochondria are not 100% efficient. Therefore, normally about 1% of the oxygen you breathe in is eventually converted to corrosive free radicals, or ROS, by the mitochondria. This 1% may not sound like much; however, this translates into the creation of 100,000 free radical attacks on your mitochondria's own DNA each and every day. This is a natural and normal process even in the most healthy of cells. In other words, as with many things in life, there is a boon and a bane to the use of oxygen for energy production.

To survive this normal free radical onslaught, your mitochondria have developed their own internally generated, or endogenous, protective antioxidants. This means that your mitochondria produce their own effective scavengers to soak up the free radicals that are normally created in the production of ATP. It's as if they have their own fire department to watch over this burning of calories to keep it slow and even. But, for your mitochondria to effectively produce these protective antioxidants in high enough levels, they need adequate levels of micronutrients and ATP to manufacture them. For example, your mitochondria utilize zinc, copper, and manganese to create extremely important endogenous antioxidants. Remember that your mitochondria at their healthiest still create 100,000 free radical attacks per day on their own DNA. When your tissues are under stress from a poor diet, chronic inflammation, or diseases such as diabetes, your mitochondria produce damaging free radicals at much higher levels, possibly without adequate internally produced antioxidants.

If you are eating a Standard American Diet (SAD) of overly processed, devitalized foods that are rich in empty calories and deficient in micronutrients, you will also produce more free radicals in your cells and less of your own antioxidants to protect your cells. Given this situation, your mitochondria become more susceptible to the more than 100,000 daily free radical attacks. It's like restricting the flow of water to the fire department. This lack of adequate antioxidant protection in your mitochondria speeds up the natural aging process of your tissues, causing a loss of your vitality and making you more susceptible to chronic pain and degenerative diseases. For healthy aging, a return of vitality, and the ability to overcome your chronic pain, it is important to perform a metabolic tune-up to your mitochondria, fully discussed in chapter 14.

What makes the mitochondria so central to chronic pain and degenerative diseases is the fact that when mitochondria become injured by free radicals, they tend to join the other side in your struggle for optimal health. One reason for this is that injured mitochondria leak out a much greater number of free radicals into your cells. Another reason is that they lose some of their ability to defend themselves against free radicals. This double whammy in turn creates more free radical damage to the already injured mitochondria of those tissues and organs involved. You can see how this can become a vicious cycle in your body. The DNA of your mitochondria (mtDNA) manages the energy production process and the vitality of your cells. Because of this, with every free radical attack that causes damage to the mtDNA, the cells are less able to produce the energy needed to maintain a healthy, vital state. This is what is known as a feed-forward cycle in biology.

Possibly you have heard of homeostasis, which is defined as the maintenance of a dynamically stable internal physiological condition in the human body. In a feed-forward cycle, some part of this process loses its check-and-balance and begins to accelerate its own decay. A very good parallel to this in nature is the present melting of the permafrost in the Arctic tundra. There are now huge quantities of methane that are locked up in the permafrost. As temperatures rise from global warming, this methane is released. The problem with this is that methane gas is a greenhouse gas that is 20 times more potent than carbon dioxide. So, as carbon dioxide builds up, increasing global temperatures, there is an increased thawing of the permafrost and an accelerated release of methane from the Arctic tundra. Because the methane released is 20 times more potent, it leads to acceleration in the greenhouse effect, warming the planet more, releasing more methane, leading to a feed-forward cycle in the warming of our planet. What is ecologically happening on the microcosm to your cells is happening on the macrocosm to our planet.

In this light, it is easy to see the importance of properly managing the healing response called inflammation and the process of oxidation. Shutting down or blocking either one means disease and death, and letting them burn out of control means eventual disease. The ideal route, therefore, is to eat a diet and live a lifestyle that assists in the management of these metabolic processes if we desire to heal our pain and prevent the development of degenerative disease. To assist you in this journey, I have laid out below a quick reference guide on how to manage chronic inflammation and oxidative stress. This assistance through the utilization of nutraceuticals becomes even more important in future chapters, as we begin to understand the impact of insulin resistance and toxic chemicals in our environment on chronic inflammation, oxidative stress, and the development of chronic myofascial pain disorders. Nutraceuticals are utilized because they go beyond simple vitamin supplements to specifically treat metabolic dysfunction and disease. Nutraceuticals are defined as foods or parts of foods (phytonutrients, herbal extracts, vitamins, minerals, fatty acids, etc.) used in combination to target specific health conditions, either in treatment or prevention.

Quick Reference Guide to Managing Oxidative Stress

Section 4 details how you can overcome the vicious cycle of oxidative stress and systemic inflammation. Here is a sneak peak at what you can start doing to protect yourself.

Probably the most common symptoms of free radical or oxidative stress and systemic inflammation in your body are general loss of vitality, muscle ache, joint pains, and headaches, along with a nagging fatigue. Individuals will commonly complain of poor mental function, irritability, and depression. Also, symptoms of immune dysfunction are present, such as a lowered resistance to infection and increased allergies. When your doctor has ruled out any possible pathological cause for any of the above symptoms, consider the following:

Things to Do to Reduce Oxidative Stress and Systemic Inflammation Resulting in Mitochondrial Injury

1. Minimize all exposures to environmental toxins: air (install HEPA filters), water (filter your tap water), and food (eat organic); see chapter 17 for details.
2. Stop smoking and reduce exposure to secondhand smoke.
3. Remove or severely limit charbroiled foods.
4. Remove excess sugars and simple carbohydrates from your diet.
5. Reduce internal toxins by overcoming dysbiosis of the gut (see chapter 16 for details).
6. Reduce exposure to molds and fungi in your immediate environment.

7. Reduce your stress and practice deep breathing to increase oxygenation of your tissues.
8. Improve your liver and cellular detoxification systems.

Nutraceuticals Shown to Combat Oxidative Stress and Systemic Inflammation (see chapters 14–18)

- Mixed vitamin E (400 IU daily)
- Mixed carotenoids, such as beta-carotenes
- Selenium (100 to 200 mcg daily)
- Vitamin C (2,000 mg daily)
- Vitamin D (400 to 1,200 IU daily)
- Vitamin A (5,000 to 10,000 mg daily)
- Vitamin B complex
- Zinc (15 to 75 mg daily)
- Curcuminoids from the herb turmeric
- Green tea polyphenol extract
- Milk thistle herb
- Ginger extract

What Does This Mean for Me?

- Inflammation is a healing response.
- Chronic inflammation is a disease process connected to chronic pain and the development of degenerative diseases.
- Chronic inflammation and oxidative stress can become a vicious feed-forward cycle.
- This chronic inflammation and oxidative stress can be controlled by how I choose to eat and live.

6

The Painful Side of Sweetness

Questions to Consider:

1. How does our SAD diet add to the incidence of chronic myofascial pain?
2. What is a high glycemic diet, and how does it add to chronic pain and chronic disease?
3. How do I know if I am developing insulin resistance, and how do I overcome it?
4. What is metabolic syndrome, and what kinds of health problems does it cause?
5. How do I know if I am developing metabolic syndrome?

According to the Centers for Disease Control (CDC), more than 2 out of every 3 adults and 1 out of 3 children in the United States are overweight or obese, and the number only continues to climb. Our Standard American Diet, high in refined carbohydrates and sugars, is creating a modern plague of obesity and type 2 diabetes. There are nearly 21 million Americans suffering from diabetes, and most of them have type 2, previously called adult-onset diabetes. Because it is now being diagnosed in increasingly younger patients, it is no longer referred to as "adult-onset" diabetes but as type 2 diabetes. Recently, the National Institute of Health estimated that as much as a third of these individuals with diabetes are unaware that they have the disease. Astonishingly, the CDC announced on June 15, 2003, that as many as one out of every three children born in the year 2000 will eventually develop diabetes.

This explosive epidemic of obesity and diabetes is directly related to the diet and lifestyle we now follow in the modern world. I can say this with confidence because I know what any human geneticist also knows: human genetics could not change so dramatically in a mere fifty years. One recent study shockingly stated that one out of every two Americans have or will develop a pre-diabetic condition known as insulin resistance or metabolic syndrome. Insulin resistance puts you at risk for most of the chronic degenerative disorders of today: diabetes, hypertension, coronary heart disease, stroke, and cognitive decline, as well as colon and breast cancer.[62] Additionally, and more important to the subject of this book, this condition of insulin resistance or metabolic syndrome predisposes you to chronic inflammation, oxidative stress, and, subsequently, chronic muscle and joint pain.

The Roots of Our Sugar Addiction

Why these shocking statistics? Possibly because we love and indeed are addicted to sweets. They taste good and give us a quick energy boost. But sugar and simple carbohydrates, in all their guises, can truly be addictive. That we are drawn to sugars because of the importance blood glucose plays in the proper functioning of our nervous system cannot be overemphasized. Our nervous system can only burn glucose to satisfy its high-energy demand. Our 400 hungry muscles also need glucose in high levels to perform all the necessary work that is demanded of them. In fact, our muscles consume about 70% of the available blood glucose to produce high quantities of ATP for all the work they do. This is one reason why you begin to develop chronic muscle pain and fatigue with insulin resistance and diabetes; you are losing your efficiency at bringing in fuel to your muscle cells to produce energy necessary for muscle function.

This does not mean we should consume simple carbohydrates and sugars! But this high demand for healthy complex carbohydrates in our diet does explain why our tongue and brain are so drawn to the sweet flavor. In evolutionary terms, this may have been a benefit to our survival. Beneficial complex carbohydrates found in nature will release a very slight sweet taste when chewed thoroughly and mixed with the

62 D. T. Villareal and J. O. Holloszy, "Effect of DHEA on abdominal fat and insulin action in elderly women and men," *JAMA* 292, 18 (Nov. 10, 2004): 2243–48.

amylase (a carbohydrate-digesting enzyme) in our saliva. Having a tongue sensitive to this extremely mild sweetness and a brain that demands more would benefit the survival of our foraging ancestors by driving them to consume natural whole foods high in complex carbohydrates. This physiological setup may have also helped our survival by drawing us away from bitter foods in nature that may have contained poisonous alkaloids.

What Is a High Glycemic Diet?

Once the food industry giants realized that they could lead us around by our tongues and maximize their profits, there was no stopping them. By the close of the last century, the average American consumed a record average of 154 pounds of caloric sweeteners per year. This amounts to a little more than one-third of a one-pound bag of sugar per day per person! That's about fifty-three teaspoons of simple sugars eaten each day.[63] Most of us find this hard to believe because we know we don't have our hands in the cookie jar or sugar bowl that much. It is important to re-examine this belief by looking at the labels on your food. Look for any thing that ends in -ose, which means it's a simple carbohydrate or sugar. Examine closely and you will see sugar disguised as sucrose, fructose, glucose, dextrose, maltose, and lactose. It's also important to realize that sugar is sugar, no matter how it is named or how natural it is. Natural cane sugar, dehydrated cane juice, sucanant, maple sugar, honey, corn syrup, whole barley malt: it's all sugar. This is not to say a small amount of a natural sweetener is going to kill you, but quantity does change quality—you *can* get too much of a "good" thing!

-ose = a simple carbohydrate or sugar

- Sucrose, fructose (high-fructose corn syrup), glucose, dextrose, maltose, lactose
- Also natural cane sugar, dehydrated cane juice, sucanant, maple sugar, honey, corn syrup, and whole barley malt: natural but still a simple carbohydrate

63 USDA Economic Research Service, "Food consumption, prices, and expenditures, 1970–1997," statistical bulletin no. 965 (April 1999).

These refined simple carbohydrates and sugars have a high glycemic index. The glycemic index of a food measures how fast and how high a specific food will raise your blood sugar level. The higher the glycemic index of a food, the higher your blood glucose will rise and the greater the level of insulin in your bloodstream. In general, the more processed and refined a carbohydrate is, the higher its glycemic index and the more detrimental it is to your health. A resource to help understand the low glycemic diet and the glycemic index of specific foods can be found at www.glycemicindex.com.

Refined carbohydrates and sugars have a high glycemic index, while complex carbohydrates from whole foods have a comparatively low glycemic index. Whole foods with complex carbohydrates include your fresh vegetables, 100% whole grains (rice, wheat, oats, barley, etc.), legumes, seeds, and nuts. Processed and refined carbohydrates are found in foods such as white rice, white bread, donuts, cakes, and muffins not made entirely from 100% whole grain. In the United States, it is legal to label a product as "whole grain" if it contains only 51% whole-grain flour. So a product with only 51% whole-grain flour, but with 49% white processed refined flour, can be labeled "whole grain" and will still have a high glycemic index. An increased intake of high glycemic foods leads to chronic inflammation and pain, obesity,[64] diabetes, heart disease,[65] cognitive impairment, dementia,[66] and cancer (colon, breast, prostate, and pancreas).[67] With this impressive list, high glycemic foods may be something you will want to pay attention to.

How a High Glycemic Diet Creates Problems

A diet high in glycemic foods is the primary cause of the epidemic rise of insulin resistance, also known as metabolic syndrome or Syndrome X. Eating a diet high in glycemic foods creates chronic elevated levels of blood sugar even before you develop

64 M. B. Schulze, J. E. Manson, D. S. Ludwig, et al., "Sugar–sweetened beverages, weight gain and incidence of type 2 diabetes in young and middle–aged women," *JAMA* 292, 8 (2004): 927–34.

65 H. M. Lakka, D. E. Laaksonen, T. A. Lakka, et al., "The metabolic syndrome and total and cardiovascular disease mortality in middle-aged men," *JAMA* 288, 21 (2002): 2709–16.

66 K. Yaffe, A. Kanaya, K. Lindquist, et al., "The metabolic syndrome, inflammation and risk of cognitive decline," *JAMA* 292, 18 (2004): 2237–42.

67 E. E. Calle, C. Rodriguez, K. Walker–Thurmond, and M. Thun, "Overweight, obesity and mortality from cancer in a prospectively studied cohort of U.S. adults," *NEJM* 348 (2003): 1625.

diabetes. High blood-sugar levels are detrimental to your health, so your body quickly reacts by producing high levels of insulin to drive down the blood glucose level. All the cells of your body, especially muscle and nerve cells, need glucose to enter the cell to produce the ATP we discussed earlier. The problem is that at your cell membranes, glucose is yelling in Russian "let me in," but your cell membranes only speak English. Luckily you have a translator called insulin, which along with a glucose tolerance factor (containing the mineral chromium) communicates with your cell membranes to allow blood glucose to enter the cells of your body.

By eating a diet high in glycemic foods, you can create problems with this complex arrangement. Highly refined carbohydrate foods and sugars are broken down very quickly into simple glucose and then absorbed directly into the bloodstream almost immediately. This in turn causes your blood glucose levels to shoot up, causing a sugar spike. Your body then overcompensates by releasing too much insulin from your pancreas into your bloodstream. This high insulin level will drive your blood sugars down precipitously, causing a low blood-sugar state or the symptoms of hypoglycemia. Also, the excess insulin can cause symptoms of its own. At this point, with hypoglycemia and high insulin levels, you feel lethargic, tired, cranky, irritable, and hungry again. Now you're dying for a quick lift, causing you to reach for the donut or candy bar, washed down with a caffeinated, highly sweetened beverage. This causes another sugar spike, and the whole vicious cycle starts all over again, as shown below:

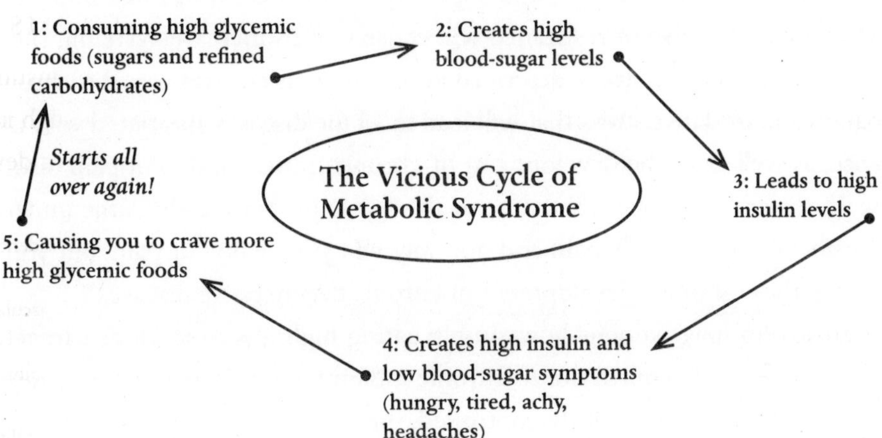

At each turn of this vicious cycle, you create periods of too much glucose and insulin in your bloodstream. Even with the high levels of insulin, not all of the available glucose can be absorbed into your cells for energy production; it is instead turned into fat and stored around your waist. Then there is the bottom of your cycle, where not enough blood glucose is available for your nervous system, causing mood swings and fatigue. This constant vicious cycle resulting in the overproduction of insulin eventually leads to the cells of your body not listening to your insulin. Through the exhaustion of your pancreas, eventually you are unable to produce enough insulin to keep your blood- sugar levels stable. You have now joined the growing ranks of Americans with type 2 diabetes. There are many things you can do, especially when you are not yet insulin- dependent, to turn this disease around. This vital program to regain your health is covered in greater detail in chapters 14 through 17.

Pain, Disease, and Aging from Insulin Resistance

Prior to the development of type 2 diabetes, the vicious cycle created by a high glycemic diet starts you down the road of insulin insensitivity and subsequent insulin overproduction by the pancreas. At this stage, you are one of the 50% of Americans who presently have or are now developing insulin resistance or metabolic syndrome with its abnormal high levels of insulin. This metabolic syndrome will cause the health problems already mentioned, such as obesity, hypertension, high triglycerides, low HDL (good) cholesterol, heart disease, and some types of cancer. But most important to our discussion here, insulin resistance will cause you to increase systemic silent inflammation and oxidative stress, described in the previous chapter. It is this chronic inflammation and oxidative stress that will lead to all the diseases associated with insulin resistance, as well as to the development of chronic muscle and joint pain disorders. This again returns to the central theme of this book: properly address the underlying mechanisms of your chronic pain and not only will you heal your pain, but you may also prevent the continued development of chronic degenerative disease.

For those who may wonder how simply eating high-glycemic foods can actually damage your cells and contribute to chronic inflammation, here's the short answer: when blood sugars are not tightly controlled, the high availability of glucose in your blood causes this glucose to be attached to structural or enzyme proteins in your cells.

If you recall, this is similar to free radicals attacking enzymes and structural proteins in your tissues. This attachment of glucose to proteins has a fancy name called AGEs (short for advanced glycosylated end products). AGEs are aptly named because they do definitely increase your aging process and the development of chronic degenerative disease. So, in a sense, the more white flour products and sugar you eat, the more you wrinkle on the inside and outside! In diabetes, it is the attachment of glucose to structural or functional proteins in the body that causes many of the side effects, such as heart disease, blindness, loss of sensation, and poor wound healing.

One of the primary ways that AGEs create all these problems is by attaching to cell membranes and turning on a gene for inflammation. You may remember from chapter 2 how the COX-2 enzyme created prostaglandins that turned on inflammation. Too much sugar in your blood creating the formation of AGEs triggers COX-2 production, leading to chronic inflammation. This makes chronic myofascial pain much more probable, so it's vital that you have effective strategies to lower blood sugar levels, combat insulin resistance, and prevent the formation of AGEs if you hope to overcome your chronic pain, prevent degenerative disease, and not age quickly from AGEs.

Diagnosing Metabolic Syndrome

One excellent way of diagnosing and monitoring your formation of AGEs is testing your blood for hemoglobin A1C(HbA1C). This lab test measures your blood sugar control by measuring your rate of AGE formation over the last ninety days. The more glucose you have floating around in your blood, the more glucose you attach to your hemoglobin, which parallels your formation of these AGEs in your tissues. For optimal health, you should have less than 4% hemoglobin A1C. If your hemoglobin A1C is between 5.5 and 6%, you have insulin resistance. If you have a hemoglobin A1C of over 6.5%, you are now in the diabetic range, and over 7% you are in serious tissue risk from AGEs. Ask your doctor to run a hemoglobin A1C for you.

To know if you are developing insulin resistance, it is helpful to run other diagnostic blood tests. The first is a fasting blood sugar test, which should not be over 100 mg/dL, and the second is your fasting insulin test, which should not be over 10 uU/L. Having blood sugar levels over 110 mg/dL indicates hyperglycemia and increases your risk for a deadly heart attack by up to five times and your risk of death from a stroke by as much as fifteenfold. A fasting glucose test is usually part of any normal blood test panel; ask your doctor what your last results were.

The second test is hsCRP, which stands for high-sensitivity C-reactive protein. This test measures chronic inflammation in your body and is highly associated with insulin resistance. Ideally, hsCRP should be under 1 mg/L (milligram per liter of blood), and for optimal health it should be under 0.5 mg/L. An hsCRP over 1 mg/L is associated with greater risk of chronic inflammation and insulin resistance. The hsCRP blood test should not be done if you've had a recent injury, trauma, or infection, because you are trying to measure a baseline of your inflammation level. Again, ask your doctor to run a hsCRP for you.

Another helpful indicator of insulin resistance is changes in your blood fats. Triglycerides are blood fats that can be easily stored as body fats around your waist, and they increase from eating sugars and simple carbohydrates. Triglycerides in your blood should be under 150 mg/dL. Your good cholesterol (HDL) should be greater than 35 mg/dL for men, 40 mg/dL for women. Your triglyceride-to-HDL ratio is probably the best indicator of metabolic syndrome; your ratio must not be greater than three to one. A triglyceride-to-HDL ratio larger than five to one has been shown to be very predictive of insulin resistance. Triglycerides and HDL cholesterol are usually part of a normal chemistry panel, so ask your doctor what the last actual numbers were, and figure out your own triglyceride/HDL ratio.

Signs That You May have Insulin Resistance

1. Fatigued and achy
2. Crave sweet, sugary foods
3. Hypoglycemic symptoms of irritability, night sweats, dizziness, and heart palpitations
4. You feel wiped out and fatigued after eating meals with simple carbohydrates or sugars
5. Central obesity or apple-shaped, with waist as big or bigger than your hips
6. High blood pressure
7. Chronic fungal infections, e.g., athlete's foot or fungal infections of the toenail

Are you Developing Metabolic Syndrome?[68]

1. Your blood pressure is greater than 130/85
   or you are on blood pressure meds

2. Waist measurement: men > 40″, women > 35″
   (measured at the largest diameter; no cheating!)

3. Your waist-to-hip ratio is > 0.90/1 for men, 0.85/1 for women: measure the waist and the hip; divide the waist measurement by the hip measurement (e.g., waist/hip, 35/42 = 0.833). Metabolic syndrome makes you apple-shaped!

4. Body fat percentage: Men = 16–29%; women = 22–37%

5. Fasting blood glucose level:

   90–100 mg/dL indicates pre-insulin resistance
   100–125 mg/dL indicates insulin resistance
   Greater than 125 mg/dL indicates diabetes

6. Fasting blood fats indicate insulin resistance when:

   Triglycerides: Greater than 150 mg/dL

   HDL cholesterol: men less than 40 mg/dL;
   women less than 50 mg/dL

   Triglyceride/HDL ratio greater than 3/1

7. Hemoglobin A1C (an AGE you can measure):

   a HbA1C greater than 5.5% is optimal;
   5.5–5.9% indicates metabolic syndrome;
   6–6.9% indicates diabetic with good control;
   7–7.9% indicates diabetic with fair control;
   > 8% indicates poor diabetic control & tissue damage

8. Fasting insulin greater than 10 mg/dL is indicative
   of hyperinsulinism and insulin resistance

9. HsCRP measures low-grade chronic inflammation: optimal is less than 0.5 mg/L, normal is less than 0.7 mg/L; greater than 1 mg/L indicates increased risk to many chronic diseases

---

68 Partially based on standards from the NCEP (National Cholesterol Education Program–Adult Treatment Panel) and the NIH (National Institute of Health World Health Organization).

Stopping Metabolic Syndrome from Ruining Your Life

To stop insulin resistance or metabolic syndrome from contributing to your chronic pain and destroying your health, you must first improve your diet by replacing high glycemic foods with low glycemic foods: whole foods that contain only complex carbohydrates and high fiber. Start by eliminating all refined white flour, white rice products, and sugars from your diet. To accomplish this, you must eliminate sodas, sweetened drinks, junk food, and highly processed foods. It is also important to eliminate artificial sweeteners, for many of them can trigger an insulin response and also increase your cravings for sweets. It is also very important to eliminate all trans-fatty acids and hydrogenated oils because they can also promote insulin resistance.

There are specific natural strategies for increasing your insulin sensitivity at your cell membranes, and these will be covered in detail in chapters 14 and 15. You will learn the importance of supplementation with magnesium, chromium, biotin, alpha-lipoic acid, vitamin E, and omega-3 fatty acids to improve insulin sensitivity. Also covered will be specific herbal supplements that will help you prevent and even overcome the challenge of high blood sugars and insulin resistance.

Things to Do to Reduce Your Insulin Resistance

1. Eat a low glycemic diet: eliminate sugars, refined flours, and simple carbohydrates from your diet (see www.glycemicindex.com).
2. Stop drinking sodas and other sweetened drinks.
3. Remove processed foods and junk food.
4. Stop all artificial sweeteners: they can fuel your cravings for sweets and trigger an insulin response from brain signals.
5. Eliminate all trans-fatty acids and hydrogenated oils.
6. Limit caffeine intake to herbal teas that have beneficial flavinoids.
7. Limit alcohol to three to four drinks per week.

Nutraceuticals That May Improve Insulin Sensitivity

With a low glycemic diet, consider:

1. Magnesium (600 to 1,200 mg daily)
2. Chromium (800 to 1,200 mcg daily)
3. Biotin (40 to 60 mg daily)
4. Vitamin C (2,000 to 8,000 mg daily)
5. Vitamin E (800 to 1,600 IU daily)
6. Alpha-lipoic acid (300 to 800 mg daily)
7. B_6 pyridoxine (150 to 250 mg daily)
8. Vitamin B complex
9. Omega-3 fatty acids (3 to 9 grams of the EPA/DHA fraction)
10. Gymnema sylvestre extract (250 mg per meal)
11. Green tea extract (300 mg daily)
12. Panax ginseng extract (5% ginsenosides—300 mg daily)

What Does This Mean for Me?

- I need to protect myself and my family from the coming tsunami of insulin resistance that is washing over our society, with devastating health effects.
- If I have a growing waistline and elevated blood pressure, I need to address insulin resistance to heal my chronic muscle and joint pain.
- Insulin resistance is something I can prevent or overcome by natural means, before it becomes full-blown diabetes.

7

Our Injured Earth, Your Injured Self

Questions to Consider:

1. Are we exposing ourselves and our children to increasing levels of toxic chemicals?
2. Are these toxic chemicals affecting our health and the health of our children?
3. Could the chronic inflammation and oxidative stress associated with myofascial pain be an indication of low-grade chemical exposure?

Imagine that you live in the pristine, green Northwest of North America; you choose to live a very healthy lifestyle by exercising, not smoking, and growing much of your own food organically. Then imagine how you would feel if a government study revealed that you had high levels of environmental toxins and organochlorine pesticides in your body. Also, your children were found to have high concentrations of PCBs, known to cause birth defects, cancer, and neurotoxicity, as well as damage immune and cardiovascular systems. Imagine how disappointed and frustrated you would feel! How could this have happened to this family, you might ask yourself, and how much is this toxic nation affecting me and my family?

The Toxic Nation

This was one family's surprise when the Environmental Defense Toxic Nation project was completed and published in June 2006 (you can find it at www.toxicnation.ca).

The goal of this project was to determine the level of chemical contamination in five families across Canada. Blood and urine samples were taken from children, parents, and grandparents of five Canadian families to determine the burden levels of sixty-eight toxic chemicals. At least forty-six of these toxic chemicals were detected in these families and even in children as young as ten years old. These chemicals included thirteen different PCBs (polychlorinated biphenyl), five different PBDEs (polybrominated diphenyl esters), nine organochlorine pesticides, four organophosphate insecticide metabolites, five different PAHs (polycyclic aromatic hydrocarbons), and five heavy metals. What this study fully demonstrated was that even if you live in a "clean and green" environment and follow a healthy lifestyle, you are exposed to harmful chemicals in the air, water, and food system that can build up in your tissues; this process is called bioaccumulation.

Toxic Families

In June of 2006, the Environmental Defense Toxic Nation project[69] found:

- 46 different environmental chemicals
- 38 carcinogens (cause cancer)
- 23 hormone disruptors (block your hormones)
- 38 reproductive/developmental toxins (interrupt normal development in children)
- 19 neurotoxins (toxic to the nervous system)

Each adult in this study averaged thirty-two chemicals detected, and on average twenty-three of these toxic chemicals were detected in each child volunteer. Most surprising was that all of the children had detectable levels of PCBs and many organochlorine pesticides that were all banned well before the children were even born. This shows that these chemical toxins persist in our environment for many years after they have been banned.

This is why these chemical toxins in our environment are referred to as POPs, or persistent organic pollutants. These chemicals are referred to as *organic* only because they contain carbon. They are *persistent* because they are very resistant to being broken

69 www.toxicnation.ca.

down and made harmless by exposing them to light, water, or chemical degradation. In fact, research has established that it can take as long as a century for these POP chemicals to break down and become harmless.[70] This extremely slow breakdown allows these chemicals to stay stable and thus circulate throughout our world in air, water, plant, and animal tissues. This characteristic allows them to readily bioaccumulate up the food chain and concentrate in top predators, even in remote places. Consequently, the aboriginal peoples of northern Canada have some of the highest levels of POPs found in their tissues.[71]

What About the Children's Health?

The encouraging news from this EDF Toxic Nation study was that the children's numbers of and concentrations of outlawed PCBs and organochlorine pesticides were lower than those present in their parents. This provides strong evidence that progressive government actions taken to eliminate toxic chemicals do decrease bioaccumulation in people's tissues; however, it may take many generations for this to be fully realized. This should encourage us to get involved in organizations fighting to limit or remove these deadly chemicals. However, it was disconcerting, if not surprising, to discover that many of the children in several of the families were more contaminated than their parents with the pollutants that are still in use today. This helps to further verify that children do accumulate toxic chemicals more readily than adults.

Children's vulnerability to environmental toxins is multifactorial. Pound for pound, children drink more liquids, eat more food, and breathe more air than adults, causing them to take in proportionately much higher levels of pollutants.[72] Children also live closer to the ground, where they are exposed to more toxins that are concentrated in low-lying layers of air, dust, soil, and carpets. Also, a child's ability to detoxify and excrete certain toxins is not as mature as an adult's. For example, the fetus and newborn do not have fully developed metabolic pathways to biotransform or detoxify absorbed toxic chemicals.[73] Additionally, children are vulnerable to the absorption of toxic chemicals and heavy metals through multiple avenues, such as their digestive tract, lungs, and skin, which are at this time of life extremely porous to the absorption

70 B. E. Fisher, "Most unwanted," *Environ Health Perspect* 107 (1999): A18–25.

71 C. D. Sandau, P. Ayotte, E. Dewailly, et al., "Analysis of hydroxylated metabolites of PCBs and other chlorinated phenolic compounds in whole blood from Canadian Inuit," *Environ Health Perspect* 108 (2000): 611–16.

72 K. Cooper et al., "Environmental standard setting and children's health," Canadian Environmental Law Association and Ontario College of Family Physicians, Toronto (2000), 51.

73 Ibid., 35.

of these toxins.[74] One example is lead; an adult will absorb about 10 to 15% of the lead contained within a meal, whereas a developing child and a pregnant woman can absorb as much as 50% of the lead in the same meal.[75]

What About All This ADD/ADHD and Depression, or Why Is Everyone on Prozac?

As children are undergoing rapid neurological growth and development, their delicate neurological tissues are more easily disrupted. I find it so tragic and horrifically comedic that parents will play Mozart to the fetus, then fight tooth and nail to get that child in the very best preschool, all in an effort to ensure that their child gets ahead later in life. Yet, in the meantime, these same parents ignore the chilling effect of toxic chemicals and heavy metals on their child's developing brain. Just one example is the chemical bisphenol-A that leaches out of the plastic of their baby's bottle or cup and into the fluid the infant is drinking. In chapter 17, you will discover ways of testing and assisting the body's removal of such chemicals.

POPs and heavy metals such as lead are much more damaging to the developing fetus and child because of the immaturity of their physiology. This is especially true from conception to birth, when the rapidly developing tissues of the fetus and child are extremely susceptible to chemical damage. This damage at the cellular level generally takes place through mechanisms we have already discussed, such as free radical damage and a chronic inflammatory response. In particular, the brain and nervous systems of the fetus and child are exceedingly vulnerable to this type of damage. These delicate and vital neurological tissues are not fully developed until age twelve, making them extremely vulnerable to damage over an extended period. To make matters worse, the brain cannot readily repair itself.

Neurotoxic chemicals are numerous in our environment and even our homes, from organophosphate insecticides, organochloride pesticides, PCBs, PBDEs, VOCs, to heavy metals. They invade our body and our children's bodies through water, food, air, clothing, cleaning and personal care products, as well as carpet and furniture. Research has demonstrated that these neurotoxins detrimentally affect the brain development and function in several ways. These effects manifest as intellectual deficits, causing low-

74 K. Cooper et al., "Environmental standard setting and children's health," Canadian Environmental Law Association and Ontario College of Family Physicians, Toronto (2000), 51.

75 Government of Canada, "Children's health and the indicators and measures–country report: Canada," (2006), http://www.cec.org/files/PDF/POLLUTANTS/CountryReport–Canada–CHE_en.pdf.

er school performance and IQ scores, as well as cognitive and motor deficits.[76] These deficits can present themselves in various ways, such as learning disabilities, dyslexia, autism spectrum disorder, and attention-deficit hyperactivity disorder (ADHD). These neurotoxins most commonly cause behavior problems, especially an inclination toward violent outbursts.[77] The *New England Journal of Medicine* reported that children exposed to PCBs in the womb had lower average IQ scores and delayed reading comprehension at age eleven, a neurotoxic impact that will last through adulthood.[78] Knowing this, when we look to the difficulties that now face our schools, are we ready to consider that our modern lifestyle of "better living through chemistry" may be poisoning our children and our future?

Neurotoxins in Our Environment

- Include insecticides, pesticides, PCBs, PBDEs, VOCs, and heavy metals
- Enter humans through water, food, air, clothing, personal products, carpet, and furniture
- Their effect on brain development and function includes:
  —intellectual deficit, causing lower school performance and IQ scores
  —cognitive and motor deficits
- Their deficits include:
  —learning disabilities
  —dyslexia
  —autism spectrum disorder
  —attention-deficit hyperactivity disorder (ADHD)
  —violent outbursts

76 Canadian Partnership for Children's Health and the Environment (CPCHE), "Child health and the environment: a primer," (August 2005), 21. www.healthyenvironmentforkids.ca.

77 Ibid.

78 J. L. Jacobson and S. W. Jacobson, "Intellectual impairment in children exposed to polychlorinated biphenyls in utero," *NEJM* 335, no. 11 (1996): 783–89.

So, is there any real proof that we are actually accumulating these neurotoxins, hormone disruptors, respiratory toxins, reproductive and developmental toxins, or carcinogens in our tissues? Unbeknownst to most individuals, the U.S. government has been looking into this for over a quarter of a century. These persistent organic pollutants normally build up in the fat tissues of all animals, including humans. From 1970 to 1989, the U.S. Environmental Protection Agency (EPA) measured the actual levels of toxic chemicals in the human body as a part of the National Human Adipose Tissue Survey, or NHATS.[79] This study has been analyzing the levels of chemical toxins in the fat tissues sampled from cadavers or gathered from elective surgeries (e.g., liposuction).

The most startling fact of this study is that the most toxic chemicals known to man are now found in 100% of all samples taken. The number-one toxin found is also one of the most deadly toxins known: dioxin. In addition, 98% of all samples show levels of DDE, a breakdown product of DDT, a toxic compound that has been banned in the United States since 1972. Toxic PCBs (polychlorinated biphenyls), known to contribute to intellectual deficit and behavioral problems, are found in more than 82% of the population. Is there any question why we are now seeing an epidemic of ADHD, autism spectrum disorders, and emotional and behavior disorders? Yet these disorders are just the tip of the iceberg. Underneath are millions more individuals who unknowingly suffer with an injured nervous system, and their only symptoms are chronic myofascial pain, fatigue, lack of mental clarity, and feeling down!

How Bad Is It?

Do not despair; knowledge can empower us! This information is meant to empower, not overwhelm; forewarned is forearmed. One of the greatest challenges I have found, even with the most health-conscious patients, is that individuals simply do not want to believe that they are living in a toxic world. Possibly it is just too much to handle after facing the detrimental effects of our Standard American Diet. Or maybe we are afraid of being associated with some green "tree hugging" extremist. But probably it is just our inability to give up our addiction to "better living through chemistry." The problem, however, is that the science is in, and it is conclusive; the other inconvenient truth is that we are living in a toxic world.

79 This study can be reviewed at http://cfpub.epa/gov/ncea/cfm/recordisplay.cfm?deid=55204.

There is something, however, that you can do for yourself, your children, and your children's children. If you do not believe in the validity of this research, just take a good look around you and notice the effect our "better living through chemistry" is having on our children and even our own health. Have you ever wondered about the dramatic decline in sperm counts, the growing difficulty for some women to conceive, and the explosion of fertility clinics in our modern world? Or what about the explosive growth of neurodegenerative diseases, such as Alzheimer's and Parkinson's disease?

EPA National Human Adipose Tissue Survey (NHATS)

- Measures levels of chemical toxins stored in human fat tissues
- Analyzes the fat from cadavers and elective surgeries
- 5 of the most toxic chemicals found in 100% of fat samples analyzed are:
  —(1) OCDD-dioxin, (2) Styrene, (3) 1,4-dichlorobenzene, (4) Xylene, (5) Ethylphenol
- 9 other toxic chemicals were found in 98% of the fat samples:
  —including benzene, toluene, ethylbenzene, DDE, 3 dioxins, and 1 furan
- PCBs (polychlorinated biphenyls) were found in 80% of the U.S. population

The difficulty in understanding the magnitude of the problem is that the vulnerability to any given chemical is based on one's own biochemical individuality, their personal genetic profile. The efficiency of detoxification and removal of toxins from the body can vary as much as 700% from one individual to another, even within the same family. This is just one reason why there are 300 million different biochemical reactions to the "toxic nation" we live in, one for each individual. The spectrum stretches from the healthy, young, genetically well-endowed "detoxifier"—you could dip this person into a chemical vat, pull them back out, and they would be okay—to the chemically sensitive individual who is so compromised with regard to their ability to detoxify that they literally have to live in a bubble of protection. When you walk down the cleaning product and detergent aisles or past perfume counters, perhaps you get headaches or just do not feel well. All of us are somewhere on this continuum.

Wherever you are along the spectrum, you can lower your toxic chemical burden. Make your personal environment less toxic by simply buying green (e.g., cleaning solutions, clothing, household items, and foods) and purchasing a quality household water filter. Also, you can add botanicals and nutrients to help your body safely remove toxic chemicals stored in your body; details are outlined in chapter 17.

The Warning Had Been Sounded

In their seminal work *Our Stolen Future*, Theo Colburn, Diane Dumanoski, and John Peterson Myers established that the incidence of specific pathologies, such as cancer, reproductive impairment, and neurodegenerative diseases, have risen dramatically since World War II. Through their research, they have related the precipitous increase of these pathologies to the explosion of endocrine-disrupting chemicals in the environment. Since World War II, more than 80,000 chemicals have been introduced into the world's environment. In fact, pesticides and herbicides as we know them today did not exist before World War II. Interestingly, the organophosphate pesticides of today were originally developed as nerve gases for World War II, and herbicides, such as 2, 4-Dichlorophenoxyacetic acid (known as 2, 4-D) were created to destroy Japanese rice fields. Immediately after World War II, these chemicals were put into commercial production for large-scale agricultural, home, and garden use, and mosquito eradication programs. Presently, organic phosphate insecticides are banned in England, Sweden, and Denmark. In the '90s, the Clinton administration began moves to ban these deadly chemicals in the United States; however, by 2006, the Bush administration reversed that direction.

Almost a half-century ago, the very perceptive Rachel Carson wrote the groundbreaking work *Silent Spring*, which brought to the forefront of public awareness our chemical contamination of the earth. As far back as 1962, Carson warned us: "For the first time in the history of the world, every human being is now subjected to contact with dangerous chemicals, from the moment of conception until death."[80] Carson went on to advise us of toxic bioaccumulation: "Like the constant dripping of water that in turn wears away the hardest stone, this birth-to-death contact with dangerous chemicals may in the end prove disastrous. Each of these recurrent exposures, no mat-

80 *Silent Spring*, 1.

ter how slight, contributes to the aggressive buildup of chemicals in our bodies and so to cumulative poisoning."[81]

Carson warned us fifty years ago of the stupidity of relying on short-term, high-dose research studies in determining the effects of toxic chemicals. The problem is that this is not how most people are exposed to toxic chemicals. Because of the ubiquitous nature of a multitude of pollutants in our life, we are exposed to low doses of multiple chemicals every day we live. Little has been done on examining the health effects of low exposure to multiple toxic chemicals over a period of years, which is exactly what we and our children have to deal with in real life each day.

How We Become Polluted

From the moment we awaken until we are tucked safely back into our beds, we are exposed to some of the most harmful chemicals in use today. Your mattress may contain flame-retardant PBDEs that are known to cause cancer and may disrupt hormone function. If your bed sheets or clothes you put on that morning are wrinkle resistant, they have been treated with formaldehyde, another chemical that is known to cause cancer and possibly many other illnesses, such as those involving the respiratory system. There are also flame-retardant PBDEs in the carpets and curtains of your bedroom.

Once you reach the kitchen for breakfast, there are more sources of toxic chemical exposure to delineate than there is room available in this chapter. For example, the food you eat may contain the toxic chemical bisphenol-A if your food came in contact with any plastic, such as food wrap or the plastic lining of canned food. Bisphenol-A has been shown to cause reproductive damage and birth defects, and lead to prostate and breast cancer in adulthood.[82] In a very recent study, published in January 2006, it was discovered that the endocrine-disrupting chemical bisphenol-A causes insulin resistance in mice.[83] Recall from chapter 6 that insulin resistance will cause increased oxidative stress and chronic inflammation, leading to the development of chronic muscle and joint pain disorders, besides being the precursor to diabetes and all its health consequences.

The meal that you ingest, whether it is breakfast, lunch, or dinner, will have low doses of heavy metals, pesticides, and other persistent organic pollutants. If you eat a completely organic diet, it will definitely reduce your exposure to pesticides and herbicides.

81 *Silent Spring*, 173.

82 www.environmentaldefense.ca/: Toxic nation: a report on pollution (2005).

83 A. Paloma et al., "The estrogenic effect of bisphenol-A disrupts pancreatic beta cell function in vivo and induces insulin resistance," *Environ Health Perspect* 114 (2006): 106–12.

But because heavy metals and persistent organic pollutants are found throughout the environment, all the foods you eat contain some of these contaminants, no matter where they are grown. As much as 94–99% of your intake of persistent organic pollutants, such as PCBs, comes through food, so eating only organic foods and beverages can definitely lower your exposure. The largest exposure to these persistent organic pollutants comes from the consumption of breast milk, fatty meats, dairy products, and fish.[84]

Breakfast, Lunch, and . . . POPs?

94–99% of your POP exposure comes through your food:

- The largest exposure comes through breast milk, meats, dairy products, and fish.
- Eating only organic foods and beverages can definitely lower your exposure.
- Eating lower on the food chain (e.g., grains, legumes, vegetables, and fruits) can lower your exposure to chemical toxins.

Stepping into the bathroom, you are flooded by an overwhelming number of toxic chemicals, especially through your personal care products. There are some 4,000 different petroleum-based chemicals, called simply "fragrances," in our personal care products that have been proven to affect your central nervous system, trigger asthma, and cause cancer. In addition to this, phthalates are used in these synthetic fragrances to extend your scent's staying power. Recent research has shown that these phthalates disrupt your hormones and can cause birth defects in male reproductive organs. These toxic phthalates are very persistent in our environment and have been found in everything from household dust to drinking water, meat, and dairy products, as well as the blood and milk of humans.

These multiple various toxic chemicals in your environment—in our water, air, and soil—are absorbed into your body through your lungs, skin, and digestive system. Chemical pollutants that are carried in our air are absorbed not just through our lungs, but also through skin contact. Dust in our houses or workplaces can be a significant

84 K. Cooper et al., *Environmental Standard Setting and Children's Health* (Toronto: Canadian Environmental Law Association and Ontario College of Family Physicians, 2000), 51.

carrier for toxic chemicals. One study in the United Kingdom found that household dust samples contained chemicals such as phthalates, bromated flame-retardants, and other toxins.[85] By the time you slip back into your wrinkle-resistant sheets on your flame-retardant mattress at the end of the day, you have been exposed at low levels to hundreds of different toxic chemicals.

In fact, by the time the average woman steps out of her house in the morning, she has exposed herself to more than 126 different toxic chemicals through her personal care and beauty products. Commonly used beauty products may be directly contributing to our suffering from chronic pain. A long-term controlled trial with forty-eight women who suffer with the muscle pain of fibromyalgia syndrome found that their symptoms were significantly decreased when they reduced the use of cosmetics. After two years, the experimental group that reduced their cosmetic exposure had a significant improvement in their pain, sleep, and stiffness. The women reported that they had better physical function and improved well-being.[86] This study is not saying that fibromyalgia is caused by cosmetics, but as we have seen, the chemicals they contain will increase oxidative stress and systemic inflammation that leads to myofascial pain.

Our fears of these chemicals have always been focused on birth defects and cancer. However, recent research is now showing that physical disease and visible birth defects may not be our most imminent dangers. Actually, our primary health risk is from low-level exposure to these toxic chemicals in our environment affecting the function of our nerves and hormones by damaging the neuroendocrine system. Low-level exposure to these environmental toxins does affect our central nervous system and can affect emotional and behavioral changes in individuals. Low-level exposure to these environmental toxins can also decrease your resistance to infection, and they can increase your susceptibility to autoimmune disorders. One need only look at the exploding statistics for asthma and other autoimmune disorders to understand the importance of this fact. It is now estimated that 23.2 million Americans and 300 million individuals worldwide suffer with asthma. The rate of asthma is now climbing 50% every ten years, according to the Fourth World Asthma Meeting in Bangkok. It is interesting to note that autoimmune disorders, such as systemic lupus, Crohn's disease, psoriasis, MS, and rheumatoid arthritis, are highly associated with chronic inflammation and oxidative stress in your

---

85 Greenpeace Research Laboratories, "Consuming chemicals: hazardous chemicals in house dust as an indicator of chemical exposure in the house," (May 2003), http://eu.greenpeace.org/downloads/chem/consuming%20chemicals.pdf.

86 B. Sverdrup, "Use less cosmetics, suffer less fibromyalgia?" *J Women's Health* 13, no. 2 (March 2004): 187–94.

tissues. This may be one factor in the connection between accumulating chemical toxins in our tissues and the increasing epidemic of chronic pain disorders, autoimmune disorders, and degenerative disease.

For health-care professionals or individuals who want more information on the connection between low-level toxic chemical exposure and chronic pain disorders, I highly recommend that you review the research by Iris R. Bell and Carol M. Baldwin at the University of Arizona. They have found that low-level toxic chemical exposure can elicit central sensitization of the nervous system, which I describe more fully in the next chapter in its connection to chronic pain disorders. In one particular study, they found that 1 out of 5 to even 1 out of 2 individuals with fibromyalgia and/or chronic fatigue syndrome has severe chemical intolerance or sensitivity. In this study, they established that even a low-level presence of environmental toxins in your tissues can cause chronic muscle pain and fatigue.[87] If you suffer with a chronic myofascial pain and/or fatigue disorder, please pay particular attention to chapter 17, which contains specific strategies to enhance your detoxification capacity and ways to protect you and your family from chemical exposure.

What Does This Mean for Me?

- On a daily basis, I am exposed to low levels of toxic chemicals that affect my health.
- These toxic chemicals increase systemic inflammation, oxidative stress, and insulin resistance in my tissues, making me more prone to chronic myofascial pain and degenerative disease.
- I can help heal my pain and improve my health by lessening my exposure to these chemical toxins and improving my detoxification capability.

87 Bell, Baldwin, and Schwartz, "Illness from low levels of environmental chemicals," 74S–82S.

8

How It All Comes Together Neurologically

In the ancient world it was said that "all roads lead to Rome." If this book was the ancient world, then this chapter and section 2 would be Rome, for all the previous chapters lead to this juncture. It is here that all previous information comes together into a practical way to help you understand your pain and transform your life for the better. In this chapter, we explore in detail the actual physical source of your chronic pain. In the coming chapters, I will focus in on the hurt you experience in the form of back pain, neck pain, shoulder pain, headaches, or the all-over pain of fibromyalgia—any recurrent pain that leads you to taking drugs that are ultimately detrimental to your health—and teach you how to physically treat it.

Stress: The Source of Your Pain

In review, the nerve receptors that sense your recurrent pain in your body are called nociceptors. These nociceptors are woven like chicken wire throughout all of your myofascial tissue. *Myo-* means "muscles" and *-fascial* refers to the connective tissue that envelops your muscles and comes together to form your tendons and ligaments. As previously discussed, this all-important myofascial tissue is the network that holds your bones together and moves them so you can stand up and move about.

Because they hold your bones together and pull on them to move you through space, these myofascial tissues come under constant acute and repetitive physical stress. Your myofascial tissues are also under constant chemical stress because they are continually bathed in 25% of your bodily fluids. So whatever is "out there" in your body—dietary excesses of alcohol, sugar, etc.; nutritional deficiencies; dysbiosis; environmental toxins;

stress hormones; and the free radicals and inflammation they all create—directly and quickly affects your myofascial tissues. Emotional stress on your myofascial tissues manifests physically as muscle tension and chemically through the stress hormones circulating throughout your body (more on the chemicals of emotions in section 3). The nociceptors woven throughout your myofascial tissues will warn you of these physical and biochemical stressors in your body by registering this distress as pain. This is why I emphasize that the actual physiological condition of your myofascial tissues foreshadows events unfolding in the tapestry of your overall health. Well-nourished, flexible, and resilient myofascial tissue reflects a generally healthy condition. This is easily known to you through having well-nourished, flexible, strong, and pain-free muscles and joints throughout your body.

The Nerve of Pain

Embedded throughout your myofascial tissues are two major types of nerves: the motor and sensory nerves. Exiting out of your spine and terminating in your muscles are the motor nerves. These nerves do pretty much just what they sound like: they "motor" you about by making your muscles contract. Then there are the sensory nerves, with sensory receptors embedded throughout your myofascial tissues. These nerves travel from your myofascial tissues back to your spine. They also do just as their name states: they "sense" things. Some of these sensory receptors sense how much pressure and tension are placed on them, so you can "sense" where you are in space and if you are moving or standing still. And, most important to our discussion here, they help you know if you are putting too much strain on your myofascial tissues.

The other very important sensory receptors are the nociceptors, the free nerve endings laced throughout your tissues that detect any stress or damage. Injury or the threat of injury to your myofascial tissues registers as pain in your brain. These nociceptors have some very special characteristics in regard to chronic pain, as previously discussed in detail in chapter 4. Recall that these receptors do not adapt to a continuous stimulus, like your sense of smell does, and that they can also become hypersensitive. To continue the comparison, if your nose worked like your nociceptors, instead of adapting to a smell in a room and eventually no longer registering it, your nose not only would continue to detect the bad smell but register it hundreds of times stronger. This would occur in your sensory system, even though the odor in the room stayed at the same exact level.

Because of this complex neurological involvement, your myofascial tissues are collectively described as the neuromyofascial system. *Neuro-* refers to the motor and sensory nerves that control the muscle, or *myo-*, and *-fascial* is for the fascia that holds the muscles together and maintains their overall health. Due to the fact that these neuromyofascial tissues are the primary source of nearly all chronic pain, they will be our primary tissues of interest throughout the rest of this book. Furthermore, when chronic pain is discussed, the term generally used is musculoskeletal disorders, but a more accurate term is neuromyofascial disorders.

The distinction here is important. For example, if you have chronic pain in your skeleton, the bones themselves, you are probably dealing with a pathology such as a bacterial infection, tumor, or something else really nasty that could kill you; this must be ruled out by your doctor. In general, this is not the chronic pain condition that you would want to self-treat through wellness care, so this fact should remove the skeletal part of our term. The term *musculo-* leaves out the all-important fascia, including the tendons and ligaments that they form. Then there are the all-important joints that cause so many of us pain from the condition known as arthritis, a general term simply meaning "inflammation of the joint [articulation]." Because the cartilage that makes up your joints does not contain any nociceptors, cartilage cannot sense inflammation or cause pain. Therefore, when you have joint pain or arthritis, you generally have pain coming from the neuromyofascial tissues, e.g., muscles, tendons, ligaments, and their nociceptors, which immediately surround the joint complex (e.g., shoulder, hip, knee, etc.).

A Rose by Any Other Name

When you have an injury or damaged tissue in your body, it is referred to in health care as a lesion. There are many common terms utilized to identify the primary lesion of chronic pain in our myofascial tissues, such as "muscle knot" and "trigger point." Muscle knot tells part of the story because there are contracted muscle fibers within these lesions, and trigger point also tells part of the story because they do in fact trigger local and distant pain. These terms are inadequate, however, because these pain-causing lesions contain multiple tissues in the form of hundreds of contracted muscle cells, abnormal fascial changes, hypersensitive nociceptors, abnormal motor nerve endings, and even changes in your spinal cord and certain areas of your brain.

It is these hyperirritable tissues (muscle knots, trigger points) and their neurological reflex that cause you chronic pain, muscle tension, and increased stress response, and eventually affect the homeostasis or smooth running of your entire body.

I have looked for a term that would bring a greater appreciation and a deeper understanding for this lesion that causes so much pain in society. For my patients and in my lectures to doctors, I like to use the most descriptive term that conveys the deepest understanding. The term that best describes this pain-causing entity is the neuromyofascial lesion, or the NML. By continuing to refer to the source of your chronic pain as the neuromyofascial lesion, it will remind you of the components of your chronic pain that must be properly addressed to achieve health and wellness: nerve, muscle, and fascial tissue.

Neuromyofascial Lesions (NMLs)

The pain-causing lesion containing multiple tissues equals:

- Hundreds of contracted muscle cells
- Abnormal physical and chemical changes in the fascia
- Hypersensitive nociceptors
- Abnormal motor nerve endings
- Changes in your spinal cord
- Changes in certain areas of your brain

Why the Big Deal over Terminology?

When we have the capability to name something, we often confuse that ability with real understanding. If we can take a concept or thing and nail it down with a term, we assume that we now have some comprehension of what it is. An example is one we used before. We say "I have dermatitis" and think we know what the problem is. But do we? Again, *dermatitis* is Latin for "skin inflammation," which really tells us very little of the underlying causes that must be addressed to heal it. The same thing holds true for "defining" the source of our pain using words such as muscle tension, muscle knots, trigger points, or phrases like "I have a catch in my back" or "my back went out." These terms actually tell us very little about the multiple underlying factors involved in our chronic pain. The term neuromyofascial lesion brings to mind that there are multiple tissues and multiple metabolic problems in these tissues that must be properly treated to heal your chronic pain.

Our word *water* is another good example of losing the essence of an important reality in a simple term. We believe we understand water when we say the word *water*. We can even go on to say that water is composed of two gases, two molecules of hydrogen and one molecule of oxygen, or in other words, H_2O. We also know that because of its unique molecular structure it acts as a universal solvent, and possibly we can name other defining factors about this thing called water. But, what if we contemplated water more deeply for just a moment? When first grasped, water seems extremely weak as it runs through your hands, yet with patience it can carve out the Grand Canyon. Even though water nourishes every living thing, it seeks out the humblest of ground wherever it resides. In the *Tao Te Ching,* Lao Tzu says water in its essence is most like the Tao: seemingly weak but infinitely powerful, nourishing all but yet most humble. The word *water* is useful but does not get to the essence of what water actually is.

The lesson learned from the essence of water is one that can serve us as well throughout the rest of this book, especially in the body/mind/spirit section. You may wonder why this lesson of "naming mistaken for understanding" is so important. My answer is that we easily dismiss out of hand what we think we comprehend without truly grasping its depth. As Mark Twain most shrewdly pointed out, "It ain't what you don't know that gets you into trouble. It's what you know for sure that just ain't so." This is an especially important concept for those who suffer with chronic pain and fatigue. When a doctor tells you, "Oh, you just have (fill in the blank: muscle tension, insomnia, depression, muscle knots, tendonitis, trigger points, etc.)," it not only minimizes the suffering you are going through, but more importantly it limits a doctor's ability to properly treat your chronic pain and fatigue. Usually, the next statement that comes out of their mouths is "We'll fix that up with (fill in the blank: NSAIDs, Prozac, sleep medication, electrotherapy, laser therapy, etc.)."

Possibly a therapy can bring you some relief, but if the underlying mechanisms that caused your chronic pain are not addressed, the discomfort will tend to linger and maybe even return with a vengeance. In the previous chapters, I described in detail the primary mechanisms connected to our diet and lifestyle that lead to not only the development of chronic pain but also degenerative disease. These causative metabolic factors created by a lifestyle of overconsumption and undernutrition are chronic silent inflammation, oxidative stress, insulin resistance, and environmental toxins. If you are given a therapy for your chronic pain, whether drug or physical in nature, and are not taught how to change the underlying causes, you often end up going backwards. To paraphrase an old saying, you can give a hungry family a fish and they eat for a day, but teach them how to fish and they will eat for a lifetime. This book is designed to show you how to "fish," not just find temporary relief; my goal is to empower you to transform your life and heal your pain!

Your Brain and the NML

The neuromyofascial lesion is the underlying problem that causes you stiffness, pain, and even weakness. The neuromyofascial lesion, again, is composed of muscle, fascia, and your nervous system, from the nociceptors embedded in these painful, tight tissues all the way up to your brain. Your neuromyofascial lesions involve tight, bunched, tense muscle tissue, but this knotted tissue does not exist in a vacuum. This painful, knotted-up tissue that triggers your pain is connected through sensory nerves directly to your spinal cord. Your spinal cord is the first stopping-off point for the signals from your myofascial nociceptors. Here the signal can die if the distress is not that threatening and the signal is weak. If the distress is truly threatening your tissues, the signal will be strong enough to cross over the synapse to another nerve. From here, the signal travels up a nerve to connect to various parts of your brain.

It is here, in the brain, where your chronic pain starts to get really interesting. The second neurological stop is deep in the center of your brain at the sensory switching station, the area called the thalamus. From your thalamus, the neuromyofascial lesions are actually connected into your emotional brain, known as the limbic area. Here is where the connection is made between pain and your emotions. Also, from your thalamus, your neuromyofascial lesions are connected to your body's homeostasis (status quo) control center in your brain, called the hypothalamus. Your hypothalamus exerts control over your organs, glands, and blood flow through your autonomic nervous system and endocrine system. The hypothalamus is also in control of your stress response through your sympathetic nervous system and your adrenal glands (all of this will be made much clearer in chapter 19). The point here to realize is that your pain is not just happening in your muscles and joints, but more importantly, it's happening in different areas of your brain as well.

Through these important neurological connections, you can now see how these pain-causing neuromyofascial lesions are intimately connected to your emotions and your stress response—actually, to the whole balanced functioning of your body. From the thalamus, your neuromyofascial lesions, or trigger points, are then connected to your sensory and motor cortex. It is only here, when the warning signal of physical and chemical distress in your myofascial tissues finally reaches the outer sensory cortex of your brain, that you actually experience the sensation of pain. Please note that this means before signals from your trigger points reach the sensory cortex and shout "PAIN," they will stimulate lower areas of your brain, causing tension and an increased stress response in your body without you even being fully conscious of it. Multiple NMLs are constantly firing into areas of your brain, creating deleterious effects on your health even without stimulating conscious pain. This explains why individuals tend to feel more relaxed and have an overall improved sense of well-being after a myofascial treatment has removed numerous muscle knots.

Dietary Promotion of Painful NMLs

Your diet and lifestyle choices can also have a significant impact on your central nervous system (spinal cord and brain) through the neuromyofascial lesion. Here is how it works. Dietary excesses, internal toxins from dysbiosis, environmental toxins, and nutritional deficiencies create chronic inflammation and oxidative stress in your myofascial tissues. As described in chapter 5, low-grade inflammation and oxidative stress can become a vicious feed-forward cycle. Oxidative stress in your myofascial tissues turns on genes that manufacture cytokines (cell messengers) that create chronic inflammation at the cellular level. This low-grade inflammation in your myofascial tissues ends up creating more free radicals, which in turn generates more cytokines, creating more low-grade inflammation, generating more free radicals—and on and on it goes.

A central component of myofascial pain disorders is this vicious feed-forward cycle of oxidative stress and low-grade inflammation that builds up until it chronically stimulates the nociceptors in your myofascial tissues. The activation of nociceptors is a signal to your spinal cord of low-grade cellular damage or tissue distress in your myofascial tissues from this feed-forward cycle. If the signal gets past the spinal cord, it goes up to your thalamus and then to the different areas of your brain. When the signal reaches your limbic system and hypothalamus, it can increase your emotional and stress response to life in general, with or without the perception of pain. When the signal gets past your thalamus and stimulates your sensory cortex, you experience the sensation of pain (more on this in chapter 19). This neurological response of your brain signaling pain is extremely important to your survival; however, the vicious feed-forward cycle of oxidative stress and chronic inflammation, triggered by dietary and lifestyle factors left unattended, will eventually cause degenerative disease in your body.

There are two central themes of this book. First, the metabolic causes of your chronic pain are the engines of your demise from degenerative disease, such as heart disease, cancer, diabetes, and neurodegenerative disorders, such as Alzheimer's, dementia, and Parkinson's. Second, the presence of neuromyofascial lesions, or trigger points, can directly affect the overall health of your body through their input into your central nervous system. Therefore, the warnings—experienced as chronic pain, indicating that there is ongoing distress in your tissues—should prompt you to change your diet and lifestyle choices that cause this distress. The problem in our society is that we swallow 30 billion over-the-counter tablets of NSAIDs in a desperate attempt to escape our chronic pain and avoid the discipline needed to truly heal. In chapters 14 through 17, I will provide a dietary, lifestyle, and nutritional program to overcome your chronic myofascial pain.

The History of the Trigger Point, or NML

The recognition of therapeutic tender points in the body was described as far back as the Tang Dynasty (AD 618–978) in China by the renowned physician Sun Ssu-Miao. In his textbook, he actually describes tender points not fixed in position or running along acupuncture meridians but appearing on the body when it is stressed, diseased, or injured. Sun Ssu-Miao wrote that these points were found in tissues that looked normal but were spontaneously tender, and when detected by palpation the patient would cry out "aah shi," meaning "ah yes" or "hurts good." Today in the East, these trigger points are still referred to as "aah shi" points. This description of stressed or injured myofascial tissue parallels the modern understanding of trigger points, or what I refer to as the neuromyofascial lesion.

These knotlike neuromyofascial lesions have been recognized and written about in Western medical literature for over 150 years, using various terminologies to define them. In 1938, the work of J. H. Kellgren, published in the prestigious *British Medical Journal,* proved scientifically to the medical community that not just nerves but also irritated muscle and fascia could produce pain in the area of involvement, and more importantly refer pain to distant regions. By injecting irritating chemicals in only the muscle and fascia at the top of the neck below the back of the skull, he reproduced the symptoms of neck pain, stiffness, and headaches all the way into the forehead. Sound familiar? When he injected irritating chemicals into the muscles and fascia of the low back, he was able to reproduce the symptoms of back pain with sciatica to the foot, without touching a nerve![88] This research should have had tremendous impact; pain of the low back is experienced by 85% of Americans and is the leading cause of disability in adults under the age of forty-five. Yet his ground-breaking work was generally ignored by the medical community at the time, and it still is today. The inability to incorporate this research on trigger points into medicine has led to a great deal of unnecessary medication and surgeries, causing an enormous amount of unnecessary suffering.

In the 1940s, Dr. Janet Travell began publishing research on what she called the trigger point, which is the most common term in use today in both popular and professional articles. She continued to be a leading pioneer in this field, doing extensive research and publishing up until her death in 1997. Travell's research partner was Dr. David G. Simons, and in 1983 they wrote the first volume of their definitive textbook, called *Myofascial Pain and Dysfunction: The Trigger Point Manual.* Well into his eighties, Dr. Simons is still researching and writing to improve our understanding of chronic myofascial pain and trigger points.

Sadly, since Dr. Travell's "trigger point" has become the primary defining term for this multifaceted neuromyofascial lesion, this complex problem is now seen as a discrete point living by itself, lurking somewhere out in your muscles. However, through the research presented in this book, we have come to realize that this pain-causing abnormal tissue is not a distinct point but more a region of tissue that contains contracted

---

88 J. H. Kellgren, "Observations on referred pain arising from muscle," *Clinical Science* 3 (1938): 175–90, and "A preliminary account of referred pains arising from muscle," *British Medical Journal* 1 (1938): 325–27.

muscle cells, anomalous fascia, multiple hypersensitive nociceptors, and abnormally functioning motor nerve endings. Also, these chronic neuromyofascial lesions have the ability to constantly fire impulses into various brain structures, creating far-reaching effects on your body and health with or without conscious pain. And finally, the underlying abnormal metabolic factors that set you up for multiple chronic pain-causing NMLs, or trigger points, are the same metabolic factors that set you up for degenerative disease. So do not relieve your pain only for a moment in time by turning to a NSAID prescription; heal your pain for a lifetime and bring about real wellness in your life by applying the strategies outlined in this book.

How Pain-Causing Muscle Knots Form

Any acute or recurrent physical stress (injury), chemical stress (toxic exposure or nutritional deficiency), or emotional stress can lead to the formation of contracted taut bands in muscle tissue. These taut bands are the tight, ropey tissue you can sometimes feel in your own muscles. At first, these taut bands are painless, but eventually they will begin to shorten your muscles and alter your movement patterns.

These taut bands are hundreds of contracted and shortened muscle fibers in a small area of the muscle. As you can imagine, this squeezes out the blood from the tissue and obstructs good blood flow into the muscle fibers. This loss of blood in your muscle tissue means there is a reduction of oxygen and nutrients. This reduction of oxygen and nutrients will cause the muscle cells of the taut band to run low on energy, or ATP. The vital importance of ATP and its role in chronic muscle pain and fatigue was discussed in detail in chapter 5. In that chapter, we discussed how oxidative stress and chronic inflammation can make it difficult for your muscle cells to produce adequate ATP (energy). Lowered energy in your muscles means lowered vitality and the development of muscle pain and fatigue. Any further physical, chemical and/or emotional stress will cause these taut bands to begin to form pain-causing myofascial trigger points by causing hypersensitization of the nociceptors contained within them.

Abnormal metabolic distress of oxidative stress and chronic inflammation in your myofascial tissues sets you up for the formation of taut bands and subsequently pain-causing myofascial trigger points. This metabolic distress, discussed in chapter 5, is caused by diet and lifestyle, things you have direct control over. Later, in section 4, we will discuss what you can do with your diet to reduce your metabolic distress and overcome chronic pain and the development of degenerative disease.

It is this lowered energy state in the taut muscle fibers that allows any added physical, chemical, or emotional stress to cause the formation of pain-causing neuromyofascial lesions. This formation is partially due to the dysfunction of sensory and motor nerve endings in the muscle fibers of a taut band. Abnormal nerve endings in your muscles are what create the painful nerve reflex of trigger points from muscles and tendons to your spinal cord, as previously discussed.

This dysfunction of your sensory nerve endings in your myofascial tissues is called peripheral sensitization. It is a fitting term, because it is happening out in the myofascial tissues, or the periphery of your body. Specifically, the nociceptors of your peripheral nervous system in your myofascial tissues are becoming more sensitive. For example, with chronic low-back pain, the peripheral sensitization of NMLs in your lumbar muscles are constantly bombarding your spinal cord and brain, creating your chronic pain disorder.

Surprisingly, it actually takes energy, or ATP, to relax contracted muscle cells; therefore, reduced energy levels in taut bands create a self-sustaining vicious cycle. Taut bands of NMLs have inadequate energy to relax, causing them to remain taut and painful until they are physically released. The neurological reflex from dysfunctional nerve endings in these self-sustaining contracted NMLs continues to create and maintain your chronic pain. The greater the number and intensity of these trigger points with dysfunctional nerve endings you have firing into your spinal cord (e.g., low back), the greater your low-back pain will be.

The longer these trigger points fire into your spinal cord, the greater chance actual biochemical changes will take place in your nervous system, and you will develop a chronic pain memory in the spinal cord. This functional change in the neurons of your spinal cord is known as neuronal plasticity, which is the primary factor behind chronic pain disorders, whether regional (as in chronic low-back pain) or the global pain of fibromyalgia. The functional changes of neuronal plasticity in your spinal cord are called central sensitization. This is fitting because the changes are in your central nervous system, and they cause your perception of pain to become more sensitive. This is what is going on in your central nervous system when it develops the memory of chronic pain—"central sensitization" of your spinal cord and brain!

The good news is that you can unlearn this chronic pain. First, with trigger point therapy, begin to remove the NMLs or trigger points that are firing into your spinal cord, causing it to become sensitized. For example, in chapter 10 I will show you the usual patterns of myofascial trigger points that commonly cause back pain problems. Find and use a trigger point tool that works best for you to remove these trigger points, as described in chapter 10. This will physically remove the NMLs of peripheral sensitization firing into the spinal cord of your low-back region. Then incorporate the dietary changes and add the nutritional and herbal supplement discussed in the chapters that follow. With this common-sense scientific approach, you can begin a program that, over time, can change the peripheral and central sensitization that is causing your chronic pain.

For other regions of chronic pain, such as shoulder or arm problems, you do the same thing by applying the information presented in chapter 11. In this chapter, you will find the keys to unlock the mystery of your recurrent shoulder problem before you end up with rotator cuff surgery. Then, in chapter 13, you will discover a self-care tool kit to help you overcome nagging stiff-neck tension headaches or a painful upper back. If you have multi-regional pain syndrome or fibromyalgia syndrome, then you will want to pay special attention to chapter 18.

How Myofascial Trigger Points Cause Your Chronic Pain

1. Physical, chemical, or emotional stress causes chronic muscle fiber contraction, creating a painless, taut band.
2. Contracted muscle fibers squeeze out blood and reduce blood flow, reducing available energy (ATP) in the muscle cells.
3. Poor energy levels do not allow muscle fibers to relax, creating a self-perpetuating taut band.
4. Any added physical, chemical, or emotional distress to the taut band creates trigger points with abnormal nerve endings (peripheral sensitization).
5. Abnormal nerve endings create a neurological reflex to the spinal cord and brain.
6. This neurological reflex eventually creates physiological changes in the spinal cord and brain, creating a pain memory (central sensitization).
7. Chronicity of primary trigger points can create satellite trigger points, causing your pain to spread to other areas.

The NML: Very Common, Never Normal!

Multiple research studies have established without a doubt the existence of the myofascial trigger point. The NML is extremely common, but it is not a "normal" finding. Contrary to the belief of many individuals, research has conclusively established that normal muscles do not contain taut bands of contracted muscle cells and are not normally tender to deep palpation. Healthy, normal muscles and fascia do not show any abnormality under the microscope, are not tender when firmly palpated, and especially do not refer pain to other areas when pressed. These abnormalities are specific indications of a NML, or myofascial trigger point, in your tissues.

Studies led by Mohammed B. Yunus at the University of Illinois College of Medicine utilized muscle biopsies of trigger points in myofascial pain syndrome and fibromyalgia patients. Electron microscopic examination found abnormal mitochondrial findings in 8 out of 10 patients.[89] The major role that the mitochondria can play in the occurrence of chronic myofascial pain has been discussed throughout this book, particularly in chapter 5. Dr. David G. Simons's research in 2002 found specific electrical activity from the abnormal motor nerve ending in the active myofascial trigger point. This research helped to further establish the existence of the myofascial trigger points and demonstrate the involvement of the nervous system in its continued maintenance.[90] This is just a very small sample of the volume of research scientifically establishing the existence of myofascial trigger points—very common, but never normal.

Primary trigger points are active hyperirritable tissues in your problem area that spontaneously cause a local deep ache and refer pain to a distal area; for example, a shoulder NML causing pain down your arm, a hip NML causing leg pain, or a neck NML referring pain into your head. Patients who have experienced pain due to heart attacks, broken bones, or kidney stones have reported that their myofascial pain from active trigger points can be just as severe as pain from these ailments. So no one should ever underestimate the suffering you are going through with chronic myofascial pain of your back, neck, or extremities. It is especially life-altering when this becomes a problem all over your body, as in fibromyalgia syndrome.

---

89 M. B. Yunus, U. P. Kalyan–Raman, and K. Kalyan–Raman, "Primary fibromyalgia syndrome and myofascial pain syndrome: clinical features and muscle pathology," *Arch Phys Med Rehabil* 69, no. 6 (June 1998): 451–54.

90 D. G. Simons, C. Z. Hong, and L. S. Simons, "Endplate potentials are common to midfiber myofascial trigger points," *Am J Phys Med Rehabil* 81, no. 3 (Mar 2002): 212–22.

The Active NML, or Primary Trigger Point

Just how common are these active trigger points in an individual complaining of pain? In one study, a neurologist examined around 100 patients from a community pain medical center and found that nearly 100% of them had at least part of their pain caused directly by myofascial trigger points. In 3 out of 4 of these pain patients, the myofascial trigger points present were diagnosed as the primary cause of all their pain.[91] In another study, 283 patients admitted to a comprehensive pain center were examined by a neurosurgeon and a psychiatrist, and 85% of these patients were given a diagnosis of myofascial trigger points as the primary cause of their chronic pain.[92] These and many other studies indicate how primary the neuromyofascial lesion is in chronic pain disorders.

NMLs that actively generate pain are designated as active trigger points. These active myofascial trigger points are always tender; they also cause stiffness and weakness in the muscle and usually refer pain upon digital pressure. These are usually the easiest and most important myofascial trigger points to find and thus to begin the process of reducing your symptoms. For example, let us say you are one of the millions of Americans suffering with recurrent back pain. You can find a very common active trigger point in the waist of your low back by simply resting your hands on the top of your bony pelvic brim, with your thumbs pointing behind you. Now rotate your hands and apply pressure with your thumbs into the muscles on each side of your backbone. The muscle is located approximately one hand-width away from the bony bumps of your lumbar spine. This is an important supportive muscle of your low back called the quadratus lumborum, and many times it contains active myofascial trigger points. Try working up and down the length of the muscle and toward and away from your spine to find the most exquisite active myofascial trigger points. If you cannot get enough pressure, try lying on a tennis or golf ball. Once you find an active trigger point, digital pressure will cause pain in the area and refer pain to your lumbosacral spine and buttock. You will find complete self-treatment programs for this and many more problematic muscles in your low back in chapter 10.

---

91 R. D. Gerwin, "A study of 96 subjects examined both for fibromyalgia and myofascial pain," *J Musculoskeletal Pain* 3, suppl. 1 (1995): 121.

92 D. A. Fishbain, M. Goldberg, B. R. Meagher, R. Steele, and H. Rosomoff, "Male and female chronic pain patients categorized by DSM–111 psychiatric diagnostic criteria," *Pain* 26 (1986): 181–97.

Another great example, if you have shoulder and/or arm pain, is a muscle in the middle of your shoulder blade. To find this active trigger point in your right shoulder, take your left arm and reach across your chest under your right armpit and around to the back of your right shoulder blade. You can assist your reach by taking your right hand, grabbing your left elbow, and pulling your left arm across your chest; this is also an ideal stretch for the left shoulder. In this position, probe with your left fingertips in the middle of your right shoulder blade, applying firm pressure to any possible nodules you find. You may discover that one or more myofascial trigger points refer pain into your shoulder joint and even down your arm. By this time, you may be realizing that the number-one problem with self-care to the trigger spot area is the extreme difficulty in applying adequate pressure to release the NML. It turns out that there are some very good self-care trigger point tools on the market today to facilitate self-treatment; these tools and their application will be discussed in chapters 9 through 13.

The Lurking NML, or Latent Trigger Point

Removing the active trigger spots or NMLs is very important in reducing your symptoms. They are easy to find because they spontaneously create pain symptoms on their own. Usually, patients come to see me and point right to their active NMLs. Often the patients report trying to pressure-treat them by lying on golf balls or leaning against door knobs. The problem with myofascial therapy is that frequently recurrent muscle and joint pain problems never seem to fully clear up when treating just these primary trigger points. One of the main reasons for this is the existence of the hidden trigger point areas in your myofascial tissues. These types of myofascial trigger areas are extremely common, and they can be very numerous. They are commonly referred to as latent myofascial trigger points, though I refer to them as lurking NMLs. They are always there in your tissues, causing stiffness and tension, but because they do not create spontaneous pain, they often go unnoticed.

Remember, though, that even while the signals from the lurking NMLs are not reaching the conscious sensory cortex, causing perceivable pain, they can reach your lower brain centers. Stimulating your lower brain center's latent trigger points can cause an increased stress response and alter your homeostatic balance. Most importantly, these lurking NMLs in your back or neck muscles keep the myofascial tissues and spinal cord of those regions sensitized, or primed. You then only need to bend over to get groceries out of your car trunk to cause many of these latent trigger points to go active and cause your severe pain. Another reason this happens is because even though lurking NMLs do not cause spontaneous pain, they have all the other characteristics of active myofascial trigger points, such as shortening and weakening of the muscle tissue. This can cause altered movement patterns, which can set you up for an acute pain episode and perpetuate your pain. Because of their hidden nature, undetected latent trigger points end up causing a tremendous amount of recurrent pain. The usual problem is that once the active trigger points are under control, therapy is not continued to remove the surrounding latent trigger points. By remaining hidden in the myofascial tissues, they can reactivate the primary trigger points again.

Possibly you may be wondering how prevalent these so-called latent or lurking myofascial trigger points are in your muscles. Numerous studies have shown them to be quite prevalent, even in pain-free, healthy individuals. For example, Dr. A. E. Sola and his associates studied 200 Air Force cadets. In this study, the average age was around twenty years old, half were male and half were female, and all of them were pain free. Upon examination, however, these individuals were found to have latent trigger points in their shoulder girdle muscles. In other words, through their neck and shoulder areas they had areas of myofascial tissue that were not causing them conscious pain but were firing into their central nervous system, causing them stiffness and tension and setting them up for future problems.[93]

Now that we have looked at the underlying causes of chronic myofascial pain, it is time to move on to treating its causes. In chapters 9 through 13, we will explore the patterns of active and latent trigger points that cause common chronic pain problems and how to specifically remove them. Then, in chapters 14 through 18, we will discover what can be done to overcome the metabolic challenges of chronic myofascial pain.

---

93 A. E. Sola, M. L. Rodenberger, and B. B. Gettys, "Incidence of hypersensitive areas in posterior shoulder muscles," *Am J Phys Med* 34 (1955): 585–90.

Book Two

THE TRIANGLE OF HEALING: PHYSICAL/BIOCHEMICAL/SPIRITUAL

By now you have examined the map thoroughly and are ready to begin the journey to heal your pain. To accomplish this, you must walk this path looking after all aspects of yourself: the physical, biochemical, and spiritual / emotional natures of your being. However, in the end, they also must be spiritually integrated; you cannot leave any aspect of yourself behind and expect to be whole and healthy. To heal, you must address the entire triangle of your health and well-being.

All too often in our health care today, we find these aspects of the self being treated separately and many times ignored altogether. It becomes even more problematic when we are treated by clinicians who specialize only in one part of the physical self. On the other hand, we may see a health-care provider who addresses our emotional well-being but is unable to take into account the effects that physical pain or poor dietary choices have on our emotions.

My goal with this comprehensive guide is that it address all three aspects of the self and their impact on healing your pain. To simplify this daunting task, I have divided this second part of the book into three sections, each addressing one leg of the balanced triangle of your health and well-being: physical, biochemical, and spiritual.

Section 3

Physically Healing Your Pain

In this section, we examine the physical foundation of chronic pain: the neuromyofascial lesion (NML), better known as the trigger point. In chapter 9, you will learn exactly what these pain-causing trigger points are and how you can remove them.

This book is vastly different and entirely unique from other books on myofascial pain. It is based on my research and many years of clinical experience, allowing me to provide you with the specific muscle patterns of dysfunction at the root of your chronic pain. For example, in chapter 10, you will learn the typical muscle patterns of dysfunction that lead to chronic low-back, hip, and leg pain.

In chapters 11 through 13, we will explore the patterns of muscle dysfunction involved in mid-back, shoulder, and arm pain, as well as those involved in neck pain and headaches. A key to understanding upper body myofascial pain syndromes is found in the beginning of chapter 11. Here I specifically examine the role of the misunderstood shoulder blade in chronic upper body pain.

I have found that generally patients are unable to heal their chronic pain if they ignore the physical aspects of their recovery. It is important for you to remove all your trigger points, the physical source of your neuromyofascial pain syndrome. However, once they are resolved, it is impossible to find complete recovery without addressing the underlying metabolic factors, and those answers are found in section 4.

9

Self-Care 101 for Myofascial Pain Syndromes

Even though the vast majority of all musculoskeletal pain is benign, it is vital for anyone who has pain, acute or chronic, to have a proper physical exam and workup by a qualified doctor. It is important to rule out the possibility of any hidden fractures, tumors, or infections that may be at the source of the pain. However, it is estimated that less than 5% of all musculoskeletal pain stems from fractures, tumors, and infection, while just another 5% of musculoskeletal pain cases are caused by nerve-root problems, such as disc herniation. If your pain does arise from one of these causes, you will want to know and have it properly treated.

But this leaves well over 90% of all musculoskeletal pain arising from a dysfunction of the myofascial tissues (muscles, tendons, and joints). The primary cause and most-ignored factor in this 90% is the myofascial trigger point. Respected pain researchers Melzack and Wall have stated that myofascial trigger points are often the major factor in the cause and/or maintenance of chronic pain states.

However, you may have more than one problem at a time, so just because you have a myofascial pain syndrome does not mean you cannot also have an associated pathological process or disease. Therefore, it is mandatory that any individual with a chronic pain syndrome receive a proper diagnostic workup by a competent doctor to rule out all other disorders. Once you know that your musculoskeletal pain of the back, neck, shoulder, and hip (or whatever) has a myofascial trigger point component, it is beneficial for you to start on a home program of deactivating these triggers of pain.

The Neuromyofascial Lesion of a Myofascial Pain Syndrome

A myofascial pain syndrome will manifest when you develop multiple neuromyofascial lesions, or trigger points, in a region, creating the characteristic deep ache and stiffness in the area involved. These NMLs are specific areas of hyperirritable tissues in muscles and tendons that cause five major things to happen:

- First, the tissue becomes painful and/or tender locally, but it then can refer pain to other areas of your body.
- Second, myofascial trigger points will cause your muscles to shorten, causing stiffness and reduced range of motion.
- Third, myofascial trigger points can weaken the involved muscles.
- Fourth, this pain, stiffness, and weakness in a muscle group will cause you to develop altered patterns of movement. This puts abnormal stress on other muscles and joints, causing you to form more myofascial trigger points, thereby further spreading your muscle and joint pain problems.
- Fifth, over time, this altered biomechanics can accelerate wear and tear on the joints controlled by the involved muscles, leading to osteoarthritic changes.

An example of this is a low-back myofascial pain syndrome with multiple neuromyofascial lesions in the core muscles that support your lumbar spine, causing pain and stiffness in your low-back region. These myofascial trigger points in your muscles and tendons of your low back could also refer pain into your buttock, hip, or even down your leg to the foot. Another example is a myofascial pain syndrome of your shoulder and neck area, with trigger points causing recurrent pain and stiffness. These myofascial trigger points in the muscles and tendons of the shoulder-girdle region could also refer pain down your arm, to your hand, and even up into your neck and head.

People with myofascial pain syndromes usually have a history of an acute injury (slip, fall, car accident, etc.) or a repetitive stress injury at work or at play (e.g., computer work, data entry, golf), all made more chronic by underlying metabolic problems discussed in detail in chapters 5–8. The presence of this regional myofascial pain syndrome is usually brought to your attention whenever you use or overuse that region of your body containing the NMLs. You can also become aware of your regional myofascial pain syndrome when a health-care provider examines and palpates your myofascial tissues, finding trigger points that reproduce your symptoms in that area. H. P. Meyer reported in a 2002 study that "failure to recognize myofascial pain syndrome often leads to over-investigation, unnecessary medical intervention, and iatrogenic [physician-caused] harm with serious cost implications."[94]

These regional myofascial pain syndromes are equally present in both males and females, whereas the global pain of fibromyalgia syndrome strikes women at least ten times more than men (see chapter 18 for more on fibromyalgia syndrome). However, myofascial pain syndrome is substantially more common and can be quite disabling, and at times it can lead to fibromyalgia syndrome. One study reported as much as 22% of individuals who suffered a whiplash injury causing a regional myofascial pain syndrome went on to develop fibromyalgia syndrome.[95]

FINDING THE NML, OR MYOFASCIAL TRIGGER POINT

Figure 9.1

s mark the neuromyofascial lesions, or trigger points; the shading indicates areas of referral pain, darker meaning more intense pain; this figure shows the trigger points for the upper and lower trapezius muscles and their common referral patterns

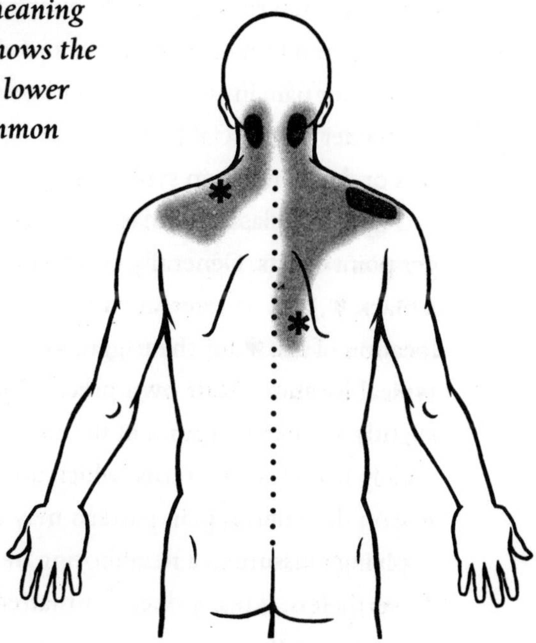

94 H. P. Meyer, "Myofascial pain syndrome and its suggested role in the pathogenesis and treatment of fibromyalgia syndrome," *Curr Pain Headache Rep* 6, no. 4 (August 2002): 274–83.

95 D. Buskila, L. Newmann, G. Vaisberg, D. Alkaley, and F. Wolfe, "Increased rates of fibromyalgia following cervical spine injury: a controlled study of 161 cases of traumatic injury," *Arthritis Rheum* 40, 3 (March 1997): 446–52.

To experience the neuromyofascial lesion, or NML, just take your right hand, reach across in front of you, and grab your left upper shoulder, the fleshy area that connects the bottom of your neck to your shoulder area. With a pincer grasp between your thumb and forefinger, squeeze the tissue along that muscular ridge. You may begin to feel tissue that is tender, lumpy, or nodular. With squeezing pressure, you may find local tenderness and pain that refers up the side of your neck, maybe even to the back of your head or above your eye. This is one of the most common NMLs, or trigger points, found in the human body, and because of postural stress it is generally there whether you are experiencing pain or not. This NML commonly causes muscle tension, stiff neck, neck pain, and headaches. Please refer to figure 9.1 for the position of this trigger point in the upper trapezius muscle and its common referral pattern.

You can also identify your pain-causing NMLs by gently stroking the tissues in painful areas of your body with your fingertips. In the areas of a NML, the muscle tissue in the immediate vicinity will feel tense or ropey under your fingertips. These are the taut bands discussed on chapter 8, and within them, you may find fingertip-sized areas that are nodular and quite tender. If one moves a fingertip or two away from this spot, the exquisite tenderness generally disappears. When pressured, the fingertip-sized region increases tenderness in the area, and with sustained pressure will generally cause referral pain, or pain in an area distant from the pressured spot. When you apply pressure to the tender myofascial trigger point, local and referral pain is created that often resembles or duplicates pain symptoms you are experiencing.

This is the classic myofascial trigger point, which can be found mapped out on trigger point charts. Generally, the myofascial trigger point on these charts is indicated by a black ✱, and its referral pain is indicated by a shaded area. Just remember that the location of the ✱ for the trigger spot and shaded-in area for the referral pain is only the typical location. Your own precise location for the myofascial trigger spot may vary slightly, so search around in the muscle. In addition, the referral area of pain can vary widely from the diagrams, which are only examples of a typical distribution. Another reason the referral pain pattern may differ from the chart is that you may actually be applying pressure to a neighboring muscle with a completely different referral pattern. Nevertheless, it really does not matter because you want to remove *all* myofascial trigger points in the area.

Finding a Treatment Point, or NML

With the muscle relaxed, you can locate a trigger point by probing the tissue with your fingers, thumb, or a trigger point therapy tool, until you find a spot that under firm pressure evokes or exacerbates the symptoms you have. You know you are on a treatment point when moderate pressure creates local tenderness with referral sensations to other parts of your body or extremities—sensations such as tingling, aching, sharp pain, and/or numbness. The decrease within sixty seconds of this discomfort with therapeutic pressure will also signal that you are correctly on a treatment point. Probe along the lines indicated in the following diagrams and described in the text correlating to your problem area to find the trigger points causing your pain. You can move to the right or left and up or down along or off each of these lines to find the exact locations of your pain-causing trigger points.

Reference Guide for Common Lower Body Pain-Causing NMLs

Hip/Leg Pain—Follow diagonal line A (see figure 9.2, next page) from the bony bump in back of your pelvis to the bony bump in front of your pelvis. Starting at the front bony bump and moving backwards, you can check the tensor fasciae latae muscle and through the gluteus minimus, medius, and maximus muscles along line A. This line of common myofascial trigger points is closely related to the outline of the opening of your back pocket of your jeans. Trigger points along line A are related to low-back, hip, and leg pain; a description of these trigger points and their symptoms can be found in chapter 10. The piriformis muscle can be found about a hand-width below the middle of line A. This muscle creates a wide variety of symptoms collectively called the piriformis syndrome; a description of this can also be found in chapter 10. Right above this back bony bump of the sacroiliac joint of the pelvis is the erector spinea muscles, right next to the lumbosacral spine along line B in figure 9.2. These muscles cause a great deal of low-back pain, and their description also can be found in chapter 10.

Low-Back Pain—Check through all the muscles listed above in the hip/leg pain section for active and lurking NMLs. Then check along line B, top to bottom, next to the bony, spinous bumps of your low back, for erector spinea trigger points (paraspinal muscles). Never apply pressure directly on these bony bumps. To apply enough pressure to be therapeutic, you may need to use a tennis ball, golf ball, or trigger point therapy tool. Then carefully check along line C, which runs from the middle of your lumbar spine across your low back, parallel to the top of your pelvis. Here you will find very important trigger points in the quadratus lumborum muscle that are related to low-back pain. Many times, NMLs in the quadratus lumborum are the starting point for low-back pain. The quadratus lumborum is famous for creating myofascial trigger points in the gluteus medius and minimus muscles; see chapter 10 for a complete explanation.

Figure 9.2

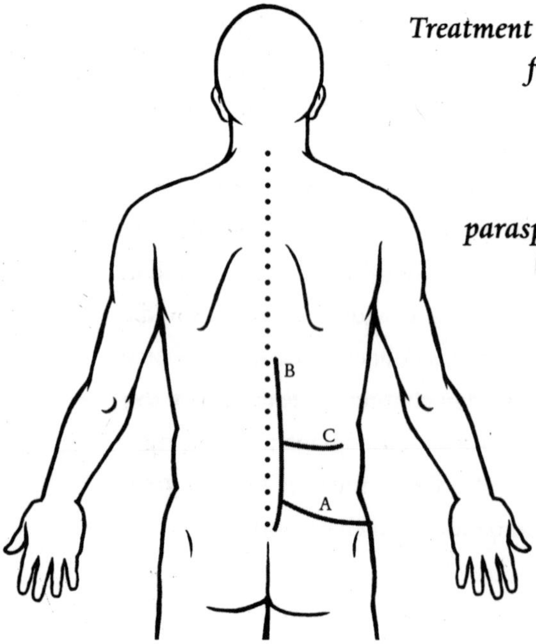

B
C
A

Treatment areas for low-back/hip-leg pain: from left to right, line A indicates gluteus maximus, medius, and minimus muscles; line B indicates lumbosacral paraspinal and erector spinea muscles, and line C indicates the quadratus lumborum muscle

Reference Guide for Common Upper Body Pain-Causing NMLs

Figure 9.3

Treatment areas for headaches and for pain in the mid-back, shoulder, arm, and neck areas; Line D indicates thoracic paraspinal muscles; Line E indicates rhomboid and mid-trapezius muscles, also levator scapula near the top (near G); Line F indicates infraspinatus, teres major and minor, and deltoid muscles; Line G indicates upper trapezius and supraspinatus muscles; and Line H indicates upper trapezius, levator scapulae, and cervical paraspinal muscles; suboccipital muscles are located at top of line H

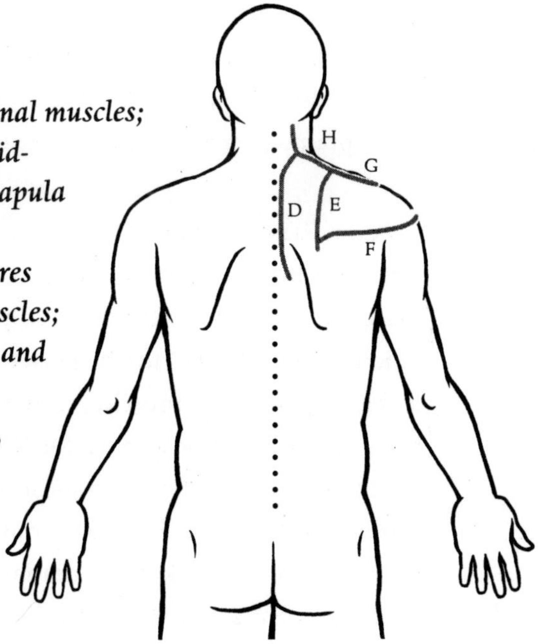

Upper and Mid-back Pain—Check along line D, two finger-widths lateral to the bony, spinous bumps of your mid-back, for any active or lurking NMLs along your thoracic spine's paraspinal muscles. Then carefully check along line E, just inside and parallel to the medial border of your shoulder blade, to find active and lurking NMLs in your rhomboid and mid-trapezius muscles. These two muscles are commonly involved in chronic upper and mid-back pain. Also near the top of line E, the levator scapula muscle attaches to the upper inside corner of your shoulder blade, a muscle that commonly causes upper-back pain and neck stiffness. Please see chapter 12 for a detailed explanation of these important muscles and other common NMLs involved in chronic mid-back pain.

Shoulder and Arm Pain—Carefully check all the muscles for mid-back pain listed above along lines D and E, because in chronic shoulder pain these muscles almost always contain active and lurking NMLs. Then follow diagonal line F from the bottom inside border of the shoulder blade across to the front top tip of your shoulder to check for TPs in your infraspinatus, teres major and minor, and through the posterior and anterior deltoid muscles. If you follow along this line, you will check the major muscles involved in shoulder-arm pain disorders; please see chapter 11 for complete details. Also follow line G, at the top of your shoulder, to check TPs (trigger points) in the supraspinatus and upper trapezius muscles.

Neck Pain and Headaches—Make sure you check all of the muscles listed above for upper, mid-back, and shoulder pain along lines D, E, F, and G. Often, muscles along these lines contain NMLs that can produce neck pain and headaches. Then carefully follow diagonal line G up the neck to line H to look for NMLs in your upper trapezius and levator scapulae muscles. Also, thoroughly check line H, next to the bony, spinous bumps of your cervical spine, for NMLs in your cervical paraspinal muscles. Continue checking up to the all-important suboccipital muscles right under the skull bone at the top of line H. The suboccipital muscles that connect your upper cervical vertebrae to the back of your skull are among the most common causes of chronic myofascial headaches. For a comprehensive examination of NMLs that can create neck pain and headaches, see chapter 13.

Physically Treating the NML, Your Source of Chronic Pain

People generally find electric massagers and heating devices to be relaxing. It feels good, so it makes them feel better for a short while. Because of this, massage lotions and electric massagers, some even with heat, are extremely popular. This is especially apparent around Christmas, when people buy these items as gifts for friends and family who are hurting. However, in my clinical experience and in research, these approaches have NOT been found to remove pain-causing, deep myofascial trigger points. This is important to realize if you *really* want to end your suffering caused by NMLs.

Numerous research studies have found deep manual pressure, generally referred to as trigger point therapy, to be one of the most effective ways to rid oneself of myofascial pain.[96] It may not be as pleasing as heat and vibration, but it is much more effective. Furthermore, a recent research study found that a home-care program of pressure trigger point therapy followed by a sustained stretch to the muscle was as effective as in-office treatment for overcoming the challenge of chronic pain; this research was conducted on forty adults with neck and upper back pain.[97] I have personally found that when individuals have an effective way to self-treat and over time remove their myofascial trigger points, they can overcome even the most disabling chronic muscle and joint pain problems!

Modern research has established that sustained, deep manual pressure applied to these myofascial trigger points has a dramatic therapeutic effect by quickly eliminating pain, relaxing tissues, and improving range of motion. This has become known as trigger point therapy, and it is now practiced around the world by chiropractors, doctors of osteopathy, medical doctors, physical therapists, occupational therapists, and massage therapists. You will hear this manual trigger point therapy to the neuromyofascial lesion referred to by many different names: pressure massage, pressure therapy, myotherapy, acupressure, myofascial release, ischemic compression, and many more.

Basically, the technique is the same in all of these differently named therapies. Once you have located the neuromyofascial lesion, or trigger, area, apply a sustained pressure of sufficient force and time to inactivate the lesion. The amount of pressure and length of time of each treatment varies considerably, depending on the individual, the muscle being treated, and the state of the tissues being treated. *Never* apply trigger point therapy, or myotherapy, over any tissues that have an open wound or are infected, lacerated, bruised, or unhealthy in any way. If you are on certain medications that cause you to bruise very easily, it is important for you to check with your doctor before applying any form of trigger point therapy.

---

96 T. A. Garvey, M. R. Marks, and S. W. Wiesel, "A prospective, randomized, double–blind evaluation of trigger-point injection therapy for low-back pain," *Spine* 14, no. 9 (September 1989): 962–4 . C. A. Hong, "New trends in myofascial pain syndrome," Zhonghua. Yi Xue Za Zhi (Taipei) 65, no. 11 (Nov 2002): 501–12. C. R. Hou, L. C. Tsai, K. F. Cheng, K. C. Chung, and C. Z. Hong, "Immediate effects of various physical therapeutic modalities on cervical myofascial pain and trigger–point sensitivity," *Arch Phys Med Rehabil* 83, no. 10 (Oct 2002): 1406–14.

97 W. P. Hanten, S. L. Olson, N. L. Butts, and A. L. Nowicki, "Effectiveness of a home program of ischemic pressure followed by sustained stretch for treatment of myofascial trigger points," *Phys Ther* 80, no. 10 (Oct 2000): 997–1003.

Proper Self-Care Trigger Point Therapy

To properly apply trigger point therapy, it is important to completely relax the muscle as you apply direct, sustained pressure to the trigger point. Pressure should be applied and held on the trigger point for about thirty to sixty seconds. The amount of pressure applied needs to be sufficient to create discomfort and possible referred pain, duplicating your symptoms, but it should not bruise your tissues or create intolerable pain. As the discomfort lessens, you can gradually increase your pressure slightly. Usually the tenderness and referral pain will dissipate within sixty seconds, and you will notice considerably less pain and stiffness in the area afterwards. This lessening of the spot tenderness and improvement of your symptoms tells you that you were on a myofascial trigger point. The process of myotherapy is accomplished with pressures in ounces in small, thin muscles to twenty or thirty pounds in large muscles, such as the buttocks.

Trigger Point Therapy

- Gently stroke fingertips over the muscle until a nodule or knot is found that creates some local tenderness and possible referral pain.
- Skin surface should be healthy, without any signs of infection, open wounds, bruises, or lacerations.
- Apply sustained pressure with thumb or trigger point tool, creating local tenderness and possible referral pain.
- Sustain pressure for up to one minute; as discomfort lessens, you may gradually increase your sustained pressure.
- Do not overdo it; start gentle at first, and do not hurt yourself!
- Proper pressure ranges from ounces over thin, delicate muscles to as much as 30 pounds over large, thick muscles, such as the buttock.
- To fully remove the NMLs, this treatment will need to be repeated daily or every other day (sometimes for weeks in very chronic tissues).

If your pressure therapy fails to bring you immediate relief, it may be because of one or more of the following factors. The most common reason is because the myofascial trigger point is either too irritable or too chronic. These very chronic myofascial pain syndromes will require many applications of pressure therapy, sometimes over weeks or months, to completely overcome the pain-causing NMLs. The second most common reason is that insufficient pressure or time was utilized in treating the trigger points. Sometimes the therapy does not bring relief because too much pressure was utilized, causing you to tense your muscles and block the therapeutic response.

The third most common reason for the lack of complete relief is the fact that latent trigger points in the region are not being treated. Remember from chapter 8 that these lurking NMLs generally do not cause conscious pain but still fire into the spinal cord. This allows them to prime the nervous system, leading to the return of pain-causing, active trigger points in the region. Because of this, they must be hunted down and removed for complete recovery. The most important reason to consider for the lack of response to trigger point therapy is the presence of metabolic factors, as fully discussed in section 2 of this book. Therefore, it is important for you to add dietary and nutritional therapeutics to your regime of trigger point therapy to achieve maximum results, as explained in detail in chapters 14 to 17.

The final reason for the lack of response to trigger point therapy, which should always be considered first, is that there may be an underlying organic disease causing the perpetuation of your trigger points. This is why it is important to have a complete workup by a competent doctor to rule out any possible pathological reasons for your chronic pain before starting your own self-care program of nutrition and trigger point therapy. Moreover, with innovative self-care trigger point tools and products now on the market, you can easily begin a home-care program of trigger point therapy.

Is Trigger Point Therapy Not Working for You?

If underutilization of therapy (most common reason)...
then self-treat TPs every day until tenderness is gone.

If TP pressure is too light or short in length of time applied...
then slightly increase pressure or hold for up to even 2 minutes.

If pressure is too hard, causing muscle tension to block treatment response...
then lighten up; go more slowly, with less pressure.

If presence of underlying metabolic factors, as discussed in
section 2 of this book exist…
then reread section 2 and apply diet, nutritional, and
lifestyle changes as outlined in section 4 of this book.

If hidden or latent TPs missed, priming the return of pain…
then seek out hidden TPs in the region not
actively causing pain, and remove them.

If underlying organic disease…
then always have a complete workup before beginning
or continuing any self-care wellness program.

Why Trigger Point Therapy Is So Effective

To fully understand why this form of pressure therapy is so effective in treating the neuromyofascial lesion, it is important to review the myofascial tissues you are treating. As discussed in chapter 4, your myofascial tissues are composed of three primary components: collagen, elastin, and ground substance. Collagen is a biological material that is as tough as steel, and in the neuromyofascial lesion, or trigger point, these collagen fibers become shortened and form scar tissue cross-links. In addition, the all-important ground substance of the myofascial tissue transforms from a fluid state to a more gelatinous condition, sort of like concrete, in your trigger points. Therefore, the NML is a region of knotted, shortened, contracted, and congealed tissue with irritated nerve endings firing pain impulses to the spinal cord.

When you apply sufficient, deep, sustained digital pressure to this knotted-up trigger spot, you actually change these three tissue components; for example, you stretch the collagen and release its cross-linkages. Also, with a sustained pressure of generally one minute or more, you change the ground substance from a gelatinous state to a more fluid state, which is vital in treating the pain-causing NMLs. These physical changes in the myofascial tissue, achieved with sustained, deep pressure directly on the point, allow you to then stretch the muscle and actually release the underlying taut band. This is why it is vital to stretch the tissue after applying trigger point therapy.

Creating these changes in the taut band with sustained pressure and stretching will substantially increase blood flow in and metabolic toxins out of the myofascial tissue. One primary way this happens is by creating this more fluid or soluble state in the ground substance, allowing oxygen and nutrients to move into the myofascial trigger points. With increased oxygen and nutrients, the muscle tissue can now produce adequate ATP energy, allowing it to relax. Deep pressure therapy is one of the most effective ways to remove neuromyofascial lesions and their chronic pain, especially when used with proper diet, nutrition, and lifestyle changes to overcome the underlying metabolic factors.

You can now see why rubbing the surface with a massage lotion, a vibrating massager, a heating device, or even an expensive vibrating lounger is not going to change the tissue of a single trigger point, let alone change the numerous primary and hidden neuromyofascial lesions involved in chronic pain states. However, as effective as trigger point therapy is, to be *truly* effective it takes repeated treatments over time, with stretching of your muscles after each treatment. The problem with this is that it is very expensive to have someone properly do this for you over many treatment sessions. This is especially true if the therapist were to release all primary and hidden trigger points involved in a chronic back pain, neck pain, or shoulder-arm pain case, and particularly in cases of fibromyalgia. The answer is to turn this amazingly effective therapy into a home-care program with a comprehensive self-treatment system.

The vital importance of utilizing self-treatment in overcoming myofascial trigger points in chronic pain disorders becomes apparent when you understand how these NMLs are multiple and develop in distinct patterns. For example, in chronic back pain, multiple specific muscles are involved, each containing numerous myofascial trigger points, as will be illustrated in chapter 10. The same is true if you have a recurrent shoulder-arm pain or neck pain with headaches—as usual, there are multiple muscles involved with numerous trigger points.

I have found that patients, given a little training and a self-treatment trigger point tool, can take the time to search out all of the multiple trigger points and remove them. At 60 to 100 dollars per treatment session, it can easily become wildly expensive to have numerous therapy sessions to remove all the primary and secondary myofascial trigger points involved in the myofascial pain syndrome. There are various trigger point tools on the market today that you can purchase for home self-care trigger point therapy. My years of clinical experience helping numerous patients out of chronic myofascial pain motivated me to invent a self-care system for the easy and effective removal of multiple NMLs.[98]

The Neuromyofascial Patterns of Chronic Pain Disorders

To get an idea of how patterns of multiple NMLs develop, stand with your feet shoulder-width apart and hands at your side. Let your weight fall slightly forward at your ankles with a tiny, slight bend at your waist. Make this move extremely small; just get the sense of your weight going forward. Notice how your toes dig in, your calves tighten up, your thigh muscles slightly fire, mild tension occurs in the buttock muscles, and a real tightening of your back muscles all keep you from falling forward, flat on your face. So even with this extremely slight movement, everything from the plantar fasciae under your foot to posterior calf muscles, hamstrings in your thigh, gluteal pelvic muscles, and muscles of your low back contracts to hold you in dynamic balance. This is not just for academic interest; if you are an individual who suffers with low-back pain or chronic foot pain, this may relate directly to you.

I have seen numerous patients who have been through the mill with various foot supports, cortisone injections into their heel spurs, and tons of anti-inflammatory medication in a desperate search to relieve their chronic foot pain. If there is a loss of one of the three normal arches of your foot, proper, flexible foot orthotics are vital.[99] Proper, flexible foot orthotics are not only important for overcoming chronic foot and calf pain, but myofascial pain syndromes all the way through to your back.

Loss of the normal arches of your foot throws off your biomechanics and can even make your pelvis unlevel when one arch is dropped more than the other. To understand the importance of this, please see the section in chapter 10 on the unlevel foundation and back pain. The problem, though, is that those foot orthotics are not usually the complete answer. From the little experiment described above, you saw how your toes dug in and the myofascial tissues under your foot and in your calf were activated.

---

98 Named after the mythological bird that rose again out of her own ashes, I have called it the FENIX Self-Care System. A full explanation of this device can be found at www.fenixstopspain.com.

99 You can find custom-made foot orthotics for around $100 through companies such as FootSmart (www.footsmart.com; click on *foot supports & insoles*, then *custom orthotics*).

This happens every time you lean forward to take a step in walking. But remember, there are other muscles firing higher up in your pelvis and low back.

I have found that this is key in overcoming chronic foot pain in many patients over the years. First off, the pain in their feet was primarily coming from muscles in the back of their calves. When the myofascial trigger points were removed from their calf muscles, their foot pains were quickly relieved. However, the primary reason the calf muscles formed trigger points was because of hidden trigger points up in the pelvic gluteus minimus muscle, and the gluteus minimus formed trigger points because of primary trigger points up in the quadratus lumborum back muscle. These muscles, with diagrams, will be explained in greater detail in chapter 10. My point here is that a seemingly isolated problem in the bottom of your foot may relate to interconnected neuromyofascial strands all the way up your leg, buttock, and in your low back.

Try this experiment again, standing with your feet shoulder-width apart and hands at your side. Try leaning back ever so slightly, and feel the muscles in the front of your calf (where people get shin splints) tighten up, all the way up to your abdominal muscles that keep you from falling backwards. These are the interconnected neuromyofascial strands that run up the front of your lower body to help with dynamic balance and support. From this demonstration, you can see that you have interconnected neuromyofascial strands in the front and back of your lower body. These interconnected neuromyofascial strands also run on your lateral sides to keep you from tipping from side to side.

These neuromyofascial strands are also involved in the upper half of your body—for example, in your shoulder girdle and arm. Imagine swinging a tennis racket and all the muscles from your chest down the inside of your elbow and wrist firing to swing the racket forward. Consider the interconnected muscles starting at your mid-back and shoulder blade and down the back of your arm, the outside elbow contracting to pull the racket back. Imagine, if you will, a motor vehicle accident in which your head snaps forward and back, and the interconnected muscles from your low back all the way up to the back of your skull that can be stretched and torn from this forceful flexion. These are the same interconnected neuromyofascial strands that can become very fatigued and painful from sitting at your desk with your head slightly bent forward all day.

The proper treatment of these neuromyofascial strands in chronic myofascial pain disorders of the back, neck, and extremities will be explored in detail in chapters 10 through 13. Again, as with the metabolic underlying problems of chronic pain, you may think it is your clinician's role to know this. However, through my clinical and teaching experience, I have found that it can be extremely difficult to find clinicians who have this understanding—or the time and motivation—to work through these neuromyofascial patterns of chronic pain disorders. Also, as stated before, you can only see what you are looking for, and most clinicians are not looking for the metabolic or muscular patterns that can plague you with such chronic pain and health problems. However, the knowledge of these metabolic and myofascial patterns of pain may be the solution to the riddle of your chronic pain, so let's get started on the journey to a new and better life today!

10

Conquering Your Low-Back Pain and Sciatica

You are not alone if you suffer with chronic low-back pain; approximately 8 out of every 10 Americans experience low-back pain during their lifetimes.[100] This disabling disorder is second only to the common cold for visits to a doctor and is a major cause of lost work time.[101] It is also the fifth most frequent cause of hospitalization and the third most common reason patients undergo surgery.[102] At any one time about one-third of us are experiencing some form of back pain, affecting men and women equally. Low-back pain strikes the young as well as the elderly, with an increase in occurrence of back pain from the third decade to the sixth decade of a person's life. For many, these back attacks tend to resolve within about six weeks; however, for many others, the pain will reoccur. Back pain commonly happens more than once to individuals, with recurring episodes increasing in severity and chronicity. If your low-back pain continues to return or a single episode lasts longer than six weeks, you are developing a chronic low-back pain problem. Chronic low-back pain is the most costly benign condition to treat in industrialized countries, and surprisingly it is the most common cause of disability in persons younger than forty-five years of age.

You may be wondering why this disorder is so extremely common and difficult to resolve, especially if you are someone who suffers from chronic low-back pain or if it is part of your fibromyalgia syndrome. To understand the underlying causes of this

100 B. Vallfors, "Acute, subacute and chronic low back pain: clinical symptoms, absenteeism and working environment," *Scand J Rehab Med Suppl 11*(1985): 1–98.

101 American Chiropractic Association website: www.acatoday.com (patients/back pain facts & statistics).

102 www.ninds.nih.gov/.

very common chronic pain disorder, it is important to understand a little bit about the anatomy and function of your low-back region, and lumbar spine in particular. The primary reason that we suffer so much back pain is because we are animals that sit and stand up against gravity all day long. This places a tremendous burden on your spinal column and back muscles; in fact, your back muscles are always working hard to maintain your posture, whether you are quietly sitting or standing actively engaged.

How Your Back Is Built

Your lumbar spine is composed of individual bony vertebrae stacked upon each other and held together by tough fascial bands called ligaments. These individual lumbar vertebrae are separated by your lumbar discs. To picture these discs, imagine a jelly-filled donut. The dough surrounding the jelly represents the tough fibers of your discs called the annulus, and the jelly in the center is what is known as the nucleus pulposus. If you have a lumbar disc herniation, these annular fibers of the "donut" have weakened and cracked, letting the "jelly" leak out. If this jellylike material leaks out and compresses a nerve exiting your spine, you have extreme nerve pain and may possibly require surgery. It is important to note here that your spinal discs are made up of connective tissue and therefore are composed of the three same components: collagen, elastin, and ground substance, discussed in detail in chapter 4. Therefore, the overall health of your spinal discs and the prevention of their degeneration and herniation relates to the same mechanisms of all connective tissue health discussed earlier.

In chapters 4 and 5, we found that our SAD diet of overconsumption and undernutrition, internal toxins from dysbiosis, and environmental toxins create metabolic stress that can produce systemic inflammation and oxidative stress. We further discovered that the three components of your connective tissue that make up your muscles, tendons, and ligaments are easily damaged by oxidative stress and chronic inflammation. Dietary and lifestyle choices therefore can negatively affect the health of your spinal discs, hence you can improve the health of your spinal discs by making healthier choices, as outlined in this book. The healthier your spinal discs are, the greater stress they can take without herniating or degenerating. This is extremely important because the rate of spinal surgery is soaring within the United States. According to the U.S. Centers for Disease Control and Prevention, from 1979 to 1990, cervical spine surgery increased 45% and the lumbar surgery rate increased 33%.[103] For many different reasons, if you live in the United States, you are five times more likely to end up with spinal surgery than if you live in the United Kingdom.

---

103 H. Davis. *Spine* 19, no. 10 (May 15, 1994): 1117–23.

The Patterns of Pain

What I am about to share with you is more important than you can ever imagine if you suffer with reoccurring or chronic low-back pain. After years of clinical practice, I have found the cause and the answer to the vast majority of low-back pain. What I am sharing with you is the culmination of years of reviewing research and seeing patients with back pain. Also, after years of lecturing to doctors and therapists, I have found that this approach to back pain is not very well understood and is generally ignored by healthcare professionals. The primary cause of low-back pain is an initial muscular imbalance in the core muscles that keep you upright.

This muscular imbalance has various causes, including an unleveled pelvis from a short leg or poor conditioning or overuse of the supportive muscles of your low back. This muscular imbalance—along with other factors, such as poor diet, lack of aerobic exercise, and problematic genetics—will eventually lead to degenerative changes in your lumbar spine. Genetics does make the underlying causes of health problems more difficult to comprehend. But, if you will recall from chapter 3, in the subsection "Dancing with Your Genes," we explored how dysfunction and disease arise from how we interact with our genetic tendencies through diet and lifestyle choices. In fact, it has been shown that degenerative disc disease and back surgeries themselves run in families.[104] I have found that even with a family history of degenerative disc disease, when you restore muscular balance you can overcome the challenge of your chronic pain and prevent the possibility of back surgery.

A very important thing to realize is that this muscular imbalance of the low back tends to occur in certain predictable patterns that you can easily discern. If you ignore these patterns, your low-back pain will not clear up or will tend to return. In these patterns, there are certain muscles that tend to start the pain and dysfunction of your low back, such as the quadratas lumborum. This back muscle then refers pain into other muscles and creates hidden secondary myofascial trigger points, such as the gluteus medius in the buttocks. If you find a primary pain-causing myofascial trigger point in the quadratus lumborum muscle and remove it, but leave the secondary, hidden trigger points in the gluteus medius muscle, your back pain will return.

You may be wondering why you need to learn this in such detail. It is because you may find it extremely difficult to get a doctor or therapist who understands and can locate these disabling, painful, imbalanced muscle patterns. However, once you find

104 P. N. Sambrook, A. J. MacGregor, and T. D. Spector, "Genetic influences on cervical and lumbar disc degeneration: a magnetic resonance imaging study in twins," *Arthritis Rheum* 42, no. 2 (Feb 1999): 366–72.

them yourself, you can easily remove them with a self-care trigger point therapy tool and free yourself from years of recurrent pain and possible spinal degeneration!

Anatomy of a Low Back

Your lumbar spine forms a flexible, bony column that supports everything from the waist up: your head, upper extremities, and internal organs, all while standing on just two feet. Unlike your mid-back with the thoracic spine and rib cage, your low back has no lateral, or front-to-back, bony support. This gives your low back its much-needed flexibility to bend and rotate; however, this decreases its stability. Your lumbar spine's primary stability against the pressure of gravity comes from your core back muscles that act like guy-wires dynamically holding you upright. These muscles are under a constant burden and work overtime to stabilize your body, allowing you to remain upright while you sit, stand, walk, jump, and run. It is easy to see that without proper conditioning, your back muscles can get overworked and become painful. You do not let your car go long without maintenance; if you do, it soon stops working. It's the same with your back. If you do not keep your core back muscles in shape, strong and flexible, they soon develop the painful muscle knots, or NMLs, we have been describing. Also, the higher your metabolic stress levels from chronic inflammation, oxidative stress, and insulin resistance, the greater your chances are of developing pain-causing NMLs in your low back.

The development of these myofascial trigger points in the supportive muscles of your back causes these muscles to become painful, shortened, and weakened, affecting the function of your spine. When the spine does not move and function smoothly, the spinal facet joints and discs of the low back can wear out prematurely. It is like the front end of your car; if the linkages (muscles) are out of alignment (too tight), your tires (joints and discs) will wear out prematurely. Therefore, the most important thing you can do if you suffer from chronic back pain, even if your spinal joints and discs are already developing degenerative arthritis, is to remove the multiple myofascial trigger points in the supportive muscles of your low back. I know this personally to be effective because I suffered with chronic low-back pain that disabled me. I also had a degenerative disc between the bottom lumbar vertebra and the sacrum (L5–S1) with mild degenerative changes in the facet joints at this level. By reducing my metabolic stress level and removing or lessening NMLs in my quadratus lumborum, gluteus medius and minimus muscles, I overcame my chronic back pain. I have also done this with numerous low-back patients who also had osteoarthritis in their lumbar spines.

An Unlevel Foundation: LLI

You can imagine the damage caused to your house if the foundation was not level. Well, the same holds true for your body. One of the most common causes of overworked supportive low-back muscles is the presence of one leg being physically shorter than the other, a condition called "leg-length inequality," or LLI to clinicians. This condition of leg-length inequality will cause an unlevel foundation in your low back, activating myofascial trigger points from your pelvis all the way up your back to your head. Leg-length inequality is extremely common. One study of 359 individuals without back pain found that even 56% of them had LLI of 3/16 of an inch or less, while 44% had one leg at least 3/16 of an inch or more shorter than the other leg.[105]

LLI commonly contributes to your low-back pain by creating more chronic strain on the muscles and fasciae of the low back. In this same study, they examined 653 individuals with low-back pain, and about one-third of them had one leg shorter than the other by at least 3/8 of an inch. From clinical observation and published studies, it seems that having one leg 3/8 of an inch or shorter than the other is significant enough to cause problems for the low-back muscles and joints. Having one leg shorter than the other also contributes significantly to the development of osteoarthritis in your hip joint, most frequently on the long-leg side. Research has found that as much as 81% of individuals with osteoarthritis of the hip joint have one leg shorter than the other.[106] The increase in arthritis on the long-leg side is generally because of the increased pressure on that hip joint.

If you have chronic low-back pain or you are concerned about developing arthritis in your back or hip, it is important that you are properly checked for LLI. Research has shown a strong correlation between LLI and low-back pain determined by x-ray but no correlation when determined by a physical exam.[107] Therefore, it is vital to see a doctor who thoroughly understands the biomechanics of the low back and radiographically examines you for LLI. I have seen numerous patients who had been everywhere looking for answers to their chronic or recurrent low-back pain, hip pain, or sciatica, only to find after thorough examination and x-ray that they had one leg slightly shorter than the other. Placing a heel lift of the proper thickness in the shoe of the short leg leveled their foundation. Then systematically removing the trigger points in the supportive

---

105 O. Friberg, "Clinical symptoms and biomechanics of lumbar spine and hip joint in leg lengthening inequality," *Spine* 8 (1983): 643–51.

106 J. P. Gofton and G. E. Trueman, "Studies in osteoarthritis of the hip: part two. Osteoarthritis of the hip and leg length disparity," *Can Med Assoc J* 104 (1971): 791–99.

107 P. F. Grundy and C. J. Roberts, "Does unequal leg length cause back pain?" *Lancet* 2 (1984): 256–58.

muscles of the low back aggravated by the short leg, especially the quadratus lumborum, helped many patients overcome years of back pain.

However, you may notice signs indicating that you may have one leg shorter than the other. One indication is that you will tend to stand with the foot of the long leg forward and most of your weight on the shorter leg. Or you may find yourself standing with your feet wide apart and your hips and pelvis shifted to the shorter leg side. If you find you do this and you have pain when standing or walking, you probably have one leg shorter than the other, creating an unlevel foundation. If this is your case, then find a qualified doctor to determine if this is an aggravating factor to your headaches and chronic myofascial pain syndrome in your hips, low back, mid-back, shoulders, and neck. In figure 10.1, A indicates the posture taken to balance out a long right leg. Figure B illustrates the distortion and pressure placed upon the hip, low back, mid- back, shoulders, and even the neck when you have a short leg. Figure C demonstrates a balanced foundation when a proper lift is placed under the short leg.

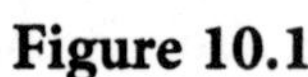

Figure 10.1

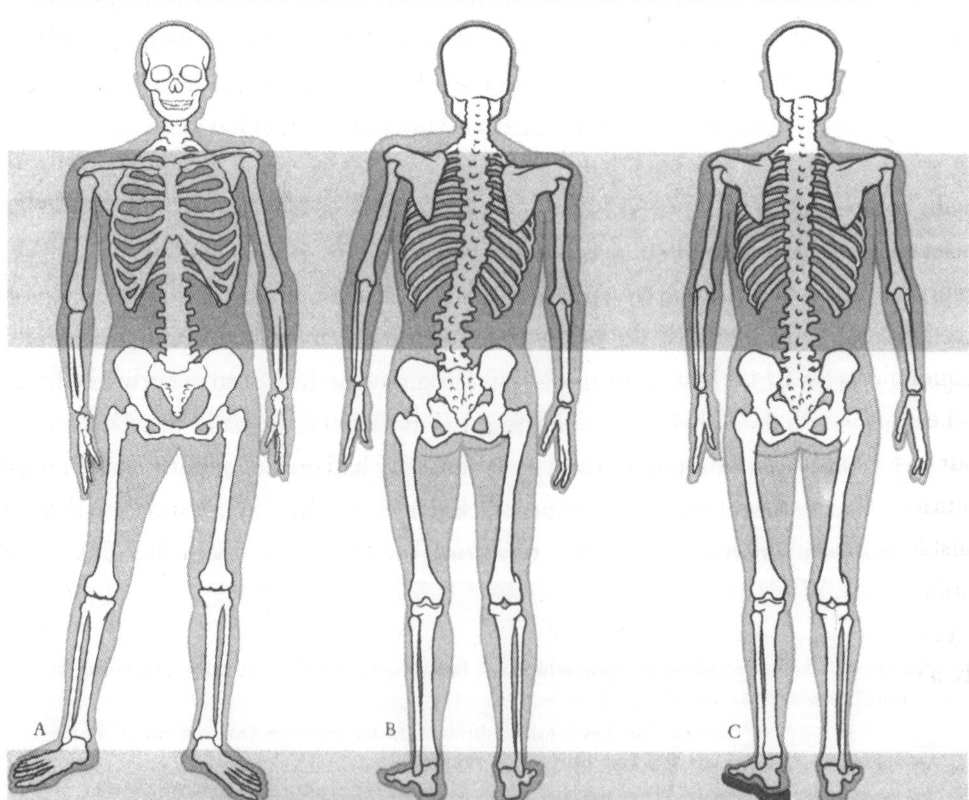

The Quadratus Lumborum Muscle

Figure 10.2

Trigger point locations of quadratus lumborum muscle are generally found along line C

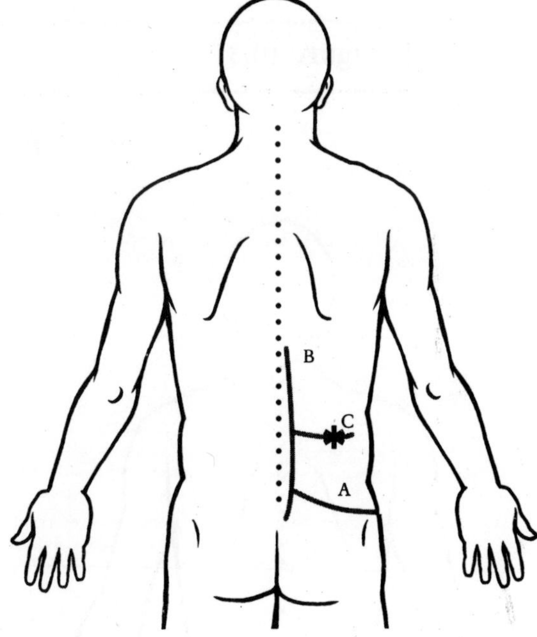

Chronic pain centered in the low back is commonly called lumbago. It is primarily muscular in origin and most commonly caused by two muscles, the quadratus lumborum in the low back and the gluteus medius in the buttock area. Numerous studies have shown that the quadratus lumborum muscle, in particular, is one of the most frequent causes of pain in your low back.[108] This is the muscle you were instructed to find earlier in chapter 8. Again, it is easy to find by resting your hands on the top of your pelvis, called the iliac crest. Have your fingers pointing forwards and your thumbs pointed backwards. Probing with your thumbs in the fleshy sides of your low back at waist level, you will find this all-important stabilizing back muscle on each side of your lumbar spine. The quadratus lumborum muscle runs from your bottom rib to the top of your pelvis in a crisscross pattern. Trigger points in this muscle can be found generally along line C in figure 10.2, above. NMLs in this muscle cause pain in the area and

108 D. G. Simons and J. G. Travell, "Myofascial origins of low back pain. 2. Torso muscles," *Postgrad Med* 73 (1983): 81–92.

refer pain down into the very low back and buttock area, as illustrated in figure 10.3. Neuromyofascial lesions in this muscle, when severe enough, will make it difficult for you to turn over in bed or stand for long periods of time without experiencing low-back pain.

Figure 10.3

Location of quadratus lumborum trigger points and common referral patterns

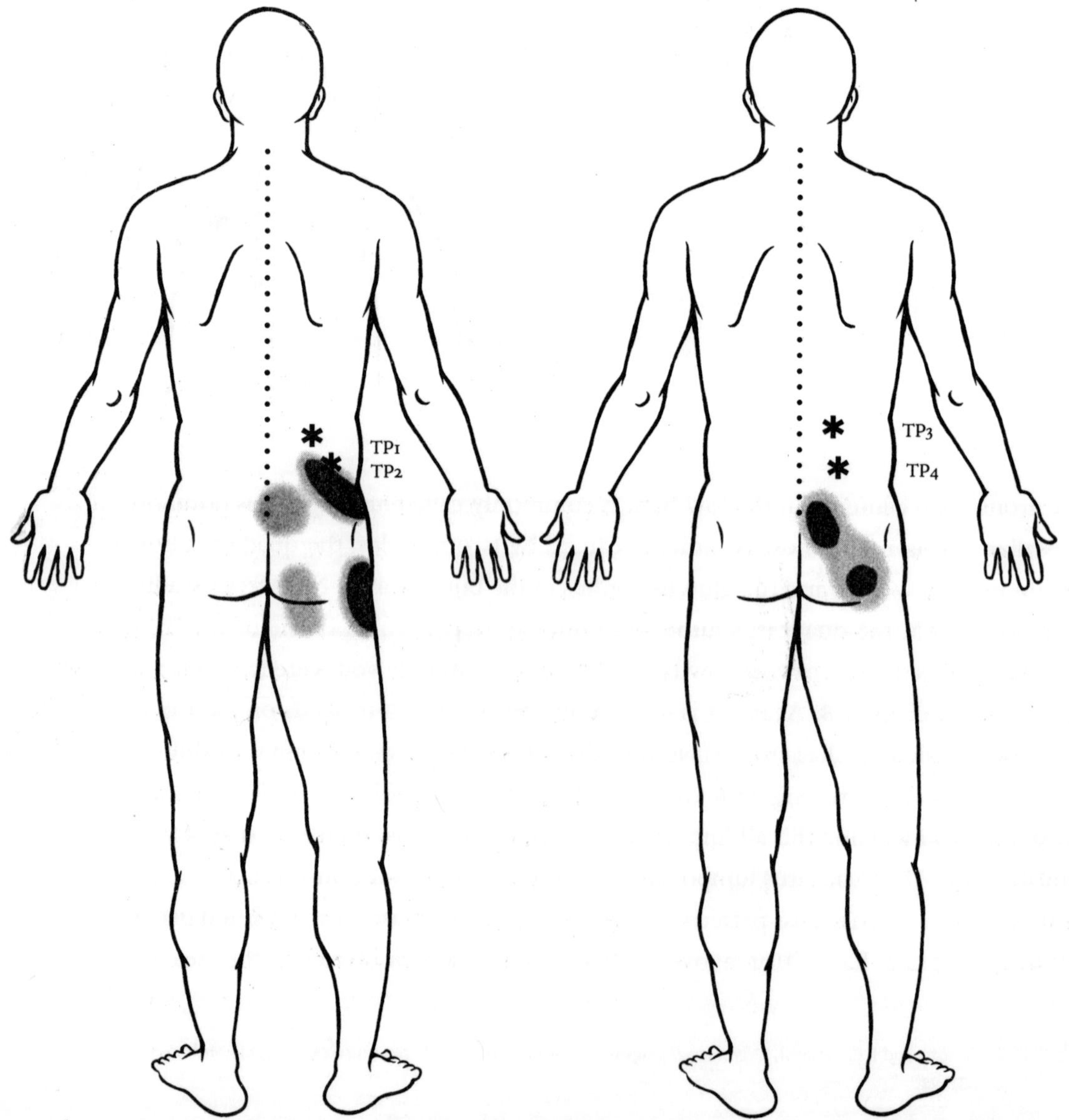

Trigger points are commonly created or activated in the quadratus lumborum when you experience trauma from a fall or motor vehicle accident, or when you simultaneously bend over and reach to one side to lift or pull on something. The second most important factor in creating, activating, or perpetuating trigger points in the quadratus lumborum is the presence of leg-length inequality, as previously discussed. Again, if one of your legs is slightly shorter than the other, it creates an unlevel foundation for your low back and everything above it. This unlevel foundation from a short leg is one of the most important factors for you to correct if you have a chronic myofascial pain in your low back, especially involving the quadratus lumborum muscle.

Figure 10.4

Self-administered trigger point therapy to quadratus lumborum trigger points

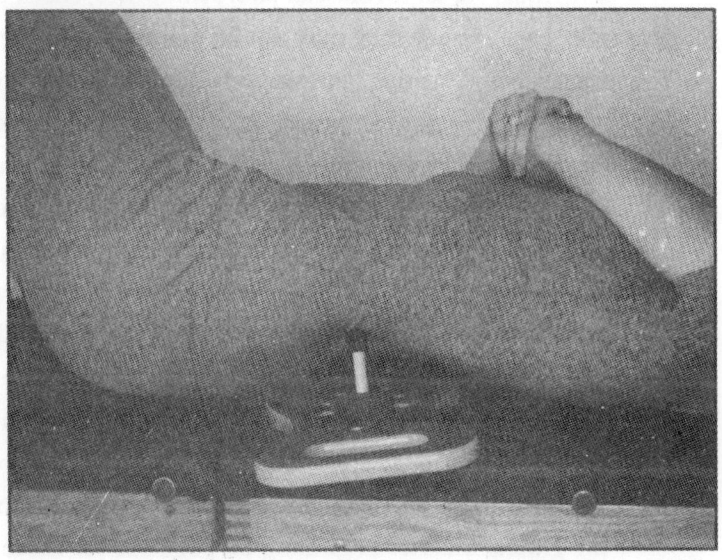

You can self-treat these myofascial trigger points of the quadratus lumborum by utilizing a tennis ball or golf ball on a carpeted floor. Simply place the ball on the floor, then lie down next to it on your side and gently roll back onto it until you are applying some light pressure to the trigger point creating your back pain. You may have to adjust where the pressure is applied by moving the ball up or down the muscle and towards the spine or away from the spine until you find the exact tender spot. There are trigger point tools to help you more accurately treat these myofascial trigger points, such as the one I invented called the FENIX Rehab System. To see how the FENIX is utilized to treat the quadratus lumborum, see figure 10.4.

Why Trigger Point Therapy Sometimes Fails

Often trigger point therapy fails because the muscles associated with the primary muscle of pain are ignored or undertreated. For example, the quadratus lumborum is one of the most common causes of low-back pain, and the most common muscle secondary to it is the quadratus lumborum on the *other* side of the spine, even if you are not experiencing pain on that side. The reason for this is that both quadratus lumborum muscles work as a team on each side of your lumbar spine to stabilize your back. So, if you have chronic right low-back pain and find multiple trigger points in the right quadratus lumborum, make sure you check the *left* quadratus lumborum for hidden or latent myofascial trigger points aggravating your *right* side. This is a good lesson to remember for all myofascial pain syndromes; check the same muscles on the opposite side, even though they may not be painful—yet. The reason for this is that myofascial trigger points on the opposite side neurologically fire into the same spinal cord level, increasing the pain response. Also, trigger points on the opposite side can affect the biomechanics of the general region, exacerbating your myofascial pain.

What makes the quadratus lumborum muscles so important to your chronic low-back pain is that this muscle very commonly activates secondary myofascial trigger points in other muscles. The second most important ancillary muscles to the quadratas lumborum are found in the buttock on the same side, called the gluteus medius and gluteus minimus muscles. When these three muscles gang up on you, it is very common to have severe pain at the base of your back in the lumbosacral spine with pain down your leg, or sciatica. This three-muscle syndrome is very commonly the cause of failed low-back and even failed surgical low-back syndrome. Please see the section on the gluteal muscles beginning on page 142 for more detailed instructions on location and treatment of their myofascial trigger points.

Myofascial trigger points in your quadratus lumborum are also frequently associated with the muscles that run along each side of the spine called the lumbar paraspinal muscles. These muscles run in layers, generally called the deep and superficial layers. If you have low-back pain and find trigger points in your quadratus lumborum muscle, slide in closer to the bony bumps up your spine, called the spinous processes, and check for myofascial trigger points.

The Lumbar Paraspinal Muscles

Figure 10.5

The lumbar paraspinal muscles, located along each side of the spine, may house trigger points that affect low-back pain; note that the trigger points shown are for the right side only but they do run along each side of the spine

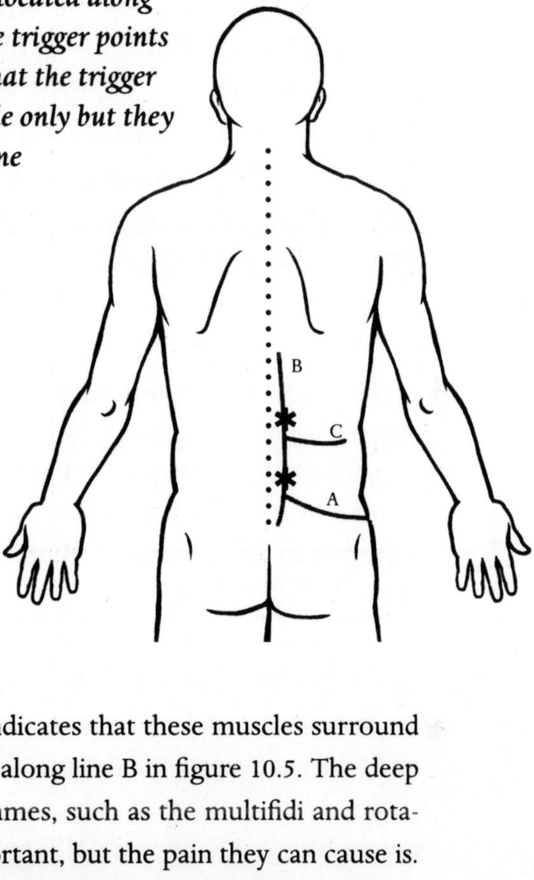

The prefix *para-* means "around," and *spinal* indicates that these muscles surround the lumbar spine on each side; they can be found along line B in figure 10.5. The deep paraspinal muscles of your spine have various names, such as the multifidi and rotator muscles. Their names are really not that important, but the pain they can cause is. These small, individual muscles act to rotate, laterally bend, and extend the vertebrae of your back, and a trigger point in them can make you feel like your back is "out of place." Trigger points in these muscles create a deep ache right in the area and can make you feel "stiff as a board." The nerves that leave your spine and go to the surrounding skin must traverse these muscles. If these paraspinal muscles, deep or superficial, contain multiple myofascial trigger points, they can entrap or pinch these nerves, causing strange sensations in the skin of your back. Patients who need to have their spines repeatedly adjusted generally have chronic and even fibrotic changes in these deep muscles of the spine.

Frequently, I have seen patients with chronic low-back pain who have been x-rayed and found to have osteoarthritis in their lumbar spines. It was then generally assumed that the osteoarthritis was the cause of their chronic low-back pain, and they were then put on NSAIDs for the arthritis. The reality, though, was that they had multiple chronic myofascial trigger points in the deep lumbar paraspinal muscles, aggravated by the loss of normal movement because of the osteoarthritis. When the chronic NMLs of the paraspinals were removed, the spinal joints manipulated to improve motion, and exercises given to restore range of motion, even some of the most elderly patients overcame their pain and returned to the activities they once enjoyed.

Figure 10.6, below, shows an ideal way to treat the paraspinal muscles on each side of the spine at the same time with the FENIX Rehab System. This is very helpful because these deep multifidi and rotator paraspinal muscles tend to be involved bilaterally. With this trigger point tool, you can easily move up and down the spine, treating all the involved paraspinal muscles in any region of your back. In figure 10.6, the individual is slowly laying down on two short rubber-tipped therapeutic digits angled in at 60 degrees to specifically treat the paraspinal muscles.

Figure 10.6

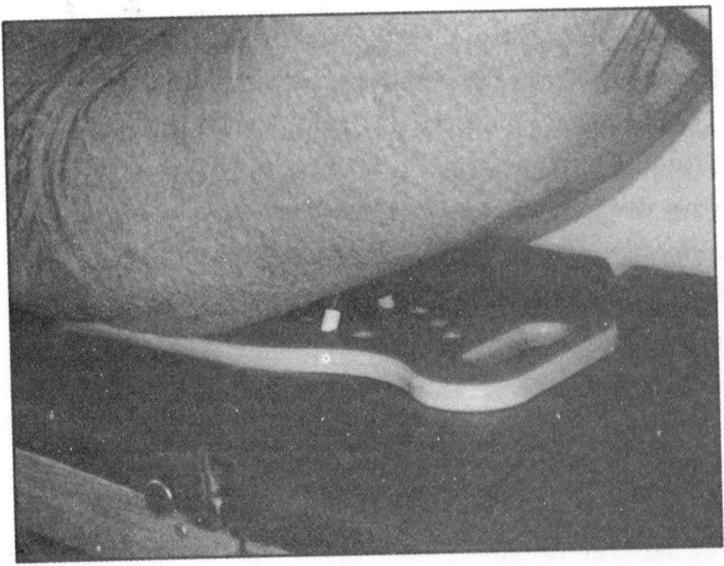

Applying self-care to lumbar paraspinal muscles' trigger points

Figure 10.7

Location of multifidi and rotator trigger points in the deep paraspinal muscles; examples given for just two levels, but trigger points are found at each vertebra level the entire length of your spine

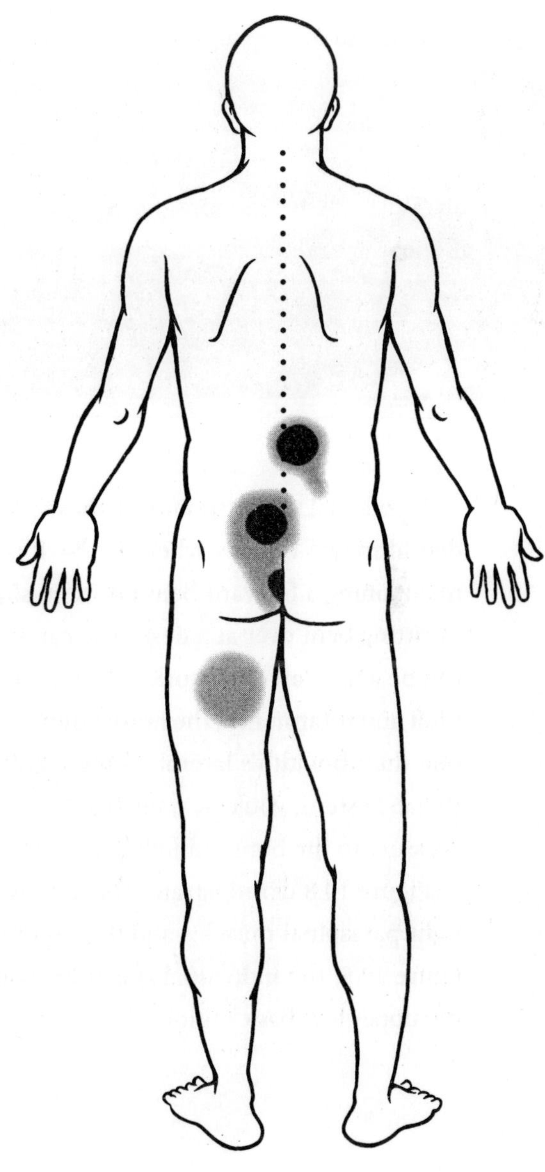

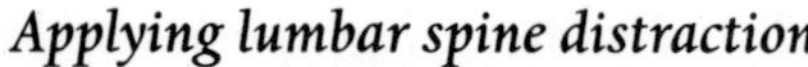

Figure 10.8

Applying lumbar spine distraction

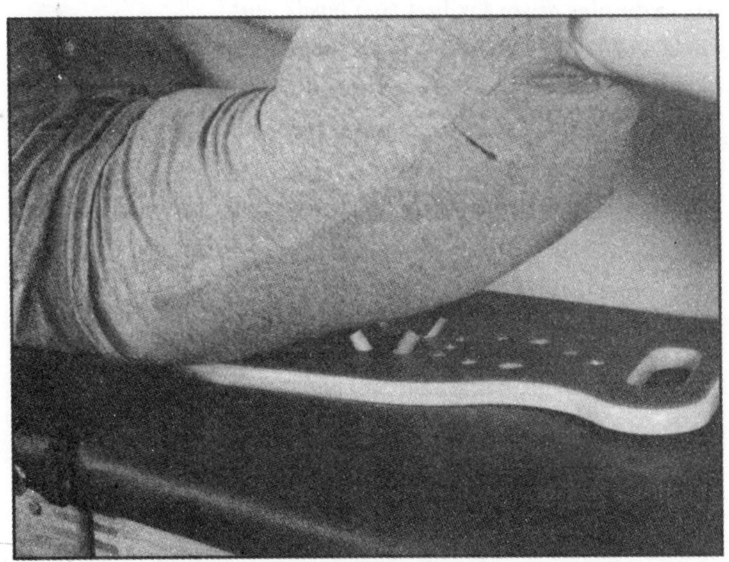

Myofascial trigger points of these paraspinal muscles are generally caused by a sudden lifting of objects when the back is twisted or flexed. Another common cause is maintaining a forward-bent position, slightly rotated, such as standing at a workbench or sitting bent over at a desk. You can see why these trigger points are so common and can be aggravated by work. To locate these deep paraspinal muscles, such as the multifidi and rotator, find the bony bumps of your low back, the spinous processes, and go one thumb-width's lateral. Using a golf ball or trigger point tool, such as the FENIX Rehab System, you can apply trigger point therapy to release these NMLs. Never apply pressure to the bony spinous processes.

Figure 10.8 demonstrates the unique way the FENIX Rehab System can stretch the tight paraspinal muscles and traction the spine by utilizing four therapeutic digits. In figure 10.8, the individual is gently laying down on four digits to apply distraction to the upper low-back region.

CASE STUDY

Samuel was in his early sixties and nearing retirement. He loved golf and to play with his grandchildren, but he was no longer able to do either of these activities. His primary complaint was of severe low-back pain and pain in his right leg; the doctor said he had "spinal arthritis." He was on a prescription of NSAIDs that was beginning to bother his digestive system, and it never really got rid of his pain. I examined his lumbar x-rays and found that he did have degenerative changes in his L4 and L5 discs and the associated spinal facet joints. However, his lumbar CT scan showed no entrapment of the exiting nerve roots of his lower spine from a disc herniation or arthritic bone spurs to explain his leg pain. His neurological exam also showed no neurological deficits. Part of his exam findings showed severe multiple myofascial trigger points in the L4/L5 deep paraspinal muscles and the gluteus medius and minimus muscles. Diagnostic pressure applied to the lumbar paraspinal multifidi muscles at L4 and L5 reproduced a great deal of his low-back pain, along with the trigger points in the right gluteus medius muscle. Pressure on the myofascial trigger points in the right gluteus minimus reproduced his leg pain.

Spinal manipulation to restore joint movement, along with deactivation of these myofascial trigger points with home trigger point therapy, nutritional support to reduce systemic inflammation and oxidative stress, and exercises totally resolved Samuel's condition. The degenerative changes were still present on x-ray, but the actual cause of his pain had been removed. Samuel found that because of the spinal arthritis affecting his low back's range of motion, his trigger point would return, but not as bad as before. He found that he no longer needed any pain meds if he occasionally self-treated his trigger points and stretched his low-back muscles.

The Gluteus Medius Muscle

Figure 10.9

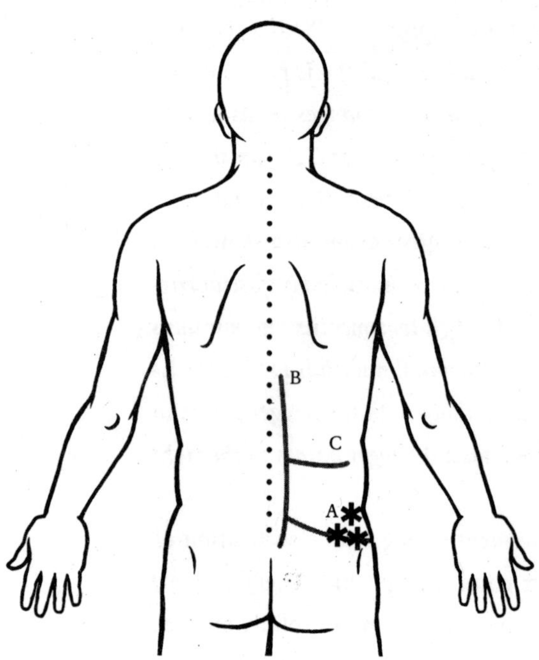

Trigger point locations of the gluteus medius muscle; top ✱ indicates gluteus maximus

Just underneath and to the lateral side of the gluteus maximus muscle lies the most underrated muscle when it comes to low-back pain, the gluteus medius muscle.[109] Myofascial trigger points in this muscle will refer severe pain to the base of your low back and over your sacrum. These trigger points are generally located along line A, as indicated by the ✱s in figure 10.9. In clinical practice, I have seen numerous patients with chronic lumbosacral pain for which they have had various treatments, from drugs to injections and sometimes even surgery. After a thorough physical examination, however, I would find that they had undiagnosed multiple myofascial trigger points in their gluteus medius and quadratus lumborum muscles causing their chronic pain.

As previously mentioned, the gluteus medius in the pelvis, along with its sister muscle, the minimus, have a close relationship with the quadratas lumborum muscle in the low back. In my experience, when this triad of muscles is unhappy, it creates a majority of the cases of chronic or recurrent low-back and leg pain. Most of the time, the quadratas

109 D. G. Simons and J. G. Travell, "Myofascial origins of low back pain. 3. Pelvic in lower extremity muscles," *Postgrad Med* 73 (1983): 99–108.

lumborum muscle develops myofascial trigger points first and then refers pain into the gluteus medius and minimus muscle area, causing secondary or satellite trigger points within them. Also, research by A. E. Sola shows that the gluteus medius triggers can also be primary at times and can create secondary trigger points up in the quadratus lumborum muscle.[110] Sola goes on to state that the gluteus medius is a very commonly involved muscle that rarely acts on its own; it usually involves other muscles as a functional unit. As in the case with Samuel, I cannot emphasize enough the importance of searching out the quadratas lumborum, the paraspinal muscles, and the gluteus medius and minimus muscles for myofascial trigger points when you have low-back, hip, and leg symptoms.

Figure 10.10

The three primary locations of gluteus medius trigger points and common pain referral patterns

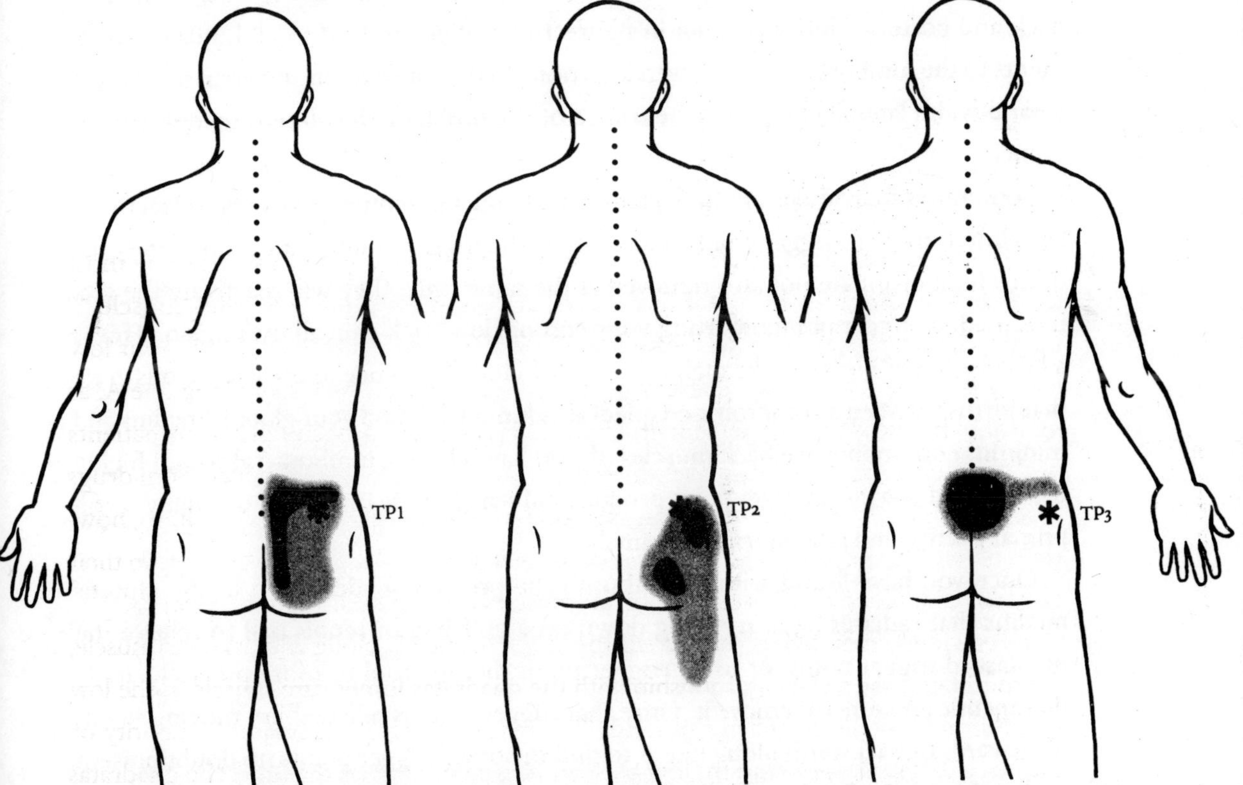

110 A. E. Sola, "Trigger point therapy, chapter 47: Clinical procedures in emergency medicine," edited by J. R. Roberts and J. R. Hedges. Philadelphia: W. B. Saunders, 1985, 674–86.

To find these all-important myofascial trigger points, as before, place your hand on the top of your pelvis at the iliac crest, with your fingers pointing forwards and your thumb backwards. Now slide your hand off your pelvic rim down about 1 to 2 inches, and your forefinger and thumb will be tracing a line around your pelvis where these trigger points are primarily located. Lift up your hand and poke with your thumb along that line from back to front until you find a reactive NML. Another way to find these all-important trigger points is to trace a line right over the opening of the back pocket of your pants. The pocket opening generally overlies the most active gluteus medius trigger points, and just lateral to the pocket opening resides the gluteus minimus trigger point. See figure 10.10 for the three primary locations of these key NMLs.

You may have noticed in figure 10.10, when compared to figure 10.3, that the ✱ marking the outer gluteus medius primary trigger points #2 and #3 are right where the quadratus lumborum refers pain to. This is how NMLs in the quadratus lumborum create secondary trigger points in the gluteus medius muscle. This pattern of secondary trigger points in the gluteus medius can create severe pain at the base of the low back and posterior hip, as shown in figure 10.10. This can lead to all kinds of treatments to the lumbosacral spine, even injections to the spinal joints, when in reality just a hand-width laterally pinpoints the source of the problem: the gluteus medius trigger points.

Sometimes individuals are lucky enough to find a practitioner who will deactivate the gluteus medius trigger points. However, if the trigger points hidden up in the quadratus lumborum are not also removed at the same time, they will reactivate the gluteus medius trigger points, starting your chronic low-back pain all over again. This is a little gem that I learned through my years of clinical practice: there is a vicious cycle that forms between a compromised quadratus lumborum and your gluteus medius and minimus core supportive back muscles. If you have chronic lumbosacral pain, I highly recommend you get a trigger point product and search these muscles thoroughly for all primary active and hidden trigger points.

Once you have found with your thumb the primary tender NML in the gluteus medius that radiates pain, try lying down on a golf ball or tennis ball to release the myofascial trigger point, or use a trigger point therapy tool to more precisely apply therapeutic pressure to remove it. Once that trigger point is released, try moving slightly forwards or backwards along line A to find the other trigger points no doubt present in the gluteus medius (see figure 10.9). Do not be surprised if you find another spot with exquisite tenderness that is unbearable; it may refer pain into your hip or into the lumbosacral spine. Multiple trigger points in the gluteus medius are quite common and almost always severe, besides being chronic. These gluteus medius NMLs are central for most symptoms in the low back, pelvis, hip, and thigh; I cannot emphasize this enough—you need to thoroughly search for these primary trigger points. If you move more forward along line A as indicated in figure 10.9, towards the front of your pelvis you may find another exquisitely tender area that may shoot pain down your leg. Here you have found a trigger point in your gluteus minimus muscle. Because this muscle tends to send severe pain down to the leg, it is commonly called the "pseudo sciatica muscle."

In figure 10.11, the model is applying trigger point therapy to the number one trigger point of the gluteus medius muscle. You can see how easy it is to treat trigger points all along line A with the FENIX Rehab System by just lifting up your buttocks from the surface you are lying on and shifting your position. With this technique, you can shift out more laterally on the digit and treat the gluteus minimus and even the tensor fasciae latae muscle.

Figure 10.11

Trigger point therapy to gluteus medius TP1

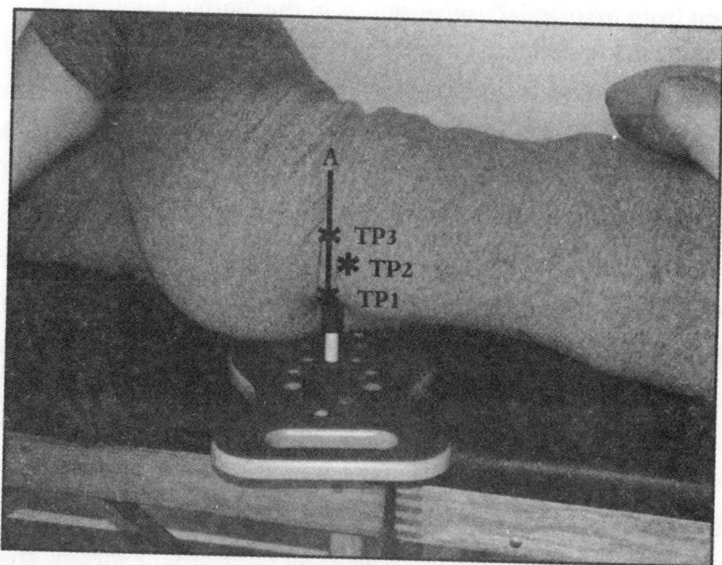

The Gluteus Minimus Muscle

The gluteus minimus attaches below the pelvic brim on the outside of your bony pelvis and connects to the top of your femur at the bony protuberance of your hip called the greater trochanter. It is called the minimus because it is the smallest of the gluteal muscles, but many times it is the most painful. Like the gluteus medius, it functions in supporting the pelvis in the weight-bearing position, such as in standing, walking, and running. Because of this, individuals will often complain of hip pain that may cause a limp during walking. Pain coming from your gluteus minimus is often excruciating and very persistent.

The primary trigger points of the gluteus minimus are generally found along the line described for the gluteus medius but towards the lateral end of this line. Again, if you utilize the opening of your back pocket to find the gluteus medius trigger points, you will find the gluteus minimus on the lateral outer edge of the pocket opening. Myofascial trigger points in the gluteus minimus muscle refer pain into the lower buttock and down the lateral side, knee, and into the ankle. By examining the drawing of the referral pain of the gluteus minimus in figure 10.12, you can see why many individuals complain of posterior hip problems and sciatica.

Sciatica, however, is not a diagnosis; it is a *symptom* that must have its cause identified by a proper neurological workup. True sciatica comes from direct irritation to the nerve roots that make up the sciatic nerve or irritation to the sciatic nerve itself in the pelvis. Leg pain from myofascial trigger points in the gluteus minimus is "pseudo sciatica" because it does not actually involve the sciatic nerve, but it can be just as painful and disabling. The differential diagnosis between the two conditions can usually be made by a careful history and an orthopedic and neurological examination. These trigger points of the gluteus minimus and medius muscles are frequently aggravated by prolonged immobility. This shows up when you sit at a desk or drive for a long period of time with your foot on the gas pedal, causing you to develop severe hip and leg pain.

Examining figure 10.12 closely and comparing it to figure 10.3, you will again see that the ✱s showing the location of the gluteus minimus trigger points are right where the lateral NMLs TP1 and TP2 of the quadratus lumborum refer pain. This is why the quadratus lumborum so often activates secondary trigger points in the gluteus minimus and medius. Therefore, if you find trigger points in one of these muscles, you must thoroughly check the other two muscles. If you remove the trigger points in your gluteus minimus, causing your leg pain to go away, but leave the lurking trigger points hidden in your quadratus lumborum or gluteus medius, your leg and hip symptoms will

Figure 10.12

Primary locations of the gluteus minimus trigger points, with referral pain in the buttock, hip, and down the leg

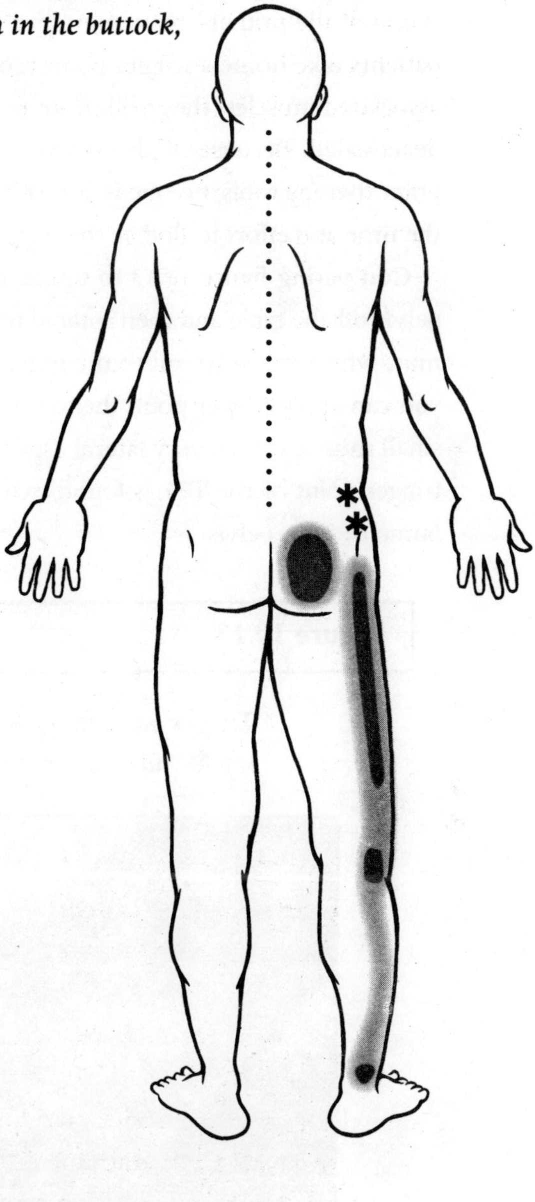

generally return. This often happens in trigger point therapy; a practitioner removes the primary active trigger points, lessening the symptoms, but for various reasons the hidden trigger points lurking in associated muscles are not found and removed. This is one of the primary reasons trigger point therapy fails a patient. I have found that if patients take home a trigger point tool and work carefully through their primary and associated muscles, they will more readily discover all the trigger points that must be deactivated. Because of this, I am a strong advocate of patients using home trigger point therapy tools; no one is as motivated as a chronic myofascial pain patient to take the time and effort to find *all* the trigger points at the root of their problems.

Comparing figure 10.13 to figure 10.11, you can see that the model has lifted her pelvis off the table and then rotated to apply trigger point therapy to the gluteus minimus, which is just lateral to the gluteus medius. By moving out more laterally again, you can apply trigger point therapy to the tensor fasciae latae (TFL) muscle. This is a small muscle on the very lateral aspect of the pelvis at the end of line A. The primary trigger point of the TFL is found two finger-widths behind and below the front bony bump of your pelvis.

Figure 10.13

Trigger point therapy to gluteus minimus trigger points; top ✱ indicates tensor fasciae latae trigger point

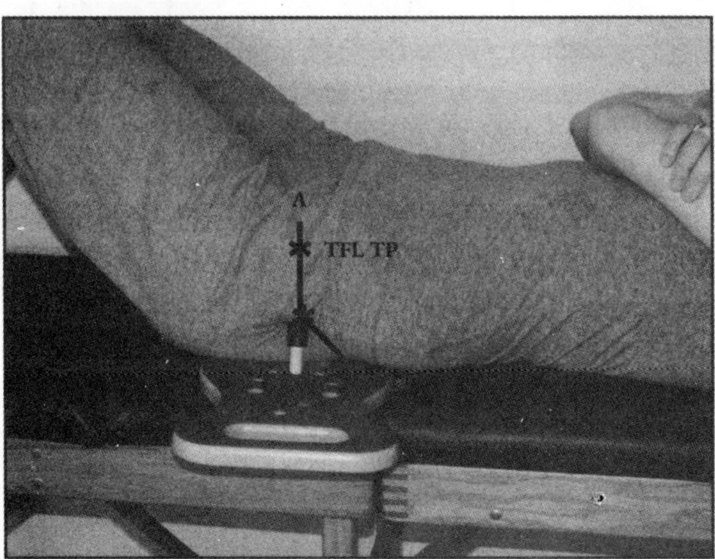

Case Study

This particular case I know quite well, because it is my own personal story. I developed severe and disabling low-back and hip pain that would radiate all the way into my foot, creating numbness and tingling. Because of my association with health-care professionals, I was able to see some of the best in neurology, radiology, and chiropractic. I had numerous orthopedic, neurologic, and radiographic examinations, along with a CT scan and an MRI examination of the lumbar spine. It was found that I had some moderate degenerative changes in my bottom lumbar disc with some mild osteoarthritis of the spinal facet joints. The pain was excruciating and went on for years. At one point, I had a neurosurgeon inject cortisone into my lower lumbar facet joints, but of course that did not correct the problem. I did have occasional trigger point therapy sessions that brought some relief, but the pain eventually returned.

Years of suffering helped motivate me to create a self-care device to accurately treat the myofascial trigger points throughout my low back. This suffering helped to give birth to the FENIX Rehab System, which allowed me to treat the numerous myofascial trigger points in my low back in a systematic way. I found that the deep paraspinal, multifidi, and rotator muscles referred pain into my quadratus lumborum muscles and activated trigger points in them. I also found that the quadratus lumborum muscle referred pain into the gluteus medius and minimus muscles and activated them. It was my gluteus medius that created my severe, crippling lumbosacral pain and my gluteus minimus that created my severe leg pain. Because of this pattern of muscular imbalance, I could not sit longer than fifteen minutes without experiencing excruciating lumbosacral pain and pain down into my foot.

After more than a decade of this recurring chronic pain, I found complete relief by simply doing the things outlined in this book. First, I began to systematically deactivate these myofascial trigger points with the FENIX Rehab System. I found treating myself every day to be the most helpful. I was already eating a very good whole foods organic diet, so to this I added specific herbal supplements to help with the chronic low-grade inflammation and oxidative stress caused by my own genetic predisposition. In a period of approximately two months, I was able to sit as long as I wanted and do virtually all the things I once did before, without the pain of the last ten years. So to all of you who suffer with chronic or myofascial pain: because of my personal experience, my experience with so many patients, as well as my daughter's recovery from fibromyalgia, I can't emphasize enough how important it is to apply this program of proper self-care.

The Piriformis Muscle

The name *piriformis* comes from the Latin *pirum* (pear) and *forma* (shape), because the muscle is actually pear-shaped. Your piriformis muscle is part of a group of six muscles deep in your buttocks that externally rotates or turns your hip outward. Of these six external hip rotator muscles, the piriformis is the largest and most important. It can also cause you the greatest amount of misery because it can entrap important nerves and blood vessels deep in your pelvis, causing the dreaded piriformis syndrome. One of these nerves, the sciatic nerve, passes right underneath the piriformis muscle, and in some individuals it passes right through the muscle. Because of this, a tight piriformis containing myofascial trigger points can pinch or irritate the sciatic nerve, creating a true case of sciatica.

The piriformis muscle and its five other sister muscles are found deep in the pelvis under the gluteal muscles. It originates from underneath the sacrum and runs over to attach to the hip joint at the greater trochanter. From figure 10.14, you can see it has two major trigger points. TP2 is at the origin next to the sacrum, and the sacrum plays a role as the central "keystone" of your pelvis. TP1 is near the piriformis muscle insertion by the hip joint, at the greater trochanter. By examining the referral pattern, you can see that TP2 tends to create a great deal of pain at the sacroiliac joint and TP1 throughout the posterior hip. The outer trigger point (TP1 in figure 10.14) should always be considered if you are suffering with posterior hip pain, while the inner trigger point (TP2) next the sacrum should be considered if you have chronic sacroiliac irritation and pain. Often, when going for the deep inner trigger point of the piriformis next the sacrum, you will also be hitting a very common trigger point in the gluteus maximus that overlies it. It really doesn't matter because the symptoms of both are very similar, and your goal is to remove with trigger point therapy whatever NMLs are in the area, creating pain.

Figure 10.14

Primary locations of piriformis trigger points (right) and location of piriformis muscle and sciatic nerve (left)

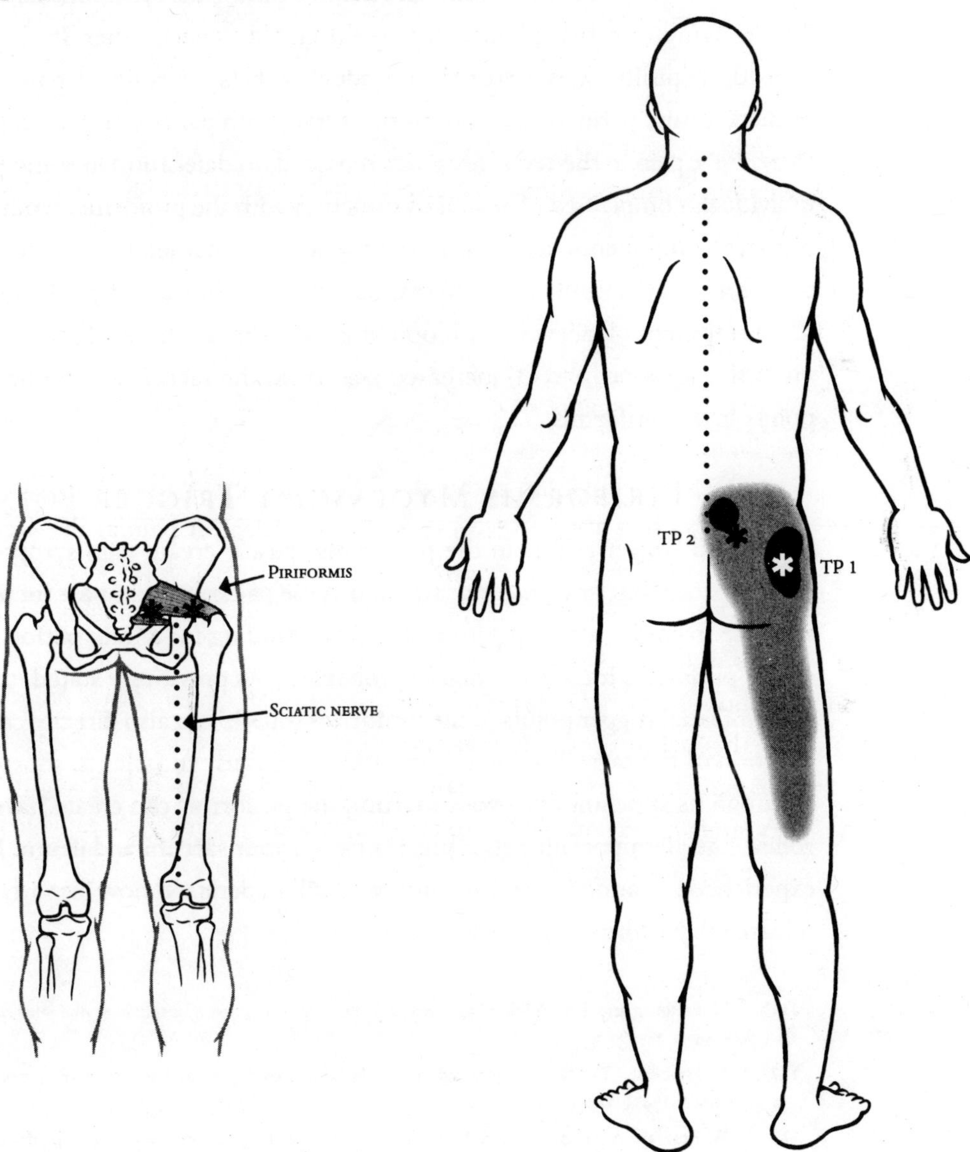

Piriformis Syndrome

As far back as 1934, the piriformis syndrome has been described in medical literature.[111] As early as 1937, Freiberg developed a surgical release for this piriformis syndrome to relieve its symptoms, but by 1941 he began to look for other reasons for the cause of this syndrome.[112] In 1974, researchers defined piriformis syndrome as characterized by bizarre symptoms that seemed totally unrelated to each other. In the study, they described the piriformis syndrome as producing the symptoms of pain in the low back, buttock, groin, perineum, and posterior thigh, with pain extending to the leg and foot. Puzzlingly, pain in the rectal area was reported on defecation in some patients.[113] Also, individuals complained of sexual dysfunction with the piriformis syndrome. The three primary components of the piriformis syndrome that lead to all these bizarre symptoms are (1) symptoms from myofascial trigger points in the piriformis muscle itself; (2) entrapment of nerves and blood vessels under a tight piriformis, leaving the pelvis at this location; and (3) increased pain from the sacroiliac joint because of trigger points in the piriformis.

Piriformis Myofascial Trigger Points

Myofascial trigger points in the piriformis muscle create pain symptoms in the low back, buttock, hip, and posterior thigh. If these pain symptoms are increased when you sit, arise from the sitting position, or while standing for a long period of time, NMLs of the piriformis muscle are highly probable.[114] As previously stated, the development of myofascial trigger points in the piriformis muscle can also directly cause painful dysfunction of the sacroiliac joint. The NMLs will cause muscles to shorten and weaken. Through its attachment to your sacrum, the piriformis can create havoc with the sacroiliac, the all-important pelvic joint between your sacrum and ileum. If you have ever experienced a painful sacroiliac joint, you will understand how important the ability to release the piriformis muscle is.

---

111 A. H. Freiberg and T. H. Vinke, "Sciatica and the sacroiliac joint," *Journal bone and joint surgery* 16 (1934): 126–36.

112 A. H. Freiberg, "The fascial elements in associated low back pain and sciatic pain," *Journal bone and joint surgery* 3 (1941): 478–80.

113 E. W. Retzlaff, A. H. Berry, A. S. Haight, P. A. Parente, H. J. Lichty, et al., "The piriformis muscle syndrome," *J Am Osteopathic Association* 73 (1974): 799–807.

114 Ibid.

Figure 10.15

Self-administered trigger point therapy to left piriformis trigger point (TP2)

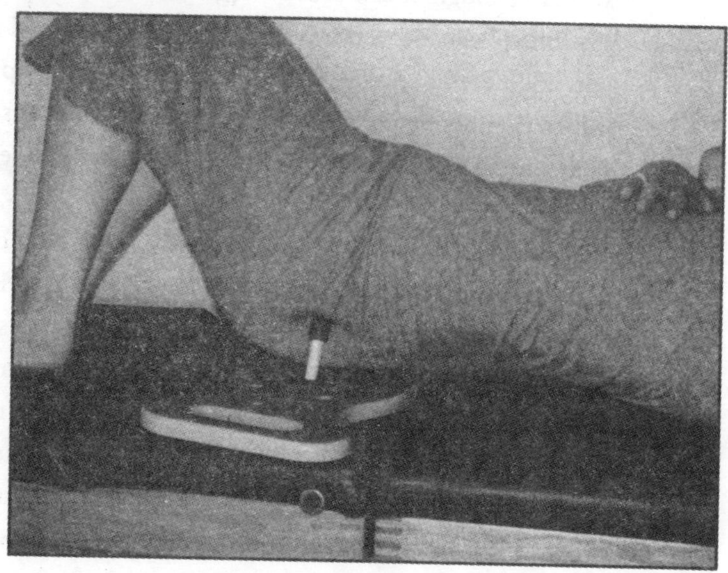

Case Study

John came to see me after a couple years of trying to track down a cure for what he called his sacroiliac problem: he suffered with severe buttock pain. He had been through the medical mill, utilizing different anti-inflammatory drugs, injections into his sacroiliac joint, and numerous attempts to end the pain through spinal manipulation. On examination, I found John to have a shortened and weakened piriformis muscle that was affecting his sacroiliac joint. After placing him on a home program of trigger point therapy and stretches, I was able to manipulate the sacroiliac joint and restore its normal function. This returned John to a pain-free state, allowing him to return to his golf game. John did find that he needed to treat his piriformis muscle with a trigger point tool on an occasional basis to keep him pain-free.

Piriformis Nerve and Vessel Entrapment

Sometimes, severe buttock pain can come from the piriformis muscle entrapping the superior and inferior gluteal nerves and blood vessels that exit there. If this entrapment is severe enough, it can cause the gluteal muscles to weaken or atrophy.[115] The piriformis muscle can also entrap the important pudendal nerve, which can cause perineal pain and possibly sexual dysfunction. In the male, pudendal nerve entrapment may also cause impotence, while in the female it can cause painful intercourse.[116] This pudendal nerve entrapment can also cause either gender to experience pain in the groin region.

The major entrapment by this muscle, which can cause so much pain and even lead to unnecessary surgery, is direct irritation of the sciatic nerve as it starts its journey down the back of your thigh. When the piriformis syndrome entraps or irritates the sciatic nerve, the symptoms are easily confused with a herniated lumbar disc. A good neurological workup showing either the absence or marked weakness of Achilles tendon reflex will suggest a herniated lumbar disc. When the piriformis muscle enlarges by being held in a contracted, shortened state because of multiple myofascial trigger points, it can put pressure on the sciatic nerve. Numerous research and case studies have reported that pressure on the sciatic nerve from the piriformis muscle can create pain and numbness projecting all the way to the foot.[117] Stein and Warfield reported a case where the patient even had loss of position sense, producing an abnormal gait mimicking a severe neurological disease.[118]

The challenge is that the piriformis muscle usually does not only reveal itself as a single problem. Usually the piriformis syndrome lays underneath a mass of multiple myofascial trigger points within the gluteus minimus, medius, and maximus muscles. Recall that the gluteus medius and minimus muscle trigger points are usually related to quadratus lumborum NMLs higher up in the low back. Through my clinical years, I've seen innumerable patients who have suffered for years with low-back pain and sciatica, and some who had been through a failed low-back surgery. Generally, I have found that a great deal of work had to be done in removing the trigger points within the gluteus

---

115 M. R. Rask, "Superior gluteal nerve entrapment syndrome," *Muscle Nerve* 3 (1980): 304–7.

116 Lazarou, Pomeranz, and Corey, "Incidents," 1200–5.

117 R. P. Hallin, "Sciatic pain and the piriformis muscle," *Postgrad Med* 74 (1983): 69–72.

118 J. M. Stein and C. A. Warfield, "Two entrapment neuropathies," *Hosp Pract* (January 1993): 100A–100P.

medius and minimus muscles and the aggravating quadratas lumborum muscle in the lumbar spine. Once this had been accomplished, I could get at the underlying piriformis syndrome deep in the pelvis. This physical program of care must be combined with an overall wellness program of improved diet and exercise, as described in section 4.

This myofascial pattern involving these multiple muscles of the low back and pelvis has accounted for a great deal of suffering in patients who made their way to my clinic and have been helped naturally. So even if you have degenerative disc disease with arthritis in your lumbar facet joints, make sure you have someone thoroughly check out the possibility of a piriformis syndrome before more drugs, injections, and surgery are prescribed. Or right now take a tennis ball or trigger point tool, if you have one, and search out your quadratus lumborum, gluteus medius and minimus, and piriformis muscles for this disabling, painful myofascial pain syndrome.

Now that I have shown you how to remove the primary dysfunctional muscle patterns found in low back; hip, and leg pain, you will want to know how to keep these muscles strong and healthy. To accomplish this, you can utilize simple stretches and strengthening exercises using an inexpensive exercise ball. If you like, you can start out with a thick sofa cushion until you purchase an exercise ball.

Rehab Exercises for the Core Muscles of Your Low Back

Check with your doctor before doing any home-care program. Perform these exercises in three light sets of 8–12 repetitions daily. Only do as many as you are comfortable with, and do not cause yourself any further pain with these exercises. They are specifically designed to strengthen the core muscles that keep you comfortably upright: the erector spinea, quadratus lumborum, gluteal, and abdominal muscles. Your abdominal muscles are the anterior support that opposes the action of your low-back muscles. Together, your abdominal and back muscles keep you balanced in an upright position. Also, strong abdominals keep the interabdominal pressure high, giving your low back the support it needs.

Figures 10.16-20

10.16: Tractioning out the low back; hold for as long as comfortable (2–5 minutes)

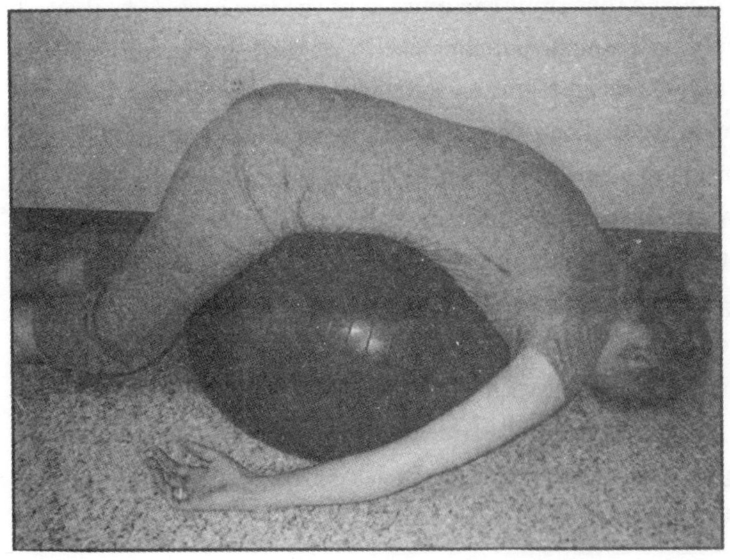

10.16

10.17: Stretching for lateral back stabilizers, the quadratus lumborum, and the gluteus medius and tensor fasciae latae

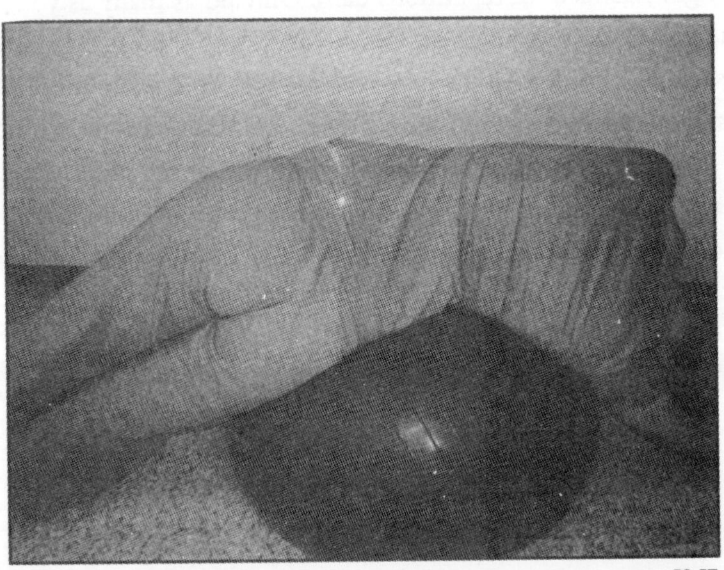

10.17

10.18: Reverse abdominal crunches strengthen the abdominal muscles

10.18

10.19: Strengthening core low-back muscles, gluteus maximus and erector spinae; focus on lifting leg with your buttocks, not your thigh

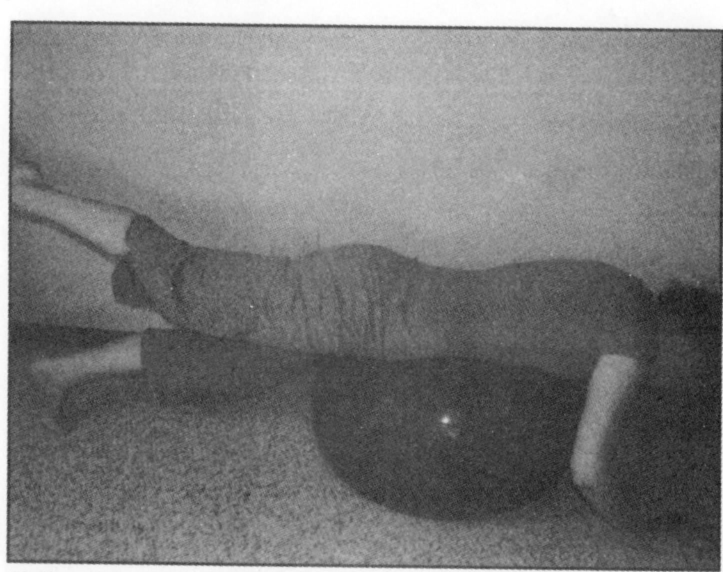

10.19

10.20: Strengthening the lateral stabilizers of pelvis and low back, the gluteus medius, and quadratus lumborum muscles

10.20

11

Solving the Mystery of Your Chronic Shoulder and Arm Pain

Chronic myofascial pain in your upper body generally manifests in two primary areas, the shoulder girdle and the neck, with or without headaches. From my clinical experience, there are two anatomical factors that hold the key to understanding the mystery of these chronic pain conditions: the freedom of movement in the shoulder joint and the tremendous weight of the head, averaging about twelve pounds. Cracking the code of these anatomical factors in your upper body pain can unlock the key to your suffering.

To comprehend the significance of the first anatomical factor, take your left index finger and follow your right collarbone into the middle of your body, where it attaches to your chest at the upper sternum. Your left index finger is now touching your right sternoclavicular joint, the joint where your collarbone joins your sternum, which is about the size of your fingertip. Please refer to figure 11.1 for an anatomical description of the shoulder girdle complex.

Figure 11.1

Right shoulder joint anatomy, anterior view

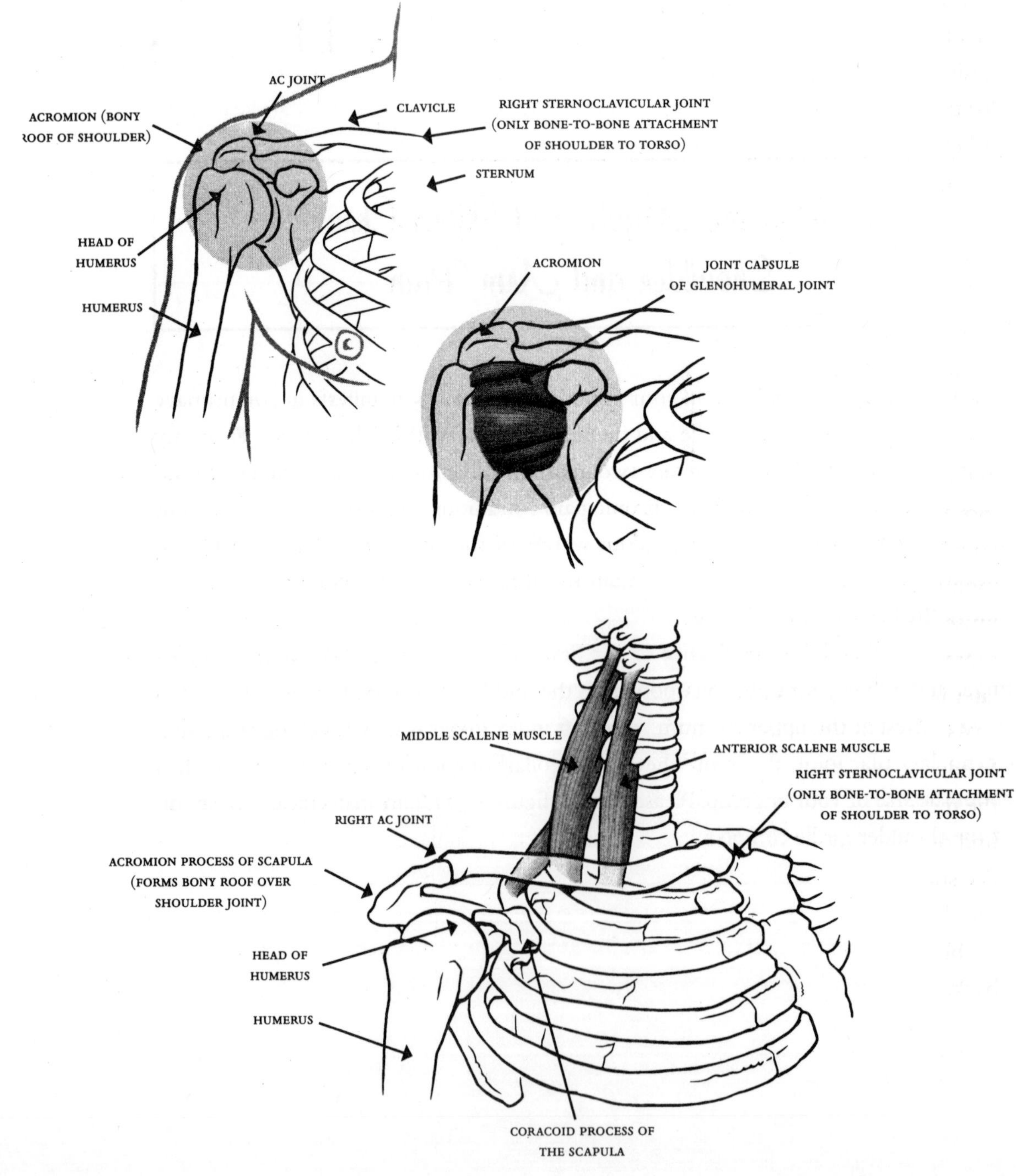

AC JOINT
ACROMION (BONY ROOF OF SHOULDER)
CLAVICLE
RIGHT STERNOCLAVICULAR JOINT (ONLY BONE-TO-BONE ATTACHMENT OF SHOULDER TO TORSO)
STERNUM
HEAD OF HUMERUS
HUMERUS
ACROMION
JOINT CAPSULE OF GLENOHUMERAL JOINT

MIDDLE SCALENE MUSCLE
ANTERIOR SCALENE MUSCLE
RIGHT STERNOCLAVICULAR JOINT (ONLY BONE-TO-BONE ATTACHMENT OF SHOULDER TO TORSO)
RIGHT AC JOINT
ACROMION PROCESS OF SCAPULA (FORMS BONY ROOF OVER SHOULDER JOINT)
HEAD OF HUMERUS
HUMERUS
CORACOID PROCESS OF THE SCAPULA

The Challenge of Having It Both Ways—Mobility and Stability

What is fascinating about this small sternoclavicular joint is that it is the only bony attachment for your whole upper extremity. Just think about what that means for a moment; your hand, forearm, arm, shoulder joint, shoulder blade—the entire shoulder girdle complex—has only this one bone-to-bone joint attachment to your body. Except for this small fingertip-sized bone-to-bone joint, your entire shoulder girdle complex is held together, and to your torso, only by muscles. This makes your shoulder joint unique among all the major joints of your body; it relies on muscles and tendons rather than bones and ligaments for its support, stability, and integrity. This is the key to understanding its chronic myofascial pain tendencies.

There are four major muscles, commonly referred to as the rotator cuff, that perform a majority of the work to move your arm through space and to maintain the integrity of your actual shoulder joint. But for these four vital rotator cuff muscles to work properly, four other important muscles must perform a complex and surprisingly contradictory task. These four muscles must fully stabilize your shoulder blade while at the same time allowing it to freely and correctly rotate on your rib cage as your arm moves. Why is this important? Because two of these muscles that stabilize and move your shoulder blade, the upper trapezius and levator scapula, contain the most commonly found myofascial trigger points. It is the upper trapezius and levator scapula muscles that create the vast majority of upper back, neck, and even head pain. Much more will be explained regarding finding and treating these two important muscles later in this chapter.

As unstable as this sounds, it makes complete sense once you realize the amount of freedom of movement that this anatomical arrangement gives you. Just try performing the movements you can do with your shoulder with any other joint; you will quickly find out how impossible it can be. Of course, having this great flexibility does sacrifice stability, meaning you are prone to acute injury and/or repetitive stress injuries in the shoulder-joint complex. Therefore, it is not surprising to find that shoulder-joint problems are the second most common work-related injury, second only to the low back.[119]

---

119 F. T. McDermott, "Repetitive strain injury: a review of current understanding," *Med J Australia* 144 (1986): 196–200.

Because of this unique anatomy, the shoulder can easily be injured if it is made vulnerable by underlying muscular imbalances in either the rotator cuff muscles that move your arm or the four muscles that stabilize and move your shoulder blade (scapula). These muscular imbalances are primarily caused by myofascial trigger points (hyperirritable tissue in muscles) that lead to a shortening and weakening of the involved muscles. Because of the complexity of the shoulder girdle, trigger points readily form in one or more of its four rotator cuff muscles: the infraspinatus, teres minor, supraspinatus, and subscapularis muscles, and/or scapular stabilizers: the trapezius, levator scapula, rhomboid, and serratus anterior.

Chronic Shoulder Pain: Where It All Begins

Usually this myofascial instability causes only a minor ache and/or restricted movement that can be ignored—that is, until you overstress your shoulder, causing you serious pain and driving you to see a health-care provider. Generally, patients believe that their shoulder problem began at that painful point and never realize that this muscular imbalance and shoulder instability had been developing over months or even years. One study on 75 pain-free schoolchildren found that 57% of the boys and 40% of the girls had exam findings indicating instability already present in their shoulder joints.[120] This research study, as well as others, indicates that instability in the shoulder can preexist for years before the pain appears. It is vital for proper rehabilitation to realize that even if your pain has only been there for weeks, the underlying myofascial instability of your shoulder has been there for many months or even years. Therefore, as with all myofascial pain disorders, give yourself some time to realize real pain relief with a self-care program of trigger point therapy and stretching and strengthening exercises.

Another complicating factor is that once you injure your shoulder, whether acute or repetitive, your body begins to lay down adhesive fibers between the muscles to protect the injured tissues. These adhesions between the muscles and fasciae begin to severely restrict your shoulder motion, exacerbating the restriction started earlier through muscle imbalance. The preexisting myofascial trigger points, along with secondary myofascial adhesions, continue to decrease the strength and restrict function of

---

120 R. J. Emery and A. B. Mullaji, "Glenohumeral joint instability in normal adolescents. Incidence and significance," *Bone Joint Surg Br* 73, no. 3 (1991): 406–8.

your shoulder. Through this process, the preexisting problem of myofascial instability will lead to pain and dysfunction that spreads to your arm, mid-back, and neck, and may even cause a "frozen shoulder."

The details of how your shoulder-girdle muscles become imbalanced is vital in practical ways to anyone suffering with headaches and chronic pain of their shoulder, mid-back, upper back, and neck. Furthermore, from my many years of clinical practice and teaching, I have found that shoulder dysfunction and its rehabilitation is not well understood. This lack of understanding on the part of many clinicians can make it difficult for you to find a health-care practitioner properly educated in the treatment of this area. Also, you may just find it a bit interesting to see how your shoulder girdle works.

SHOULDER IMPINGEMENT SYNDROMES

The primary job of your four rotator cuff muscles and your four shoulder blade stabilizers is to keep your shoulder joint properly aligned in an extremely wide range of positions. The presence of myofascial trigger points in any of these shoulder girdle muscles will disrupt their ability to keep your shoulder joint complex properly aligned. This can lead to many problems. Imagine a sophisticated, complex gear system just slightly out of proper alignment; eventually it would begin to create wear and tear in the gears. Your shoulder girdle complex is like this when myofascial trigger points begin to affect the length and strength of any one of these eight shoulder girdle muscles. The muscular imbalance and subsequent dysfunction will eventually lead to parts of your shoulder joint complex wearing out. Generally, the first to go are the rotator cuff tendons.

The Role of Shoulder Abduction

The movement of your shoulder that is most commonly disturbed is abduction of your arm. Shoulder abduction is the raising up of your elbow from your side to do work in front of you or to the side of you. A good example of full abduction is the front crawl stroke in swimming, in which you bring, or abduct, the arm up next to your head. If you have myofascial trigger points in one or more of your rotator cuff muscles, weakening and shortening them, the head of your humerus (arm bone; see figure 11.1) can ride high in your shoulder joint, creating an impingement syndrome, where it will pinch and grind the tendons and bursa of your rotator cuff against the bony root of the shoulder joint called the acromion (see figure 11.1). Another reason this impingement syndrome takes place is because myofascial trigger points can develop in the muscles stabilizing your scapula. When this happens, the restriction does not allow the acromial process (acromion) of your shoulder blade to rotate out of the way of the elevating humerus. This causes the tendons and bursa again to become impinged between the humerus and the bony roof of the acromion.

This very simplistic explanation of beginning muscular dysfunction in your shoulder joint is the primary way that myofascial pain syndrome develops in the shoulder girdle area. In fact, according to Kalb, 95% of all shoulder pain cases are attributed to the tendons of these rotator cuff muscles becoming pinched between two bones, the humerus and acromion, when we raise our arms.[121] These "impingement syndromes" of the shoulder are the most common type of shoulder problem, causing pain and dysfunction in the shoulder girdle and arm.

Furthermore, if the muscular imbalances caused by myofascial trigger points in the rotator cuff or scapular muscles are not removed, this impingement syndrome will constantly wear away at the tendons and bursa of the shoulder joint, which ultimately can lead to degenerative tendonitis. Because of this impingement syndrome caused by myofascial dysfunction, a great deal of unnecessary arthroscopic surgery of the shoulder is done in the United States. In practice, I have found that when you remove all of the active and hidden myofascial trigger points throughout the shoulder girdle and restore the length and strength of the muscles, many patients can avert arthroscopic surgery—especially when the myofascial dysfunction is caught early enough.

This simple problem of muscular imbalance of the shoulder joint not only leads to degenerative tendonitis of the shoulder, but it is also connected to unrelenting neck and mid-back pain problems. The key to all of these common upper body chronic pain disorders is the lowly and ignored shoulder blade, and very little is written about its role and importance in chronic pain disorders. In fact, abnormal function of your shoulder blade through muscular imbalance may right now be playing a major role in your shoulder, arm, mid-back, and/or neck pain with headaches. Here's how.

121 R. L. Kalb, "Evaluation treatment of shoulder pain," *Hosp Pract* (1998): 119–22.

The Humble Shoulder Blade

Your scapula acts as a dynamic keystone to all actions involving movement of your upper extremity and neck. Your shoulder blade must perform two contradictory functions at the same time: it must provide dynamic stability while providing controlled mobility. To perform these contradictory functions, there are four primary muscles that run from the spine of your mid-back and neck to attach to the medial, or inside, border of your shoulder blade. From top to bottom, these four stabilizing muscles are the trapezius, levator scapula, serratus anterior, and rhomboid (see drawings and descriptions below for exact locations):

Figure 11.2

The four scapula stabilizer muscles: (1) trapezius, (2) levator scapula, (3) rhomboids, and (4) serratus anterior, and the direction of their pull to rotate the shoulder blade in a controlled fashion; they can either elevate the acromion away from the rotator cuff or depress it into the rotator cuff

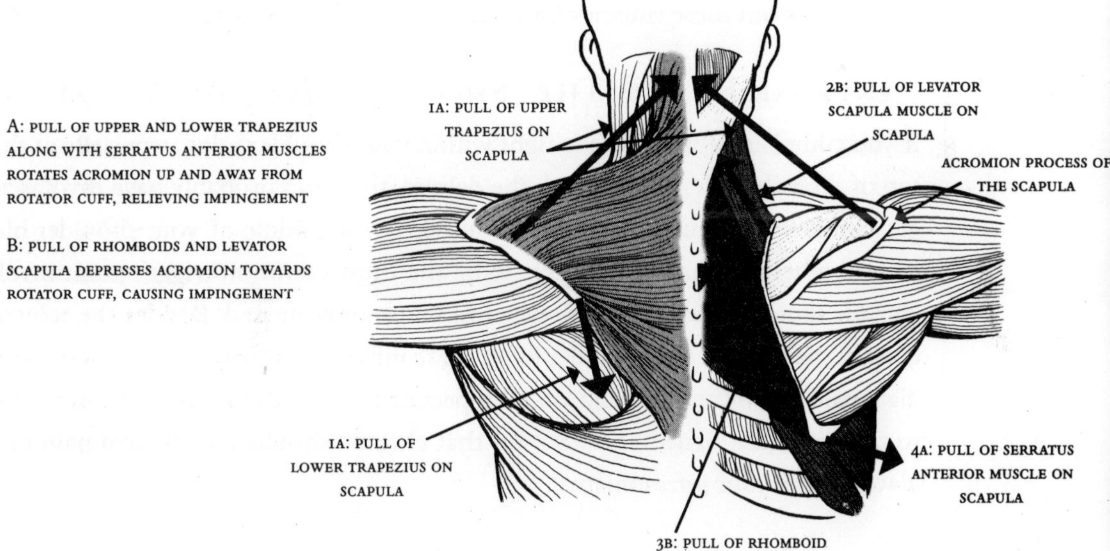

The lateral rotator cuff muscles run from your shoulder blade to your arm bone, or humerus. These four rotator cuff muscles actually move your arm. From this description, you can see that the shoulder blade sits in the middle of these eight important muscles, helping them to perform their all-important functions of dynamic stability and controlled mobility.

These eight muscles work in synchrony to move the scapula and humerus in harmony, maintaining, at all times, what is known as normal scapulohumeral rhythm.[122] When any of these eight muscles contain myofascial trigger points, this vital scapulohumeral rhythm is compromised and your shoulder begins to dysfunction.[123] This disruption of your normal scapulohumeral rhythm, over time, will lead to chronic myofascial pain and stiffness of your shoulder joint, mid-back, upper back, and/or neck. Therefore, if you suffer from any chronic pain and/or stiffness of your upper body, it is extremely helpful to check these eight muscles for the presence of trigger points, and then remove them. If these muscles are not normalized, eventually the instability from the improper functioning of your shoulder blade muscles can lead to a disabling shoulder injury or degenerative changes. One study found that 100% of shoulder joint instability, pain, and dysfunction could be traced to abnormal shoulder blade function.[124] Therefore, if you wish to recover from your recurrent shoulder, mid-back, or neck pains, check out these muscles for hidden trigger points right away!

Infraspinatus: The "Shoulder Joint Pain" Muscle

If you complain of a deep ache right within your shoulder joint, especially at the front top of your shoulder underneath the deltoid, then you probably have myofascial trigger points in your infraspinatus, the muscle in the middle of your shoulder blade. In clinical practice, I have found this to be the most common trigger point involved in chronic shoulder pain and the one most commonly missed. Besides the referral pain deep in the front of the shoulder joint, these infraspinatus trigger points commonly radiate pain down the front and lateral aspect of the arm to the lateral forearm and even to the hand (see figure 11.3). So, for that chronic shoulder joint–arm pain problem, *always* check your infraspinatus.

---

122 W. B. Kibler, "Role of the scapula in the overhead throwing motion," *Contemp Orthop* 22 (1991): 525–32.

123 J. DiVeta, M. L. Walker, and B. Skibinski, "Relationship between performance of selected scapular muscles and scapular abduction in standing subjects," *Phys Ther* 70 (1990): 470–6.

124 W. B. Kibler, "The role of the scapula in athletic shoulder function," *Am J Sports Med* 26 (1998): 325–37.

Figure 11.3

Typical trigger point locations and referral pain for infraspinatus muscle

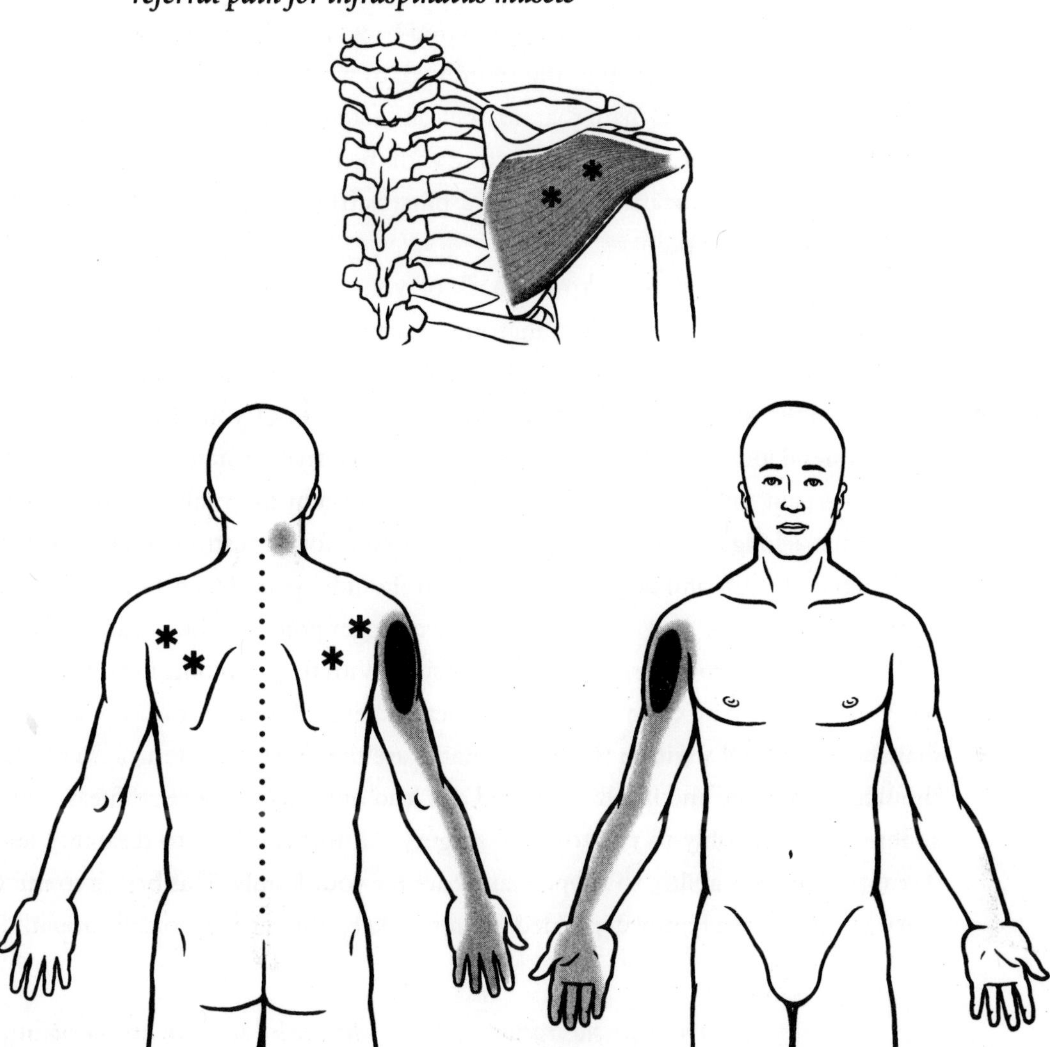

Additionally, this muscle also can radiate pain into the back of your upper neck and head. This is one reason why myofascial problems with the muscles that govern your scapulohumeral rhythm can lead to neck pain and headaches. Something else that is generally overlooked is that the infraspinatus can be a key factor in mid-back pain. Not only can this muscle refer pain into your mid-back, but also a tight infraspinatus can cause mid-back muscles, such as the rhomboid, to work overtime. So, if you have that nagging chronic mid-back pain that no one can seem to find the cause of, do yourself a favor and check out the infraspinatus along with the rhomboid muscles; refer to figures 11.3 and 11.4 for the location of the infraspinatus trigger points and 12.1 and 12.2 for the rhomboid trigger points.

The infraspinatus attaches to the back of your shoulder blade and runs laterally to attach to your humerus. This anatomical arrangement allows your infraspinatus muscle, when contracted, to externally rotate your arm and stabilize the head of the humerus in the shoulder joint capsule during movement of your arm (see figure 11.1, glenohumeral joint capsule). Because this muscle externally rotates your arm, you may experience pain and symptoms whenever you stretch it by internally rotating your arm, such as in reaching into your back pocket or hooking your bra strap in the back. If these movements are stiff and difficult or cause you shoulder pain, you probably have NMLs in your infraspinatus. You also know you have trigger points in the infraspinatus if you find that you have trouble sleeping on your side. With trigger points in your infraspinatus, you will find pain deep in your shoulder and even down your arm when lying on that shoulder. NMLs within the infraspinatus are the most common cause of chronic shoulder–arm pain, and if left untreated can lead not only to more stiffness, pain, and suffering, but possibly to rotator cuff surgery. All this can lead to disability and the disruption of your ability to support and care for your family. This brings to mind the story of Jim, whose family depended on him to keep them economically afloat.

Case Study

Jim was a 42-year-old tractor mechanic who needed strength and flexibility in both of his shoulders to do the work necessary to bring home a paycheck. His income was the family's entire basis for rent, heat, light, clothes, and food—in other words, their survival. Jim had been suffering on and off with right shoulder pain that radiated into his arm, mid-back, and up his neck, on and off for over three years. His rotator cuff pain and disability had become so severe that it was difficult for him to work. He had very poor insurance coverage, but he did try many different medical approaches in overcoming his chronic condition—courses of NSAIDs, physical therapy, exercises, cortisone injections—and he was now facing the possibility of surgery. When Jim first came to see me, he was quite despondent; he just did not have the financial resources to cover the costs involved in surgery and his subsequent rehabilitation, plus all the time off without paid medical leave.

After a physical examination, I found Jim to have multiple NMLs within his infraspinatus muscle, causing shortness and weakness, which led over time to his rotator cuff tendon impingement syndrome. What surprised Jim was that all the severe pain he felt deep in the front of the shoulder joint came from a muscle on the back of his shoulder blade. I began a course of myofascial therapy for the infraspinatus and subscapularis and showed him how to do self-administered trigger point therapy to these rotator cuff muscles. Jim began to experience immediate results with the myofascial therapy, restoring function and reducing his pain.

Lab work showed Jim's blood had elevated levels of hsCRP, illustrating that he had low-grade systemic inflammation and elevated F2-isoprostanes, ideal markers for oxidative stress. Jim's blood also showed lab findings consistent with insulin resistance. The systemic inflammation and oxidative stress were primary factors in making his myofascial pain so chronic, which was fueled by his insulin resistance, as explained in chapters 5 and 6. Following a dietary and nutritional supplementation program (outlined in chapters 14 and 15), Jim was able to normalize the underlying metabolic factors that contributed to his chronic myofascial pain. This metabolic dysfunction was also undoubtedly leading him down the path to degenerative disease. Follow-up lab tests showed his insulin resistance to be corrected; subsequent lab markers for chronic inflammation and oxidative stress were no longer elevated. Jim's case illustrates how these chronic myofascial problems can be a signal of deeper metabolic issues that need to be addressed. It is also why a team effort is needed between the clinician and the patient to fully overcome the challenge of a chronic myofascial pain disorder. Jim stopped chasing simplistic answers, quick relief, and medical "magic," and actually healed his pain through a holistic, commonsense approach. So can you!

Figure 11.4

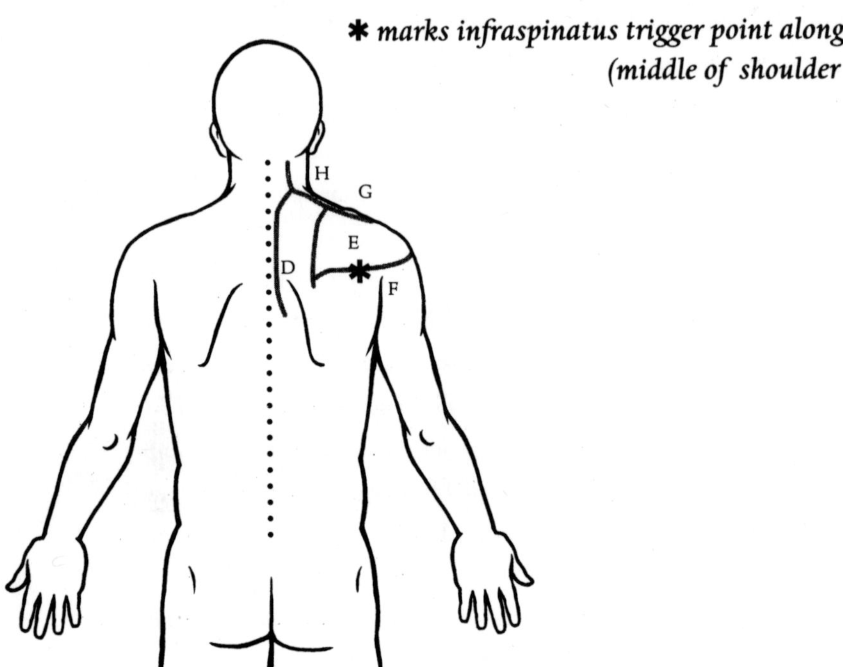

To find these common trigger points, all you need to do is find the middle of your shoulder blade, as indicated in figure 11.4 in the middle of line F. For your right infraspinatus, take your left hand and reach across your chest, under your armpit, and touch the middle of your right shoulder blade. Then poke around in the muscular tissue until you find a tender point. With a little more pressure, you may find referral pain to the front of your shoulder or even down your arm. If you cannot apply enough pressure, then use a tennis or golf ball or a trigger point tool, such as the FENIX Rehab System, as demonstrated in figure 11.5. To remove the trigger points, apply direct pressure, as described on pages 120 to 124. After applying trigger point therapy to the infraspinatus muscle, stretch the muscle, as indicated in figure 11.6. As explained in chapter 9, pages 122 to 124, this trigger point therapy creates actual changes in the tissue, allowing the trigger points to stretch and release.

Figure 11.5

Self-administered trigger point therapy to infraspinatus trigger points

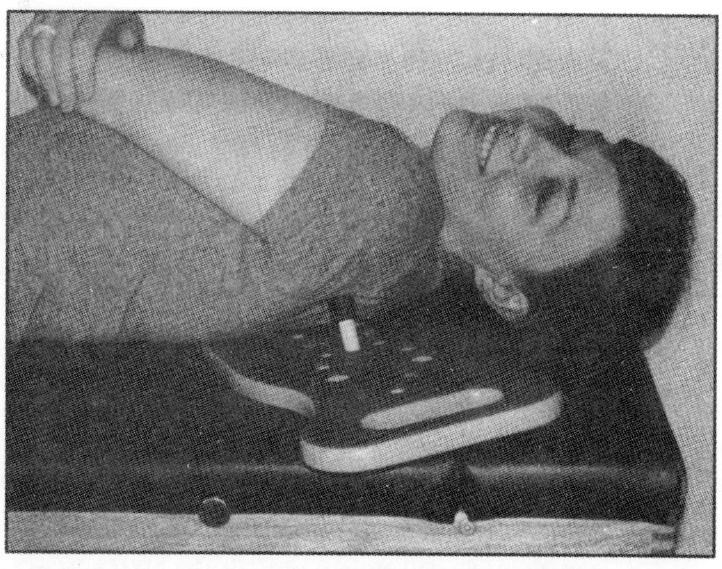

Figure 11.6

Stretch for the infraspinatus muscle

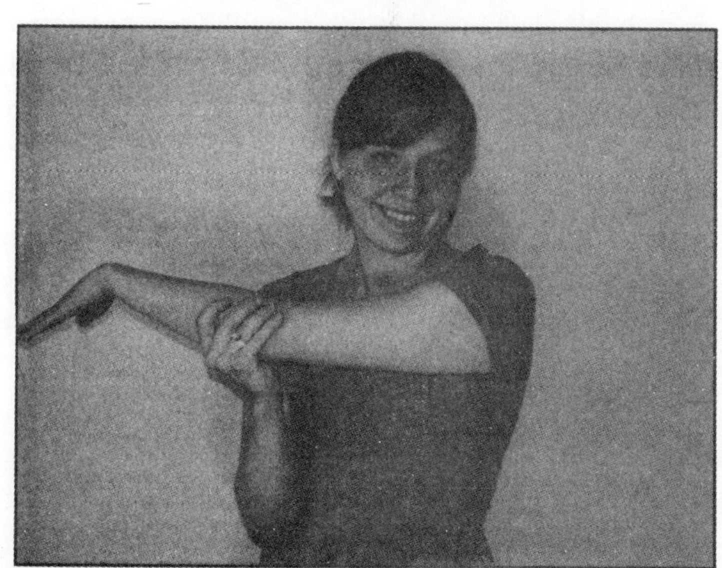

After years of treating individuals with chronic shoulder joint and arm pain, I cannot emphasize enough the importance of searching out this muscle for trigger points. It is one of the most important muscles in maintaining proper scapulohumeral rhythm. Myofascial trigger points in the infraspinatus can lead to shoulder instability and many different types of shoulder problems. Remember that the referral pattern and marked locations of these trigger points in figures 11.3 and 11.4 may vary from individual to individual. Also, once you find a trigger point and deactivate it, remember to move slightly off it in other directions to find the other trigger points nested within the muscle; myofascial trigger points are always multiple in nature.

Infraspinatus "Little Brother": The Teres Minor Muscle

If you move down to the bottom edge of your infraspinatus, you will come upon a trigger point (TP3 in figure 11.7). This trigger point is in the "little brother" of the infraspinatus, the teres minor muscle. It is called the "little brother" because it looks and acts just like a little infraspinatus muscle right at its lower border. This muscle with trigger points is usually found *after* you have removed the trigger points from your infraspinatus muscle. When you remove the NMLs from your infraspinatus, the pain in your shoulder joint and down your arm tends to go away, but you may then start to notice a deep ache in the back of your shoulder joint. Or you may be treating myofascial trigger points in the infraspinatus and find one at the lower edge that refers a severe pain into the back of your shoulder joint; this is the teres minor muscle. It's really not that complicated to find these tender muscle knots that create referral pain, and once you find them, simply remove them with self-administered trigger point therapy. Again, you know you are on a trigger point if within 30 to 60 seconds the tenderness and referral pain feel like they are "melting away."

Figure 11.7

TP1 = primary supraspinatus muscle/tendon TP
TP2 = primary infraspinatus muscle TP
TP3 = primary teres minor muscle TP

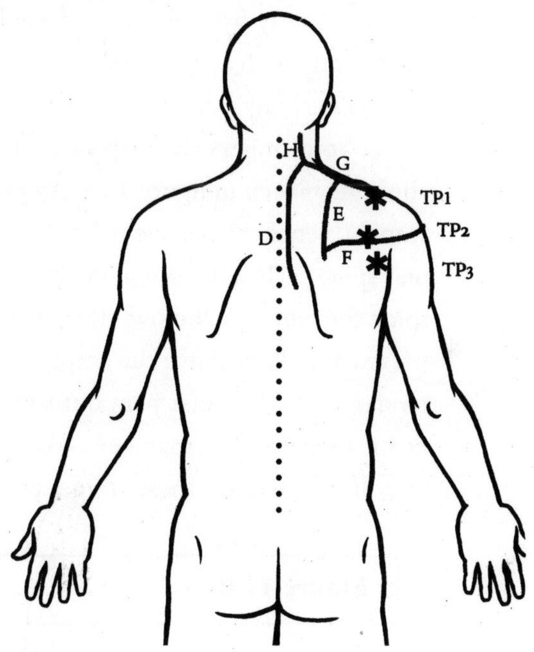

Supraspinatus Muscle: The "I Think I Have Bursitis" Muscle

The supraspinatus muscle attaches to the top of your shoulder blade and runs laterally to insert at the top of the humeral head, right above the attachment of the infraspinatus tendon. Because of its anatomical position, contraction of this muscle abducts, or lifts, your arm away from the side of your body. To find your left supraspinatus, take your right hand, reach across your chest over the top of your left shoulder and place your fingers on the bony ridge at the top of your shoulder blade, as demonstrated in figure 11.8.

Let your fingers slide upward off the bony spine into the muscular hollow right above it, as seen in figure 11.9. Anatomically, this bony ridge is called the spine of the scapula, hence the muscle right above it is the *supra-*, or "above," the *-spinatus,* or "scapular spine." This, of course, makes the large muscle on your shoulder blade below the spine the *infra-*, or "below," the *-spinatus,* or "scapular spine." With your fingers in the muscular hollow above the scapular spine, poke downward and determine if there are tender knots that refer pain out to your shoulder or elbow joint. To get enough diagnostic pressure, you may need to use a trigger point tool; it is impossible to use tennis or golf balls to treat these trigger points in the supraspinatus.

Figure 11.8

Finding the left supraspinatus trigger point (located at top of the shoulder blade, above the bony ridge)

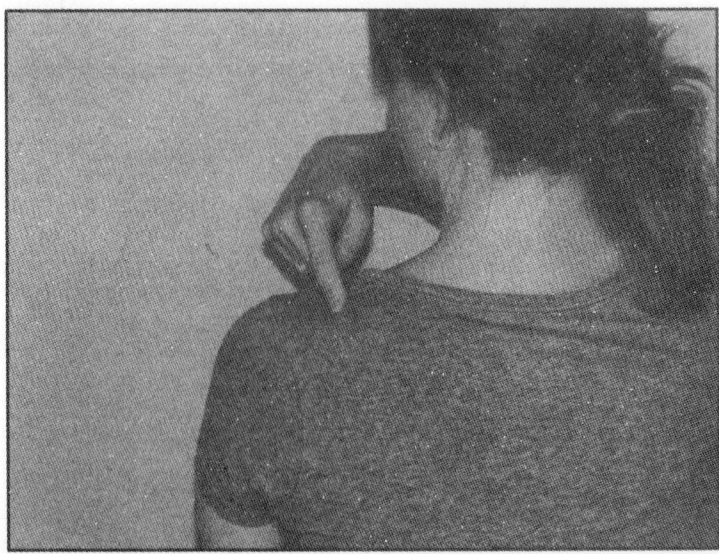

Figure 11.9

Typical supraspinatus trigger point locations

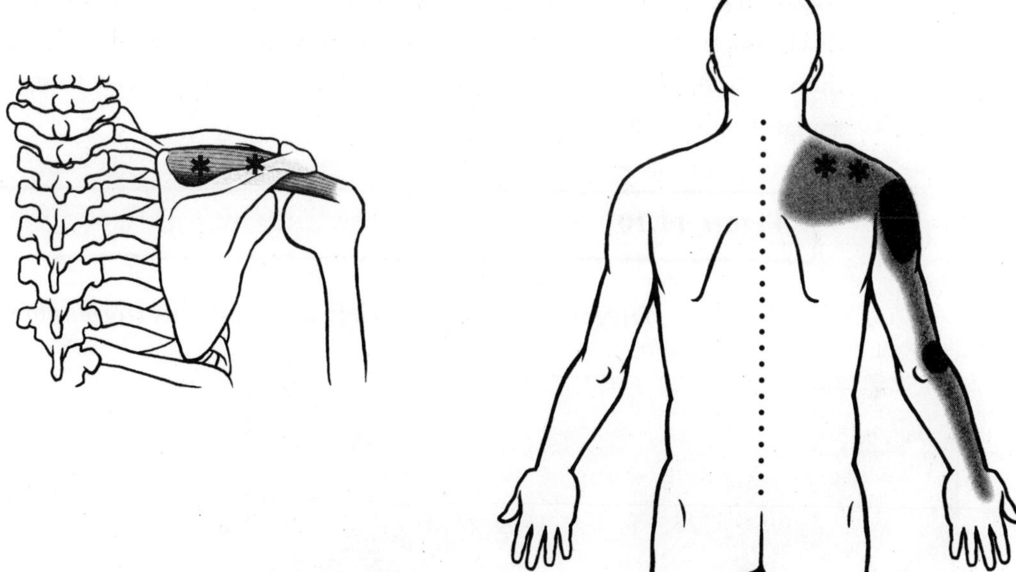

As indicated above, trigger points in the supraspinatus muscle cause a deep ache in the middle top of your shoulder joint; patients usually come in saying they have "bursitis." Clinically, I have not found this muscle to be as important in shoulder joint pain problems as its larger brother, the infraspinatus, but it is one that you will want to check after you have removed trigger points in the infraspinatus and teres minor muscles. If your shoulder pain also has an element of lateral elbow pain, this is one muscle you will want to make sure to search for NMLs. Sometimes trigger points in the supraspinatus will refer pain down the outside of your arm to concentrate at your elbow on the lateral side. This pain will often feel like tennis elbow, or lateral epicondylitis. Or, more importantly, the referral pain from the supraspinatus can create secondary trigger points in the muscles that attach at your elbow, aggravating a chronic tennis elbow problem. So, if you have tennis elbow, make sure to carefully check out the supraspinatus muscle on the same side.

In figure 11.10 below, you can see that with the proper trigger point therapy tool, such as the FENIX Rehab System, you can easily get the right angle to specifically treat the supraspinatus. Here the tool is out on the lateral aspect of the supraspinatus, where its tendon begins. The juncture where the muscle meets the tendon is the most common place for trigger points to manifest in this muscle and cause shoulder pain. As always, make sure you fully stretch the myofascial tissues after doing trigger point therapy. In figure 11.11, the model demonstrates the proper way to stretch the supraspinatus muscle after trigger point therapy.

Figure 11.10

Trigger point therapy to left supraspinatus trigger points

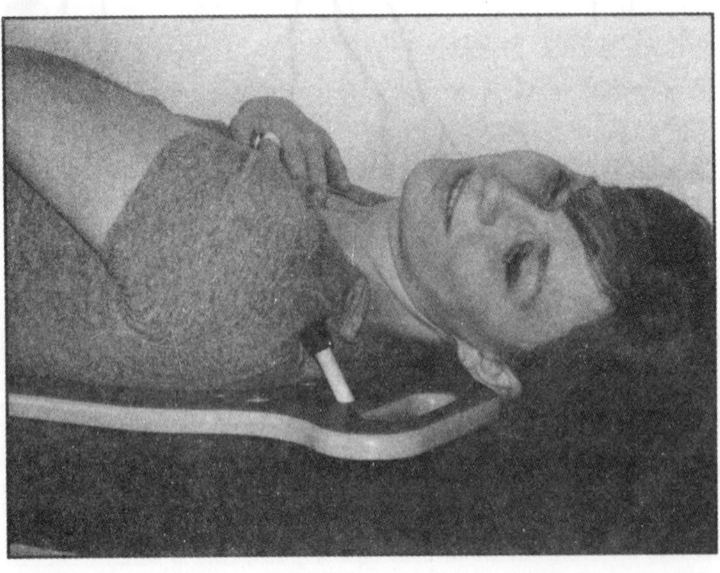

Figure 11.11

Supraspinatus stretch;
if muscle is too restricted,
use a rolled-up towel between hands

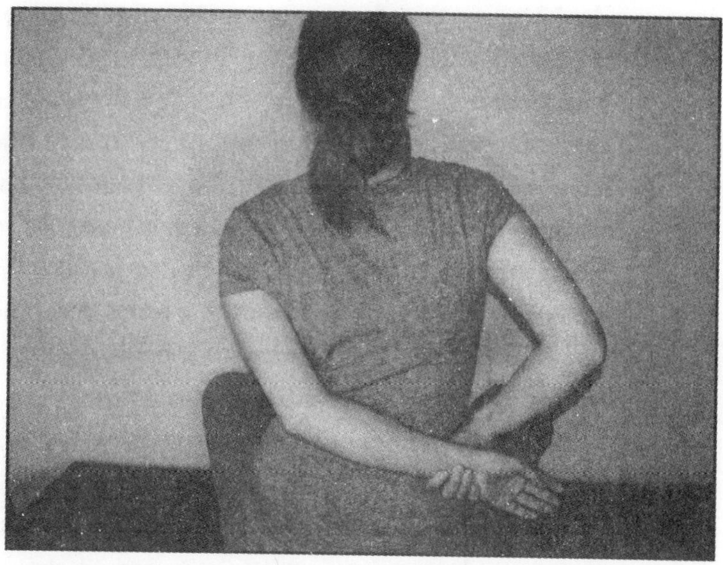

Trigger points in the supraspinatus can disturb your sleep at night when you attempt to lie on your side. Trigger points in the supraspinatus can also sometimes give you a snapping or clicking sound around the shoulder joint on movement. I have found that this frequently goes away when myofascial trigger points of the supraspinatus and infraspinatus are removed. Research has found that the supraspinatus muscle is one of the less frequently involved shoulder girdle muscles.[125] I rarely find the supraspinatus to act up on its own, but it is a muscle you may want to check after cleaning out other trigger points in the shoulder girdle muscles.

125 A. E. Sola, M. L. Rodenberger, and B. B. Getty, "Incidence of hypersensitive areas in posterior shoulder muscles," *Am J Phys Med* 34 (1955): 585–90.

Subscapularis Muscle: "My Arm Is Frozen" Muscle

This is a very special muscle, for many different reasons: (1) it's the last of the four rotator cuff muscles we will discuss, (2) it's extremely hard to get at and treat, (3) it plays a major role in shoulder problems, and (4) left untreated, it can cause a "frozen shoulder," a severe disorder that can make your life miserable. The subscapularis muscle is just as it sounds: *sub-*, meaning "under," and *-scapularis,* meaning "scapula," it is the muscle that covers the entire surface on the underside of your shoulder blade. From here, the subscapularis runs upward and out to insert at the anterior portion of the humeral head, the front top portion of your arm bone. This anatomical arrangement allows it to do two primary functions. It internally rotates your arm and adducts it, or brings it down, to your side. This motion is classically illustrated by twisting your arm around to get in your back pocket, a move that includes internal rotation and adduction of your arm. This movement is made possible by contracting the subscapularis, but it also stretches your infraspinatus muscle.

The complete opposite move stretching the subscapularis would be to brush or comb the hair on the back of your head, a move involving contraction of the infraspinatus and teres minor muscles, causing external rotation of the arm. Actually, the infraspinatus and teres minor work in concert with the subscapularis muscle to perform its second major function, keeping the head of your humerus, or arm bone, properly in the shallow glenohumeral joint of your shoulder (see figure 11.1 for details). This is a vital part of that scapulohumeral rhythm that we discussed earlier in this chapter.

In review, when you raise your arm to do virtually anything above the waist, muscles of the rotator cuff must keep the head of the humerus from being pulled up and hitting the bony roof of the shoulder joint. This bony roof is called the acromion process, and this is where the tendons and joint capsule can become pinched and damaged between it and the head of the humerus (see figure 11.1). This problem is called an impingement syndrome, and, as previously stated, research by Kalb and others has found that as much as 95% of shoulder pain comes from this impingement syndrome. The infraspinatus and teres minor muscles on the back of your scapula, and your subscapularis on the front of your shoulder blade, act as checkreins on each side of your humerus, keeping it from riding up and hitting against the acromion process. Please refer to figure 11.12 to help visualize the role of the subscapularis muscle in keeping the head of the humerus from hitting the acromion process.

Figure 11.12

Subscapularis trigger point locations, top, and pain referral pattern, bottom

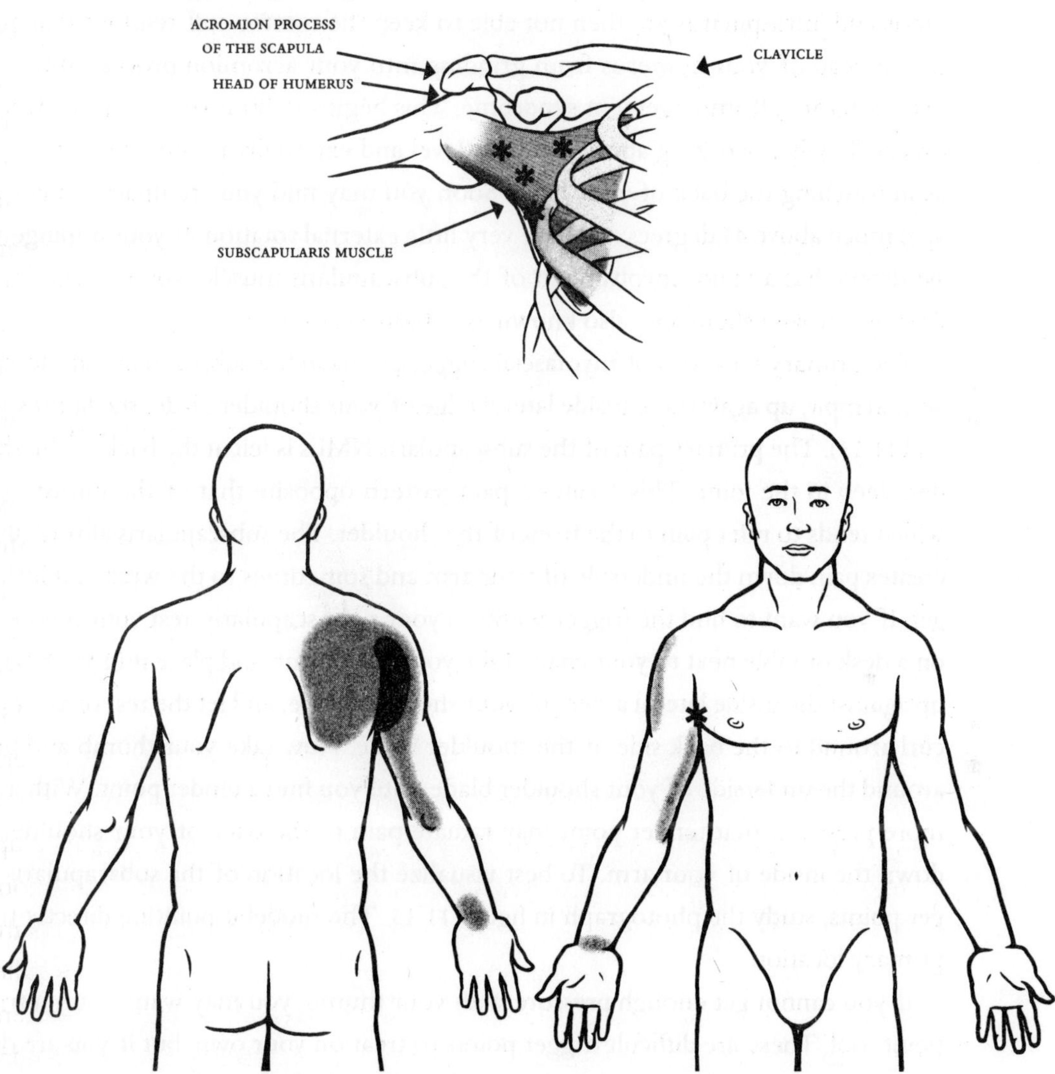

Through repetitive exertion, forceful overhead lifting, or acute injury, you can activate multiple myofascial trigger points in your subscapularis muscle, as well as the other rotator cuff muscles. These active NMLs will frequently cause the muscles to shorten and weaken, throwing off their normal function. This means that the subscapularis and infraspinatus are then not able to keep the rotator cuff tendons that attach to the head of your humerus from grinding into your acromion process, thus creating a rotator cuff impingement syndrome. This begins to limit your range of motion, especially when working above shoulder level and externally rotating your arm, such as in touching the back of your head. Soon you may find you are unable to get your arm much above 45 degrees and have very little external rotation. If your impingement syndrome has a major involvement of the subscapularis muscle, you can develop the dreaded "frozen shoulder," also known as adhesive capsulitis.

The primary locations of myofascial trigger points in the subscapularis are found in your armpit, up against the inside lateral edge of your shoulder blade (see figures 11.12 and 11.13). The primary pain of the subscapularis NMLs is felt at the back of the shoulder, deep in the joint. This creates a pain pattern opposite that of the infraspinatus, which tends to refer pain to the front of the shoulder. The subscapularis almost always creates pain down the underside of your arm and sometimes to the wrist and little finger. If you want to find the trigger points in your right scapularis, rest your right elbow on a desk or table next to your chair. Take your left thumb and place it in your armpit, up against the inside lateral aspect of your shoulder blade, and let the rest of your hand curl around to the back side of the shoulder blade. Now take your thumb and probe around the underside of your shoulder blade until you find a tender point. With a little more pressure, that tender point may radiate pain to the back of your shoulder and down the inside of your arm. To best visualize the location of the subscapularis trigger points, study the photograph in figure 11.13. The model is pointing directly to the primary location.

If you cannot get enough pressure with your thumb, you may want to try a trigger point tool. These are difficult trigger points to treat on your own, but if you are developing a frozen shoulder, this muscle must be released of all its trigger points by you or a therapist.[126] NMLs in this rotator cuff muscle can become quite stubborn, and it will

126 The FENIX Rehab System does an excellent job in reaching this trigger point, and the accompanying DVD shows step-by-step how to tackle this muscle.

need a great deal of repetitive trigger point therapy, followed by stretching, to heal this muscle over time. In figure 11.14 , the model demonstrates how easy it is to treat the subscapularis muscle with the FENIX Rehab System.

Again, it is always vital to stretch the myofascial tissue after applying trigger point therapy. In figure 11.15, the model shows how to specifically stretch the right subscapularis. In this demonstration, she is showing how an individual with adhesive capsulitis can utilize a rolled-up towel to assist in the stretching.

Figure 11.13

Finding the left subscapularis trigger point

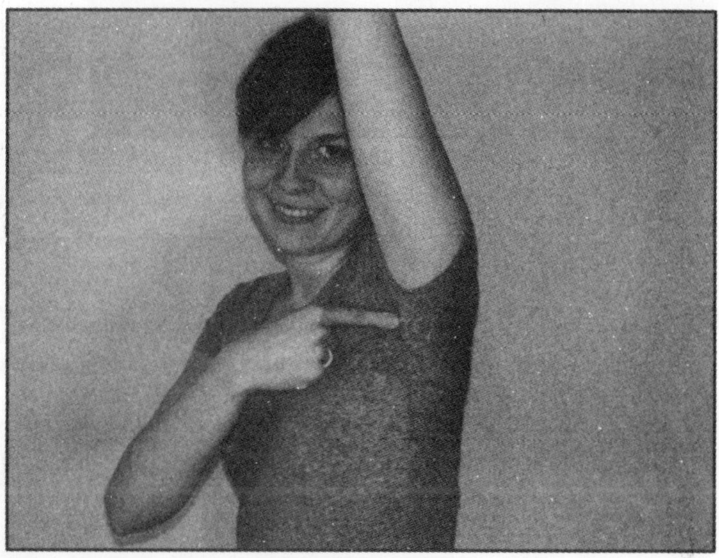

Figure 11.14

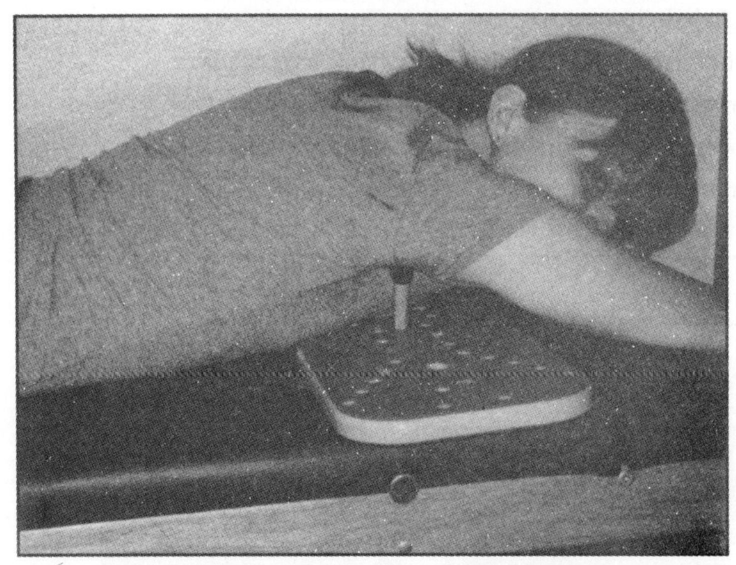

Self-administered trigger point therapy to the right subscapularis trigger points. Pressure is applied under the arm, up against the underside of the shoulder blade. If you have any questions on the location, always check with your doctor or therapist.

Figure 11.15

Right subscapularis stretch; use a towel if you can't grab other wrist

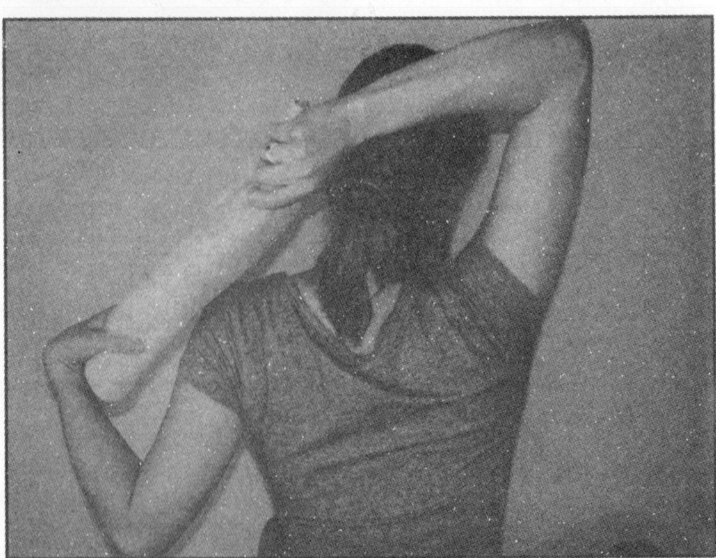

Case Study

Barbara was a 46-year-old schoolteacher who realized over a period of time that she was unable to brush her hair with her right arm. Thinking that it would clear up, she ignored it until she was unable to use her arm because of the pain and stiffness. By the time I saw her, she had developed a full-blown case of adhesive capsulitis of the right shoulder. This condition was making her life completely miserable and was interfering with her job. It was not until this point that she realized how much she used her shoulder throughout the day, such as writing on the whiteboard. She had previously seen an MD, who prescribed NSAIDs, cortisone injection, and physical therapy—however, without much progress.

Barbara fit the general pattern of idiopathic "frozen shoulder": individuals tend to be in their forties and are more likely to be female. On examination, I found that all of her shoulder girdle muscles were involved with multiple NMLs, causing tenderness, shortening, and weakening of these vital muscles. The muscle most involved and no doubt the instigator of her entire problem was her right subscapularis. By slowly working my way through the multiple trigger points within the subscapularis muscle and aggressively applying a passive stretch to it, we began to slowly increase her range of motion. This would have been impossible without her applying daily trigger point therapy at home to her subscapularis, pectoralis major, and also the infraspinatus muscle with a home-care trigger point therapy tool.

In "frozen shoulder," or adhesive capsulitis, because of its reactive inflammatory nature that leads to progressive fibrosis within the soft tissue, I usually find an underlying metabolic problem. Because of this and her complaints of irritable-bowel-like symptoms, it made me suspect the possibility of intestinal dysbiosis. A urinary organic acid profile was done to check for abnormal overgrowth of an unfavorable microflora in her small intestine. Her test results showed high levels of indican in her urine, which is a good indication of intestinal bacterial overgrowth. She also had a presence of p-hydroxyphenylacetate in her urine, which is a strong indication of clostridium, or other anaerobic bacteria, as a source of dysbiosis. When we treated her gut by removing the dysbiosis and inoculating her bowel with beneficial bacteria, not only did her irritable-bowel-like symptoms vanish, but so did many of her other health problems, such as recurring headaches, muscle aches, and chronic fatigue. The details of treating dysbiosis will be covered in greater detail in chapter 16.

12

Nagging Mid-Back Pain and the Great Entrappers

After examining the four rotator cuff muscles and the role they play in chronic shoulder pain problems, we now turn our attention to that all-too-common nemesis, nagging mid- and upper-back pain. Perhaps you have experienced that sensation of carrying the world around on your shoulders—that nagging, irritating ache that will not go away. Some of the most important muscles involved in this chronic pain syndrome are the four medial shoulder blade stabilizing muscles, discussed in chapter 11. Recall that the four lateral rotator cuff muscles—the infraspinatus, teres minor, supraspinatus, and subscapularis—originate on the scapula and insert on the head of the humerus, and that 9 times out of 10, shoulder pain problems arise from impingement of the tendons of these four muscles.

Using the shoulder blade as their base, these four rotator cuff muscles pull on your humerus to move your arm in various directions. However, to be able to perform this function properly, your shoulder blade must be held dynamically stable as a platform for these four rotator cuff muscles..Acting as a platform for your rotator cuff muscles allows the muscles to move your shoulder joint through all its planes of motion. Complicating this is the fact that your shoulder blade must also move and rotate in a controlled manner as you raise your arm. This again is the scapulohumeral rhythm discussed earlier. As the shoulder blade is rotated on your rib cage, the muscles that perform this complicated and demanding function of dynamic stability and controlled mobility are the rhomboids, levator scapula, trapezius, and serratus anterior. Because of the demand placed on these four scapula-stabilizing muscles, they can develop severe, nagging myofascial pain disorders. A common example would be experiencing severe mid-back and neck pain while working at your desk or sitting at your computer.

Rhomboids: The Midbackache Muscle

The paired rhomboid muscles on each side of your backbone attach to the bottom vertebra in your neck and run down to the middle of the thoracic spine; from there, they run laterally to attach to the medial, or inside, border of your shoulder blade. By contracting the rhomboids, you pull your scapula towards your mid-back; however, their major role is to stabilize and control the rotation and movement of your shoulder blades. Because of the angle of its muscle fibers, when a rhomboid is contracted, it turns your shoulder joint (the glenoid fossa) and the acromion process downward, towards the humeral head and the rotator cuff tendons attached there. Recall from chapter 11 (see figure 11.2, p. 165, for illustration of rhomboid muscle and its pull) that the impingement syndrome is a primary factor in about 95% of shoulder pain problems, and the underlying cause of this is the pinching of the rotator cuff tendons between the head of the humerus and the acromion process.

Here is the important point: if your rhomboid muscle becomes shortened and stiff because of multiple trigger points, when you raise your arm the rhomboid does not allow the acromion process of your shoulder blade to move out of the way of the elevating humerus. This causes the tendons of the rotator cuff and bursa to become pinched or caught between the head of the humerus and the acromion process, causing inflammation, pain, and eventually degenerative changes in your shoulder.

This rhomboid myofascial imbalance is complicated, for two reasons. First, trigger points in the rhomboid muscle do not refer pain into your shoulder joint and therefore often go undetected in shoulder joint problems. Rhomboid trigger points cause a chronic ache in the mid-back and along the border of the shoulder blade. The second factor that complicates this shoulder joint problem is that myofascial trigger points in the rhomboid muscles generally are not obvious. They are usually difficult to detect until you have removed trigger points in other shoulder girdle muscles, such as the infraspinatus, levator scapula, and trapezius.

The primary trigger points of the rhomboid muscle can be found right along the medial border of your shoulder blade, along line E, as shown in figure 12.1. From the referral pattern, you can see how they can cause you a nagging mid-back ache.

Figure 12.1

Rhomboid muscle trigger point locations and symptom referral patterns

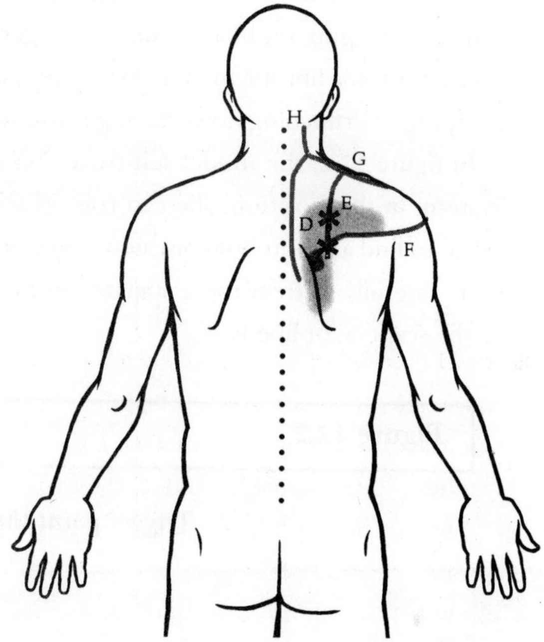

These are trigger points that are virtually impossible for you to palpate yourself, but once you apply pressure to them with a trigger point tool they will definitely let you know they are there. They usually can be found by leaning the inside border of your shoulder blade against a tennis or golf ball until a tender spot is discovered. Trigger points in the rhomboid alter shoulder movement, creating an impingement syndrome and/or a nagging mid-back pain that is generally not relieved by rest. Also, the presence of chronic fibrotic myofascial trigger points in the rhomboids sometimes creates a snapping or crunching noise during movement of your shoulder blade.

In figure 12.2, the model self-treats her rhomboid muscle with the FENIX Rehab System. In this position, she can roll off the therapeutic digit to move up and down line E to find all rhomboid or mid-trapezius trigger points in the area. Or she can move more laterally to treat the associated infraspinatus trigger points found in the middle of the scapula, or line F.

Figure 12.2

Trigger point therapy for rhomboid muscle

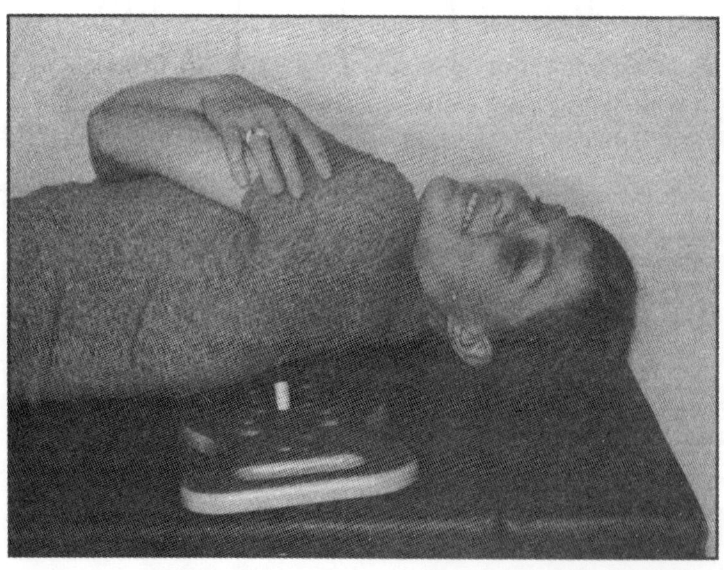

Rounded Shoulders, Mid-back Pain, and the Pectoralis/Rhomboid Relationship

To remove the rhomboid myofascial trigger points, you may find you have to remove the NMLs in your infraspinatus first. This is very important because myofascial trigger points in the infraspinatus muscle will actually refer pain into the rhomboids and cause secondary trigger points in them. Also, multiple trigger points in the infraspinatus shorten the muscle, pulling your shoulder blade away from your mid-back, stressing the rhomboid muscle and causing NMLs to form.

Another factor that comes into play here is the shortening of the chest muscles, the pectoralis major and minor, adding a pulling stress to the rhomboid muscles in your mid-back. This can all lead to a rounded shoulder problem, which can develop from poor posture, sitting bent over at a desk, or from weight lifting and the overdevelopment of the pectoralis muscles. I have seen numerous individuals who had lived for years with chronic, nagging mid-back pain, and almost always their myofascial problem had been missed.

To recap, if you have chronic mid-back pain that just will not go away, check for a rounded shoulder posture. If this is present, make sure you remove all trigger points from the infraspinatus muscle on your shoulder blade and the muscles at the front of your shoulder, the pectoralis minor and major muscles. With a rounded shoulder posture, your pectoralis muscles have shortened, and before you can lengthen them you must remove any NMLs that are present. After removing the trigger points, begin stretches for your shortened pectoralis muscles in your chest, as described in the next section.

Case Study

When John first came in to see me, he looked and sounded as if he was carrying the world on his shoulders. John was a 38-year-old desk worker who reported a bilateral deep ache in his mid-back, especially on his right side. This problem had gone on for years. He had tried various means to alleviate his pain, such as NSAIDs, rehab exercises, new mattresses, different pillows, a very expensive vibrating chair, and even some psychotherapy after becoming convinced that the pain was all in his head. His frustration drove him in to see me because I was an acupuncturist and he was now ready to try anything. After doing a comprehensive neurological, orthopedic, and myofascial examination, I found the source of his problem.

John's pain-causing primary myofascial trigger points were located deep in his rhomboid muscles and the deep muscles around his spine, the multifidi and rotator. Part of the cause for this was a shortening of his chest muscles, specifically the pectoralis major. The pectoralis muscles had shortened through years of being hunched over at a desk, and this rounded shoulder and mid-back posture put a great deal of strain on his rhomboid and thoracic paraspinal muscles. Also, there were chronic NMLs in his infraspinatus muscle, and when they were examined they referred pain back into his rhomboid muscle area. Because of the forward pull on the shoulders by the shortening of his pectoralis major chest muscles, there was also a chronic strain on his rhomboid muscles.

With intensive bilateral trigger point therapy to the rhomboid muscles and the muscles around his thoracic spine, John began to feel immediate relief. He soon realized, however, that complete recovery could not be gained until he removed the active trigger points in his infraspinatus muscle in his shoulder blades and those of the front of the shoulder in his pectoralis muscles. Once the trigger points began to lessen in his chest muscles, aggressive stretching and postural training allowed him to bring his shoulders back and take strain off his mid-back. This postural change was also made possible through strengthening his infraspinatus and rhomboid muscles to help support a more neutral position with his shoulders.

John was quite frustrated and angry that he had suffered for years with this pain. He also wondered why he had been told for years to keep taking different NSAIDs when they were damaging his gastrointestinal tract. This eventually caused him to take another drug for his GERD, or gastroesophageal reflux disorder. John was also quite upset when he learned that recent studies indicated a possible connection between long-term NSAID use and hypertension. He had started taking a blood pressure medication over the last year and was now taking Viagra because of the side effects of sexual dysfunction from the antihypertensive drug. After years of clinical practice, seeing thousands of patients who had suffered for years with myofascial pain or muscle and joint pain problems, I know John's story to be the rule and not the exception. The vicious cycle of myofascial pain from NMLs leading to reliance on NSAIDs (e.g., ibuprofen) to get through the day, leading to drug side effects needing to be treated with other medications, is an all-too-common story. This is not to fault modern medicine, but how it is utilized. Modern medicine is best at emergency medicine and disease care when there is a life-threatening pathology. But when symptoms are caused by dysfunction and not pathology, look to wellness care.

Pectoralis Minor and Major Muscles

In regards to the function of your shoulder girdle complex, the pectoralis major and minor muscles play a vital role. These two muscles, as just described, greatly affect your posture and can even affect your breathing. Additionally, these muscles often cause symptoms of chest pain that can be mistaken for lung and heart problems. However, with these symptoms, never self-diagnose; make sure a competent doctor rules out any possibility of pathology in these vital organs.

The large pectoralis major runs from the middle bone of your chest, or sternum, over to your humerus, and when it contracts, it pulls your arm across your chest and internally rotates it. This action is opposite to that of your infraspinatus, which runs from the back of your shoulder blade out to your humerus, draws your arm away from your chest, and externally rotates it. Therefore, you can see that if you have trigger points shortening the pectoralis major in front, the result can cause irritation to your shoulder girdle complex, specifically as it opposes the infraspinatus. Please recall that the infraspinatus is one of the most commonly involved muscles in shoulder joint pain. In order to correct a chronic shoulder joint problem, it is often helpful to remove trigger points at the front of your chest in the pectoralis major, and stretch it out to relieve pressure on the infraspinatus and rhomboids.

Common Pectoralis Symptoms: What to Look Out For

Myofascial trigger points in these two pectoralis muscles tend to cause pain over your chest, anterior shoulder, and sometimes down the inside of your forearm to the ring and little fingers. You can imagine how disconcerting this can be when the myofascial trigger points are in the left pectoralis muscles over your heart. These chest wall pains often make individuals feel as if they are having a heart attack. In fact, numerous studies have shown that the intensity, quality, and distribution of pain from trigger points in these anterior chest muscles can mimic true cardiac pain in almost every detail.[127] Of course, anytime you have chest pains, you must rule out any possibility of a cardiac problem. Furthermore, having severe myofascial trigger points in these chest wall muscles does not exclude the possibility of an underlying cardiac disease, so always check it out! As far back as 1936, hypersensitive spots in the muscles of the chest were found to be responsible for pain that persisted following an acute heart attack.[128]

These chest wall muscles on the front aspect of your shoulder can create medial elbow pain problems and also produce symptoms mistaken for carpal tunnel. These anterior shoulder muscles have been known to cause such severe numbness in the forearm hand and fingers that they have contributed to the misdiagnosis of carpal tunnel syndrome. I have seen many patients who have had carpal tunnel surgery, some who even had multiple surgeries, when in reality they had myofascial pain syndrome with an entrapment of the nerves higher up. These symptoms generally come primarily from the small pectoralis minor underneath the larger pectoralis major muscle. The pectoralis minor muscle runs from your second, third, and fourth ribs up to the bony process of your scapula called the coracoid process (see figure 12.4). The pectoralis minor is not a major scapula stabilizer, but because of its attachment to your shoulder blade's coracoid process, it does work at times to help stabilize it.

If you reach up to the front of your right shoulder with your left hand and feel right below the outer end of your collarbone, you will palpate the coracoid process (as seen in figure 12.4). This part of your shoulder blade protrudes like a bony thumb under

127 T. J. Reeves and T. R. Harrison, "Diagnostic and therapeutic value of the reproduction of chest pain," *Arch Intern Med* 91, no. 5 (1953): 8–20. S. H. Rinzler, *Cardiac Pain* (Springfield, Illinois: Charles C. Thomas, 1951).

128 J. Edeiken and C. C. Wolferth, "Persistent pain in the shoulder region following myocardial infarction," *Am J Med Sci* 191 (1936): 201–10.

the skin on the front of your shoulder joint. Because the coracoid process is attached to your shoulder blade, when the pectoralis minor contracts it pulls the shoulder blade forward and down if it is not countered by other muscles, such as the rhomboid. This is how a short, tight pectoralis minor can put a strain on your rhomboid muscles in your mid-back. Trigger points can shorten the pectoralis minor muscle, pulling your shoulder forward and down, causing a rounded and slumped shoulder posture. If you have a shortened pectoralis minor and major causing this round shoulder problem, generally you will not be able to correct your posture until these myofascial trigger points are removed. As you release the myofascial trigger points in the pectoralis major and minor, you can begin to stretch these muscles out to improve your posture.

Pectoralis Minor Syndrome: Entrapping Nerves and Vessels

The coracoid process and the pectoralis minor tendon attaching to it create a tunnel through which the nerves and blood vessels of your upper extremity travel. Because of this, the pectoralis minor muscle can create troubling neurological and vascular problems in your forearm, wrist, and hand.[129] Again, this is commonly misdiagnosed as, or can complicate, carpal tunnel syndrome. The pectoralis minor creates these problems by entrapping nerves and blood vessels exiting underneath it, similar to how the piriformis muscle in your pelvis creates the problematic piriformis syndrome. You tighten the pectoralis minor over the tunnel by moving your arm away from your chest and externally rotating it, for example, when combing or brushing the back of your head. When the pectoralis minor is shortened by myofascial trigger points, this motion can compress the exiting axillary artery and brachial nerve plexus under the taut muscle, making arm symptoms of numbness, pain, and tingling worse. Many individuals notice they have a problem when they work with something above their heads or fall asleep with their arms over their heads.

Symptoms can vary, depending on which parts of the brachial nerve plexus are compressed. Commonly, you get severe numbness and abnormal sensations in the fourth and fifth digits of your hand when the medial part of your brachial plexus is compressed by the pectoralis minor. This pectoralis minor syndrome can also cause

129 D. Rubin, "An approach to the management of myofascial trigger point syndromes," *Arch Phys Med Rehabil* 62 (1981): 107–10.

severe numbness and abnormal sensations in the lateral aspects of your forearm, palm, and first three digits of your hand. These symptoms of numbness and tingling in the palm and first three fingers duplicate the symptoms found in carpal tunnel syndrome. There may also be some swelling in the carpal tunnel of your wrist, exacerbated by the entrapment of the brachial plexus by the pectoralis minor. This swelling may be reduced when the pectoralis minor is released. I found that patients many times can bypass carpal tunnel surgery when they improve their diets, take specific herbs to lessen the swelling, adopt better work posture, and go through a specific manual therapy program for the upper extremity and cervical spine. This manual therapy could include trigger point therapy, stretching and strengthening the involved muscles, and manipulation of the involved joints.

Finding and Treating Pectoralis Trigger Points

In most individuals, the pectoralis muscles tend to be quite tender, especially with the presence of myofascial trigger points. Because of the thin structure of the pectoralis muscles, the NMLs present usually do not need a great deal of pressure to deactivate them, so go easy. Usually you can reach across with the opposite fingertips and pressure-treat the trigger points that are present. In men, the pectoralis major is usually quite easy to find right underneath the skin. In women, the upper half is usually easily palpated, whereas the lower half of the pectoralis major muscle is covered by the breast tissue, which must be gently moved aside to locate any NMLs. The pectoralis minor is underneath the upper half of the pectoralis major muscle (see figures 12.3 and 12.4 for details).

Figure 12.3

Typical trigger point locations in the pectoralis major and symptom referral patterns

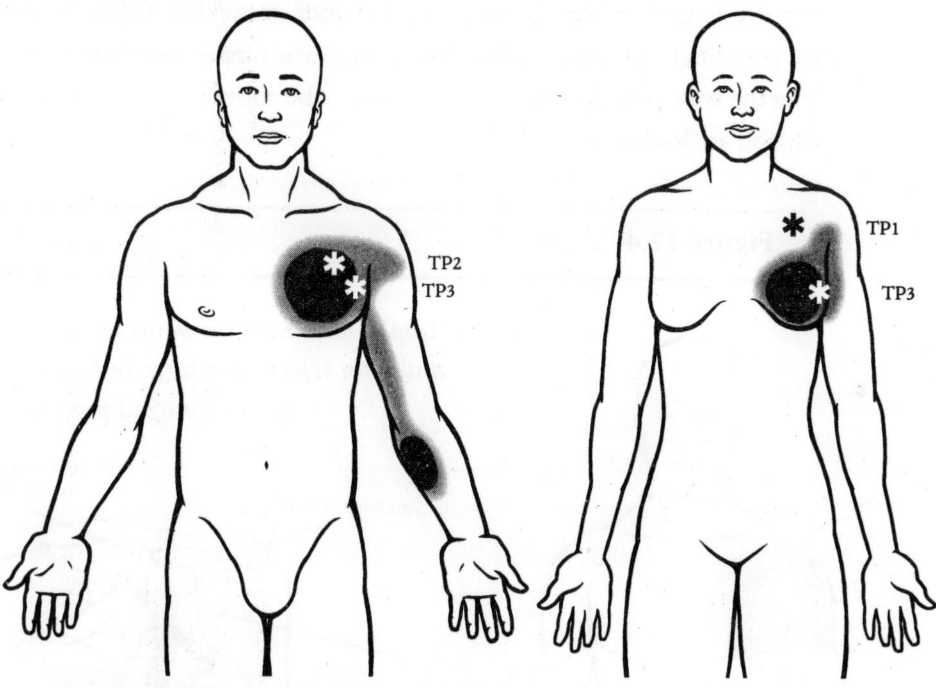

The three bands of the pectoralis major and their primary trigger points

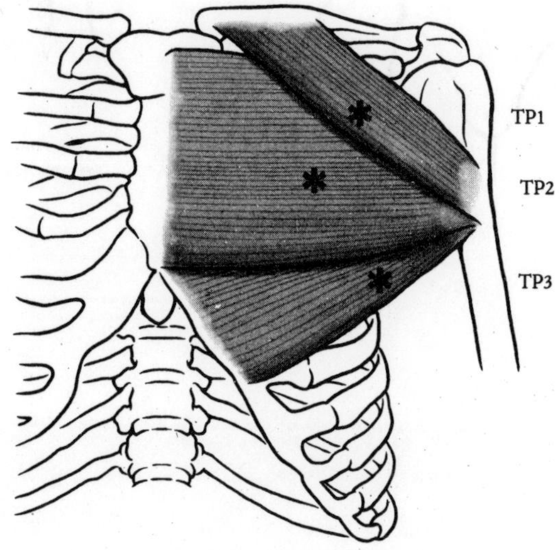

To locate trigger points in your right pectoralis minor muscle, take your left hand and follow your collarbone out laterally to near its end. Just below the lateral end of your collarbone on the front of your shoulder is the coracoid process of your shoulder blade; see figure 12.4. This was found earlier in the chapter and feels like a large marble or protruding, thumblike bony projection under your skin. From the coracoid process, take your fingertips diagonally down towards the nipple, searching out for tender spots along the way. Once you find a tender spot, a bit more pressure may create the referral pain you are looking for.

Figure 12.4

Pectoralis minor trigger point location and pain referral pattern; in figure, X marks coracoid process

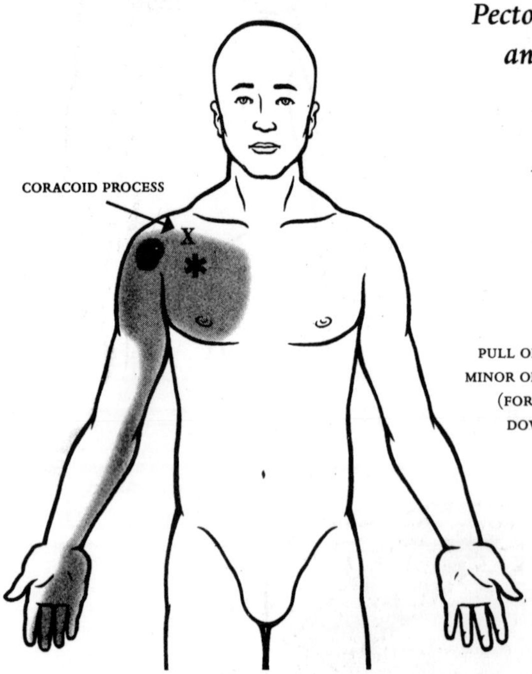

CORACOID PROCESS

X

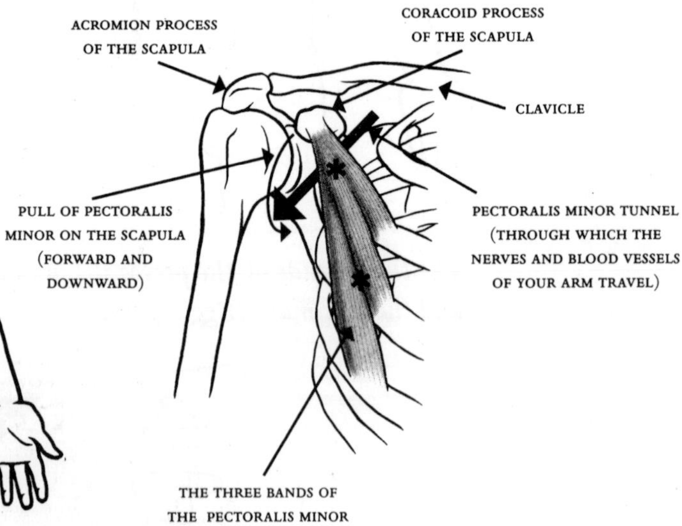

ACROMION PROCESS OF THE SCAPULA

CORACOID PROCESS OF THE SCAPULA

CLAVICLE

PULL OF PECTORALIS MINOR ON THE SCAPULA (FORWARD AND DOWNWARD)

PECTORALIS MINOR TUNNEL (THROUGH WHICH THE NERVES AND BLOOD VESSELS OF YOUR ARM TRAVEL)

THE THREE BANDS OF THE PECTORALIS MINOR

Figure 12.5

Self-administered trigger point therapy to pectoralis muscle

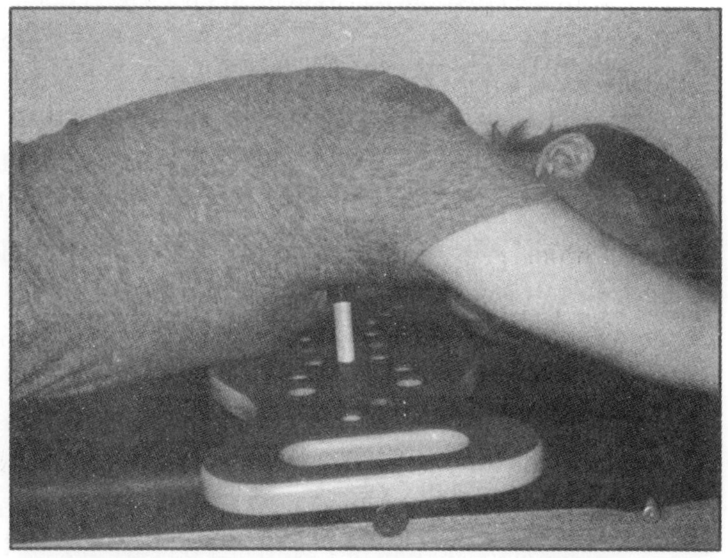

When palpating this area, generally the first muscle tenderness you will feel is the pectoralis minor muscle, which attaches to this coracoid process and lays underneath the edge of the pectoralis major. If you have trigger points here, you will experience referral pain to your shoulder and down the inside of your arm to your hands and fingers, as indicated in figure 12.4. If you have trouble with numbness and tingling in your forearm, hand, and fingers, you may find that this duplicates some of your symptoms. This muscle often works in concert with the scalene muscles in your neck, which can also pinch vital nerves and vessels going down your arm. The location of the scalene muscles and their referral pattern can easily be seen in figure 12.6.

As you continue to move diagonally down from the coracoid process towards your nipple, you will come across other tender spots located in the pectoralis major muscle right underneath your skin. These trigger points can be found throughout the pectoralis major muscle from your upper humerus to your sternum. These NMLs tend to concentrate pain right in the area of your chest; however, these trigger points may also refer pain into your shoulder and down into the medial aspect of your forearm and hand (see figure 12.3 for details of location and referral patterns of the pectoralis major). Again, both pectoralis muscles can usually be deactivated by reaching across with your opposite hand and applying fingertip pressure to the muscles.

In figure 12.5, the model is applying trigger point therapy to the pectoralis muscle with the FENIX Rehab System. With a trigger point tool, it is less fatiguing to self-treat multiple trigger points, but you must go very easy and use light pressure because the muscle is quite thin and easily bruised.

Scalene Muscles: The Great Entrapment

Chronic pain and numbness throughout the shoulder and upper extremity quite frequently comes from myofascial trigger points in the scalene muscles.[130] The three scalene muscles start at the top of your first rib and run up to attach to the vertebrae of your neck. Situated like this, they can either flex your neck or lift up on your rib cage to assist with breathing. Through a small gap between the anterior and middle scalene runs the brachial plexus, containing the vital nerves and blood vessels of your arm, forearm, hand, and fingers. Please refer to the diagram of the three scalene muscles found at the bottom of Figure 11.1 on page 162.

As with all muscles, when trigger points are present, they tend to tighten and shorten the scalene muscles. Because of their anatomical arrangement, when myofascial trigger points are present in the scalene muscles, they can literally squeeze or pinch the neurovascular bundle traveling between them, causing a neurovascular entrapment. This entrapment of the nerves and blood vessels will disturb the nerve and blood flow down through your upper extremity, causing swelling, pain, tingling, numbness, and burning sensations in your arm and hand.[131] This assortment of symptoms caused by this compression of the nerves and vessels exiting your neck and going down your arm is properly diagnosed as a thoracic outlet syndrome.

Many times, patients have come to me with the diagnosis of carpal tunnel, and some have even had one or more surgeries on their wrist. However, after a complete workup, they have been found to have a thoracic outlet syndrome. Often these patients also have a pectoralis minor syndrome in conjunction with the scalene muscles' involvement, and only very minor swelling in their carpal tunnels. Because these other myofascial syndromes and complicating metabolic factors were ignored, their surgeries were usually a failure and their symptoms were not relieved.

---

130 C. Long, "Myofascial pain syndromes: part two; syndromes of the head, neck and shoulder girdle," *Henry Ford Hosp Med Bull* 4, 1 (March 1956): 22–28.

131 Rubin, "An approach," 107–10.

Figure 12.6

Scalene trigger point location and symptom referral patterns

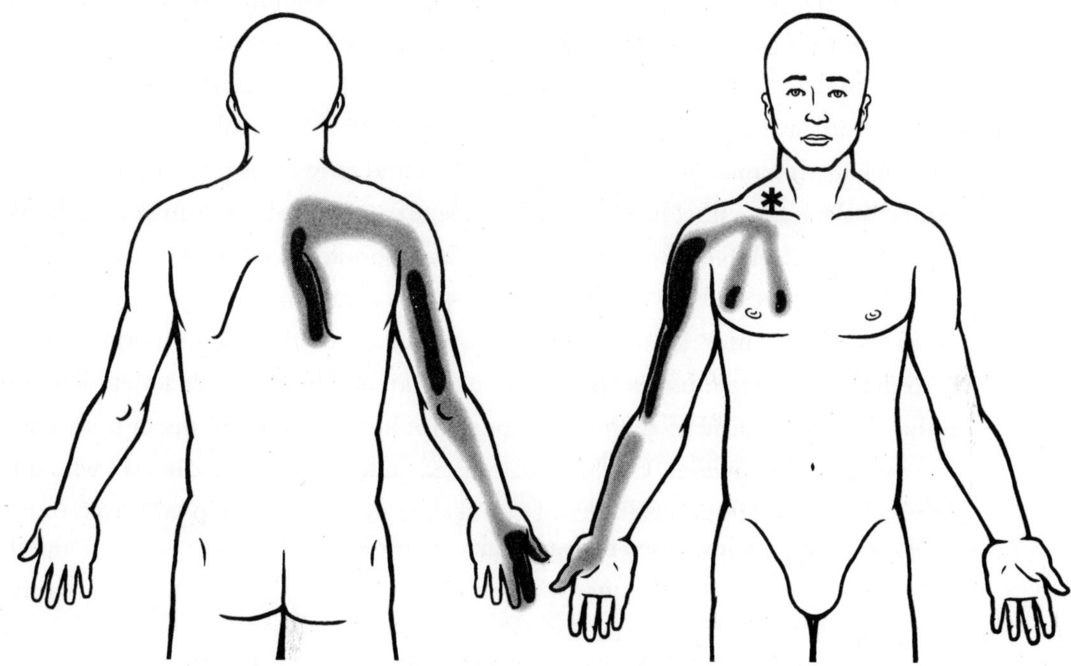

One thing I emphasize to doctors that I teach is that a patient is allowed to have more than one thing wrong. The pectoralis minor syndrome and the scalene muscles entrapment syndrome frequently go hand in hand, because scalene muscles will cause satellite, or secondary, trigger points in the pectoralis minor muscle. Also, the same underlying postural factors that promote trigger points in the scalene muscles also activate NMLs in the pectoralis minor. Therefore, if you are suffering with the above-described symptoms of a thoracic outlet or pectoralis minor syndrome, find a clinician or therapist who understands these myofascial syndromes.

To find the scalene muscles on your right side, reach across your chest with your left hand to the inside, or medial, half of your collarbone. This part of the clavicle is found from where it attaches to the sternum and to the collarbone's middle portion. Right above this section of your collarbone, with your middle finger you will find the muscular bands of your anterior and medial scalene muscles (see ✱ in figure 12.6).

With a little pressure, you may find tenderness and referral pain down your arm, hand, and fingers (repeat for the left side using your right hand). This is especially true if you suffer from the symptoms of numbness and tingling in your arm and hand at night when you sleep. One other common referral pattern often overlooked is pain referred into the rhomboid muscle region along the shoulder blade border. I have found many patients with chronic mid-back pain to have myofascial trigger points in the scalene that refer pain right to where their nagging midbackache resides.

So, if you have unresolved issues in the upper extremity involving pain, numbness, and tingling, or a midbackache that no one can find answers for, make sure you check out the scalene muscles. I have found the scalene muscles to be a complicating factor in a very high percentage of my patients who have shoulder and upper extremity symptoms. Part of their therapy is self-treatment with a gentle pressure therapy and stretching to the scalene muscles to help release and reeducate these all-important muscles. Even though scalene muscles are difficult to self-treat, I have included their description in this chapter because of their vast importance in these types of upper body chronic pain syndromes. However, I highly recommend finding a qualified clinician who understands these myofascial disorders of the scalene muscles to help you overcome the challenge of these entrapment syndromes.

Case Study

Susan came into my clinic almost two years after a motor vehicle accident (MVA) where she sustained a severe whiplash injury to her cervical spine. Since her accident, she had been through quite an ordeal; she had suffered with the usual neck pain and headaches, but she also had severe pain and numbness into her forearm and hand. Because of her symptoms, her orthopedist suspected a herniated disc, and so she had CT scans and MRIs to try to locate the lesion for surgery. A cervical disc herniation can put pressure on the nerve root, causing pain down the arm; however, no disc herniation was found to account for her forearm and hand symptoms. Despite all the NSAID therapy, sleep medications, and antidepressants, sleep and work continued to be difficult because of the unrelenting pain and numbness in her forearm and hand—this besides the chronic neck pain and headaches.

Susan then went through a failed carpal tunnel surgery, which is not all that uncommon in cases such as this where there may be some slight swelling within the carpal tunnel. But usually this swelling is only secondary to other factors and is not the real source for the forearm and hand symptoms. I have seen several patients who not only had one failed carpal tunnel surgery but had it repeated, and still the symptoms remained. When Susan came in to see me her surgeon was considering doing carpal tunnel surgery on her other wrist because her symptoms had become bilateral. Because the first surgery on the first wrist was such a failure, Susan became desperate and decided to look beyond the standard medical approach.

After a complete myofascial, orthopedic, and neurological exam, I determined that her symptoms in the forearm and hand were not coming from her carpal tunnel. What I did discover was that Susan had a very common problem that is rarely discovered by traditional modern medicine; she had severe scalenus anticus syndrome, which had become bilateral. Because of her whiplash injury, when her neck was forcefully snapped backwards, the anterior muscles of her cervical spine were injured. This MVA injury caused severe NMLs to form into her scalene muscles, specifically the anterior scalene, causing tenderness and referral pain down her lateral forearm to the thumb and index finger. As you can see in figure 12.6, the scalene muscles commonly refer pain into the arm, forearm, and hand. But also many times the scalene muscles will refer pain in the mid-back, along the border of the shoulder blade, which was yet another symptom that plagued Susan.

Of course, NMLs in the scalene muscles cause them to tighten and shorten. When this happens in the anterior and middle scalene muscles, it can cause a physical entrapment of the nerves and arteries exiting between them and running down the arm. The entrapment syndrome was the source of Susan's numbness and tingling in her arm. This entrapment can also obstruct venous and lymphatic flow, causing slight swelling in the hands. This may possibly account for the mild swelling found in the wrist that was mistaken for the primary source of her symptoms; luckily she only had one unnecessary surgery. I'm happy to report that with trigger point therapy and active stretching on Susan's part to the scalene muscles, she was able to end her bilateral symptoms of the forearm and hand. Commonly associated with these scalene trigger points are trigger points in the sternocleidomastoid muscle (SCM), especially in cases of whiplash injury. The SCM muscle commonly creates severe headaches up into the forehead, and by Susan removing these trigger points, her headaches ceased.

13

Overcoming Upper Back, Neck, and Chronic Head Pain

We have become a society of individuals who constantly traumatize their cervical spines, so it's not surprising that more and more people are suffering with chronic myofasçial neck pain and headaches. This trauma to our neck muscles has two major causes. First, many of us sit working at desks and/or computer terminals all day. This position causes individuals to sit for long periods of time with their necks in a slightly bent forward, flexed position.

To comprehend the stress this places on your posterior neck muscles, imagine holding a twelve-pound bowling ball upright in your hand in a slightly bent forward, flexed position. It would not be long before you dropped the ball from pain and fatigue. As we sit at our desks working, our muscles along the backs of our necks are constantly straining to keep our heads in a slightly bent forward position. As any muscles will under continued stress, over time our neck muscles develop myofascial trigger points that cause us chronic neck pain, stiffness, and headaches. How prone you are to the development of this syndrome depends on your own physiology, based on your genetics, diet, and lifestyle.

The second form of trauma that is common to neck muscles in our modern society is acute whiplash injury from automobile accidents or slip/fall injuries. The acute force on your neck muscles from these incidents will cause myofascial trigger points to form, causing myofascial pain syndromes of the neck and/or chronic headaches. To understand the small amount of force needed to injure the neck, again imagine holding a twelve-pound bowling ball upright in your hand, but this time in a car traveling only thirty miles an hour. Then think of coming to an immediate stop; imagine how much force would be placed on your muscles trying to keep the bowling ball from flying forward. This is why even small accidents can produce severe and chronic injuries to your neck.

There are a wide variety of physical, physiological, and environmental factors involved in the cause of chronic neck pain and/or headaches. However, a small percentage of headaches and even neck pain can be caused by dangerous pathological processes or diseases (e.g., tumors, infections, etc.). Because of this, anyone with headaches and/or neck pain must have a proper diagnostic workup by a competent healthcare professional before beginning any home-care program!

Stressed Scapula Stabilizers Equals Neck Pain and Headaches

Moving up the inside, or medial, border of your shoulder blade, we leave behind the middle and lower shoulder blade stabilizers, such as the rhomboid and lower trapezius, and find the two most commonly painful muscles in your body: the levator scapula and upper trapezius muscles; see figure 11.2 for details. These two upper shoulder blade stabilizers are under constant postural stress, caught between keeping your head on your shoulders and maintaining the dynamic stability of your scapula. Because of this, the levator scapula and upper trapezius are the most common muscles to contain chronic myofascial trigger points. In a clinical study of the neck and shoulder girdle, it was found that the most common, pain-causing myofascial trigger points were found in the levator scapula.[132] In another study of 200 normal young adults, hidden or latent NMLs were found to be most common in the upper trapezius and levator scapula muscles.[133] So, if you have chronic pain at the base of your neck or pain that runs up the back of your neck to your head, then you need to examine these muscles for trigger points. For details on trigger point location and pain referral patterns, see figure 13.1, diagram B.

132 A. E. Sola and J. H. Kuitert, "Myofascial trigger point pain in the neck and shoulder girdle," *Northwest Med* 54 (1955): 980–84.

133 Sola, Rodenberger, and Getty, "Incidence of hypersensitive areas," 585–90.

Figure 13.1

A: Location of the levator scapula muscle and its primary trigger points

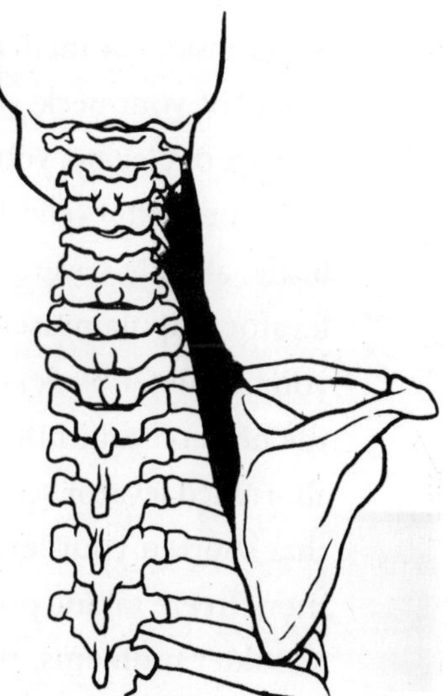

B: Trigger point locations and symptom referral pattern of the levator scapula muscle

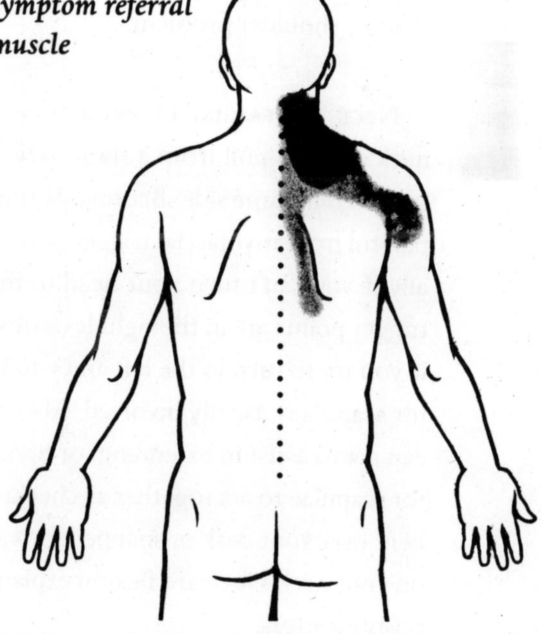

Levator Scapula: The Stiff Neck–Bad Shoulder Muscle

Shoulder Myofascial Dysfunction—The levator scapula muscle starts out at the upper inside, or medial, corner of your shoulder blade and runs up to the top four vertebrae of your neck. (For anatomical details, see figure 13.1.) This gives it the ability to pull up, or elevate, your shoulder blade and also act as an upper scapula stabilizer, hence its name *levator* (elevate) scapula. Because of the complex function of your shoulder blade, already covered in chapters 11 and 12, this places a great deal of stress on your levator scapula muscle. When the levator scapula pulls on the upper inside corner of your shoulder blade, causing it to rotate, it forces the acromion process down towards the head of your humerus and the rotator cuff tendons. This explains why a tight and shortened levator scapula can aggravate a rotator cuff syndrome. Releasing the NMLs that shorten your levator scapula can often help allow your shoulder blade to rotate more freely, taking pressure off your rotator cuff impingement. So, if you have chronic shoulder problems, this is one muscle that you want to check out after releasing the rotator cuff muscles, such as the infraspinatus and subscapularis, as described in chapter 11. This is especially true when you have chronic neck pain and stiffness with your chronic shoulder problem.

Neck Myofascial Dysfunction—The levator scapula muscle on one side of your neck also can pull from a stationary, stabilized shoulder blade and cause your neck to turn to that same side. Because of this, when the levator scapula shortens and becomes painful from myofascial trigger points, it can create a severe stiff and painful neck. Usually if you can't turn your head to the right and your neck is painful on the right, the trigger points are in the right levator scapula, as indicated in figure 13.1. And vice versa: if you try to turn to the left and you have pain and restriction on the left, your left levator scapula is usually involved. Also, the levator scapulae acting together on both sides can act to assist in extending, or bending, your neck backwards. This allows your levator scapulae to act together as checkreins on the forward flexion of your neck, whether bent over your desk or snapped forward from whiplash. This ability to act as checkreins on your neck's forward flexion explains why it is commonly injured and under constant postural stress.

As previously mentioned, we have to balance a twelve-pound bowling ball on a thin column called the cervical spine. As we lean forward over our desk, computer terminal, or workstation, muscles in the back of our neck are constantly working to keep our head from falling forward. This places a great deal of postural stress on these muscles of the posterior neck. This postural stress becomes more severe on the levator scapula when we turn and flex our head to one side; for example, when cradling a telephone between our shoulder and neck. Constantly turning to one side to look at a computer monitor as you work on your keyboard is another easy way to injure the levator scapula muscle. It is these repetitive stress motions that can easily create trigger points in the levator scapula.

Acute trauma is also a common cause of myofascial trigger points in the levator scapula muscle. In a slip/fall or automobile whiplash injury, these muscles can be damaged, causing the formation of myofascial trigger points. On the other end of the spectrum, emotional stress also has been shown to commonly contribute to the formation of levator scapula and upper trapezius trigger points. It has been found that a tense and hostile posture is unconsciously held in reaction to the belief that "I have the weight of the world on my shoulders."

Figure 13.2

Location of primary levator scapula myofascial trigger point

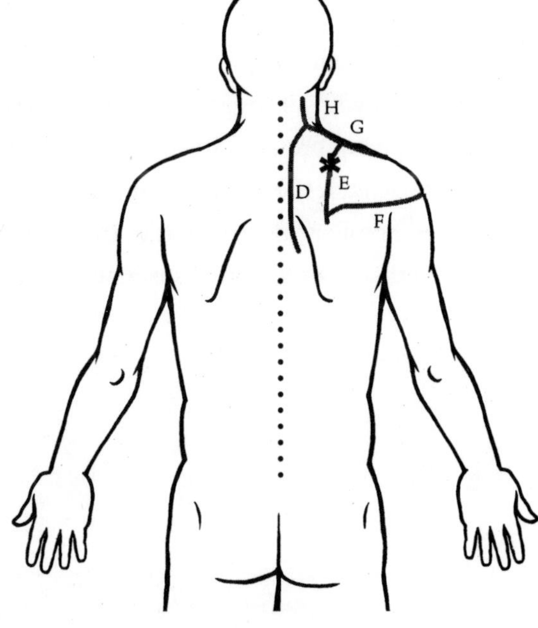

The primary myofascial trigger point of the levator scapula is generally easy to find; it's the one everyone at the office is going for when they reach over the top of their shoulder and poke around at the top of their shoulder blade. Because it is such a common trigger point, people are drawn to unconsciously massage it even as they sit at their desk and work. To find this primary NML on your left side, reach across in front of your neck with your right arm over the top of your right shoulder to find the top bony ridge of your left shoulder blade. Follow that bony ridge to the medial or inside top corner of your left shoulder blade; it's usually quite tender around it. Right at that inside upper corner of the shoulder blade is the attachment of the levator scapula, and right above it is the most common trigger point. This procedure is demonstrated by the model in figure 13.3. To find the second most common levator scapula trigger point, just follow the muscle up towards your neck with your fingertips a couple of inches. Both of these trigger points cause similar symptoms: stiffness and a severe ache around the angle of the neck. (Again, see figure 13.1 for exact locations and common referral pattern.)

To remove these problematic NMLs, you can try utilizing a tennis ball, but because of the angle of the upper back, it is usually impossible to apply enough therapeutic pressure. A trigger point therapy tool can increase the effectiveness of your self-treatment, as shown in figure 13.4. With a good trigger point therapy tool, you can completely relax the muscle while applying therapeutic pressure, a vital aspect of releasing trigger points.

As with all trigger point therapy, you are not done until you stretch the muscle after applying pressure to the trigger point. In figure 13.5, you are shown the proper way to stretch the levator scapula muscle on the left side of your neck. The best way to remember this stretch is to think about gently bringing your nose towards your armpit and holding a gentle, sustained stretch for 30 to 60 seconds.

Figure 13.3

Finding the left levator scapula trigger point

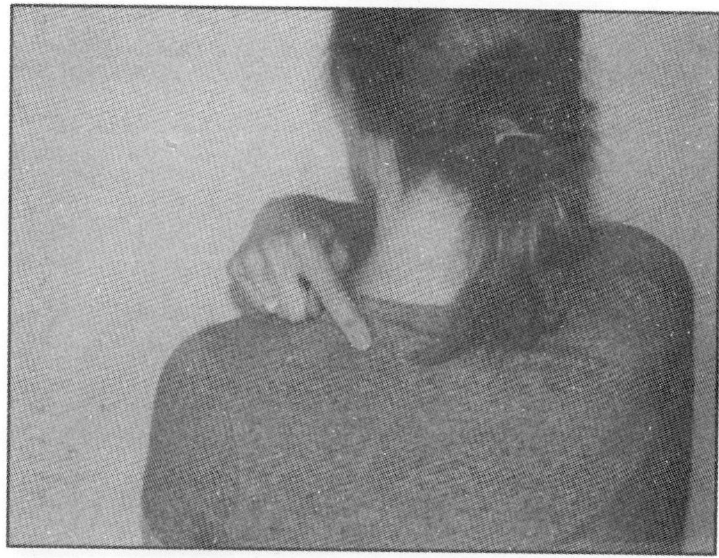

Figure 13.4

Self-administered trigger point therapy to left levator scapula

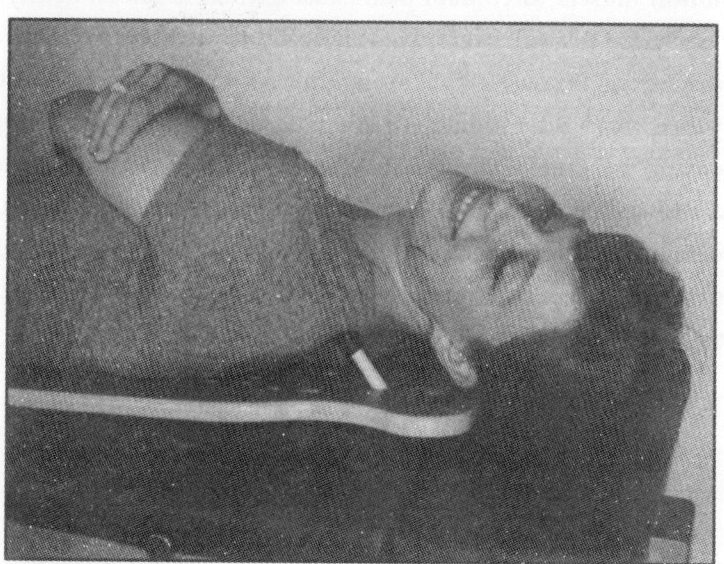

Figure 13.5

Levator scapula stretch: pull nose to armpit

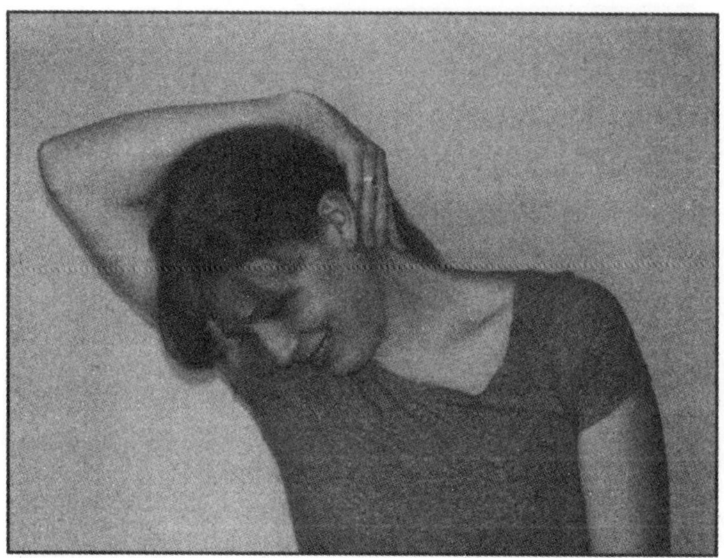

The Trapezius Muscle

As far back as 1938, research has shown the trapezius muscle of your neck to be the most common muscle to contain pain-causing muscle knots, or myofascial trigger points.[134] Yet today it is still overlooked clinically as the most frequent cause of temporal and even frontal headaches.[135] Throughout my years of clinical practice, it has been extremely rare that I did not find either a pain-causing active trigger point or a latent trigger point in the upper trapezius muscle of a patient. Virtually every patient I have examined who suffers with chronic headaches has been found to have upper trapezius trigger points that referred pain into their temple region or their forehead. NMLs in the upper trapezius are also a major source of neck pain and stiffness, as well as tension headaches.

134 M. Gustein, "Diagnosis and treatment of muscular rheumatism," *Br J Phys Med* 1 (1938): 302–21.

135 Rubin, "An approach," 107–10.

Figure 13.6

Primary upper, middle, and lower trapezius trigger points and referral patterns

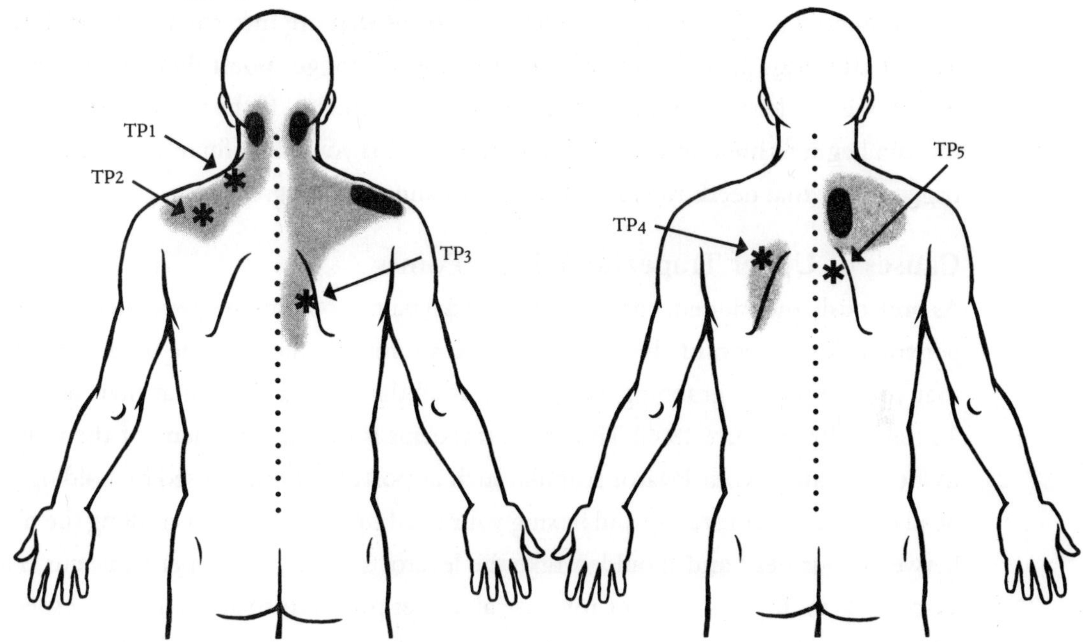

The trapeziuses are two large but very thin muscles, one on each side of your spine, that form a diamond shape. The trapeziuses run from the back of your skull outward to the tops of your shoulder blades and then down to the bottom vertebra of your thoracic spine. Because of its anatomical attachments, this muscle plays a major role as a shoulder blade stabilizer. Contraction of the upper and lower trapezius fibers will actually lift up on the acromion process and rotate the shoulder joint upwards, which can relieve pressure on the rotator cuff tendons (see page 167, figure 11.2, for details).

The trapezius muscle on each side of the spine has three parts: the upper, middle, and lower trapezius. In figure 13.6, TP3, TP4, and TP5 are the primary trigger points of the lower and middle trapezius and are located along the medial border of your shoulder blade. A very important NML, the lower trapezius primary trigger point (TP3) will tend to refer pain up your mid-back and out to the acromion process area and all the way up to the back of your head. The primary trigger points of the middle trapezius (TP4 and TP5) are right off the medial border of your shoulder blade. TP4 overlays the inner upper corner of the infraspinatus muscle on the shoulder blade, and TP5 overlays the rhomboid muscle, which resides underneath the mid-trapezius.

When applying trigger point therapy to the area along the scapula border, you may be treating multiple trigger points at the same time. Trigger points of the mid-trapezius and rhomboid both have similar referral patterns that are into the middle and upper back. This brings up a good point to remember in trigger point therapy: if you hit a spot that is tender to pressure and refers pain, then treat it. If the tenderness and referral pain begin to melt away in under a minute, then you are definitely on a myofascial trigger point that needs repetitive treatments and stretching.

Causes of Upper Trapezius Trigger Points

As previously mentioned, common myofascial pain problems are generated by the upper trapezius portion of this muscle. These are muscle fibers at the base of the neck that you see people grabbing and poking at all the time as they sit at their desk. (See TP1 and TP2 in figure 13.6.) The upper trapezius is irritated by many of the same activities that affect your levator scapula, such as postural stress caused by holding your head over a desk or rotating and flexing your head to one side when cradling the phone between your head and shoulder. Like the levator scapula, the upper trapezius is also susceptible to the formation of myofascial trigger points from acute trauma, especially whiplash. Furthermore, the upper trapezius and levator scapula muscles have a tendency to activate myofascial trigger points in each other. Due to this, these two muscles can create a vicious cycle, which is another reason why these two muscles are found to be the most prevalent for containing myofascial trigger points.

The upper trapezius muscle is also very susceptible to the formation of myofascial trigger points when there is pelvic unleveling from a short leg, as described in chapter 10. If your pelvis is unlevel from a short leg, your upper trapezius, generally opposite the short-leg side, must work constantly to keep your eyes level. So, as mentioned in chapter 10, a short leg will not only cause chronic myofascial pain in the low back but also work its way up into the cervical spine and even ultimately lead to headaches. The headaches are produced by myofascial trigger points in the upper trapezius, which commonly refer pain up into the temple or forehead area on the same side; also, there is usually posterior and lateral neck pain and stiffness.

Figure 13.7

The most common trigger point in the human body:
✱ marks primary upper trapezius trigger point #1

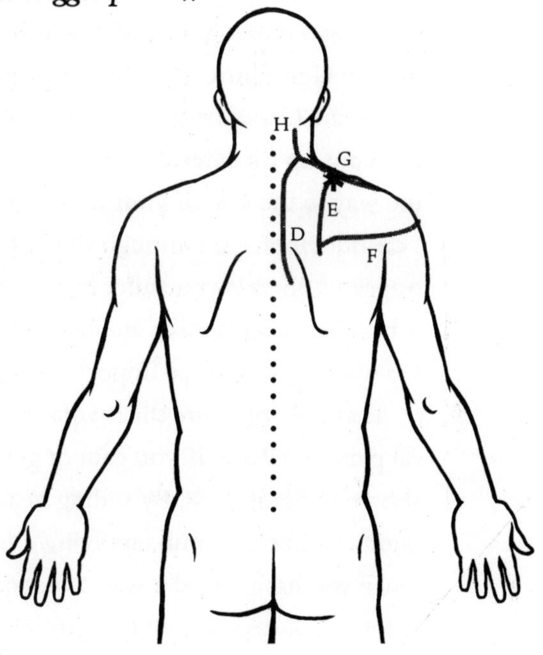

The upper trapezius NML is the easiest trigger point for you to find on yourself, especially on your dominant-hand side. You have probably already found them on yourself by instinctively poking around when you've had a stiff neck or headache. The primary trigger point is generally located where line E (medial scapula border) connects to line G, as indicated in figure 13.7. To find the NMLs in the upper trapezius fibers on your right side, simply reach across the front of your neck with your left hand to grab the soft tissues at the base of your neck, along line G. Between your thumb and fingers, grab the muscular ridge that runs from the base of your neck out towards your shoulder, and squeeze along the length until you find a tender spot. Gently apply pressure by squeezing the tender spot until you get referral pain up the side of your neck to the back of your head. You may possibly feel referral symptoms all the way to your temple or forehead. If you find an NML that exactly duplicates your symptoms, this is the trigger that must be removed first. Then move around throughout the tissues to find any associated hidden trigger points, and remove them next.

NML Location and Referral Pattern of the Upper Trapezius

You can find most of the upper trapezius NMLs by kneading the muscular ridge between your thumb and fingers. Move around by taking deeper or more superficial grasps and moving up and down the entire upper trapezius muscle ridge, as indicated by line G in figure 13.7. The myofascial trigger points in the upper trapezius fibers along line G are the major source of tension headaches and neckaches. The pain usually runs up the lateral side of your neck and can become very intense and extend all the way to the side of your head, into your temple and above your eye in the forehead. I cannot emphasize enough the importance of finding the trigger points of the upper trapezius fibers if you suffer from recurring headaches. Even severe, migrainelike headaches that cause nausea and light-headedness can have an upper trapezius component. Do not overlook these important trigger points in the upper trapezius.

As always, pressure the myofascial trigger point for up to one minute to get the referral pain to release. If you cannot get enough pressure, try using a trigger point tool, as shown in figure 13.8. By sliding headward on the treatment platform, the therapeutic digit acts like a thumb, applying a footward pressure on TP1 of the upper trapezius. Once you have found a way to adequately pressure-treat these upper trapezius trigger points, as always it is vital to stretch the myofascial tissues afterwards. This factor cannot be over-emphasized and should be thought of as part of any trigger point therapy care. This is one place that treatment in offices often fails, for rarely does a therapist take the time to do a minute stretch to the muscles after pressure treatment. In figure 13.9, you can see the proper way to stretch your left upper trapezius fibers by gently pulling your right ear to your right shoulder while stabilizing the left shoulder, and vice versa for the right upper trapezius muscle.

Figure 13.8

Self-administered trigger point therapy to the left upper trapezius trigger point #1

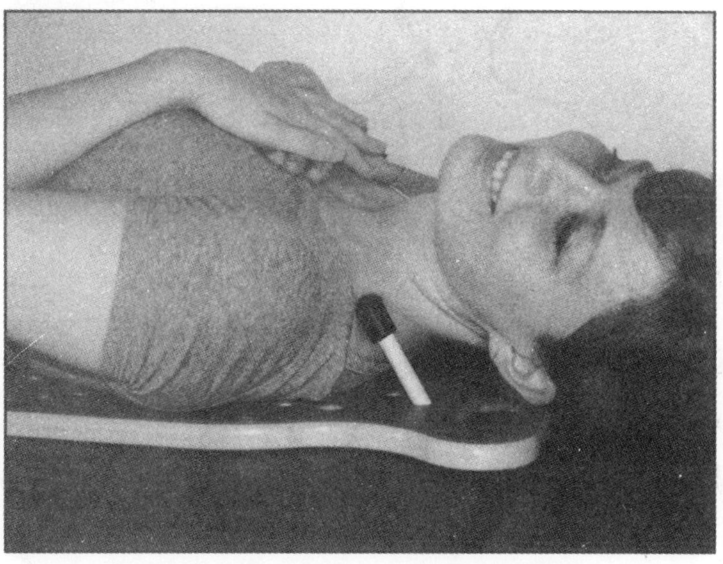

Figure 13.9

Stretch for left upper trapezius muscle, pulling ear to shoulder

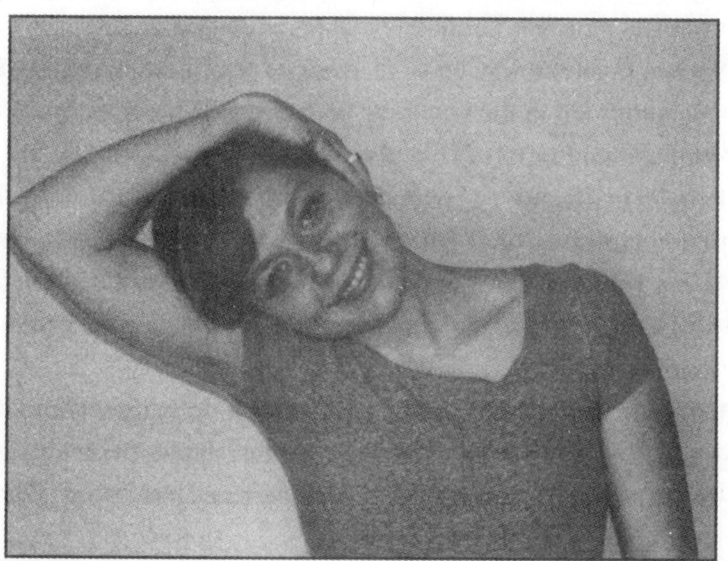

Figure 13.10

Posterior cervical & suboccipital "ache in the head" muscles and their trigger point locations

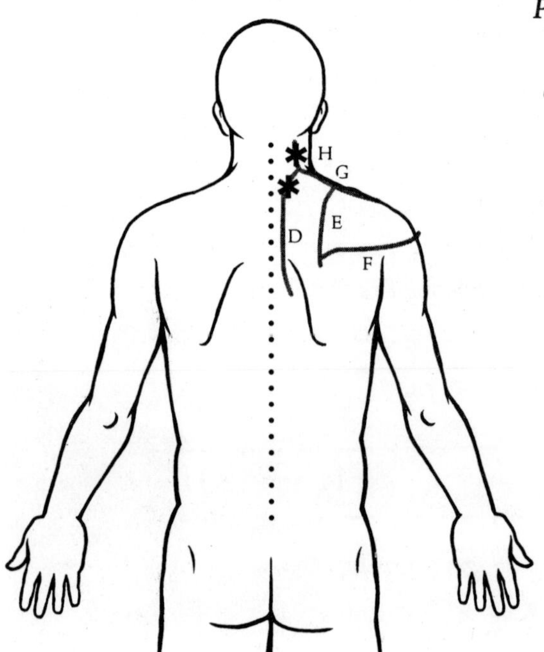

The Posterior Cervical and Suboccipital Muscles

Underneath the levator scapula and trapezius muscles lay the three deeper layers of the posterior cervical muscles. These three layers of paired muscles run from your upper back, along line D, all the way up to the back of your head, along line H, on each side of the bony bumps felt in the center of your neck. These three layers of muscles run in alternating directions, much like the plies of your automobile tire. The posterior cervical muscles in these three layers have their own special names, such as the splenii, semispinalis, longissimus, multifidi, rotators, and the small suboccipital muscles. These names are not really all that important; all you really need to do is find the painful muscle knots alongside your cervical spine that reproduce your symptoms and gently apply pressure therapy.

All three layers of these posterior cervical paired muscles work to primarily extend your neck and head backwards. This action is what allows these muscles, like the levator scapulae, to act as checkreins to keep your neck and head from falling forward when bent over your desk or work table. It is this checkrein action that causes these muscles to easily form multiple pain-causing myofascial trigger points, whether from repetitive stress at work or acute stress from a motor vehicle accident. What complicates this is that these muscles also rotate your head and neck, which can cause them further stress when you rotate and look down at your work on your desk. This work posture is very common in our modern desk-bound work environment. It is helpful to use an easel that holds up your book or documents whenever reading or doing keyboard work. To the best of your ability, place your book or documents on an easel that is not too far below your line of vision and fairly central or right in front of you at your workstation. In addition, you must also reduce the dietary and lifestyle factors that increase chronic inflammation and oxidative stress in your myofascial tissues, as will be discussed in chapter 14.

Figure 13.11

Primary posterior cervical muscle trigger point locations

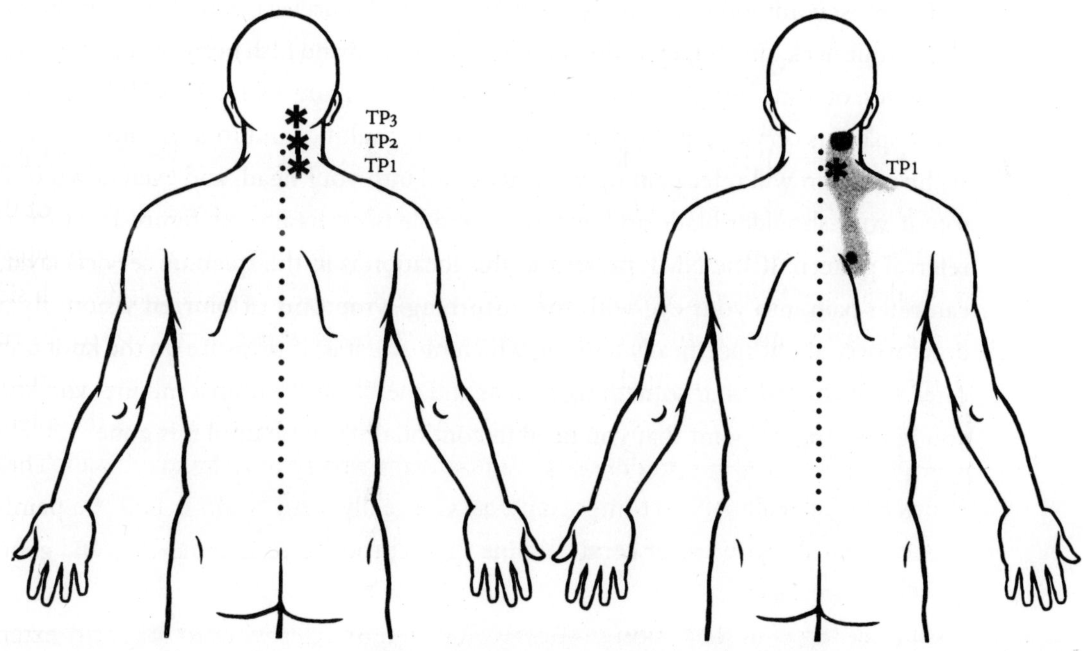

The Headache Muscles

One recent study found three risk factors that could signal a dangerous headache: (1) severe and sudden onset, (2) being over fifty years old, and (3) having abnormal neurological findings on examination. If you suffer from headaches, you must rule out any possibility of pathology as the root cause. Everyone rightfully fears a brain tumor; however, they are rarely the cause of headaches. Primarily, headaches arise from changes in the myofascial tissues of the cervical spine. So, once you have ruled out tumors, fractures, and infections, you can then start to track down the usual cause of most headaches: neuromyofascial lesions, or trigger points.

To locate the pain-causing NMLs in your right posterior cervical muscles, just reach back with your right hand and with your fingers search alongside each side of the bony bumps up the center of your neck, called spinous processes. Start at the bottom of your neck one or two finger-widths lateral to these spinous processes and work your way up to the back of your skull. When you find a tender spot, apply a little more pressure to see if it refers pain up your neck and into your head. If you cannot apply enough pressure to duplicate your symptoms, try using a tennis ball or a trigger point therapy tool.

The most common NML in the posterior cervical muscles is found right in the middle of your neck, one finger-width lateral to the fourth and fifth bony bump, or spinous processes, of your cervical spine, designated TP1 on figure 13.11. This NML is usually in the splenius cervicis, or the deepest layer in the multifidi and rotator muscles. NMLs at this location will refer pain up your neck and into your head, and even down to the top of your shoulder blade and into your middle back; again, see figure 13.11 for the referral pattern. If the NML present at this location is in the splenius cervicis layer, it can refer pain into your eye with the disturbing symptoms of blurred vision. Again, don't worry about specifically naming which muscle it is; if pressure on the knot duplicates your symptoms or something similar and melts away within a minute, you know you're on a trigger point that you need to continually release until it is gone.

Figure 13.12

Upper posterior cervical trigger point locations and referral patterns

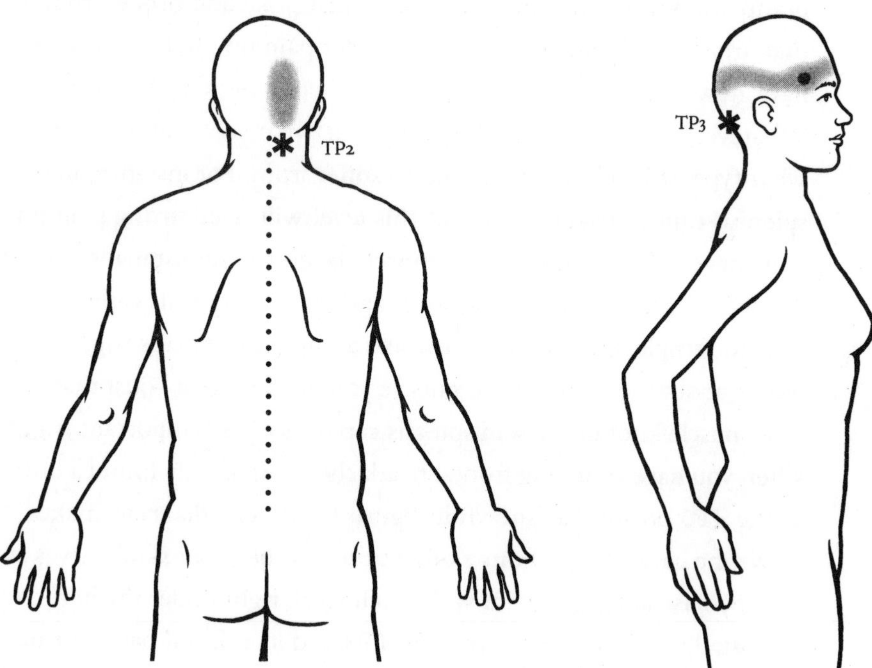

The second most common NML in your posterior cervical muscles is designated TP2 in figure 13.12. I have clinically found TP2 to be one of the most prevalent NMLs in individuals with chronic headaches. This is especially true for headaches that tend to stay in the back of your head. TP2 of the posterior cervical muscles is easy to find; simply reach behind to where the back of your head meets the top of your neck and locate that large, bony bump. Patients always ask about that bony protuberance; this bony landmark is part of your skull, specifically the occipital bone. It is called the EOP, short for *external* (because it's on the outside of your skull) *occipital* (the bone it is part of) *protuberance* (because it sticks out). This bony prominence exists because of a thick ligamentous attachment that starts there and runs down your entire spine, attaching to each spinous process of your vertebrae. We will use this bony landmark, the EOP, to find the rest of these posterior cervical muscle trigger points.

Once you have found your EOP, it's quite easy to find these important headache-causing myofascial trigger points. Just go two finger-widths lateral to the EOP and two to three finger-widths down parallel to the spinous processes of your cervical spine; now you're near the second and third cervical vertebrae. Usually this is the first bony bump you feel below your EOP. Now, just poke and probe around in the muscles in that area to find tender nodules that refer pain up the back or side of your head. You have now found a major component of your neck stiffness and chronic headaches. Whatever muscle layer has the primary active myofascial trigger points will determine what type of headaches you tend to suffer from. For instance, in the second layer, the splenius capitis, trigger points at this level will refer strong pain into the very top of your head. In the third, deeper muscle layer, the semispinalis cervicis will give you a headache at the back of your head, and the semispinalis capitis will create headaches in your temple and forehead, just like an upper trapezius trigger point. Again, do not worry about the name of the muscle you need to treat—just make sure you treat it!

A muscle knot in the semispinalis capitis is a very important trigger point to release when you have recurring frontal headaches. It is usually found a little higher than TP2, in the TP3 position as shown in figure 13.12. The diagram makes it look like TP3 is above the back of your bony skull, but remember your skull curves away from you and this myofascial trigger point will be felt to be right under the bony ridge at the back of your skull. In figure 13.12, you see TP3 and its referral pattern from the side. To specifically find this frontal-headache-causing NML, find your EOP and go two to three finger-widths lateral, slide your finger down into the soft tissue hollow felt right under the skull, and press firmly.

If you find a tender nodule that refers pain into the front, duplicating your headaches, this is a very important trigger point for you to remove completely. To get adequate pressure, it is usually easiest to treat the side with the NML with the hand from the same side. For example, to treat the right semispinalis capitis for frontal headaches, reach back with your right hand, wrapping all your fingers around the left side of your skull and placing your thumb into the muscles underneath your right skull. Now you can squeeze your hand and push with your arm to increase the pressure on the muscles of the back of your head. However, you can see from figures 13.13 and 13.14 that certain trigger point therapy tools are designed to make it much easier to treat these suboccipital muscles. The FENIX Rehab System allows you to get a good angle and apply adequate pressure to properly release these NMLs, all while completely relaxing your muscles.

Techniques aimed at treating these headache-causing muscles can be seen in figures 13.13 and 13.14. The special suboccipital lift technique shown in figure 13.14 pressure-treats the suboccipital muscles right underneath the skull while applying mild traction to stretch the contracted tissues at the top of your neck and relieve the pressure.

Figure 13.13

Self-administered trigger point therapy to the left suboccipital trigger points TP2 or TP3, depending on the position

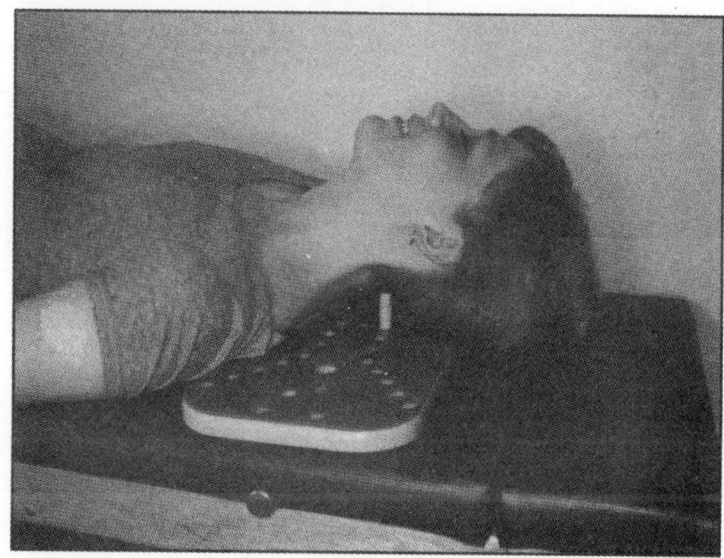

Figure 13.14

Suboccipital lift technique with two angled, paired therapeutic digits

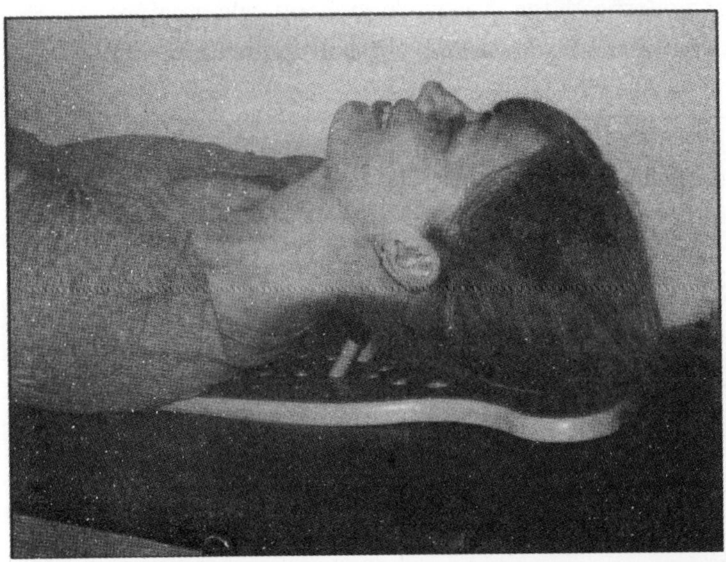

The Deep Suboccipital Muscles

Right underneath the common myofascial trigger point of the semispinalis capitis muscle lays the fourth, or deepest, layer of the upper posterior cervical muscles. These muscles would be equivalent to the multifidi and rotator muscles lower down your spine. However, these four small suboccipital muscles have a very specialized function. They keep your head and eyes perfectly level with the world around you, which can place a great deal of stress on them. These four small specialized suboccipital muscles are notorious for causing chronic hemicranial, or one-sided, headaches and can be easily identified in figure 13.15.

Each of these four muscles have specific names, but they all lie one to two finger widths below your EOP and one to three finger widths lateral to your EOP. Development of myofascial trigger points in these deep suboccipital muscles is always associated with trigger points in other major posterior cervical muscles. Therefore, it is important to search around the entire area for tender nodules that refer pain that is similar to the symptoms you suffer from. If the referral pain begins to dissipate within a minute, this is further evidence that you are on a myofascial trigger point that needs be treated. I have found that patients generally instinctively poke around back there when they have headaches.

Figure 13.15

The four deep suboccipital muscles—trigger point locations and referral pain

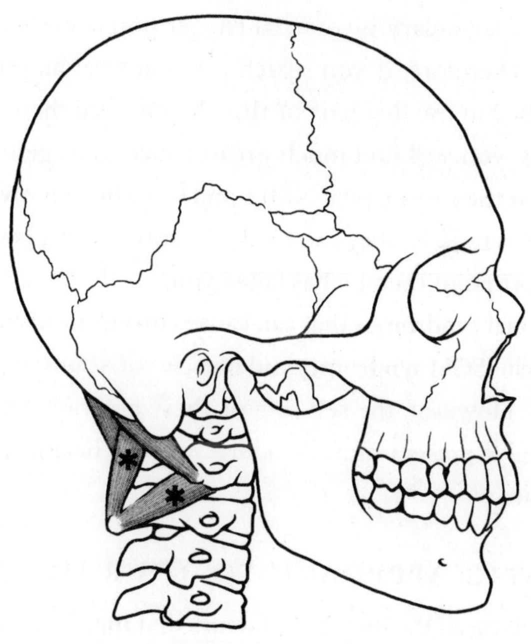

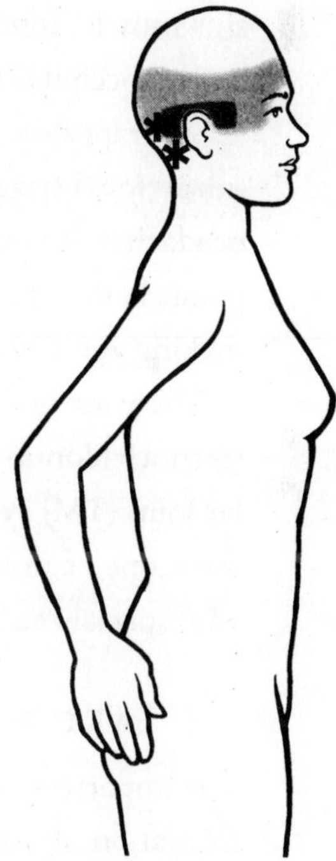

I have found throughout my years in clinical practice that headaches generally never go away until these myofascial trigger points are fully removed. In some individuals, the NMLs have been so chronic that they have developed some fibrosis within the muscle fibers. Then the best you can do then is to control these trigger points with occasional preventative therapy, thereby not allowing them to generate headaches when you're under stress. Either way, you need to search out all the different trigger points in the posterior cervical muscles, especially those underneath the back of your head. Therapeutically pressure-treat each of them for up to two minutes and then stretch the myofascial tissue for a full minute. If you do this repetitively at the end of each day or every other day, slowly you will eventually release these myofascial trigger points and overcome your chronic headaches.

One little clinical gem I have found to be true in almost every headache patient is that the most common trigger points in the human, TP1 and TP2 in the upper trapezius muscle, tend to create secondary myofascial trigger points in their referral area, the suboccipital muscles. Therefore, if you search out and treat all the NMLs in the upper trapezius, as described in the first part of this chapter, and then release all your suboccipital trigger points, you will find much greater success in getting rid of your headaches. If you only treat the suboccipital NMLs and leave hidden myofascial trigger points in the upper trapezius muscle, they can cause the suboccipital NMLs to re-form, making you feel as if trigger point therapy has failed you.

There are other myofascial syndromes that can cause chronic headaches, such as the sternocleidomastoid muscle (SCM syndrome) and muscles of your temporal mandibular joint (TMJ syndrome). However, the self-care of these anterior muscles is beyond the scope of this book, and if present must be addressed by a health-care professional who specializes in their care.

Take a Holistic Approach to Your Headaches

The importance of controlling all the metabolic factors that may be contributing to the formation of your myofascial trigger points cannot be overemphasized. It is vital for you to apply the principles outlined in chapter 14 on improving your diet to decrease oxidative stress, chronic inflammation, and insulin resistance—factors that are at the root of maintaining chronic myofascial pain syndromes. Take a more comprehensive, holistic approach to all chronic headaches: myofascial, muscle tension, migraine, or stress related. No matter what diagnosis you have been given for your chronic headache, you can benefit from trigger point therapy, improved diet, and stress reduction, as long as there is no underlying pathological process involved.

With chronic headaches, it's important to look to maldigestion, poor absorption, and the possibility of dysbiosis and food allergies. If you have dysbiosis of the small intestine, you may be absorbing toxic metabolites or byproducts from the "bad bugs" (yeast and harmful bacteria) that not only make you ache and fatigued but can also create severe toxic headaches. Also, when you are not fully digesting your food properly, you may be absorbing partial proteins in your food that can set up allergic-reaction headaches. For more information, please see chapter 15 on treating maldigestion and dysbiosis.

Besides actual food allergies, sometimes food sensitivities can play a role in chronic headaches. This is especially well known when it comes to vascular changes and migraines. Almost any food can trigger any symptom, but this is especially true with headaches. If you find you eat a food and within one to three hours you get a headache, stop eating that food! Possibly with improved digestion, absorption, and overcoming dysbiosis, you may be able to return to eating that particular food. However, until your trigger point therapy and improved diet overcome your chronic headaches, help yourself out by staying away from all foods that seem to trigger your headaches.

Section 4
Biochemically Healing Your Pain

In this section, you will find the answers to the underlying metabolic complications of your chronic myofascial pain.

In chapter 14, I will address what an ideal diet is, with tips on how to follow it. In this chapter, I also provide you with a simple nutritional jumpstart program to help maximize the physical treatment of your pain. This chapter also contains vital information, such as the importance of magnesium malate and vitamin D_3 in chronic muscle pain.

In chapter 15, you will find alternatives to the deadly NSAIDs that so many of us have come to rely on. Then, for those who suffer with more complicated chronic pain disorders, chapters 16 and 17 deal with confounding factors such as maldigestion, dysbiosis, chemical toxicity, and poor detoxification capacity. Finally, in chapter 18, we will put this all together to address the complicated syndrome of fibromyalgia.

In section 2, we discussed the many roadblocks that can impede you on your journey to a pain-free and healthy life. Here in section 4 we meet those challenges head-on with practical suggestions for overcoming the metabolic challenges of your chronic pain.

14

Eating Your Way out of Pain and into Wellness

Questions to Answer:

1. Is there a shortcut to optimal health?
2. What is the ideal diet?
3. What are some simple steps to begin real healing?

The first two sections of this book—chapters 1–8—set out to accomplish a few primary goals. To briefly recap:

First and foremost, to establish that it is not plausible that we can eat and live as we please and then expect modern medicine to have some magic bullet to pull us out of whatever pain and disease develop.

Second, to show that underlying metabolic factors of chronic myofascial pain, oxidative stress, systemic inflammation, and insulin resistance are the same mechanisms that can lead to degenerative disease. These are the common maladies of our modern society that lead to disability and premature death: heart disease, cancer, stroke, diabetes, and neurodegenerative diseases.

Third, to inspire you to make dietary and lifestyle changes that will not only help you overcome the challenge of your chronic myofascial pain but then help you prevent the development of these degenerative diseases.[136]

136 E. B. Rimm and M. J. Stampfer, "Diet, lifestyle, and longevity—the next steps," *JAMA* 291, 21 (2004): 26.

Fourth, and perhaps most important, to make real the fact that we humans and the earth are connected: that our own personal well-being cannot be separated from the overall well-being of this earth. Not that we can destroy the earth—we can't—but we can destroy our ability to live on the earth. To live our life physically and emotionally to its fullest, we must look to heal our pain and not just distract ourselves from our pain.

Healing Your Pain vs. Relieving Your Pain

Based on advertisements and infomercials in the media, we have a tendency in our society to look for "the cure-all" and "the quick fix." I even find this with patients who have literally been ground up in the medical mill, suffering with medication side effects and scarred by failed surgery. They still come to me looking for the quick fix, the single cure-all, whether it be an herb, acupuncture, or some special technique. Their hope is that I have some magic that will cure them and ask nothing of them. Sometimes it seems as if my patients wished they could drop off their body, run a few errands, and come back and pick it up, "all better now!" While we may wish for a magic bullet or single pill or nutrient that can take away our pain, the power to overcome our health challenges—and our pain—lies in a holistic approach of common sense.

The reality, as shown in chapters 2 and 3, is that there is no such thing as "pain relief." Either you momentarily hide or distract yourself from your chronic physical and emotional pain with drugs, only to have it return again, or you finally heal your pain. Please don't misunderstand: I am talking here about chronic pain that arises from dysfunction, not intractable pain from severe trauma or pathology that must be controlled with medications!

Sometimes I have tried to explain to patients who are actually willing to make the necessary changes to heal their pain that their chronic pain may have been a blessing. This may sound counterintuitive, but I have found that individuals who have suffered with chronic pain and have been through the medical mill or tried all the "natural" quick-fix gimmicks were finally ready to make substantive changes in their lives. Their chronic pain drove them to keep asking, to keep seeking, until they found real answers to their underlying health challenges. Then, and only then, because of their ordeal, were they ready and willing to make the changes necessary, changes that not only helped them to overcome their chronic pain but also helped to prevent the onset of degenerative disease.

The Core Questions to Be Answered

The core questions that must be asked by any individual hoping to overcome the challenge of their physical, emotional, and spiritual pain are *what has been damaged?* and *what will restore my vitality?* It is vitality that we seek, for it is vitality that gives us the ability to fully live life, to share our lives with others, and most of all to truly love. The very origin of the word *vitality* illustrates this for us. The suffix of the word, *-ity*, means "the quality of being," and the root comes from the Latin *vita*, meaning "life." Therefore, at its origins, our word *vitality* means the "quality of being alive, filled with life." The Webster dictionary today defines vitality as "the power to fully live." The questions, then, are what depletes this power to fully live and what then restores it.

In the first section of this book, we explored in detail the many factors that can harm or damage your vitality. What damages the vitality of an individual who experiences chronic pain and fatigue is generally not one element but an accumulation of many different factors. No clinician you see for only a few moments of your life can understand, like you do, the multiple factors that impinge on your health and vitality. That is why it is so important for you to take on the warrior's spirit in your quest for sustainable health! Become an active partner with your health-care providers in the restoration of your health and the healing of your pain. Generally, this multi-factorial problem comes down to several common considerations: (1) poor diet, (2) poor digestion and absorption, (3) toxicity from dysbiosis of your gut, (4) environmental toxins, (5) poor immune function with chronic allergies and/or infections, (6) toxic internal self-talk, and (7) genetics, a factor that influences and is influenced by the previous six factors.

The second part of this core question must then be addressed by you: *what is of the utmost importance to the restoration of my vitality?* This may include the highest-quality food, water, air, sunlight, specific nutrients for healing, activity, loving relationships, and sleep. The primary factors damaging your vitality will determine which healing elements should be focused on in your recovery. If you are eating a relatively good diet but have poor digestion, or dysbiosis, of your small intestine contributing toxins to your tissues, then these factors would be more important to start with. In general, I have found this to be the best place to start for almost everyone, because if you are not digesting and absorbing the needed calories and nutrients, it is impossible for your tissues to produce the energy you need to heal. Furthermore, if there are "bad bugs" in your gut, spilling out metabolic wastes that affect the function of your tissues, no matter how healthy you eat or how hard you try to detoxify your body, little progress will be made.

What an Ideal Diet Is

But before we examine these factors in healing, let's make sure we understand what it means to eat a good diet. This is a subject wrought with emotion and a great deal of misinformation and confusion. Perhaps you or someone you know has lost weight or felt better for a short period of time on a fad diet. Low-carbohydrate, high-protein diets, while once the rage, have now been shown in numerous studies to be detrimental to one's health over the long run.[137] Part of the confusion over carbohydrates is that to Americans, a white flour, sugary baked good is a carbohydrate—and so is 100% whole grain bread and pasta. The problem here is that these are two completely different foods with completely different effects on your body. So as not to get bogged down in the controversy, let us turn our attention to some recent studies that may clarify the subject for us.

Imagine the type of study you could design to tell you what would be the most life-giving or vitality-creating diet. The study might involve testing the effects of a specific diet on a large group of individuals over a ten-year period of time, at a time in their life when vitality is in decline. Recently there have been some very exciting studies that have essentially done just this. In one particular study, reported by the *Journal of the American Medical Association*, they investigated over 2,300 men and women, aged 70 to 90 years, in eleven different European countries.[138] They placed these elderly individuals on what researchers call the Mediterranean diet. The Mediterranean diet consists of 100% whole grains, vegetables, fruits, nuts, seeds, olive oil, and fish, and is generally low in simple carbohydrates, sugars, red meats, and saturated animal fat (see also figure 14.1).

Besides following this specific diet, these elderly individuals also adhered to healthy lifestyle practices, such as moderate physical activity, not smoking, and moderate alcohol consumption. What was amazing about this study was not only did their health

137 T. C. Crowe, "Safety of low-carbohydrate diets," *Obes Rev* 6, no. 3 (August 2005): 235–45.

138 K. T. Knoops, L. C. de Groot, D. Kromhout, A. E. Perrin, O. Moreiras-Varela, A. Menotti, and W. A. van Staveren, "Mediterranean diet, lifestyle factors, and 10-year mortality in elderly European men and women: the HALE project," *JAMA* 292, 12 (September 22, 2004): 1433–39.

parameters improve, but at the end of the decade there was a substantial drop in the death rate of the study group. There was nearly a 70% reduction in all causes of mortality and cause-specific mortality; for example, a 64% drop in death from coronary heart disease and a 60% drop in death from cancer.[139] These results have been found in other similar studies; one reported in the *New England Journal of Medicine* studied the dietary habits of 22,043 adults in Greece and found the same reduction in all cause and cause-specific mortality.[140] Never has there been anything—diet, pills, potions, or lotions—shown to be this powerful in any study! *This* is the magic bullet that everyone is looking for, but sad to say, very few of us actually put it into practice. Can you imagine the stock futures for a pharmaceutical company that created a drug that could cut in half the mortality from all causes and with only beneficial side effects? Yet this ground-breaking research seems to have been virtually ignored.

Even more important to our subject of chronic myofascial pain, adherence to a Mediterranean diet has been shown to lower the metabolic factors that can create or exacerbate chronic pain in your body. As established in the first section of this book, chronic low-grade inflammation, oxidative stress, and insulin resistance all work together to create tissue stress that eventually registers as pain in your body. One study published in the *Journal of the American Medical Association* compared two groups of individuals, one group that consumed a Mediterranean diet and another group that consumed a prudent and healthy heart diet (50–60% carbohydrates, 15–20% proteins, less than 30% total fat). The Mediterranean diet group consumed higher levels of whole grains, vegetables, fruits, nuts, and olive oil than the "healthy" diet group. At the end of two years, the individuals consuming a Mediterranean-style diet had lower levels of systemic inflammation, as well as decreased insulin resistance,[141] important metabolic factors in the cause of chronic myofascial pain.

---

139 Ibid.

140 A. Trichopoulou, T. Costacou, C. Bamia, and D. Trichopoulos, "Adherence to a Mediterranean diet and survival in a Greek population," *NEJM* 348, no. 26 (June 26, 2003).

141 K. Esposito, R. Marfella, M. Ciotola, C. Di Palo, F. Giugliano, G. Giugliano, M. D'Armiento, F. D'Andrea, and D. Giugliano, "Effect of a Mediterranean-style diet on endothelial dysfunction and markers of vascular inflammation in the metabolic syndrome: a randomized trial," *JAMA* 292, 12 (September 22, 2004): 1440–46.

Figure 14.1

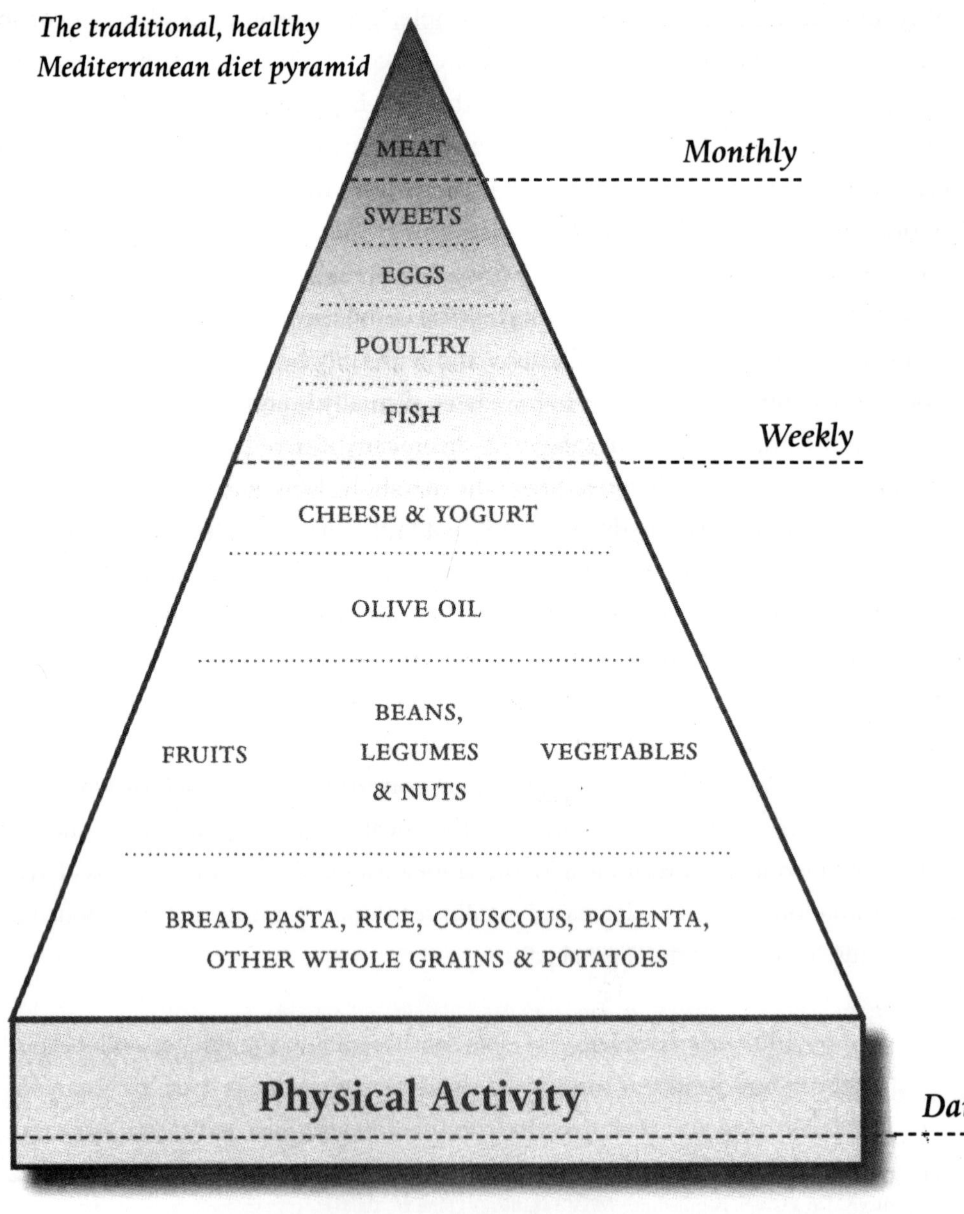

Daily beverage recommendations:
6 glasses of water, wine in moderation

How to Follow a Mediterranean Diet

The traditional diets of countries around the Mediterranean Sea are delicious as well as helpful in losing weight and lowering your risk for heart disease, stroke, insulin resistance, diabetes, cancer, and Alzheimer's, whereas the typical Standard American Diet (SAD) will increase your risk for all of these disorders as well as chronic myofascial pain. The Mediterranean diet comes from an accumulation of research into the traditional diets of countries such as Greece, Morocco, southern Italy, and Spain. It is very easy to follow a Mediterranean diet: just make unprocessed whole foods from plants the main focus of all your meals, especially those that are grown nearby. These unprocessed whole plant foods, such as grains, beans, nuts, fruits, and vegetables, are a great source of fiber, essential nutrients, and healthy phytochemicals.

The largest portions of your meals should come from fresh vegetables and 100% whole grain, such as brown rice, couscous, polenta, and bulgur, in addition to breads, cereals, and pastas. Eggplant, zucchini, tomatoes, and bell peppers are examples of excellent Mediterranean vegetables to enjoy on a daily basis. Also include beans and nuts in your diet every day; for example, bean soups, pasta with beans, hummus, and green salads with pine nuts or almond slices. To add flavor to your meals, throw in lots of garlic and onions, and spice up your food with fresh herbs, such as basil, oregano, and thyme. If you add dairy, utilize low-fat cultured products such as certain cheeses (feta, parmesan, mozzarella, provolone, part-skim ricotta and low-fat cream cheese) and yogurt; they have good bacteria that can benefit your health. As far as meat, you can add fish and seafood two or more times per week, but poultry only once a week or less. As for red meats, just a few times a month at the most is best, and make sure that these are very lean cuts. This will reduce your intake of the pro-inflammatory arachidonic fatty acid.

Utilize the healthier fats to add richness and flavor to your cooking. For example, use oils that come from cold-pressed olives and nuts. It is best to use full-flavored extra-virgin olive oil for dipping breads and making salad dressings, and then utilize light olive oil for baking. For snacks and desserts, try fresh or dried fruit and nuts. Try to remove all other sweets from your diet; keep these foods down to less than a couple times a week. And of course, to make it truly Mediterranean, drink wine in moderation with meals, especially dark red wines rich in antioxidants and phytochemicals. It should go without saying to avoid alcohol when it might put you or others at risk, such as during pregnancy, when you are breastfeeding, if you have liver or pancreatic disease, or when you are going to be driving.

The Synergy of a Holistic Approach

Imagine the tremendous synergy you can experience by utilizing a Mediterranean-style diet with specific nutritional and herbal supplements designed to lessen your pain and inflammation, along with trigger point therapy to physically release your pain-causing myofascial trigger points. This helps to answer the second part of our core question regarding what will restore our vitality. But we would also need to fully examine the first part of this core question: what has *damaged* our vitality? Again, what damages your vitality and leads to chronic pain, fatigue, and eventually degenerative disease are the metabolic factors discussed throughout the first section: oxidative stress, systemic inflammation, insulin resistance, and toxic burden.

What will help you most is to remove the primary offending agents in your diet and lifestyle that are creating this metabolic dysfunction in your tissues. Many are so obvious that it seems ridiculous to even mention them, but it is at times helpful to be reminded: processed foods, junk foods, sweets, soft drinks, and tobacco products. It may be that some of these items are impossible to completely remove because of their addictive qualities. But each baby step you take down the road towards wellness will register in your tissues and eventually show up as an overall improvement.

A healthy meal resource

- An excellent resource to help you plan out and prepare quick, healthy meals can be found at www.whfoods.org.

  To quote the website: "The George Mateljan Foundation for the World's Healthiest Foods was established by George Mateljan to discover, develop, and share scientifically proven information about the benefits of healthy eating, and to provide the personalized support individuals need to make eating the world's healthiest foods enjoyable, easy, quick, and affordable. The Foundation is not-for-profit so we can offer an independent perspective that is not influenced by commercial interests."

Baby Steps to Eat Your Way out of Pain and into Wellness

If you cannot quit smoking altogether, each day you smoke one less cigarette improves your odds for recovery. If you cannot give up your three quarters of a pound of daily sugars overnight, each day you eat a few less ounces of these simple carbohydrates, you're closer to recovery. Sometimes the transition is easier than you think; all you need do is begin to move out to the periphery of your grocery store where the fruits and vegetables live. Here, you can pick up those naturally colorful foods that do not need an ingredient label. First, simply spend more time away from the center of your grocery store, which is filled with packaged, processed foods, then toss a few more deeply colored fresh vegetables and fruits into your cart from the periphery. Second, pick up those boxed, blister-packed, and canned foods and read the ingredient labels of the foods you bring into your home. Besides being shocked and a little overwhelmed, you will become educated on what the food industry is actually putting into your body. Often I've found this to be enough to inspire my patients to become warriors and change their lives.

I like to keep things simple for my patients, to give them a fighting chance to follow any wellness program; I tend to stay away from having them compute calories or calculate food combinations based on food type, color, or their yin and yang content. At this point, don't start thinking about exacting food balances or all-organic meals. Just simply decide to start eating more foods that come from plants, smoke much less or not at all, and increase your activity level throughout the day by taking the stairs and parking a greater distance from the door of your destination. Then, when reading your food labels, put back on the shelf any foods that contain anti-nutrients or harmful foods, such as high-fructose corn syrup, artificial sweeteners, trans-fatty acids[142] or hydrogenated oils, fake fats (e.g., Olestra), and chemical food additives (artificial colors and flavors). These substances have never before been consumed by humans. In a bizarre, uncontrolled "study" on the human population, these substances have become exceedingly common only in the last few decades. You will be surprised how much this simple removal of dietary offenders can improve your health and well-being.

142 Trans-fatty acids are made by hydrogenating an oil fully or partially.

Step 1: Burn the Best Grade of Fuel

If you really value your car, you wouldn't put the wrong type of fuel in your gas tank for any reason, cost, appearance, or seductive advertising. Even though kerosene is quite a bit cheaper than gasoline and both are petroleum-based products that burn well, you still wouldn't try to burn it in your valuable automobile. You have the intelligence to understand that not all petroleum products are the same, nor do they work the same in your valuable car engine. Yet in our modern society we treat simple carbohydrate foods (aka white flour, sugary foods) as if they are equal to foods composed of complex carbohydrates rich in essential nutrients, phytochemicals, and fibers. The reality is that simple carbohydrates are not the proper fuel for the complexity of the human organism. With this awareness, you are now ready to take the next baby step forward in your quest to heal your pain and promote true health in your life.

When you read food labels, it's important to look for not only artificial sweeteners and high-fructose corn syrup but all added simple carbohydrates. The easiest way to identify these substances is to look for anything ending in *-ose,* signifying a simple sugar, such as sucrose, fructose, glucose, and dextrose. Remember these hidden sugars quickly add up to 158 pounds ingested by the average American each year, while the average American yearly consumes a total of only 8.3 pounds of broccoli.[143] This dietary pattern creates more and more obesity, insulin resistance, and diabetes in our society each year. In removing these simple carbohydrates, you will come to discover how addictive they really can be. Don't forget the biggest culprit for sugar and artificial sweeteners is ingestion of sodas and soft drinks.

After you have removed the added sugars from your diet, it is time to remove all refined grains and flours. Sweetened, refined white flour baked goods (doughnuts) and salty refined flour snacks (pretzels and chips)—are how our modern society "spells" carbohydrates. These are not health-giving, naturally occurring, unrefined complex carbohydrates; these are processed and unnatural foodlike substances that lead to obesity, insulin resistance, and diabetes. By creating insulin resistance, these food-like substances create oxidative stress and systemic inflammation, leading to conditions of chronic pain, fatigue, and eventually degenerative disease.

Simply remove these refined, processed harmful foods once and for all from your diet, and replace them with wholesome 100% whole grain, complex carbohydrate

---

143 Center for Science in the Public Interest, *Nutrition Action Newsletter* (April 1999).

foods. Make sure all your breads, pastas, baked goods, snacks, and rice state on the label "100% whole grain." These whole grain foods are more than just complex carbohydrates; they are rich in soluble and insoluble fibers vital for good health. Besides its vital fiber, whole grains contain hundreds of different phytochemicals, all beneficial to our health in many ways. These various phytochemicals are one reason why the Mediterranean diet, rich in whole grain breads and pasta, is so beneficial to your health.

Step 2: Do an Oil Change

Take as good care in maintaining your body as you do your car: do an "oil change" on the cellular engines of your body. A report from the surgeon general on nutrition and health stated that deficiencies of "good fats," excesses in "bad fats," and an imbalance in fats in general are, shockingly, involved in more than 70% of all U.S. deaths! Recently, our weight-conscious society has turned to consuming all kinds of fat-free and fake-fat products. This is extremely short-sighted, because there are certain fats that are *essential* fats, meaning life cannot go on without them. This has only fueled our diet's deficiencies in healthy fats, and because of our addiction to snack foods, fast food, junk food, and processed food, harmful fats have continued to increase in our diet. These harmful fats are the "sludge" that you must remove from your cellular engines, and include the non-food fats, such as trans-fatty acids, hydrogenated or partially hydrogenated oils, and the excess saturated fat from animal products.

The best way to drain out this sludge is to remove all these harmful fats from your diet and replace them with healthy, life-giving essential fatty acids. Trans-fatty acids are found in margarine, vegetable shortening, virtually all commercially baked goods, deep-fried foods, fast foods, and most restaurant foods. These trans-fatty acids and hydrogenated oils have been chemically manipulated so they become firmer to give you the texture of butter and, most importantly to the food industry, to keep them from becoming rancid. The problem is these trans-fatty acids and hydrogenated oils will raise your total cholesterol and lower your good cholesterol twice as much as saturated fats. These altered fats found in virtually all processed foods also increase many other risk factors connected to cardiovascular disease.[144] In a recent study, it was found that healthy omega-3 fatty acids lowered the death rate from heart disease more than the highly touted statin drugs now prescribed to lower cholesterol.[145]

---

144 W. C. Willett, "Balancing life-style and genomics research for disease prevention," *Science* 296, no. 5568 (2002): 695–98

145 M. Studer, M. Briel, B. Leimenstoll, et al., "Effect of different antilipidemic agents and diet on mortality: a systematic review," *Arch Intern Med* 165, no. 7 (2005): 725–30.

These trans-fatty acids and hydrogenated oils also promote insulin resistance and add to your risk of developing type 2 diabetes.[146] In chapter 6, we saw how highly connected insulin resistance is to the formation of systemic inflammation and oxidative stress in your tissues, which promotes pain and disease. Research has also shown trans-fatty acids and hydrogenated oils to directly raise numerous laboratory test markers of systemic inflammation, such as C-reactive protein (CRP).[147] Therefore, if you have chronic myofascial pain, such as reoccurring low-back or neck pain, chronic shoulder dysfunction, or fibromyalgia, you'll want to immediately do an "oil change" by removing these "bad fats" from your diet. Replace them with healthy essential fatty acids found in whole natural foods, seeds, nuts, vegetables, and fish.

The essential fatty acids are vital to healing your pain and creating wellness, for two basic reasons. First, they are essential in building healthy, properly functioning cell membranes throughout your body. Healthy cell membranes efficiently allow the right things inside your cells while keeping unwanted things out; for example, a healthy cell membrane binds well with insulin and allows glucose readily into your muscle or nerve cell for energy production. If you have a diet of "bad fats" as your source of building blocks for your cell membranes, they will not work effectively, and problems like insulin resistance can develop, which can lead to myofascial pain and disease. Second, essential fatty acids act as the precursor for vital cell messengers called prostaglandins, which mediate inflammation in your tissues. Therefore, certain essential fatty acids are necessary in your diet to help create prostaglandins, which control inflammation in your body. This is the exact reason why certain supplemented omega-3 essential fatty acids can help you to heal your chronic pain and promote wellness.

One of the very best ways to manage systemic inflammation and lessen chronic pain is by taking omega-3 fatty acid supplements. Studies have found that specific omega-3 fatty acids, known as EPA and DHA, from certain deep-sea fish may lower inflammation in human tissues.[148] This first came to light when it was discovered that the

146 L. Kohlmeier, N. Simonsen, P. van't Veer, et al., "Adipose tissue trans-fatty acids and breast cancer in the European Community multicenter study on antioxidants, myocardial infarction, and breast cancer," *Cancer Epidemiologic Biomarkers Prev* 6, no. 9 (1997): 705–10.

147 E. Lopez-Garcia, M. B. Schulze, J. B. Meigs, J. E. Manson, N. Rifai, M. J. Stampfer, W. C. Willett, and F. B. Hu, "Consumption of trans-fatty acids is related to plasma biomarkers of inflammation and endothelial dysfunction," *J Nutr* 135, no. 3 (March 2005): 562–66.

148 O. Eschen, J. H. Christensen, et al., "Soluble adhesion molecules in healthy subjects: a dose-responsive study using N-3 fatty acids," *Nutr Metab Cardiovasc Dis* 14, no. 4 (August 2004): 180–85.

traditional Inuit people had a very low incidence of heart disease, inflammatory bowel disease, asthma, psoriasis, and other diseases known to be of an inflammatory nature. This baffled early researchers, because the Inuit diet is extremely high in animal fats, which were thought at that time to always lead to heart disease. It turned out that their diets were rich in the omega-3 EPA and DHA that protected them from these inflammatory disorders. You can benefit from this research by supplementing your diet with EPA and DHA omega-3 fatty acids to lower systemic inflammation. However, with increased omega-3 fatty acid supplementation, it's important to add antioxidants so the fats do not get damaged by free radicals.

Numerous studies on inflammation disorders, such as rheumatoid arthritis, have shown the benefits of supplementation with EPA and DHA essential fatty acids. There have been more than thirteen different studies on utilizing omega-3 fatty acids for the pain and inflammation of rheumatoid arthritis. The amount of omega-3 EPA/DHA supplemented fatty acids in these studies was from 2.5 to 7 grams daily; all of these studies reported improvement in the test subjects. One study done at the University of Pittsburgh compared the pain relief from supplementing omega-3 essential fatty acids to taking ibuprofen on 250 patients with nonsurgical neck or back pain. This study found that patients had just as much pain relief from the omega-3 fatty acids as they did from ibuprofen, and without the side effects.[149]

Research has repeatedly shown, and I have personally found in clinical practice, that to benefit from the omega-3 fatty acid supplementation with chronic myofascial pain, it is important that you consistently take at least 3 grams of the EPA/DHA portion of the total omega-3 fatty acids supplemented on a daily basis. This level of supplementation is necessary to create adequate levels of the anti-inflammatory PGE-3 series prostaglandins in your myofascial tissues. I have found in clinical practice that many times, individuals with chronic myofascial pain or degenerative diseases need to get up to 6 grams of the EPA/DHA fraction of fish oils. The only way to do this is to purchase high-quality fish oil supplements that have per capsule 1 gram of total omega-3 fish oils in them. In these concentrated capsules, out of the 1 gram of omega-3 fatty acids, there is still only one-half gram of the needed EPA/DHA fraction. This means that you must

149 J. C. Maroon and J. W. Bost, "Omega-3 fatty acids (fish oil) as an anti-inflammatory: an alternative to nonsteroidal anti-inflammatory drugs for discogenic pain," *Surg Neurol* 64, no. 4 (April 2006): 326–31.

take two of these concentrated capsules for every 1 gram of EPA/DHA that you wish to take; 3 grams of EPA/DHA fraction would equal six concentrated capsules daily.

Much of the fish oils purchased by individuals are of low quality and low concentration, which is why some individuals state that they are not helped by taking fish oils—because they never reached adequate levels of supplemented EPA/DHA. However, the research is well established, and if you reach adequate therapeutic levels, generally you will have a beneficial response to EPA/DHA supplementation. If you want to get the minimum therapeutic dose of 3 grams of the combined EPA/DHA fraction, you need six capsules of concentrated fish oils daily; for 6 grams of the EPA/DHA fatty acids, you would need twelve capsules of the concentrated fish oils daily. I generally recommend two concentrated capsules three times daily with meals for a starting dose. If pain and inflammation aren't reduced, then I suggest increasing the dosage up to four concentrated capsules three times daily with meals.

Increasing your deep-sea fish consumption does help, but it is impractical to reach the therapeutic dosage of EPA/DHA needed to lower inflammation, for a couple of reasons. For one thing, to even get close to an adequate level of EPA and DHA, you would have to eat over 100 grams of deep-sea fish per day. But that raises the concern of ingesting toxins of farm-raised and wild fish containing heavy metals and persistent organic pollutants (POPs), such as mercury and PCBs. In chapter 7, we saw unequivocally that elevated levels of toxic chemicals in our tissues can lead to chronic myofascial pain disorders and degenerative disease. Therefore, it would be counterproductive to take in these toxic chemicals and heavy metals through increasing your intake of farmed or wild deep-sea fish to get adequate levels of EPA and DHA. This is not to say that you should never eat seafood as part of your Mediterranean diet; it has many health benefits and is an excellent source of protein.

Saving the Fish, or Going Vegetarian on the Oil Change

However, the oceans' populations of fish are being quickly depleted by an ever-growing, ever-hungry world population. For this reason, once your chronic pain and inflammation lessens, you can lower your intake of EPA/DHA and add a vegetarian source of healthy essential fatty acids. These vegetable-based omega-3 fatty acids are not as effective as fish oils in lowering inflammation, but in a healthy individual they have been shown to be beneficial in raising EPA in the body. Vegetarian sources of omega-3 fatty acids do not have the preformed EPA/DHA fractions found in the sea fish oils, but your body has enzymes that can convert a portion of the available alpha-linolenic acid (ALA) omega-3 fatty acids into EPA/DHA. Besides having their own health benefits, canola, flaxseed, hemp, and walnut oils contain high levels of ALA omega-3 fatty acids, and research shows that their long-term dietary intake may help lower your need for deep-sea fish oils. Consider adding these oils liberally to your Mediterranean diet, which should include olive oil. However, it is physiologically impossible to create high-enough levels of EPA/DHA in your body from vegetarian omega-3 fatty acids to get the same benefits of lowering inflammation as with preformed EPA/DHA from deep-sea fish oils. Therefore, if you suffer with chronic myofascial pain and/or degenerative disease, it is important that you supplement concentrated EPA/DHA derived from deep-sea fish for now.

Probably the very best way to lower the amount of EPA/DHA you need to supplement is to severely reduce arachidonic acid in your diet, the fatty acid that creates the inflammatory PGE2 series prostaglandins. The more arachidonic acid in your diet, primarily from meat and dairy, the more readily you create pro-inflammatory PGE2 prostaglandins in your tissues. This sets you up for chronic inflammation, which is connected to chronic pain and disease. Chronic elevations of PGE2 in your joint tissues cause their destruction and that of the surrounding bone. As emphasized throughout this book, there are no "bad guys" or "evildoers," only systems that get out of balance, and inflammation is necessary for fighting off infection and healing. But if you have a diet high in arachidonic acid, that's primarily all your body has to work with, so you then have a greater tendency to create chronic inflammation, leading to pain and disease. A recent study involving individuals with rheumatoid arthritis found that following a diet very low in meat and dairy products, and therefore low in arachidonic acid, reduced the signs of inflammation, such as tender and swollen joints. The study found even greater improvement when they added fish-oil supplementation to a diet low in arachidonic acid.[150]

If you are vegetarian and wish to get the benefits of "good fats" that create anti-inflammatory prostaglandins in your tissues, you can try supplementing with oils such as borage oil, black currant seed, or evening primrose that contain gamma-linolenic acid (GLA). When acted on by certain enzymes, GLA will form the anti-inflammatory

150 O. Adam, C. Beringer, T. Kless, et al., "Anti-inflammatory effects of a low arachidonic acid diet and fish oil in patients with rheumatoid arthritis," *Rheumatol Int* 23 (2003): 27–36.

PGE1 series prostaglandins. These are oils that are not generally used much in cooking or salad dressings and are best taken as a supplement. Research has shown that when these oils are supplemented with fish oils, you get an enhanced anti-inflammatory effect with less supplemented fish oil EPA/DHA needed. One study found that by combining EPA with GLA from evening primrose or borage oil, arachidonic acid was reduced and EPA levels were significantly increased, creating a balanced inflammatory response.[151] It has also been reported in other research that by combining supplementation of these "good fats," GLA with EPA/DHA, there is a 300% increase in the anti-inflammatory effect, with less fish oils needed. The dosage in these studies was around 3 grams per day of EPA/DHA and at least 1.5 grams per day of the GLA. This is a program that I highly recommend for lowering systemic inflammation and overcoming chronic myofascial pain, but again, if this is not cutting it, double your dose of the EPA/DHA and the GLA.

If you wish to stay totally vegetarian in your approach, try supplementing with as much as 13 grams or 1.5 tablespoons of pure flaxseed oil containing the omega-3 fatty acid ALA. Omega-3 ALA can be converted into the beneficial EPA if you eat a diet very low in arachidonic fatty acids from animal products and low in omega-6 fatty acids from vegetable oils. I highly recommend that you use organic canola oil for cooking and salad dressings. Canola oil contains omega-3 fatty acids in the form of alpha-linolenic acid and can now be found in butterlike spreads that do not contain trans-fatty acids. With this approach, some studies have found vegetarians to be able to produce enough EPA without supplementing fish oils.[152]

Always make sure that you're getting quality supplements that guarantee their potency as well as their purity. Sometimes this does increase the cost of treatment, but the most costly thing you can do is suffer needlessly or pay for supplements that will do you no good and may even harm you. Because essential fatty acids can be easily damaged by free radicals in your tissues, when increasing your dietary intake, it's always advisable to increase your vitamin E intake as well. However, when overcoming the challenge of chronic myofascial pain disorders, supplementation of vitamin E is vital at about 400 to 800 IU per day, and this is more than enough to protect you from any possible oxidative stress created by supplementing essential fatty acids.

---

151 J. R. Barham, et al., "Addition of Eicosapentaenoic acid to gamma-linolenic acid-supplemented diets prevents serum arachidonic acid accumulation in humans," *J Nutr* 130 (2000): 1925–31.

152 E. Mantzioris, et al., "Dietary substitution with an alpha-linolenic acid-rich vegetable oil increases EPA concentrations in tissues," *Am J Clin Nutr* 59, no. 6 (June 1994): 1304–9.

Step 3: Tuning Up Your Cellular Engines

The next vital step is to supplement your diet with the essential mineral magnesium. Within the cells of your body, the concentration of magnesium is second only to potassium, and magnesium functions to activate over 300 different enzymatic reactions. The primary enzymes activated by magnesium are those that are critical for energy production. You find magnesium highly concentrated within the mitochondria, the ATP power plants of the body. Recall that we began our discussion of the importance of muscle cell energy production, or ATP, back in chapter 5. In that chapter, we discussed in detail how chronic inflammation and oxidative stress can affect the energy production of your cells, and how these metabolic factors can deleteriously affect these energy-producing organelles of your cells.

In the mitochondria, magnesium is involved in activating enzymes that produce your ATP, and magnesium protects your mitochondria from oxidative damage. This is a key to some symptoms people experience when they are deficient in magnesium: fatigue, muscle tenderness, muscle cramps, irritability, weakness, mental confusion, insomnia, and a predisposition toward stress. These symptoms make more sense when we realize that the highest concentration of magnesium is found in the muscles, brain, heart, liver, and kidneys. In fact, a little over one-fourth of all your magnesium is concentrated in your muscles, where it performs many vital functions, especially that of energy production. For the above reasons, I make magnesium a cornerstone of my metabolic tune-up program.

Recall from chapter 8 how the pain-causing trigger point forms within the myofascial tissue. Through physical, chemical, or emotional injury or distress, thousands of muscle fibers in numerous microscopic muscle cells become chronically contracted, forming a taut band. Any further stress to these already taut bands of muscle cells will cause the formation of a neuromyofascial lesion, or myofascial trigger point. As explained in chapter 8, because it actually takes energy (ATP) to relax contracted muscles cells, these knotted-up muscle fibers cannot relax. Because magnesium is so vital to energy production in all muscle cells, any deficiency of it in myofascial tissues creates a situation where painful trigger points form more easily, leading to muscle tension, stiffness, tenderness, and weakness. If you have chronic pain of the low back or neck, or fibromyalgia, these symptoms may sound like a laundry list of your complaints.

This is why anyone suffering with a chronic myofascial pain syndrome must consider supplementation with magnesium.

How Much Magnesium Is Needed?

Although calcium gets all the press, it turns out deficiencies of magnesium within the American population may be more common. Magnesium supplementation may be far more vital for many Americans. The RDA of magnesium for healthy young adult males is 350 milligrams per day and 280 milligrams per day for healthy young adult females. The RDA is established for young adults who have no health issues, so if you are a growing youth, aging adult, pregnant, or have any sort of health disorder, such as chronic myofascial pain syndrome, the RDA does not apply to you. In Russia, the RDA of magnesium for women ranges from 500 to 1,250 milligrams, depending on their physiological demands.[153] In reviewing the available literature, this seems to be a much more realistic RDA for magnesium. Even though the RDA in the United States is set at a fraction of Russia's, Americans still are not reaching their RDA levels in magnesium. Most studies show that the average magnesium intake by healthy adults in America ranges between 143 to 266 milligrams per day, which is well below the RDA.

Part of the reason is that magnesium occurs in whole, natural, unprocessed foods, which are severely lacking in the Standard American Diet (SAD). This becomes even more obvious when you look at what foods are highest in magnesium: tofu, beans, seeds, nuts, whole grains, and green leafy vegetables. Magnesium is generally quite low in meat, dairy products, fish, and the more commonly eaten fruits. What's interesting about this is that a diet high in magnesium sounds very much like a Mediterranean diet. This may be another reason why the Mediterranean diet is so helpful in bringing about wellness.

How Do I Know if My Tissues Are Low on Magnesium?

Low magnesium levels are hard to diagnose, and physicians tend to rely on blood serum magnesium levels, which will only go below normal in severe magnesium depletion, which is a pathological condition. Like calcium blood serum levels, which remain normal in the blood while your bones become depleted of calcium, causing osteoporosis, blood serum levels of magnesium will stay normal while your tissues are being depleted. Because of this, blood levels in your serum do not reflect the amount of

153 G. E. Abraham and H. Grewal, "A total dietary program emphasizing magnesium instead of calcium: effect on the mineral density of calcaneous bone in postmenopausal women on hormonal therapy," *Journal Reproductive Medicine* 35 (1990): 503–7.

available magnesium in your muscles. Therefore, you could have all the symptoms of muscle tension, tenderness, weakness, and fatigue, and still have perfect blood serum levels of magnesium. There are more sophisticated and sensitive tests to measure actual magnesium status; one of the simplest, inexpensive ways is what's known as erythrocyte magnesium. This is a measurement of the level of magnesium inside your red blood cell. Because magnesium is stored in the cells, this provides a closer correlation to the actual levels of magnesium in your tissues.

A better test altogether is to try some inexpensive magnesium supplementation for a few months and see if your symptoms improve. Because deficiencies are so extremely common and magnesium supplementation is inexpensive, with so many positive benefits, it only makes sense to do a trial therapy instead of running numerous expensive tests. It takes about six weeks for magnesium levels to build up in your tissues, so don't expect to be all better overnight; however, many patients report improvement within days. With magnesium supplementation, they commonly report that they are handling their stress better, they sleep better, and their muscles are feeling more relaxed. I find that patients who have low tissue levels of magnesium consistently complain of muscle tension, headaches, insomnia, poor response to stress, and an exaggerated startle reflex. In other words, if a book drops or a door slams, they tend to jump a little higher than others in the room.

How Much and What Kind of Magnesium Should I Take?

Numerous well-done studies have found supplemented magnesium to be beneficial for many common disorders of our modern society: asthma, cardiovascular disease, cardiac arrhythmias, high blood pressure, intermittent claudication, abnormal cholesterol levels, insulin resistance, diabetes, chronic fatigue, fibromyalgia, migraines, tension headaches, kidney stones, PMS, and osteoporosis. This partial list of health disorders helped by magnesium, plus its role in chronic myofascial pain, makes it a primary component of any wellness program. For chronic myofascial pain, I recommend starting with a dose of around 450 milligrams of elemental magnesium per day and increasing the dose to 600 milligrams of elemental magnesium daily. This dose is around three times the level of magnesium the Standard American Diet provides, but it is actually less than what the average Asian diet supplies on a daily basis. Generally, there are no contraindications for someone taking this level of magnesium because it can be achieved in a very healthy diet; however, if you suffer with kidney disease or severe heart disease, such as high-grade atrioventricular block, do not take magnesium or potassium unless your physician orders it.

You can buy magnesium in several different forms; the difference is determined by what organic molecule it is bonded to. Magnesium, like other minerals, is bonded (or "chelated") to an organic molecule such as citrate, malate, aspartate, or glycinate. I like to utilize magnesium combined with malate or citrate because these chelating molecules are actual components of the energy-producing citric acid, or Krebs cycle, in your mitochondria. As Krebs cycle intermediates, they are necessary for the production of ATP in your cells. Malate has been shown to increase the rate that fuel for ATP production is brought into your mitochondria, which increases the efficiency of cellular energy production—vital factors in overcoming myofascial pain. Because they are Krebs cycle intermediates, they also allow magnesium to be better absorbed and utilized when compared to mineral salts, such as magnesium oxide or carbonate. Malate and citrate are also compounds that occur naturally in foods, generally in fruits. For the complaints of muscle tenderness and fatigue, such as with fibromyalgia, I prefer 150 milligrams of magnesium combined with 600 milligrams of malate per tablet. This way, two tablets taken twice daily will supply you with 600 milligrams of magnesium and 2.4 grams of malate, levels shown to be highly effective in reducing muscle tenderness, tension, and fatigue.

The Crucial Role of B Vitamins

Because of the critical role that many of the B vitamins play in energy production in the Krebs cycle, to the magnesium malate I like to add a good helping of B complex. Thiamine B_1 is so essential for good energy production and carbohydrate metabolism, it should be supplemented at 100 milligrams per day. Pantothenic acid is a B vitamin that also plays a vital role at the beginning of the energy production cycle, and it is beneficial to supplement it at 200 milligrams per day. The importance of the B vitamin pantothenic acid in this program cannot be overemphasized. One of the first signs of pantothenic acid deficiency is fatigue, and it has been shown to be important for optimal adrenal function. It has many times been referred to as the anti-stress vitamin because of its support for the adrenal gland.

Because of their importance to energy production and mitochondrial function, the other B vitamins should be included in this program by adding them to your magnesium malate supplementation. Riboflavin vitamin B_2 is crucial for energy production and helps to regenerate a vital cellular antioxidant called glutathione. Each tablet should contain about 20 milligrams of riboflavin, any more than that is difficult for your gastrointestinal tract to absorb.

The vitamin niacin, or B_3, is also essential for good energy production, regulation of your blood sugar, antioxidant protection, and for detoxification. Because of niacin's tendency to cause skin flushing and itching, I suggest that each tablet contain about 20 milligrams, for a total of 80 to 100 milligrams per day. Niacin can be used for other reasons such as lowering cholesterol, but it would need to be used at much higher levels for that purpose.

Pyridoxine, or vitamin B_6, is utilized in more than sixty different enzyme pathways in your body. As it is involved in the manufacture of neurotransmitters, it plays a critical role in brain chemistry. Because the liver does not seem to handle more than 50 milligrams a time, each tablet should contain no more than 50 milligrams, for a total of no more than 200 milligrams per day. Furthermore, studies have shown that doses greater than 2,000 milligrams per day of B_6 can produce nerve toxicity symptoms in some individuals, and long-term use of more than 500 milligrams per day of B_6 for months or years can be toxic.[154]

Another important B vitamin involved in the utilization of glucose and fatty acids for energy metabolism is biotin. Biotin is a vitamin that can be manufactured in your intestines, if you have healthy gut bacteria. Therefore, with dysbiosis resulting in fatigue and muscle pain, this may be a crucial B vitamin to add to your metabolic tune-up. Biotin has no reported side effects and no RDA level established, but I suggest adding around 1 to 3 milligrams to your program.

Folic acid is one B vitamin that entire books have been written about. Folic acid deficiency is probably the most common vitamin deficiency in the entire world. Folic acid supplementation helps to reduce your body's production of a molecule called homocysteine. Homocysteine has been implicated in many different degenerative diseases, from atherosclerosis to Alzheimer's and even osteoporosis. There have been some recent studies connecting higher levels of homocysteine in the cerebrospinal fluid of individuals who suffer with the chronic pain and fatigue of fibromyalgia.[155] For this reason, I suggest 800 micrograms per tablet in your metabolic tune-up program.

When supplementing folic acid, it is always important to add vitamin B_{12} because folic acid can mask a B_{12} deficiency. Furthermore, vitamin B_{12}, or cobalamin, plays a

---

154 M. Cohen and A. Bendrich, "Safety of pyridoxine—A review of human and animal studies," *Toxicol letters* 34 (1986): 129–39.

155 B. Regland, M. Andersson, et al., "Increased concentrations of homocysteine in the cerebrospinal fluid in patients with fibromyalgia and chronic fatigue," *Scan J Rheumatol* 26, no. 4 (1997): 301–7.

vital role in energy metabolism and nerve function, it is important to include a total of 1,000 micrograms daily in your supplementation program. Vitamin B_{12} also helps to reduce the levels of homocysteine in your body. Supplementation with vitamin B_{12} has been shown to be appropriate in everything from impaired mental function in the elderly to asthma in the young, as well as depression, diabetic neuropathy, and low sperm counts.

The combination of magnesium malate and the B vitamins at the dosages given create a supplement that is an ideal product to begin tuning up the engines of your cells, the mitochondria. I highly recommend this combination of nutrients for anyone with chronic myofascial pain of the back, neck, or extremities.[156] It has even been shown in studies to be helpful for individuals who suffer from fibromyalgia and chronic fatigue syndrome.[157] However, for those who have severe fibromyalgia and/or chronic fatigue syndrome, there will be a need for enhanced mitochondrial support, which will be covered in more detail later in the book.

The Rediscovery of Vitamin D_3

Another vital component of your metabolic tune-up is vitamin D. The newly rediscovered role in health and disease that this lowly hormonelike vitamin plays is commonly overlooked by many clinicians. This is very troubling for those who suffer from chronic muscle and joint pain problems, for recent studies have shown clearly that low serum of vitamin D levels is associated with chronic nonspecific musculoskeletal pain. You may have seen pictures of children with rickets or adults with osteomalacia from vitamin D deficiencies in poorer developing countries. Vitamin D deficiencies

---

156 Because I believe this basic metabolic tune-up, utilizing concentrated magnesium malate with specific B vitamins, is so important, I agreed to design a formula for a nutritional company. I created a product called Fibro-Ease that supplies in 2 tablets twice daily 2 grams of malate, 600 milligrams of magnesium, 200 milligrams of thiamine, 80 milligrams of riboflavin, 100 milligrams B_6, 80 milligrams B_3, 1600 micrograms of folic acid, 1,000 micrograms of B_{12}, and a whopping 400 milligrams of pantothenic acid. Along with all these beneficial nutrients, it supplies 1,000 IU of vitamin D_3. The extreme importance of this will become clear in the next section! This way, individuals can get all these important nutrients helpful in treating myofascial pain at levels high enough to be effective in just two tablets twice daily. Utilizing this formula, a month's supply for this metabolic tune-up costs you about nineteen dollars, or about sixty cents a day.

157 I. J. Russell, J. E. Michalek, J. D. Flechas, and G. E. Abraham, "Treatment of fibromyalgia syndrome with Super Malic: a randomized, double blind, placebo controlled, crossover pilot study," *J Rheumatol* 22, no. 5 (May 1995): 953–58. I. M. Cox, M. J. Campbell, and D. Dowson, "Red blood cell magnesium and chronic fatigue syndrome," *Lancet* 337, no. 8744 (March 30, 1991): 757–60.

were something that was never considered a problem in Western nations; in years past, there was more concern that people were getting *too much* vitamin D. However, recent research studies are now showing that vitamin D deficiencies in the United States are much more prevalent than once was thought.

In data from the Third National Health and Nutrition Examination Survey 1988–94, blood serum levels of vitamin D_3 were found to be below the recommended levels for a large portion of the general adult U.S. population and for most minorities. The prevalence of moderate and severe deficiencies of vitamin D was found to be much higher among women and minority populations; however, one-third of all white men had low vitamin D levels.[158] The researchers in this study concluded: "Need exists for a critical review and probable revision of current recommendations for adult vitamin D intake to maintain adequate 25(OH) D_3 levels."

The findings of this comprehensive research become even more significant in light of a recent study on individuals with chronic musculoskeletal pain, completed at the University of Minnesota. In this study, blood vitamin D levels were tested on 150 individuals, males and females aged 10 to 65 years from six broad ethnic groups. All 150 of these individuals suffered with persistent, nonspecific musculoskeletal pain. Amazingly, in these muscle and joint pain patients, 93% had deficient serum levels of vitamin D. This means that if you suffer with nonspecific musculoskeletal pain, your chances would be greater than 9 out of 10 of having a vitamin D deficiency. In this study, 100% of all African American, East African, Hispanic, and American Indian patients had deficient levels of vitamin D.[159]

The conclusion of these researchers was straightforward: "All patients with persistent, nonspecific musculoskeletal pain are at high risk for the consequences of unrecognized and untreated severe hypovitaminosis D." "Persistent, nonspecific musculoskeletal pain" is another name for the myofascial pain syndromes we have been discussing throughout this book. They are nonspecific because these individuals did not have an underlying diagnosable bone or muscle pathology to account for their pain, and persistent because they were chronic disorders. Therefore, if you have regional myofascial

158 A. Zadshir, N. Tareen, D. Pan, K. Norris, and D. Martins, "The prevalence of hypovitaminosis D among U.S. adults: data from the NHANES III," *Ethn Dis* 15, no. 4, suppl. 5 (Autumn 2005): 97–101.

159 G. A. Plotnikoff and J. M. Quigley, "Prevalence of severe hypovitaminosis D in patients with persistent, nonspecific musculoskeletal pain," *Mayo Clin Proc* 78, no. 12 (December 2003): 1463–70.

pain or the global myofascial pain of fibromyalgia, you will want to have your vitamin D_3 levels measured and/or consider supplementing with vitamin D. Ask your doctor to run a serum 25-hydroxyvitamin D blood test on you to see how deficient you might be. Not long ago, "normal" was considered 7 to 46 ng/mL of serum vitamin D, but this has recently been raised to 32 to 100 ng/mL. Many experts now believe that 40 to 100 ng/mL of serum of vitamin D is the optimal range for good health. Serum vitamin D levels over 100 to 150 ng/mL suggest toxicity and must be investigated by your physician.

It's important to remember that many studies have now found a correlation between many modern health problems and vitamin D deficiencies, including osteoporosis, chronic muscle pain, fibromyalgia, certain cancers, multiple sclerosis,[160] and even depression.[161] Always supplement with vitamin D_3 (cholecalciferol), not vitamin D_2. The dosage in various conditions runs from 500 to 2,000 IU of vitamin D_3 daily; even though there is limited toxicity, never exceed 2,000 IU per day. Do not take with vitamin A, as in cod liver oil, because vitamin A competes with the absorption of vitamin D. Recent research has suggested that vitamin D helps to lower systemic chronic inflammation and insulin resistance in tissues throughout the body. This may explain its widespread health effects and its ability to combat chronic myofascial pain disorders, so don't pass this one up in performing your metabolic tune-up.

The supplements listed below are given in per-day dosage. Where there is a range given, the dosage depends on the severity of your symptoms. If you have fibromyalgia, you would want to take the full 2.4 grams of malate, with a full 600 mg of magnesium, daily. As you improve, you may be able to cut this dosage in half. Depending on your wellness goals and the quality of your diet, you may wish to maintain yourself on this half dosage. If you search, you may find nutritional companies who have put together combination formulas close to this program.[162]

---

160 K. L. Munger, L. I. Levin, B. W. Hollis, N. S. Howard, and A. Ascherio, "Serum 25-hydroxyvitamin D levels and risk of multiple sclerosis," *JAMA* 296, no. 23 (December 20, 2006): 2832–38.

161 C. H. Wilkins, Y. I. Sheline, C. M. Roe, S. J. Birge, and J. C. Morris, "Vitamin D deficiency is associated with low mood and worse cognitive performance in older adults," *Am J Geriatr Psychiatry* 14, no. 12 (December 2006): 1032–40.

162 Fibro-Ease, by BIOSPEC Nutritionals, is a combination that I formulated for them based on this research.

Basic Metabolic Tune-up for Your Cellular Engines

- Malic acid (1,200 to 2,400 mg)
- Magnesium (glycinate / oxide; 450 to 600 mg)
- Manganese (sulfate; 5 to 10 mg)
- Vitamin B_1 (100 to 250 mg)
- Vitamin B_2 (80 mg)
- Vitamin B_6 (100 to 200 mg)
- Vitamin B_{12} (methylcobalamin; 1000 mcg)
- Folic acid (1600 mcg)
- Niacin (80 mg)
- Pantothenic acid (400 mg)
- Vitamin D_3 (cholecalciferol; 1,000 to 2,000 mg)
- Biotin (2 mg)
- Copper (gluconate; 2 mg)
- Zinc (citrate; 20 mg)

15

Spice Up Your Healing

In the previous chapters, we discovered the actual "magic bullet" that everyone has been looking for—the way to stay youthful and healthy even as we age: the well-researched Mediterranean diet. This approach to health calls for us to fundamentally change the way we look at foods—no longer as empty calories to fill us up but rather as actual parts of this sacred earth that nourish us and make us whole.

To this sound dietary base, I have suggested some very basic supplements to begin to jumpstart the healing process. For example, perform an oil change by removing all the "bad fats" in your diet and replacing them with healthy fats to jumpstart healing your pain. Supplemented omega-3 fatty acids are incorporated into your cell membranes. Here they can be acted on by enzymes to produce anti-inflammatory prostaglandins that help to manage inflammation in your tissues.

The second additions to a healthy diet were nutrients and herbs to enhance your mitochondrial function and restore your vitality. Towards this goal, I have advocated the mineral magnesium combined with malate and a specific blend of B vitamins, especially high in thiamine B_1 and pantothenic acid. The third step was to consider the supplementation of vitamin D, based on recent research on its role in chronic myofascial pain as well as myriad other modern health complaints.

After years of clinical and personal experience, I cannot emphasize enough how far this simple, basic program can take you in your attempt to heal your pain. I have seen phenomenal positive results in chronic pain patients with this program. This is especially true if you also begin a self-care program to release your pain-causing muscle knots. Whether they are in the low back, neck, or extremities, you can start out with a tennis ball or golf ball, but eventually you may want to buy a quality self-care trigger point therapy tool.

Next, instead of your usual NSAIDs, such as ibuprofen, try spicing up your pain relief with some quality herbs to help alleviate your inflammation and pain. Whether it is a substitution for your NSAIDs or part of your comprehensive approach to heal your pain and prevent disease, specific herbs, such as ginger and curcumin (also called turmeric), can be of great benefit to your overall health.

The Benefits of Healing Your Pain with Herbs

I have seen numerous times the tremendous, natural pain-relieving power these herbs can provide—the natural pain relief you seek. This can help you eliminate NSAIDs and the many dangers to your health that they bring. And not only can these herbs, such as ginger and curcumin, help relieve your inflammation and pain, they offer you side *benefits* to your health, instead of side effects. In fact, there is now strong evidence that ginger and curcumin may actually protect the stomach from the damaging effects of nonsteroidal anti-inflammatory drugs (NSAIDs), such as ibuprofen.[163]

These herbs have a long and celebrated history of their use by humanity for seasoning foods and for healing. Turmeric is native to southern India, where it has been harvested for over 5,000 years and is included as a revered member of the Ayurvedic pharmacopeia. It is commonly used today in many curry dishes. The herb turmeric comes from the deep orange root of the *Curcuma longa* plant and has a peppery, warm, and bitter flavor. This is the herb that gives curry dishes their distinctive color and, to some degree, their flavor.

No one is sure how old ginger is. Native to southeast Asia and cultivated there for millennia, ginger comes from the root of the ginger plant, *Zingiber officinale*, and comes in yellow, white, or red colors. The taste of ginger is aromatic, pungent, and hot, and found in many traditional dishes throughout the world. Ginger has been used medicinally throughout the Far East since before recorded history. The ancient Romans imported ginger from China almost 2,000 years ago, and it has been used as a culinary and medicinal herb in the West since that time.

---

163 M. A. Al-Yahya, S. Rafatullah, and J. S. Mossa, et al., "Gastroprotective activity of ginger in albino rats," *Am J Chinese Med* 17 (1989): 51–6. S. Rafatullah, M. Tariq, M. A. Al-Yahya, J. S. Mossa, and A. M. Ageel, "Evaluation of turmeric (*Curcuma longa*) for gastric and duodenal antiulcer activity in rats," *J Ethnopharmacol* 29, no. 1 (April 1990): 25–34.

The Power of Ginger Root Extract

I like to utilize standardized ginger root extracts (*Zingiber officinale*) as the base for any anti-inflammatory / antioxidant herbal supplement utilized with chronic pain patients. Chinese and Ayurvedic practitioners have relied on ginger root's anti-inflammatory properties for at least 3,000 years in the treatment of inflammatory joint diseases, such as arthritis and rheumatism. Ginger root is an excellent antioxidant, helping to scavenge free radicals from multiple sources, including drugs and environmental toxins. It is ginger root extract's ability to counteract oxidative stress and systemic inflammation that makes it so beneficial in counteracting the metabolic factors that can complicate or create chronic pain in you.

Ginger and Chronic Inflammation

Of primary importance to our discussion here is ginger's therapeutic abilities to inhibit the formation of inflammatory molecules and also have direct anti-inflammatory effect. The dried root of ginger contains approximately 1 to 4% volatile oils, which give ginger its characteristic odor and taste. These aromatic components include gingerols and shogaols, the very potent anti-inflammatory compounds found in ginger. It is these components of ginger root that are believed to explain the wonderful reduction in pain levels and improvement in mobility patients experience. In two different studies reported in the journal *Medical Hypotheses*, ginger root was found to provide significant pain relief and reduction of swelling.[164]

In the second study, 56 patients (28 with rheumatoid arthritis, 18 with osteoarthritis, and 10 with muscular pains) took powdered ginger root for their muscle and joint pain problems. In the arthritis group, more than three-quarters experienced relief of their pain and swelling. Of the patients with muscular pain, 100% experienced relief of pain, a pretty impressive result for any compound, synthetic or natural. Furthermore, none of the patients reported adverse effects from the powdered ginger root during their trial period, which ranged from 3 months to 2½ years. It was suggested by the authors of the study that at least one reason why ginger root reduces symptoms was related to reducing the prostaglandins and leukotrienes, such as PGE2 and LTB4, which cause pain and inflammation.

---

164 K. C. Srivastava and T. Mustafa, "Ginger (*Zingiber officinale*) and rheumatic disorders," *Med Hypotheses* 29, no. 1 (May 1989): 25–28. K. C. Srivastava and T. Mustafa, "Ginger (*Zingiber officinale*) in rheumatism and musculoskeletal disorders," *Med Hypotheses* 39, no. 4 (December 1992): 342–48.

In a 2005 article published in the *Journal of Medical Food,* the authors reviewed the past twenty-five years of research on ginger's anti-inflammatory properties. Multiple research studies outlined in the review established that ginger helped to manage multiple biochemical pathways activated in chronic inflammation without blocking enzymes vital for maintaining healthy tissues.[165]

A recent study reported in the *Osteoarthritis Cartilage Journal* further demonstrates the power of ginger root. This study tested ginger root's effect on osteoarthritis of the knee in 29 individuals over a 12-month period; 6 were men and 23 women, all ranging in age from 42 to 85 years. When the participants took the ginger root, they experienced less pain and the swelling in their knees (an objective measurement of inflammation) went down significantly.[166] So, if you have swollen, achy joints, you may just want to give ginger root extract an adequate trial (4 to 6 months). Additionally, a 2005 study reported that ginger extract components were quite effective in inhibiting the chemical messengers that trigger destructive inflammation in arthritic joints.[167]

Ginger and Substance P(ain) in Chronic Myofascial Disorders

Possibly one of the most exciting aspects of utilizing standardized ginger extracts for chronic pain is its ability to affect substance P in your nerves; I like to think of it as substance PAIN. Substance P(ain) is contained within some of the nerves in your body dedicated to pain, neurons that come from nociceptors. Recall from earlier chapters the role that these special nerve endings, called nociceptors, play in your chronic pain.

To quickly review, these free nerve endings are literally laced throughout your myofascial tissues and will become stimulated by the presence of any inflammatory chemicals. These inflammatory chemical messengers (e.g., PGE2) are produced in your tissues in response to any tissue damage or stress. When the stimulation of these nociceptors in the myofascial tissues of your back, neck, or extremities reaches the cortex of your brain, you experience pain! This "great alarm system" is there to protect you

165 R. Grzanna, L. Lindmark, and C. G. Frondoza, "Ginger—an herbal medicinal product with broad anti-inflammatory actions," *J Med Food* 8, no. 2 (Summer 2005): 125–32.

166 I. Wigler, I. Grotto, D. Caspi, and M. Yaron, "The effects of Zintona EC (a ginger extract) on symptomatic gonarthritis," *Osteoarthritis Cartilage* 11, no. 11 (November 2003): 783–89.

167 P. V. Phan, A. Sohrabi, A. Polotsky, D. S. Hungerford, L. Lindmark, and C. G. Frondoza, "Ginger extract components suppress induction of chemokine expression in human synoviocytes," *J Altern Complement Med* 11, no. 1 (February 2005): 149–54.

from doing harm to any injured or stressed tissues. If, for example, you tear myofascial tissues in your ankle by twisting it, you want to have the good sense not to keep damaging it by putting all your weight on it. The nociceptors do a great job of warning you with the signal of pain to stay off of it, thereby protecting the injured tissue.

As discussed earlier in this book, nociceptors are special in that they do not adapt and they can actually become hypersensitive. This means that unlike other nerve receptors, they will not shut down from continued stimulation as your nose does in response to a continued disagreeable smell. Worse yet, these nociceptors will actually become hypersensitive to the chronic stimulation. In evolutionary terms, this is helpful to human survival; it motivates us to get out and stay out of the way of harmful and damaging stimuli in our environment. This aspect of nociception does have its drawbacks, though, when the system becomes hypersensitive from the presence of multiple myofascial trigger points in your tissues, as discussed in chapters 8 and 9.

There has recently been a good deal of research on the role of substance P in the development of chronic pain disorders. It has been established that in chronic pain disorders, substance P is increased in your spinal cord. Interestingly, substance P is also increased in the nociceptive nerve endings in your tissues where you are chronically experiencing pain. For example, if you have had years of recurrent or chronic pain in your shoulder girdle and neck area, you would have increased substance P levels in that area and in the spinal cord segments that neurologically control your shoulder girdle and lower neck area.

It is also interesting to note that substance P has been found to be significantly higher in the cerebrospinal fluid of fibromyalgia patients. In one study, substance P averaged three times higher in the cerebral spinal fluid of a group of 32 fibromyalgia patients, compared to 30 individuals without fibromyalgia.[168] Other studies have found elevated substance P concentrations in the central nervous system of individuals who suffer with major depression and in those who experience severe stress.[169] These studies may

168 I. J. Russell, M. D. Orr, B. Littman, G. A. Vipraio, D. Alboukrek, J. E. Michalek, Y. Lopez, and F. MacKillip, "Elevated cerebrospinal fluid levels of substance P in patients with the fibromyalgia syndrome," *Arthritis Rheum* 37, no. 11 (November 1994): 1593–601.

169 T. D. Geracioti Jr., L. L. Carpenter, M. J. Owens, D. G. Baker, N. N. Ekhator, P. S. Horn, J. R. Strawn, G. Sanacora, B. Kinkead, L. H. Price, and C. B. Nemeroff, "Elevated cerebrospinal fluid substance P concentrations in post-traumatic stress disorder and major depression," *Am J Psychiatry* 163, no. 4 (April 2006): 637–43.

be showing us one aspect of the chemical connection between chronic pain disorders and depression experienced by so many individuals.

What is exciting about standardized extracts of ginger root is that it contains (6)-shogaol besides other active substances, such as the gingerols. What's special about (6)-shogaol is that research has shown it to reduce substance P in the spinal cords of rats.[170] This mechanism of action may explain why standardized extracts of powdered ginger have been found to be effective in chronic myofascial pain disorders and fibromyalgia syndrome. Because of these findings and my own clinical experience, I recommend that individuals utilizing ginger root extract for chronic pain disorders only utilize supplements that guarantee the quality and concentrations of their ginger root extracts.

Your ginger root extract must be specifically standardized to at least 5% gingerols and shogaols. Standardization of an herbal preparation means that the manufacturer has made sure that a certain percent of the known active ingredient is present in that botanical. This can be quite important, because not all ginger root is high in these shogaol components. It depends on how, where, and under what conditions the ginger plant was grown and prepared, so you want a manufacturer who is testing to make sure the ginger root contains at least 5% of these vital components.

Proper Herbal Supplementation

This brings up a common problem with herbal supplements. Research may show a certain herb (e.g., ginger root) with a certain concentration of active components (e.g., shogaols) at a specific daily dosage (e.g., 2,000 milligrams per day) can have beneficial effects (e.g., reduce inflammation and pain), but the herbal supplement you buy may not be of the same quality or concentration. So the questions you need to ask yourself are, am I getting the same quality herbal preparation as the study used, and am I taking it in a high enough concentration to get the results indicated in the research? In the research on ginger, for example, the researcher was using a high quality, concentrated herbal preparation, but ginger root purchased at the discount store may not have been properly handled and prepared. This is why it is important to buy standardized herbs from quality companies that you trust.

---

170 T. Onogi, M. Minami, Y. Kuraishi, and M. Satoh, "Capsaicin-like effect of (6)–shogaol on substance P-containing primary afferents of rats: a possible mechanism of its analgesic action," *Neuropharmacology* 31, no. 11 (November 1992): 1165–69.

I cannot emphasize the importance of this enough; the most expensive supplement you can buy is one that does you no good. When you try to save money by purchasing a discount herbal preparation, many times the product is not concentrated enough to give you the benefit you desire. Take standardized extracts of ginger root; some of the studies showing reduction in pain and inflammation utilized up to 4,000 milligrams of the standardized ginger per day. If your product has the usual 200 milligrams per capsule, that would mean you would need to take up to twenty capsules a day to reach the dosage used in that research. If you want results, it's important to educate yourself on exactly what type of herb and what amount was utilized in research to produce the health benefit you desire.

Much of the research on standardized ginger root extracts for chronic pain disorders utilized anywhere from 1,000 to 4,000 milligrams per day. The best results are found utilizing products that contain as much as 350 to 500 milligrams of standardized ginger root extract per tablet or capsule. Also, the ginger root extract label must state that it has been standardized to at least 5% gingerols and shogaols. Ideally, these herbal preparations to reduce chronic inflammation are combined with curcumin root extract standardized to 95% curcuminoids (more on this fascinating botanical later in this chapter).

An ideal product may be one that contains a guaranteed concentration of 500 milligrams of the standardized ginger root extract and 250 milligrams of standardized curcumin root extract. At this dosage per tablet, I generally suggest starting out at one tablet twice a day and increasing the dose over the next couple of days to two tablets twice a day, for a total of at least 2,000 milligrams of standardized ginger root extract and 1,000 milligrams of standardized curcumin root extract. If your inflammation and pain are not fully controlled, you may try increasing the dose to two tablets three times a day and even up to two tablets four times a day. Two tablets four times a day would give you a daily dose of 4,000 milligrams of standardized ginger root extract and 2,000 milligrams of standardized curcumin root extract, the upper dosage utilized in the research.

Usually within six weeks of taking this concentrated dosage of ginger root extract, you can lower the dosage to the lowest effective amount needed. This is especially the case if you utilize the complete program described in this book: a healthy Mediterranean diet, omega-3 fatty acids, and magnesium malate with B vitamins and vitamin D. However, as you will see from the other research presented in this chapter, you may want to indefinitely stay on some amount of ginger root extract and curcumin root extract for their many positive health benefits.

Case Study

Linda, a 52-year-old nurse, suffered with chronic pain in her right shoulder girdle and into her right lower neck for almost a decade. She told me that over that period of time she had seen almost 100 doctors for her pain and had only found relief in utilizing oral cortisone, which was causing her many severe side effects. On examination, she fit the common shoulder girdle pain pattern (as described in chapter 11), with chronic active NMLs in her levator scapula and upper trapezius muscles and hidden trigger points in her infraspinatus and rhomboid muscles. Utilizing home trigger point therapy, she was able to begin to lessen the intensity of the pain, but the old patterns would not go away without some extra help. It seemed obvious from her history that she had a chronic pain syndrome that involved the production of substance P in her spinal cord segments and the myofascial tissues of her shoulder girdle. I found placing her on standardized extracts of ginger containing (6)-shogaol of 1 gram four times daily helped her to overcome this chronic pain disorder.

If this isn't enough incentive to add ginger extracts to your healthy diet, then consider the fact that gingerols have been shown to inhibit the growth of colorectal cancer cells. In one study, the researcher Ann Bode noted, "These results strongly suggest that ginger compounds may be effective chemopreventative and/or chemotherapeutic agents for colorectal carcinomas."[171] In other words, ginger has the ability to prevent colon cancer and may even be therapeutic in the treatment of colon cancer! If that isn't impressive enough for you, recent studies have also shown that ginger extracts may be helpful in preventing neurodegenerative disorders, such as Alzheimer's, specifically by inhibiting the genes that create inflammation in certain areas of your brain.[172]

171 A. M. Bode, W. Y. Ma, Y. J. Surh, and Z. Dong, "Inhibition of epidermal growth factor-induced cell transformation and activator protein 1 activation by (6)–gingerols," *Cancer Res* 61, no. 3 (February 1, 2001): 850–53.

172 R. Grzanna, P. Phan, A. Polotsky, L. Lindmark, and C. G. Frondoza, "Ginger extract inhibits beta-amyloid peptide-induced cytokine and chemokine expression in cultured THP-1 monocytes," *J Altern Complement Med* 10, no. 6 (December 2004): 1009–13.

The Power of Turmeric

As powerful as ginger extract is, recent studies have shown extracts of turmeric root (*Curcuma longa*), also referred to as curcumin, to be the most powerful natural antioxidant and anti-inflammatory agent available. For this reason, I always make it a cornerstone of my herbal therapies, combined with ginger root. The only real problems with these herbs are having patients find high-enough quality concentrated extracts, and secondly, getting past the prejudice that they are "just spices." Used medicinally in adequate concentrations, together they are an extremely powerful, natural, and safe substitute for NSAIDs.

Curcumin extracts will help protect your myofascial tissues and the rest of your body against free radical damage through its strong antioxidant capacities.[173] Second, curcumin extract acts as a powerful anti-inflammatory to counteract the formation of systemic inflammation, especially when used in conjunction with 3 grams of omega-3 EPA/DHA supplementation. In numerous studies, curcumin extract's anti-inflammatory abilities have been shown to be comparable to potent drugs, like hydrocortisone, as well as NSAIDs, but without the nasty side effects or safety issues.[174] In a recent comprehensive review of the research literature done at the London Medical School, they found almost 1,500 research papers pertaining to curcumin, most of them written in recent years. In a full review of almost 300 of these research papers on curcumin, it was shown to be nontoxic, have strong antioxidant activity, and modulate numerous contributors to chronic inflammation.[175]

This special characteristic of curcumin extract, the ability to work gently on many different pathways of inflammation, is what makes it such an effective and safe anti-inflammatory.[176] In this way, herbal extracts, such as curcumin, work by making fine adjustments to manage your inflammatory pathways, creating a better, balanced

---

173 A. Ramirez-Boscá, A. Soler, M. A. C. Gutierrez, et al., "Antioxidant curcuma extracts decrease the blood lipid peroxide levels of human subjects," *Age* 18 (1995): 167–69.

174 R. B. Arora, N. Basu, V. Kapoor, and A. P. Jain, "Anti-inflammatory studies on *Curcuma longa* (turmeric)," *Ind J Med Res* 59 (1971): 1289–95.

175 S. Bengmark, "Curcumin, an atoxic antioxidant and natural NF-kappa B, cyclooxygenase-2, lipooxygenase, and inducible nitric oxide synthase inhibitor: a shield against acute and chronic diseases," *JPEN J Parenter Enteral Nutr* 30, no. 1 (Jan–Feb 2006): 45–51.

176 R. C. Lantz, G. J. Chen, A. M. Solyom, S. D. Jolad, and B. N. Timmermann, "The effect of turmeric extracts on inflammatory mediator production," *Phytomedicine* 12, nos. 6–7 (June 2005): 445–52.

response. This is especially true when we look at the multifactorial role the antioxidants in curcumin extracts play in managing chronic inflammation in your tissues.[177] This is in contrast to NSAID therapy that has no antioxidant abilities and tends to go after a vital enzyme pathway with a sledgehammer. NSAIDs work by blocking your inflammatory response, but as discussed in chapters 1 and 2, this will eventually cause tissue destruction. So, do yourself a favor and utilize an herbal product containing quality concentrated ginger and curcumin extracts to manage your chronic pain and inflammation.

Curcumin Extract: Great Support for a Toxic World

The third benefit of curcumin root extract is its ability to protect your liver from a number of toxic compounds and improve your liver's detoxification capabilities, much like the well-known herb milk seed thistle, or silymarin, does. This aspect of curcumin or turmeric root extract makes it a vital component in your regimen to overcome chronic pain and prevent degenerative diseases, especially in our modern, toxic world. In one very well-done study, researchers tested how well turmeric extract could protect the liver and increase detoxification capabilities.

In this study, rats were fed a diet containing carbon tetrachloride, a known carcinogen and toxic chemical found in our environment today. The rats were divided into five different groups: (1) a group was supplemented with turmeric extract and carbon tetrachloride at the same time, and (2) another group of rats were pretreated with turmeric extract for two weeks before being exposed to the toxic chemical carbon tetrachloride. The other three groups of rats were (3) a control group getting nothing but a healthy diet, (4) a group just receiving carbon tetrachloride in their normal diet, and (5) a group supplemented turmeric extract and a healthy diet, nothing else.

This study went on to test different liver enzymes in each of the five test groups. In group 4, the rats given carbon tetrachloride without any turmeric extract, there was as much as a 300% increase in the liver enzymes, showing stress and damage to the liver. In both groups 1 and 2, given the turmeric extracts, the liver enzymes remained well within normal, showing that curcumin had a profound protective effect on the liver. Group 2, pretreated with turmeric extract for two weeks before being exposed to the

177 S. K. Biswas, D. McClure, L. A. Jimenez, I. L. Megson, and I. Rahman, "Curcumin induces glutathione biosynthesis and inhibits NF-kappa B activation and interleukin-8 release in alveolar epithelial cells: mechanism of free radical scavenging activity," *Antioxid Redox Signal* 7, nos. 1–2 (Jan–Feb 2005): 32–41.

carbon tetrachloride, showed even better liver protection, as would be expected.[178] The good news found in this study was upheld in a recent study completed in 2000, also showing that turmeric extract protected the liver from acute and chronic carbon tetrachloride toxic chemical injury.[179]

In numerous studies, turmeric extract has been shown to improve the liver's ability to detoxify toxic chemicals, in addition to the curcuminoids' very potent antioxidant and anti-inflammatory properties. In multiple studies, turmeric extract has been shown to increase the activity of two very important liver detoxification enzymes, one being glutathione S-transferase, or GST.[180] In one study, rats given curcumin for 14 days increased the production of this primary detoxification enzyme (GST) by 16%. Another exciting finding in this study was that an important marker indicating free radical damage, called malondialdehyde, was decreased by 36%.[181]

Malondialdehyde is a by-product of free radical damage to fats in your body that causes mutations in your DNA. Your doctor can test your levels of malondialdehyde to see if you have elevated free radical damage in your tissues. It's important to remember that if malondialdehyde is elevated, you can take concentrated curcumin and retest in 3 to 6 weeks to make sure the oxidative stress is normalizing.

Turmeric extract has also been found to inhibit mutagenic cancer-causing polycyclic aromatic hydrocarbons (PAHs), which are created when society burns any carbon-based fuels, and it is found in cigarette smoke and charred, broiled meats.[182] This is all very exciting information for anyone who lives in our modern, toxic world. Since the EPA determined that the five most toxic chemicals known to man are now present in 100% of all human adipose tissues sampled, you may appreciate how vital extracts of ginger and curcumin root could be in protecting you and your loved ones.

---

178 U. R. Deshpande, S. G. Gadre, A. S. Raste, D. Pillai, S. V. Bhide, and A. M. Samuel, "Protective effect of turmeric (*Curcuma longa L.*) extract on carbon tetrachloride–induced liver damage in rats," *Indian J Exp Biol* 36, no. 6 (June 1998): 573–77.

179 E. J. Park, C. H. Jeon, G. Ko, J. Kim, and D. H. Sohn, "Protective effect of curcumin in rat liver injury induced by carbon tetrachloride," *Pharm Pharmacol* 52, no. 4 (April 2000): 437–40.

180 Biswas, McClure, Jimenez, Megson, and Rahman, "Curcumin induces," 32–41.

181 J. T. Piper, S. S. Signal, M. S. Salameh, R. T. Torman, Y. C. Awasthi, and S. Awasthi, "Mechanisms of anticarcinogenic properties of curcumin: the effect of curcumin on glutathione-linked detoxification enzymes in rat liver," *Int J Biochem Cell Biol* 30, no. 4 (April 1998): 445–56.

182 M. Nagabhushan and S. V. Bhide, "Curcumin as an inhibitor of cancer," *J Am Coll Nutr* 11, no. 2 (April 1992): 192–98.

The volume of research that has demonstrated turmeric extract's ability to counteract toxic chemicals, prevent cancer, and even inhibit cancer cell growth is beyond the scope of this book. But to restate the central theme of this book: if you naturally heal your pain, instead of just seeking quick pain relief, you'll not only conquer your pain but may also prevent premature aging and degenerative disease.

Protecting Your Heart and Brain with Curcumin

One primary example of this theme is the recent research showing that curcumin not only seems to protect against Alzheimer's but may actually help to disintegrate the beta-amyloid plaque associated with the progression of the disease. Anyone who has experienced the suffering of a loved one with Alzheimer's does want to do everything possible to prevent this tragic disorder. Research has established that a healthy diet, such as the Mediterranean diet, along with proper omega-3 fatty acid supplementation and magnesium, is beneficial not only in reducing pain and inflammation but also in the prevention of neurodegenerative disorders. In addition to this dietary program, the addition of curcumin extracts to counteract the oxidative stress and chronic inflammation of the neurodegenerative diseases seems to be a very prudent step, based on all the available research. No one wants to live their life in pain or lose their mind in the end; therefore, to fully illustrate the importance of utilizing these protective herbs, for those who are interested, I will attempt to explain some of the important findings from recent research studies.

Alzheimer's disease involves the accumulation of beta-amyloid fibrils and plaques in specific areas of your brain, such as the hippocampus. As this damage accumulates in the hippocampus of your brain, you have greater difficulty accessing memories, until you actually forget who you are. The beta-amyloid and other factors of Alzheimer's disease have been shown to be caused by oxidative damage and chronic inflammation. Multiple studies have found that curcumin root extracts can cross the blood-brain barrier and have potent anti-inflammatory and antioxidant activities, actually preventing the oxidative damage and inflammation that causes amyloid accumulation.[183]

These same studies help to illustrate how curcumin root extract can be so effective in helping individuals overcome their chronic myofascial pain. Recall from previous chapters how oxidative stress from free radicals induces chronic inflammation. These inflammatory products stimulate the nociceptors in the myofascial tissues and help to induce central sensitization of the neurons in the spinal cord and brain. This is the pro-

183 G. P. Lim, T. Chu, F. Yang, W. Beech, S. A. Frautschy, and G. M. Cole, "The curry spice curcumin reduces oxidative damage and amyloid pathology in an Alzheimer transgenic mouse," *J Neurosci* 21, no. 21 (November 1, 2001): 8370–77.

cess that leads to chronic myofascial pain disorders. Therefore, the ability of turmeric extract to prevent oxidative stress and inflammation in the central nervous system makes it a potent ally in your regimen against chronic myofascial pain.

There has been a tremendous push to market NSAIDs as protection against Alzheimer's because of the inflammation connection to the disease. However, studies have shown that turmeric root extract actually outperforms ibuprofen in this regard; also, curcumin extract inhibits oxidative damage in the brain, whereas ibuprofen does not. Not only does curcumin outperform NSAIDs, but NSAIDs can cause gastrointestinal upset and gastrointestinal bleeding, while the turmeric extract actually protects the gastrointestinal tract. It would seem silly that anyone would choose a drug over this wonderful herb. Another fascinating study just published in 2005 demonstrated the effectiveness of turmeric extract in reducing amyloid levels and effectively disintegrating beta-amyloids in living laboratory animals. This was achieved when mice with advanced amyloid accumulation in their brains were fed curcumin root extract. The researchers went on to state that this data supports the rationale for curcumin to now be used in human clinical trials, not only for preventing but also for treating Alzheimer's disease.[184]

If this wasn't enough, multiple studies have shown that turmeric root extract may help protect against atherosclerosis and cardiovascular disease, the number-one killer in the modern Western world. A study published in 2000 shows that a daily oral administration of turmeric root extract significantly decreases the "bad cholesterols," LDL and apo B, and raises the "good cholesterol," HDL and apo A, of healthy subjects. The research group went on to state that curcumin root extract actually fought atherosclerosis through its antioxidant activity, its ability to reduce fibrinogen levels, and its capacity to normalize the apo B/apo A ratio.[185] These are known to be major risk factors for the development of cardiovascular disease.[186] This study points out that curcumin root extract prevents the free radical damage to cholesterol in your bloodstream. This is major, because it is not cholesterol that damages your blood vessels; it is cholesterol that has been oxidized or damaged by free radicals. Preventing the oxidation of any

---

184 F. Yang, G. P. Lim, A. N. Begum, O. J. Ubeda, M. R. Simmons, S. S. Ambegaokar, P. P. Chen, R. Kayed, C. G. Glabe, S. A. Frautschy, and G. M. Cole, "Curcumin inhibits formation of amyloid beta oligomers and fibrils, binds plaques, and reduces amyloid in vivo," *J Biol Chem* 280, no. 7 (February 18, 2005): 5892–901.

185 Fibrinogen is a factor in your blood that allows it to coagulate, and it may be elevated secondary to systemic inflammation. When it is elevated, you have an increased cardiovascular risk and increased systemic inflammation. An elevated apo B to apo A ratio is a marker for an increased risk for cardiovascular disease.

186 J. Miquel, A. Bernd, J. M. Sempere, J. Diaz–Alperi, and A. Ramirez, "The curcuma antioxidants: pharmacological effects and prospects for future clinical use," *Arch* 34, no. 1 (February 2002): 37–46.

new cholesterol may help reduce the progression of atherosclerosis and cardiovascular disease.

The wonders of curcumin extracts could take up an entire book itself, but it's important to add here that research has also shown it to be an inexpensive, well-tolerated, effective treatment for inflammatory bowel disease.[187] Curcumin has also received a great deal of attention as a promising dietary supplement for cancer prevention and treatment, especially with colon cancer. Curcumin root extract has been found to prevent cancer in multiple ways; for example, its strong antioxidant capabilities enable it to protect the cells of your colon and their cellular DNA from free radical damage. This is vital, because the rapid cellular turnover in the lining of your colon, approximately every three days, makes the DNA of the colon cells highly vulnerable to mutations from carcinogens in your colon. When cellular DNA mutates, it can result in the formation of cancerous cells in your colon or anywhere in your body.

Also, by enhancing liver function, curcumin root extract has been shown to assist the body in destroying mutated cancer cells.[188] A study published in January 2006 demonstrated that curcumin extract can actually inhibit human colon cancer cell growth and may provide a potential therapeutic strategy for the prevention and treatment of colon cancer.[189] Numerous studies have linked the frequent use of turmeric to lower rates of prostate, breast, lung, and colon cancer.

Another very exciting study shows that curcumin extract inhibits the activation of NF-kappa B, a regulatory molecule that signals your genes to produce a variety of inflammation-causing molecules that can promote cancer cell growth. This study also points out something very important: curcumin root extract can regulate the chemical switch NF-kappa B that is "stuck in the on position" when you are suffering with chronic inflammation and pain.[190] This again emphasizes a central theme of the book:

---

187 B. Salh, K. Assi, V. Templeman, K. Parhar, D. Owen, A. Gomez-Munoz, and K. Jacobson, "Curcumin attenuates DNB-induced murine colitis," *Am J Physiol Gastrointest Liver Physiol* 285, no. 1 (July 2003): G235–43.

188 Nagabhushan and Bhide, "Curcumin," 192–98.

189 A. Chen, J. Xu, and A. C. Johnson, "Curcumin inhibits human colon cancer cell growth by suppressing gene expression of epidermal growth factor receptor through reducing the activity of the transcription factor Egr-1," *Oncogene* 25, no. 2 (January 12, 2006): 278–87.

190 S. Shishodia, H. M. Amin, R. Lai, and B. B. Aggarwal, "Curcumin (diferuloylmethane) inhibits constitutive NF-kappa B activation, induces G1/S arrest, suppresses proliferation, and induces apoptosis in mantle cell lymphoma," *Biochem Pharmacol* 70, no. 5 (September 1, 2005): 700–13.

if you work to properly heal your pain naturally, you can overcome the challenge of your chronic myofascial pain and reduce your risk for premature aging and degenerative disease as a side benefit!

Proper Curcumin Root Extract Supplementation

Hopefully, after reading the abbreviated synopsis of recent research on curcumin root extract, you are as excited about utilizing this herb in your wellness program as I am. My family and I personally supplement curcumin extract standardized to 95% on a daily basis, for many of the reasons outlined above. If you want to utilize turmeric extract to lower systemic inflammation or overcome chronic pain, you need to take a very high quality herb that is also standardized to 95% curcuminoids, the active components of turmeric. The same is true if you are looking to enhance liver function, prevent Alzheimer's disease or cardiovascular disease, or lower your risk for breast, prostate, lung, or colon cancer. The herbal formula you take should have around 300 milligrams of quality curcumin root extract standardized to 95% curcuminoids per tablet.

You need this concentration so you can easily get up to the 900 to 1,800 milligrams of curcumin a day necessary to lower inflammation and pain. For the 1,800 milligram level, you would need two tablets three times daily at this concentration. Some individuals with severe chronic pain may need to take three tablets three times daily, for a total of 2,700 milligrams of curcumin extract, to achieve the results desired. The dosage indicated for general wellness and preventative measures runs from 900 to 1,200 milligrams per day of curcumin extract standardized to 95% curcuminoids.

Don't forget about ginger root extract standardized to 5% gingerols and shogaols to lower systemic inflammation and overcome chronic pain. As previously mentioned, an effective supplement to heal your chronic pain would contain approximately 500 milligrams of ginger root extract and 300 milligrams of curcumin root extract, both properly standardized to their active ingredients. A properly designed formula at this level of concentration of standardized extracts of ginger root and curcumin root can be difficult to find. To give you some idea on the cost involved, I can utilize the formula I created for BIOSPEC Nutritionals called Inflam-Rx. This formula contains 500 milligrams of ginger root extract standardized to 5% gingerols and shogaols, 300 milligrams of curcumin root extract standardized to 95% curcuminoids, along with nettle leaf and boswellia servata extract, which are also anti-inflammatory herbs. At full strength, a

120-tablet-size bottle will last you for a full month and cost you a little under thirty dollars. That's under a dollar a day for natural pain relief that also promotes wellness and may help protect you from degenerative diseases, such as Alzheimer's, and colon cancer. Once out of pain, you may find a maintenance dose of one tablet twice a day is all you need to promote overall well-being; the cost then would be less than fifty cents a day. When you decide to start on an anti-inflammatory herb formula to replace your NSAID, shop around and read labels so as to get something similar to this in concentration and quality.

Extra Help from Harpagophytum

Generally, the program outlined in the last couple chapters—self-administered trigger point therapy to your areas of pain, a healthy Mediterranean diet, supplemented omega-3 EPA/DHA fatty acids and magnesium malate with B vitamins—will go a long way in conquering your chronic muscle and joint pain problems. This is especially true when you utilize herbal formulas containing wellness-promoting, concentrated ginger root and curcumin root extracts instead of dangerous NSAIDs. However, if you suffer with severe regional myofascial pain or conditions such as fibromyalgia, you may need an added edge in the beginning of the program. One herb that may help you overcome the challenge of your pain is the botanical called devil's claw. It is important to know its scientific name—*Harpagophytum procumbens*—to make sure you're getting the right herb.

The herb *Harpagophytum* seems to have some of its primary effect at the spinal cord, reducing the nociceptive input from your myofascial tissues. So, *Harpagophytum* is not just working on the anti-inflammatory level, but it may also be working on your central nervous system to lower your pain levels. A recent research review of twelve clinical trials found the herb *Harpagophytum* to be clinically valuable, with adverse side effects equal to that of a placebo.[191] In another study, *Harpagophytum* was tested against the COX-2 inhibitor drug Vioxx (recently taken off the market) and was found to be at least as effective, but of course much safer.[192] Generally, the different studies have found *Harpagophytum* to be most effective when standardized to a specific content of the active component harpagosides. The dose that has been found to be effective in

191 J. J. Gagnier, S. Chrubasik, and E. Manheimer, "Harpagophytum procumbens for osteoarthritis and low back pain: a systematic review," *BMC Complement Altern Med* (September 15, 2004) 4:13.

192 S. Chrubasik, A. Model, A. Black, and S. Pollak, "A randomized double-blind pilot study comparing Doloteffin and Vioxx in the treatment of low back pain," *Rheumatology (Oxford)* 42, no. 1 (January 2003): 141–48.

overcoming musculoskeletal pain is 30 to 60 milligrams of harpagosides per day. So read the label and make sure you are getting a quality *Harpagophytum procumbens* product standardized to a level of harpagosides so you can get 60 milligrams per day of the active component.

There are other herbs that are discussed in the literature for chronic inflammation and pain, such as willow bark. For multiple reasons I will not dwell upon, I prefer standardized extracts of curcumin and ginger root, based on research and clinical experience. Also, I am very partial to extracts of turmeric and ginger because of the tremendous evidence of their greater health benefits. With willow bark, I personally have not found as much research and clinical evidence to justify its use over other herbs. Also, I have concern that those who have allergies to aspirin may react severely to willow bark. I cannot emphasize enough from my own clinical and personal experience the benefit you may receive by utilizing extracts of ginger and curcumin root.

About Possible Herb/Drug Interactions

Regarding side effects or interactions of the botanicals ginger and curcumin root, they are generally regarded as safe, and they have been used in many cultures in large quantities as condiments for generations with no adverse reactions. Both of these herbs have the added benefits of keeping your blood from getting too sticky, which of course helps prevent strokes and heart attacks, much like aspirin has been shown to do. Because of the mild anticoagulant ability of these herbs, *any individual on the drug Coumadin/warfarin must not take these botanicals.* This warning also goes for the supplementation of omega-3 fatty acids that also have the protective, mild anticoagulant properties. The reality is that once you have been put on the very aggressive drug Coumadin/warfarin, you must be extremely careful in any supplementation therapy. The scope of this book does not allow the inclusion of every drug-nutrient or drug-herb interaction, so even if a drug is not mentioned, there may still be a drug-food, drug-nutrient, or drug-herb interaction. Also, new interactions are discovered all the time and may be published after the writing of this book. It is always wise for people taking responsibility for their health to seek information about interactions between a prescription drug and food, herb, or specific nutrient to talk with their pharmacists and prescribing physicians. You can also research this for yourself by going to the complementary and alternative medicine index of the University of Maryland Medical Center at www.umm.edu/altmed.

16

Conquering Maldigestion, Food Allergies, and Dysbiosis

The "Healing Your Pain" program outlined so far will work for most individuals suffering with chronic regional myofascial pain of the low back, neck, extremities, or who have headaches. However, if you have complicating factors such as maldigestion, malabsorption, dysbiosis, toxic chemical exposure, or poor detoxification capacity, you may need to address these factors along with the previously described program to once and for all conquer your pain. If one or more of these complicating factors are present in your life, you may also be dealing with more severe pain and fatigue, or even fibromyalgia syndrome (FMS) or chronic fatigue immune dysfunction syndrome (CFIDS). You may also find it difficult to cope emotionally with your life because of your severe loss of vitality. Problems with the major Ds—digestion, dysbiosis, and detoxification—will make it extremely difficult for you to absorb and utilize the nutrients you need to create healthy tissues and energy levels necessary for wellness. Complications with digestion, dysbiosis, and detoxification can also cause a self-poisoning of your metabolic pathways, again making it difficult to create healthy energy levels necessary for real wellness.

Poor Digestion, Food Allergies, and Chronic Pain

Recall from chapter 3 the step-by-step process and vital importance of proper digestion and absorption. The digestive tract is that magical place where annually 1,538 pounds of the earth's bounty comes into you and selected bits and pieces are chosen to become you. From this river of earthly elements, you constantly build and maintain your physical self, and create the energy that breathes life into you. Digestion is the process whereby you break down large molecules into smaller units for absorption and utilization. This process of digestion and absorption is the most energy-demanding thing your body does, and when you lose your vitality, one of the first places it shows up is with decreased digestive ability.

Stomach hydrochloric acid is extremely important for starting out the process of digestion and for protecting you against "bad bugs," or pathogenic organisms, setting up housekeeping in your intestines.[193] When you have low stomach acid, a condition called hypochlorhydria, you can develop the problems of maldigestion and malabsorption. One of the primary forms of maldigestion with hypochlorhydria is poor breakdown of proteins. When proteins are not fully broken down into amino acids, these partial proteins tend to be a source of food allergies. Food allergies cause a wide variety of symptoms and afflict approximately 8% of children and 2% of adults worldwide. Food allergies can cause you a variety of symptoms that range from the obvious skin and gastrointestinal problems to respiratory disorders and even emotional and behavioral problems. One of the most common problems caused by hidden food allergies is chronic fatigue coupled with muscle aches and pain. In clinical practice, I have seen this many times, and when the hidden food allergies are discovered and removed from the diet, a great deal of the musculoskeletal pain is alleviated. More importantly, these hidden allergies are usually an indication of maldigestion that must be improved for individuals to heal their pain and promote real wellness in their lives.

Improving Your Digestion and Absorption

To improve digestion and overcome the challenge of food allergies, especially when they are multiple, start with the supplementation of betaine hydrochloride capsules and pancreatic digestive enzymes. This will help promote the complete breakdown of dietary proteins. Pancreatic digestive enzymes can be found in health food stores and come from an animal source, usually porcine (pig). These tablets contain the enzymes protease, lipase, and amylase to digest proteins, fats, and carbohydrates. However, I find that with normalizing digestion in the stomach with betaine HCL, pancreatic enzymes are usually unnecessary.

193 A. Pilotto, "Aging and the gastrointestinal tract," *Ital J Gastroenterol Hepatol* 31, no. 2 (March 1999): 137–53.

Betaine hydrochloride generally comes in five-grain capsules, which is equivalent to about 325 milligrams. Supplementation of betaine hydrochloride is contraindicated if you have a prior history of or a current peptic or duodenal ulcer. However, as previously explained in chapter 3, stomach nausea and even acid reflux is often caused by a deficiency of hydrochloric acid in your stomach. So seek the assistance of a clinician knowledgeable in nutrition to determine if betaine hydrochloride supplementation would be helpful in your particular situation.

The typical signs and symptoms of low stomach acid are the 4 Bs: burping, belching, burning, and bloating after meals. The burning is from the acid reflux that is caused by having low stomach acid. Other very common signs of low stomach acid are flatulence and nausea, especially the nausea that comes after taking your nutritional supplements. One of the biggest culprits for promoting nausea is magnesium supplementation, because magnesium needs sufficient hydrochloric acid for proper absorption. So if you get nausea or diarrhea from your magnesium, it's a good indication of poor absorption of this mineral and a real need for it to be taken with hydrochloric acid. The amount of betaine hydrochloride you need per meal depends on what you can tolerate and how much hydrochloric acid your stomach is still producing. The normal stomach will produce varying amounts of hydrochloric acid, depending on what and how much it needs to digest. The stomach can produce up to 200 grains of hydrochloride; however, you should never take more 10 to 20 grains without the assistance of a nutritionally trained doctor.

Another major cause of food sensitivities and allergies is the growth of unhealthy bacteria in your intestinal tract. The growth of unhealthy microbes, or dysbiosis, creates inflammation and causes damage to the lining of your small intestine. This causes microscopic tears in your intestinal lining, allowing the absorption of undigested proteins. This absorption of undigested proteins can activate an immune response, causing you systemic inflammation. This chronic low-grade inflammation can "settle in," or attack, various tissues, causing a variety of symptoms. For example, if this food allergy-induced inflammation settles in your sinuses due to dairy protein, you can get chronic sinusitis. If the chronic inflammation tends to settle on your skin from a wheat allergy, you would find symptoms of eczema, or allergic dermatitis. This low-grade systemic inflammation can also settle in your myofascial tissues and cause you generalized aches and pains. This is why food allergies have been related to fibromyalgia and different forms of arthritis.

With this knowledge, if you suffer with chronic pain or an inflammatory disease, you may want to consider the role that food allergies or sensitivities may be playing in your health problems. To tackle these problems, first consider improving your digestion by possibly adding betaine hydrochloride and/or pancreatic digestive enzymes if you do not have a prior history of or a current peptic or duodenal ulcer. It is beneficial to find a clinician who truly understands maldigestion and malabsorption disorders to help you in this task. The next thing to do to overcome the challenge of food allergies or sensitivities is to remove any unwanted microbes in your intestinal tract and reinoculate your gut with beneficial bacteria, such as lactobacillus. This subject will be covered in greater detail in a later section of this chapter. But, the most important thing you can do to conquer any symptoms that may arise from food allergies or sensitivities is to completely remove the symptom-causing foods from your diet.

Self-Diagnosing Food Sensitivities or Allergies

To identify possible food allergies or sensitivities, it is sometimes helpful to keep a diet diary by writing down what you eat and any immediate or delayed food reactions you may experience. The problem with this approach is that some food allergy reactions can be delayed by as much as 6 to 72 hours, so if you get a reaction six hours after lunch while eating dinner, consider the possibility that the symptoms are actually coming from a food you ate at lunch or even breakfast. This is where an elimination diet can be very helpful. To follow an elimination diet, you simply remove completely from your diet the most common allergy-causing foods and any foods you suspect you are sensitive to.

Foods that tend to cause the most allergies are corn, gluten, dairy, beef, pork, citrus fruits, eggs, soybeans, high-fructose corn syrup, artificial sweeteners, various food additives, and colorants. To really test the possibility that one of these common foods is causing your symptoms, generally you must completely eliminate these foods from your diet for three weeks. A side benefit of the elimination diet, if there are allergies, is that patients tend to lose 4 to 6 pounds over the three-week trial. Part of the reason for this is that allergens tend to cause fluid retention. Fluid retention is another way to determine if you're allergic to something in a meal. If you don't get symptoms but find that your rings are tighter or you shot up three pounds after a meal from fluid retention, you may be having a food allergy reaction.

After you've completed three weeks, you will then need to slowly reintroduce the foods back into your diet one at a time to evaluate if they cause symptoms or worsen your condition. You will want to give each food three days between the reintroduction of the next. Remember that delayed food allergies can take up to three days to show up. It can be extremely helpful to find a clinician who not only understands maldigestion, malabsorption, and dysbiosis, but also has a firm grasp of diagnosing and treating food allergies. You can see that this very inexpensive way of testing for food allergies can be very slow and arduous, so you may want to consider utilizing special lab tests.

Utilizing Clinical Allergy Testing

There are special blood tests to diagnose actual food allergy reactions involving your immune system that your doctor can easily order and run for you. These blood tests, however, are not as accurate as you identifying specific foods with an elimination diet, where you actually experience the allergic symptoms. But a blood test can give you results within days instead of taking weeks to months to fully identify your problem-causing foods. The blood lab work I like to use is the ELISA test, which measures your body's production of IgE and IgG antibodies to specific foods.

The IgE antibody reaction to a food is immediate and, many times, severe. This is generally the immunological reaction that takes place when someone's throat swells shut and threatens their life just from eating strawberries. It is also the IgE allergic reaction that creates immediate hives on the skin after eating a specific food. Because IgE allergic reactions happen within minutes to a few hours after eating something, people tend to know they react to that particular food. The IgG antigen reaction is the delayed immunological response that may take up to 72 hours to manifest, making identification of the food allergy harder to spot. This is where the ELISA test can be very helpful in letting you know if a delayed food allergy may be a source of your aches, pains, and fatigue. With this test, you can check hundreds of foods and get results within days. You then need to remove those foods from your diet that the ELISA test indicates you are allergic to, and see if it makes a difference in your symptoms.

The ELISA test is not 100% accurate, but it's very convenient and about the most accurate lab test you can do for food allergies. Still, there is no better test than to remove a food completely, feel better, reintroduce the food, and finally feel worse again, to know you are either allergic or sensitive to that food or food group. It may sound overwhelming to try and track down the culprits, but the research and my clinical experience tells me that there can be tremendous payoffs if you find and remove an offending food. I have seen many patients with histories encompassing years of chronic pain have their pain vanish virtually overnight once they stopped eating a certain food or food group that was causing them problems. The medical literature is filled with studies showing that the removal of certain foods can relieve the symptoms of many common and baffling disorders: for example, attention deficit disorder,[194] migraine headaches, bedwetting, eczema, hyperactivity,[195] irritable bowel syndrome, rheumatoid arthritis, and Crohn's disease.

The Health Consequences of the Right Microbes in Your Gut

From the beginning of your small bowel to the end of your colon lives a diverse population of beneficial bacteria that actually outnumber the cells in your body. These beneficial bacteria are few in number beginning in the small bowel, but they grow in increasing numbers and concentration as you near the distal colon. Overall, you contain over 100,000 billion intestinal bacteria with a collective weight of around six pounds, making this vital gut flora the largest organ in your body. Recently, some scientists have stated that the DNA of the 400+ bacterial families present in the human intestinal tract should be included as part of the present human genome project. Their reasoning for this is that these bacteria have symbiotically evolved with the human, and continued existence of the human species is impossible without this gut flora.

These important, beneficial microorganisms synthesize important vitamins and nutrients that keep you and your digestive tract healthy, such as B_{12}, biotin, pantothenic acid, vitamin K, and butyric acid. These microbes also produce fuel for the cells of your intestinal wall, allowing them to produce adequate energy to stay healthy. This is one reason why your intestinal wall becomes damaged if you don't have adequate, healthy

194 C. M. Carter, M. Urbanowics, R. Hemsley, et al., "Effects of a few food diets in attention deficit disorder," *Arch Dis Child* 69, 5 (1993): 564–68.

195 J. Egger, C. M. Carter, J. F. Soothill, and J. Wilson, "Effect of diet treatment on enuresis in children with migraine or hyperkinetic behavior," *Clin Pediatr* 13, 5 (1992): 302–7.

gut bacteria. These beneficial bacteria also keep unhealthy microbes from growing in your intestines, and the presence of healthy bacteria helps to convert toxic substances into less-toxic forms. Another recently appreciated aspect of their beneficial behavior is their ability to improve your immune system's function.

Modern dietary patterns, medications, food additives, and toxic chemicals in our food and environment are poisoning the healthy bacteria in our gastrointestinal tract. It is now estimated that up to 20% of the U.S. population suffers with irritable bowel syndrome. This troubling and sometimes disabling functional gastrointestinal disorder, characterized by abdominal pain and altered bowel habits, has been associated with altered gut bacteria. A review of the research is now showing a correlation between irritable bowel syndrome and dysbiosis of the small intestine.[196] Recent research studies have also shown that certain specific strains of beneficial bacteria are able to improve irritable bowel syndrome.[197] In light of this convincing research, it seems strange to me that individuals with IBS, IBD, and other gastrointestinal disorders are not more aggressively treated with beneficial bacteria instead of drugs that only suppress the symptoms!

Dysbiosis is generally defined as the growth of unwanted and pathogenic microbes anywhere along your digestive tract. Small bowel bacterial overgrowth (SBBO) can have a negative effect on the delicate environment of your small intestine. Dysbiosis in the small bowel can wreak damage to the highly selective lining of the small intestine, causing increased absorption of unwanted products of metabolism, or wastes, from these unwanted microbes.[198]

Unwanted dysbiotic bacteria, yeast, and protozoa growing and multiplying in your gut produce, like all living things, waste products, cellular debris, and metabolic products. These byproducts of unwelcome microbial growth in your intestines are referred to as *endotoxins* because they are poisonous (*-toxin*) to your cells and they are produced on the inside (*endo-*). Endotoxins produced by these microbes have very fitting names,

---

196 H. R. Lee and M. Pimentel, "Bacteria and irritable bowel syndrome: the evidence for small intestinal bacterial overgrowth," *Curr Gastroenterol Rep* 8, no. 4 (August 2006): 305–11.

197 S. Nobaek, M. L. Johansson, G. Molin, S. Ahrne, and B. Jeppsson, "Alteration of intestinal microflora is associated with reduction in abdominal bloating and pain in patients with irritable bowel syndrome," *Am J Gastroenterol* 95, no. 5 (May 2000): 1231–38.

198 S. M. Riordan, C. J. McIver, D. H. Thomas, V. M. Duncombe, T. D. Bolin, and M. C. Thomas, "Luminal bacteria and small-intestinal permeability," *Scand J Gastroenterol* 32, no. 6 (June 1997): 556–63.

such as putrescine and cadaverine—you can imagine why they are called by these names! The problem is that these endotoxins are absorbed into your body and then interfere with normal cellular and body functions. The absorption of the bacterial or fungal debris and endotoxins from these harmful microbes in your small intestine can circulate throughout your body in your bloodstream. These toxic foreign materials can then attach to the surface of your cells in your tissues and cause the activation of chronic inflammation and oxidative stress.[199]

Dysbiosis and Your Chronic Pain

Here is a vital connection you may have been wondering about: yes, dysbiosis can be a major factor in your chronic myofascial pain and degenerative disease, as previously described in chapter 5. The increased permeability caused by dysbiosis in the small intestine, as previously discussed, can also increase your likelihood of food sensitivities and allergies through the absorption of partially digested proteins. These partial food proteins can then circulate in your bloodstream and be "seen" by your immune system as a viruslike foreign invader, stimulating an allergic reaction and chronic inflammation, creating muscle pain and joint degeneration!

This absorption of bacterial debris, along with their endotoxins and partial food proteins, may explain why dysbiosis is so highly associated with systemic inflammatory disorders and chronic myofascial pain. Recent studies have shown that dysbiosis is associated with many chronic pain disorders, such as IBS, regional myofascial pain syndrome, fibromyalgia, interstitial cystitis, and chronic fatigue syndrome. The fact that a high percentage of individuals actually suffer with many of these disorders at the same time adds weight to the argument that these disorders may have a shared cause in dysbiosis. Fibromyalgia, chronic fatigue, depression, and irritable bowel syndrome (IBS) are notorious for ganging up on the same individual.[200] Statistically, 81% of fibromyalgia patients report problems with bowel function,[201] and 1 out of 3 people

199 H. L. Pahl, "Activators and target genes of Rel/NF-kappa B transcription factors," *Oncogene* 18, no. 49 (November 22, 1999): 6853–66.

200 L. A. Aaron, M. M. Burke, and D. Buchwald, "Overlapping conditions among patients with chronic fatigue syndrome, fibromyalgia, and temporomandibular disorder," *Arch Intern Med* 160, no. 2 (January 24, 2000): 221–77. L. A. Aaron and D. Buchwald, "Chronic diffuse musculoskeletal pain, fibromyalgia and comorbid unexplained clinical conditions," *Best Pract Res Clin Rheumatol* 17, no. 4 (August 2003): 563–74.

201 G. Triadafilopulus, et al., "Bowel dysfunction in fibromyalgia syndrome," *Dig Dis Sci* 36, no. 1 (January 1991): 59–64.

with fibromyalgia are medically diagnosed with irritable bowel syndrome.[202] Research has now demonstrated that individuals with irritable bowel syndrome harbor bacterial overgrowth in their painful small intestines, and the removal of these unwanted microbes reduces the symptoms.[203]

Even more important to our discussion of muscle and joint pain is the very exciting research showing a strong correlation between chronic myofascial pain conditions and small intestine bacterial overgrowth. In two studies, researchers compared the lab findings between one group of individuals with irritable bowel syndrome and another group with fibromyalgia syndrome. In these two studies, an amazing 100% of the fibromyalgia patients' lab work tested positive for small intestine bacterial overgrowth, or dysbiosis. This establishes some extremely strong evidence that chronic myofascial pain disorders, at least in fibromyalgia, are caused, maintained, and/or worsened by bacterial overgrowth in the small intestine.[204]

This ground-breaking research should motivate any individual with chronic myofascial pain, especially fibromyalgia, to do everything possible to restore the healthy six pounds of good microbes in their intestines (please refer to pages 286–288 on restoring healthy bacteria in the gastrointestinal tract). This 10 out of 10 correlation between the small intestine bacterial overgrowth and the chronic muscle pain in two studies is enough evidence to indicate dysbiosis as a causative factor. This finding is even more amazing considering the fact that studies find about an 8 out of 10 correlation between chronic abdominal pain from IBS and positive lab findings for small bowel bacterial growth.[205] At first glance this is surprising, for one would have expected a stronger correlation between dysbiosis and chronic abdominal pain than between chronic myofascial pain and small intestine bacterial overgrowth.

Interestingly, these two studies found a 100% correlation between dysbiosis and fibromyalgia syndrome, and the higher the patient's measured lab results were, indicating greater bacterial overgrowth and production of the endotoxins, the worse were the presence of fibromyalgia and chronic muscle pain symptoms. So possibly the worse your fibromyalgia is, the more severe is your dysbiosis! The relationship between

202 A. D. Sperber, Y. Atzomn, et al., "Fibromyalgia in the irritable bowel syndrome: studies of prevalence and clinical implications," *Am J Gastroenterol* 94, no. 12 (December 1999): 3541–46.

203 Pimentel, Chow, and Lin, "Eradication," 3503–6.

204 M. Pimentel, D. Wallace, D. Hallegua, E. Chow, Y. Kong, S. Park, and H. C. Lin, "A link between irritable bowel syndrome and fibromyalgia may be related to findings on lactulose breath testing," *Ann Rheum Dis* 63, no. 4 (April 2004): 450–52.

205 Lee and Pimentel, "Bacteria and irritable bowel syndrome," 305–11.

dysbiosis and chronic pain has also been established by recent research on animals, published in the journal *Pain*. When the central nervous systems of rats were exposed to the endotoxins of the intestinal bacteria E. coli, amazingly these animals developed global hyperalgesia, meaning all-over pain and tenderness, just as in fibromyalgia syndrome.[206]

Those findings correlate well with my own clinical observations and those of other clinicians. Not to sound too simplistic about this complex syndrome, but generally fibromyalgia patients are individuals with a large number of pain-causing myofascial trigger points throughout their bodies, along with the complication of small intestine bacterial overgrowth, or dysbiosis. Remember that dysbiosis can cause inflammation and oxidative stress in your myofascial tissues, through the absorption of endotoxins and partial food proteins. This chronic inflammation and oxidative stress from dysbiosis sets you up for the formation of multiple pain-causing trigger points throughout your body (see chapter 8). It is also interesting to note that some of the other symptoms that irritable bowel syndrome patients often complain of, such as increased achiness, fatigue, headaches, depression, anxiety, and disruption of sleep patterns, match up well to the symptoms of fibromyalgia. Dysbiosis may be part of the source of the "sick and sore all over" complaint of fibromyalgia and chronic fatigue patients.

Other studies have shown that these absorbed bacterial endotoxins from dysbiosis can cause inflammation of your liver.[207] This leads to another problem with dysbiosis, or altered gut flora: it can overwhelm your liver's detoxification capacity, especially now in our modern, toxic world. This makes complete sense when you realize that a healthy gastrointestinal tract is your first defense against toxic substances entering your body. Besides providing an active barrier to toxic substances, your intestinal tract acts biochemically to help detoxify many toxic substances.

Finding Out What's Wrong

To create a healthy and dynamic gastrointestinal tract, it is often helpful to know the exact nature of the problem you are dealing with; therefore, some laboratory testing may be in order. Simple blood analysis by your doctor may reveal many different types of anemia, which could be related to iron, B_{12}, or folic acid deficiency, depending on the results. Sometimes these deficiencies can be related to malabsorption or chronic in-

206 K. Walker, A. Dray, and M. Perkins, "Hyperalgesia in rats following intracerebroventricular administration of endotoxins: effect of bradykinin, B1 and B2 receptor antagonists," *Pain* 65 (1996): 211–19.

207 S. M. Riordan, C. J. McIver, and R. Williams, "Liver damage in human small intestinal bacterial overgrowth," *Am J Gastro* 93, no. 2 (February 1998): 234–47.

flammation and bleeding from the gastrointestinal tract. Changes in your white blood cell count can sometimes be a sign of chronic yeast or viral infections; for example, when you have low neutrophils and high lymphocytes. When a special type of white blood cell called eosinophil is elevated, it usually indicates parasites or allergies, and further testing should follow.

Comprehensive Digestive Stool Analysis, or CDSA

An excellent test for studying the quality of your digestive system is the comprehensive digestive stool analysis, or CDSA, which can be easily ordered by your doctor. With this test, your doctor sends a sample of your stool to a lab that specializes in this specific procedure, which is not a simple stool analysis run by any general lab. From a stool sample many things can be determined by a CDSA, such as maldigestion, malabsorption, and inflammation of the gastrointestinal tract. They will also culture the stool to determine the type and number of beneficial bacteria, such as bifidobacteria and lactobacillus, to determine if supplementation of probiotic, or good bacteria, would be beneficial.

In this CDSA, they also carefully culture your stool for the presence of any harmful microbes, such as clostridium, streptococcus, nisseria, and E. coli, in your lower bowel. When dysbiosis is found through the presence of unwanted microbes, they will test what therapeutic agents are capable of eliminating them. This comprehensive digestive stool analysis will also be cultured to determine if there are any pathological yeasts and fungi present in your colon, such as Candida yeast. In general, the CDSA will cost you around 255 to 300 dollars to run. If you cannot find a doctor to run this vital test for you, go to www.crohns.net and go to the bottom link on their menu, Genova Digestive Tests, and click on it. It will bring you to a page listing the CDSA GSD1000 test kit, which you can order online. Because dysbiosis plays such a major role in chronic pain, I believe it's vital for you to be able to test for it.

There is also a CDSA with parasitology, where lab technicians will perform a thorough physical examination of your stool to look for any parasites or larvae, such as Giardia, that may be the source of any gastrointestinal or systemic problems you may be experiencing. This is a very helpful clinical lab to run if you have any gastrointestinal disturbances, but it is also extremely helpful to do if you suffer with chronic myofascial pain and/or chronic fatigue. The addition of a parasitological exam adds another 100 to 150 dollars to the CDSA, but it is very well worth it.

Urinary Organic Acid Test

One clinical lab that I find extremely easy to run and very illuminating as to the patient's underlying metabolic problems is a urinary organic acid test; this is especially helpful in diagnosing dysbiosis, or bacterial overgrowth of the small intestine. This special test is extremely important in light of the research showing a 100% correlation between the chronic myofascial pain of fibromyalgia and dysbiosis of the small intestine. It is important to point out here that the comprehensive digestive stool analysis (CDSA) really only gives you an idea of what kind of bacteria is growing in your large intestine; it can miss dysbiosis in the small intestine. Therefore, if you have chronic myofascial pain, especially that of fibromyalgia, you may want to consider doing a urinary organic acid test for dysbiosis. There are a few labs in the United States that specialize in performing this lab test, such as Metametrix in Atlanta, Georgia, and the Great Plains Laboratory in Kansas. You can find them online at www.metametrix.com and www.greatplainslaboratory.com.

Discuss the importance of these lab tests with your clinician and ask him or her to go online and review the information available at www.metametrix.com. What follows is a brief description of the urinary organic acid test for dysbiosis. It will provide you with a basis to discuss this lab test with your clinician. And if you are a health-care provider, this may act as an introduction to the subject of urinary organic acids.

If your urinary organic acid test comes back high in urinary indican, it can indicate small intestine bacterial overgrowth. Indican is a metabolite created when there are a high number of undesirable bacteria in your small intestine. Indican gets absorbed and is then excreted in your urine. Another urinary organic acid with a fancy name is p-hydroxyphenylacetate, and when it is elevated in your urine, this metabolite is a strong indication of Giardia growing in your small intestine. Many have heard of this dreaded protozoa causing great intestinal distress when hikers drink from contaminated streams. I experienced this myself once when on a wilderness excursion; I drank from a contaminated stream. From that experience, I found that after the acute attack is over, chronic symptoms can plague you for years; that is, until the Giardia is completely removed. There are many other urinary organic acids that can help you determine if your chronic pain and health problems are related to small intestine bacterial overgrowth. These urinary organic acid levels can also be utilized to see if the therapy being used to remove the unwanted microbes from your gut is actually working.

Another significant urinary organic acid is known as D-arabinitol, a known byproduct or metabolite from the pathogenic yeast Candida. When D-arabinitol is elevated in your urine, it is highly suggestive of overgrowth of the pathogenic Candida yeast somewhere in your gastrointestinal tract.[208] The general symptoms found with yeast infections are chronic fatigue, loss of energy, general malaise, and increased muscle aches and pains. Gastrointestinal symptoms tend to be bloating, gas, intestinal cramps, and altered bowel function. There has been a great deal written about Candida syndrome, and it has caused a great deal of controversy in the world of medicine. On the other hand, there has been an overdiagnosis of Candida syndrome among natural and alternative health-care practitioners. In a way, this is a disservice to those who really do suffer with dysbiosis related to Candida yeast. If you have been diagnosed with Candida syndrome, or suspect you may have it, and want to get to the truth about its possible role in your chronic pain and health problems, I highly recommend having D-arabinitol measured in your urine. If you really do have candida growing in your gut, this yeast cannot help but give off D-arabinitol, which will show up in your urine: This way, there is no guesswork about it; either you do or you do not have Candida syndrome! D-arabinitol can also be used to monitor the success of the therapeutic intervention used to remove Candida yeast from your gut.

Urinary Organic Acid Test for Dysbiosis

- URINARY INDICAN: The greater the bacterial overgrowth is in your small bowel, the higher the level of indican in your urine. Indican is normal at low levels; however, elevated urinary indican is specific for small bowel bacterial overgrowth and the health problems this can create, such as fibromyalgia.
- URINARY HYDROXYPHENYLACETATE: This organic acid elevates in your urine when general dysbiosis is present in your gastrointestinal tract.
- URINARY 2, 3-DIHYDROXYPHENYLPROPIONATE OR DHPP: An organic acid that tends to be specific for clostridia bacterial overgrowth in your intestines.
- URINARY P-HYDROXYPHENYLACETATE: Organic acid elevation specifically associated with small bowel Giardia infestation.

208 S. Tokunaga, et al., "Clinical significance of measurement of serum D-arabinitol levels in Candiduria patients," *Urol Int* 48, no. 2 (1992): 195–99.

URINARY D-ARABINITOL: This urinary organic acid is a byproduct metabolite of pathogenic Candida yeast growth in your intestinal tract. When there is elevated urinary D-arabinitol and serum D-arabinitol, it can indicate invasive candidiasis that has infested more then the gastrointestinal tract.

Getting Rid of Pain-Causing "Bad Bugs" in Your Gut

If the presence of any urinary organic acids indicating dysbiosis, such as D-arabinitol, indican, or p-Hydroxyphenylacetate, is found in your urine, you will want to start a treatment program to remove them immediately. And if any unhealthy microbes, such as Candida, Giardia, or pathological bacteria, are cultured in your comprehensive stool analysis, you will want to quickly eliminate them from your colon. To accomplish this, it's important to eat a diet that helps limit the growth of "bad bugs" in your intestines. This is accomplished by completely removing all sugars, simple and refined carbohydrates, as well as any yeasted or fermented foods from your diet. Sugars and simple carbohydrates only add fuel to the fire of the overgrowth by feeding the yeast and unwanted microbes in your gastrointestinal tract.

There are nonprescription herbs that can help kill off the unhealthy microbes growing in your intestinal tract, such as standardized extracts of oregano and the active ingredient berberine sulfate from different berberine-containing plants.[209] Also helpful as nonprescription antifungals are citrus seed extracts and caprylic acid. Various studies have also shown that ginger and curcumin root have antifungal and antibacterial capabilities.[210] Recall from chapter 15 the many tremendous benefits of utilizing standardized extracts of ginger and curcumin root for your general wellness besides treating your chronic myofascial pain. The added benefit that ginger and curcumin can also eliminate and control pathogenic organisms in your intestines makes them all the more

209 M. Friedman, P. R. Henika, and R. E. Mandrell, "Bactericidal activities of plant essential oils and some of their isolated constituents against Campylobacter jejuni, Escherichia coli, Listeria monocytogenes, and Salmonella enterica," *J Food Prot* 65, no. 10 (Oct. 2002): 1545–60.

210 C. E. Ficker, J. T. Arnason, P. S. Vindas, L. P. Alvarez, K. Akpagana, M. Gbeassor, C. De Souza, and M. L. Smith, "Inhibition of human pathogenic fungi by ethnobotanically selected plant extracts," *Mycoses* 46, nos. 1–2 (February 2003): 29–37.

important to include in your regimen. Don't forget that these herbs also reduce inflammation and improve healing of your gastrointestinal tract when dysbiosis is present.

If you are unable to remove the "bad bugs" from your gut with a natural approach, you may need to find the assistance of a physician who can help you with prescription medications. The drawback to this is that antibiotics tend to kill off the beneficial bacteria in your intestines, and chronic use of antibiotics is one of the predisposing factors in the development of dysbiosis. Recurrent use of antibiotics can also cause a vicious cycle of increased yeast or fungal growth, by eliminating the beneficial bacteria that keep Candida in check. Other prescription medications to counteract protozoa and parasites can also have some very strong side effects.

Once you have begun to eliminate the offending microbes from your gut, you will want to replace them with beneficial bacteria, generally called probiotics. The use of probiotics can have many beneficial effects on your health, besides competing with unwanted microbes and keeping them from growing in your gut. Recent studies have shown that probiotics can be very helpful in preventing and controlling the development of various disorders, such as asthma, eczema, allergies, and inflammation.[211] In general, the supplementation of beneficial bacteria will take approximately one to three months to begin to normalize the microflora of your intestines. When buying a probiotics supplement, it is usually best to buy from quality firms that guarantee their potency. Some products have been found to contain no live bacteria in the capsules because they have been damaged in processing or storage.

Try to buy brands of beneficial flora that are a mixture of freeze-dried lactobacillus acidophilus, lactobacillus rhamnosis, bifidobacteria lactis, and bifidobacteria bifidum packed in capsules. It is usually advisable to take about 6 to 9 billion organisms a day, in divided doses. In other words, if your probiotics supplement contains 3 billion viable organisms per capsule, you would need one capsule two to three time daily to achieve this desired dosage. Do not be shy about supplementation; some studies have shown that to correct severe gastrointestinal dysfunction from dysbiosis, daily doses may need to reach 30 to 50 billion viable organisms per day, which can get to be quite a few capsules.

---

211 M. Kalliomaki, S. Salminen, T. Poussa, H. Arvilommi, and E. Isolauri, "Probiotics and prevention of atopic disease: 4-year follow-up of a randomized placebo-controlled trial," *Lancet* 361, no. 9372 (May 31, 2003): 1869–71.

Never Forget Fiber

Along with adding digestive enzymes, eliminating any offending foods, and killing off intestinal pathogens and replacing them with beneficial probiotics, make sure that you also improve your overall digestion with fiber supplementation. It is extremely helpful for your digestion and to normalize your intestinal tract to increase fiber from a variety of sources. An excellent source is fresh-ground flax seeds, approximately 2 tablespoons per day. You can grind up about a cup at a time and keep it in a sealed container in your freezer. Use it on salads and vegetable dishes to add many health benefits. Another healthy form of added fiber is obtained by eating a couple handfuls of nuts each day, the best probably being almonds, walnuts, or pecans. Again, the importance of increasing fresh vegetables in your diet cannot be overemphasized; they are an excellent source of fiber, add very few calories, and are high in antioxidants and phytonutrients. The highest source of dietary fiber, surprisingly, is found in beans, which should be added to your diet for their many health benefits. It's also important to utilize a good fiber supplement containing both soluble and insoluble fibers, with no sweeteners or chemical additives. Build up the quantity of fiber in your diet slowly to avoid any gas or bloating.

17

Strategies to Enhance Detoxification and Energy Production

Through the air you breathe and the water you bathe in, you bring cell-damaging pollutants into your body. Along with the 1,530 pounds of your yearly food and water intake enter pounds of herbicides, pesticides, fungicides, food additives, chemical preservatives, and industrial chemical contaminants. Annually, we each absorb an enormous load of toxic substances from the outer environment. Furthermore, there are endotoxins from unhealthy bacteria in your gut that get absorbed into your bloodstream. All these toxic substances will eventually be challenged by your liver in the attempt to render them harmless and remove them from your body. In fact, 75% of all the blood that reaches your liver comes directly from your intestines and other abdominal organs. The other 25% of the blood that reaches your liver is from the rest of your body (skin, lungs, brain, etc.), which also must be detoxified. This toxic exposure means that your liver is under a constant challenge to keep your inner environment as toxin-free as humanly possible.

Liver: The Answer to All Questions

There is an old joke in human physiology classes that whenever you don't know the answer to a question, just put down "the liver." This usually works, because the liver is an extremely complex organ that performs many metabolic functions for the body, especially those involved with detoxification. The liver must handle and render harmless a wide range of toxic chemicals from your modern environment, as well as toxins produced in your own body. Even the healthiest human in a pristine environment 10,000 years ago naturally produced a wide range of noxious chemicals and hormones that had to be neutralized by the liver. The liver had evolved to handle this natural background level and type of internally produced toxins. However, this detoxification was only possible if the individual had adequate nutrients to support proper liver detoxification.

Now, at a time of overconsumption of empty calories and undernutrition of needed nutrients, we modern humans are having difficulty handling our own internally produced metabolic byproducts and hormones. This becomes more complicated when we suffer from "bad bugs" growing in our gut, producing copious endotoxins, adding to our liver's workload. Add toxic chemicals from our modern environment and you now have a liver desperately in need of assistance. In this chapter, we will outline a comprehensive program to help you do exactly this.

Your liver plays multiple roles in the complex drama of detoxification: (1) it filters blood to remove large toxins, (2) it synthesizes and excretes bile to help carry away fat-soluble toxic substances, and (3) it uses a two-step enzyme process to remove unwanted chemical compounds from your body. Approximately every minute, two quarts of blood are filtered by your liver, initially removing as much as 99% of the bacteria and toxins. Your liver can become slightly damaged by drugs, medications, or alcohol. This will, in turn, increase by a factor of 10 the number of toxins getting through your liver without being detoxified.

The liver's second detoxification process utilizes the liver's manufacture of about one quart of bile per day. This bile helps you to digest fats, but it also acts as a carrier to wash fat-soluble toxic substances out of your body and into your intestines for excretion. However—and this is a very important point—if you have constipation, these toxins washed out in your bile sit around in the bowel and get reabsorbed back into your bloodstream. This is why it is so important to have one to two good bowel movements each and every day! This excretion of toxins through your bile can also be a problem if you have dysbiosis; the "bad bugs" can modify the toxins in the bile to more damaging and even carcinogenic forms. The way to maximize this second type of liver detoxification is to naturally promote (1) good bile flow, (2) good bowel movements every day, and (3) the removal of any unwanted microbes from your intestines.

Phase 1 and Phase 2 of Liver Detoxification

Protection and enhancement of the third role of detoxification performed by your liver will be a major focus of the rest of this chapter. This third detoxification process of your liver takes place in two steps involving enzymes, simply called phase 1 and phase 2 enzymes. Phase 1 will directly neutralize some chemicals and make them water soluble so the kidney can pass them out of your body in the urine. But, most of the enzymes in phase 1 convert toxic chemicals to another chemical form that can be handled by the phase 2 enzymes. The only problem with this part of your liver's detoxification system is that going from phase 1 to phase 2 creates tremendous amounts of free radicals, which must also be quenched with antioxidants in your liver before they cause damage. Therefore, the more toxins you expose yourself to, the harder your liver works and the more free radicals it generates. This is why antioxidants are so extremely helpful in protecting the liver from damage and enhancing detoxification. Many of the nutritional supplements and herbs discussed in this comprehensive program act as very strong antioxidants.

The other important function of these nutritional supplements and herbs that we will discuss is to enhance the quantity of something called glutathione, also known as GSH. This makes these nutraceuticals extremely helpful to your detoxification, because glutathione is used as a primary detoxification route for many chemicals in phase 2. Glutathione is also one of your body's most important and powerful antioxidants. This 1–2 punch combination of enhancing detoxification and protecting against free radical damage in every cell of your body makes GSH a very important compound. A deficiency of specific nutrients and exposure to drugs and toxic chemicals have been shown to deplete levels of glutathione in your liver and tissues. For example, deficiencies of vitamin B_2, selenium, and zinc can lower your glutathione levels, as well as exposure to cigarette smoke and the common drug acetaminophen, as found in the popular pain reliever Tylenol.

Glutathione can be increased in your tissues through dietary sources found in fresh fruits, vegetables, and fish, and by your body synthesis. Certain nutrients have been shown to help increase the body's levels of tissue glutathione, which greatly enhances your liver's ability to detoxify toxic substances. For example, in one study, 3 grams of vitamin C per day raised glutathione in white blood cells by 400%. Because of the pain and inflammation that low levels of chemical toxins can create in your myofascial tissue, it is vital to enhance your detoxification capabilities. This becomes an even more important issue when we realize the number of degenerative diseases associated with the exposure of our tissues to toxic chemicals.

How Chemical Toxins and Endotoxins Can Lead to Pain

If you live or work in an environment loaded with toxic chemicals, or overburden your liver with drugs, smoking, or excessive alcohol consumption, you compromise your liver's ability to remove toxins from your body. The same thing is true if you have unhealthy bacteria and/or fungus in your gastrointestinal tract dumping endotoxins into your system and thereby overwhelming your liver. This condition will then lead to a liver that is overtaxed and unable to keep up, allowing toxins from various environmental sources to accumulate in your tissues. When these toxic substances accumulate in your tissues, they will act as free radicals, creating oxidative stress that in turn activates a chronic inflammatory response. Byproducts from this induced chronic inflammation will act as free radicals, creating more oxidative stress. As explained in much greater detail in chapter 5, this oxidative stress and the chronic inflammation it creates can cause a feed-forward cycle. This vicious cycle of oxidative stress and chronic inflammation not only stimulates nociceptors causing pain but can eventually affect your cells' ability to produce adequate energy in tissues. If this takes place in your muscles, they will become painful, stiff, and easily fatigued, partly through the formation of multiple myofascial trigger points.

This is the direct connection between externally and internally produced toxins and nutritional deficiencies causing a feed-forward cycle of oxidative stress and inflammation leading to chronic pain and fatigue. Therefore, by improving your diet and lifestyle, and limiting the amount of toxic substances you expose yourself to, you can begin to heal your chronic myofascial pain. After normalizing the bacteria in your gastrointestinal tract, so you are no longer poisoning yourself, make sure your liver has all the help it needs to maximize its detoxification capabilities. To fully understand how vital it is to maximize your ability to properly detoxify in this toxic world, you may want to review chapter 7.

THE CHALLENGE BEFORE US

We now live in a time different from all others in history, as we discussed in chapter 7. All humans now harbor measurable toxic substances or foreign chemicals in their tissues, whether they are organic farmers in Canada or Inuits up on the polar cap. It is sad to say that now even newborns are not exempt from this horror. A study spearheaded by the Environmental Working Group measured the chemical contamination of the blood from the umbilical cord of newborns. In that study, they tested for 413 different toxic chemicals; they found 287 chemicals present in umbilical cord blood samples, with a range between 154 to 231 chemicals per child. These 287 chemicals found within the blood of newborns do have serious ramifications; 217 of the chemicals are known toxins to the brain and nervous system, 208 of the chemicals will cause developmental problems in children, and 180 of these chemicals cause cancer in humans or animals.[212] This horrendous legacy that we leave our children through our addiction to "better living through chemistry" must be soberly examined and action taken as a society if we hope to be truly healthy ourselves. It is also why we must stop looking for some magic in a drug or supplement to get us out of our pain. The healing of our pain is connected, now, to the healing of this earth!

Another quick example of the toxic burden we choose to place on our health is the use of volatile organic compounds (VOCs), such as the antifungal preservative parabens. These preservatives, known as methylparaben, ethylparaben, butylparaben, and propylparaben are found in our medications, toiletries, cosmetics, foods, and other sources. One primary source of these toxic chemicals is the parabens we absorb from the deodorants we use. Recent, alarming studies have found that parabens accumulate in breast tissue, and they are found in higher concentrations in breast biopsies of women with breast cancer.[213] This is just one small example of how the 4 million synthetic compounds and 80,000 industrial chemicals found in our twenty-first century can enter our bodies and wreak havoc. Today, all human beings on this earth store toxic chemicals in their tissues, and the innate detoxification capacities of these tissues are being exceeded. The question, then, is how you can protect yourselves and your loved

212 You can find this complete study, and many other studies of the toxic burden we modern humans carry in our tissues, by going to http://archive.ewg.org/reports/bodyburden2/.

213 P. D. Darbre, A. Aljarrah, W. R. Miller, N. G. Coldham, M. J. Sauer, and G. S. Pope, "Concentrations of parabens in human breast tumors," *J Appl Toxicol* 24, no. 1 (Jan–Feb 2004): 5–13.

ones from this onslaught. This question becomes even more pressing if you suffer with fibromyalgia or chronic fatigue.

Assessing Your Toxic Exposure

It can be helpful to clinically assess your toxic burden and detoxification capacity with laboratory tests. There are functional medicine tests that your doctor can do to assess, for example, if genetically you have less-effective detoxification pathways. Or you can test for heavy metal toxicity by measuring the amount found in your red blood cells or a hair sample. One of the simplest and possibly most effective ways to understand your exposure and detoxification capabilities is to have a urinary organic acid test done by your doctor. This is the same urinary organic acid test discussed in the previous section on dysbiosis, except that other metabolic organic acids are tested for in your urine.

Organic acids tend to reveal more about your metabolism than many other lab tests, and they are easy to perform. Since the early 1990s, there have been research studies showing that a urinary organic acid test can be more sensitive than blood tests.[214] This metabolic profile can be easily ordered by your doctor, and all you do is simply collect your first morning urine to be sent into the lab. These different urinary organic acids, as you have seen, can have complicated and difficult names to pronounce, but a discussion of a few of them may help you understand their importance and be able to discuss them with your doctor.

Glucaric acid is a byproduct predominantly from your liver's detoxification pathways, and its elevation in your urine suggests overworked detoxification pathways. If glucaric acid is elevated, you will want to examine your life for potentially toxic exposures that you will then want to reduce. Generally, increased glucaric acid in your urine is caused by exposure to pesticides, herbicides, fungicides, petrochemicals, alcohol, and drugs. If glucaric acid is elevated, you will want to fully examine your home and work environment for possible sources. You will need to stop using chemical-based personal care products and switch to natural, "green" deodorants, perfumes, and lotions. You may want to make sure your water is filtered through reverse osmosis and eat only organic foods. You will need to stop smoking and reduce all second-hand smoke and

214 J. Lindenbaum, D. G. Savage, S. P. Stabler, and R. H. Allen, "Diagnosis of cobalamin deficiency: II. Relative sensitivities of serum cobalamin, methylmalonic acid and total homocysteine concentrations," *Am J Hematol* 34, no. 2 (June 1990): 99–107.

alcohol in your life. Another organic acid elevated in your urine from exposure to toxic chemicals is something called 2-methylhippurate. This organic acid specifically elevates in your urine when you have a recent exposure to a common chemical solvent called xylene. This very common solvent is found in paint thinners, building products, fuel and exhaust fumes, and industrial degreasers and solvents. If this organic acid, 2-methylhippurate, is elevated in your urine, check carefully for possible exposure to solvents.

Chemical Exposure, Free Radicals, and Pain

Another method of assessing if you have possible exposure to toxic chemicals is to measure for oxidative stress. Please recall from chapters 5 and 7 how toxic environmental chemicals act as or create free radicals in your tissues. Free radicals in your myofascial tissues stimulate nociceptors, causing the sensation of pain. These free radicals also activate genes in your cells that turn on inflammation. These inflammatory products, as previously discussed, are the main stimulators of nociceptors in your muscles and joints. Therefore, oxidative stress from chemical toxins can lead to chronic myofascial pain. Enough free radicals present in your tissues will cause damage to the lipids and proteins of your cells. These damaged lipids and proteins will act as free radicals themselves, creating a feed-forward cycle. Also, free radicals will damage the nucleic acids of your DNA, which can lead to mutations, which can be measured through elevation of a urinary organic acid.

To measure the amount of free radical damage to fatty acids in your cell membranes, your doctor can measure the level of F2-isoprostanes in your blood or urine. This is the most reliable way to know the amount of oxidative stress going on in your body.[215] Then, to determine if oxidative stress from chemical exposure is damaging the DNA of your cells, your doctor can measure the level of a specific urinary organic acid called 8-OHdG, short for 8-hydroxy-2'-deoxyguanosine. This may sound a little complicated, but the clinical importance of knowing if your cells are under attack from free radicals cannot be overemphasized. This is especially true if this damage is affecting the DNA of your cells, so ask your doctor about testing to see if your urinary 8-OHdG is elevated.

---

215 P. Montuschi, P. J. Barnes, and L. J. Roberts, "Isoprostanes: markers and mediators of oxidative stress," *FASEB J* 18, no. 15 (December 2004): 1791–1800.

There are other functional tests that can be done to assess your toxic burden, oxidative stress, and detoxification capacity. These assessments are all very important to run if you suffer from chronic myofascial pain, fibromyalgia, chronic fatigue syndrome, or multiple chemical sensitivity syndromes. This is only a brief introduction to the subject of assessing your toxic burden; it is important to find a clinician who understands the importance of these very helpful lab tests. Do some research online, then call around to find a practitioner in your area who understands these functional tests and practices a more functional approach to health care. If you have a multiple compound fracture in your leg, you need an orthopedic surgeon. However, when you have multiple metabolic problems causing you chronic pain and fatigue, you need the information contained within this book and possibly the help of a specialist in functional health care.

Three-Step Program to Reduce Toxic Chemicals, Oxidative Stress, and Inflammation

If you have chronic pain or fatigue and suspect that oxidative stress and chronic inflammation caused by toxic chemicals may be playing a role in your disorder, there is no danger in implementing my three-step program without running expensive lab tests. This three-step program is just common sense that can help to improve anyone's wellness program. There are four primary categories of toxins that your body must constantly render harmless and/or remove: (1) chemical toxins (e.g., drugs, POPs), (2) toxic heavy metals, (3) endotoxins from microbial growth (e.g., bacteria, yeast, protozoa, and other organisms), and (4) and the natural break-down products of hormones and protein metabolism in the body. Toxic chemicals and heavy metals can gain entry into your body through many different avenues: outdoor air pollution, drinking water, and indoor air pollution at work and home. Worker exposure to chemicals is now designated to be among the top four threats to human health.[216]

The air you breathe enters your body through your lungs, bringing in air pollutants with each breath, and the concentration of toxic chemicals depends on where you live. The burden that air pollutants place upon our health is tremendous. Adverse health effects include the development and exacerbation of asthma, loss of lung func-

216 R. Metzger, J. L. Delgado, and R. Herrell, "Environmental health and Hispanic children," *Environ Health Perspect* 103, suppl. 6 (September 1995): 25–32.

tion, impaired neurobehavioral development (e.g., ADHD), and death.[217] It has been estimated that particulate air pollution generated by motor vehicles and the burning of coal, fuel oil, and wood causes over 100,000 deaths per year in the United States.[218] Pesticides, herbicides, industrial solvents, and other toxic chemicals are now found within our public water systems, and they enter our body through drinking, bathing, and cooking.

If you or your clinician have determined through lab tests or your health history that chemical toxins or endotoxins may be playing a role in your chronic pain disorder, it is vital for you to bolster your detoxification system. Your detoxification system is made up of multiple organs, including your skin, lungs, intestines, liver, and kidneys. Your skin must protect you from and detoxify surface chemical threats, such as from lotions, cosmetics, or bathing. Your lungs, of course, must protect you from and detoxify any indoor or outdoor airborne pollutants that enter with every breath you take.

Your intestines have a role in protecting you from two sources of toxins: (1) chemicals that entered your body with the foods and liquids you take in, and (2) endotoxins produced by unhealthy microbes in your gut. Any toxic chemicals or endotoxins that get past your skin, lungs, or intestines are then challenged by your liver and kidneys. Your liver will handle any toxic substances from the exterior or interior of your body and send it through the two-step process of phase 1 and phase 2, to prepare it to be excreted from your body. Your kidneys then take the water-soluble form of this toxic substance and excrete it in your urine, finally ridding it from your body.

Step 1: Eat a Healthy, Organic Diet

There are specific strategies that you can adopt to enhance your detoxification capabilities and improve your ability to heal your pain. To accomplish its vital work, first your detoxification system must receive adequate and balanced levels of (1) macronutrients (e.g., complex carbohydrates, proteins, fats), (2) fiber, and (3) micronutrients (e.g., vitamins, minerals, and phytochemicals). Without adequate quantities of these needed nutrients, your detoxification system breaks down, leaving you vulnerable to chemical toxins, heavy metals, and endotoxins in your personal environment. With this, we go

---

217 D. B. Coultas and W. E. Lambert, "Air pollution," *Curr Opin Pulm Med* 1, no. 2 (March 1995): 89–95.

218 S. Chalupka, "Environmental health: an opportunity for health promotion and disease prevention," *AAOHN J* 53, no. 1 (January 2005): 13–28.

back to a consistent theme: to be healthy and free of pain, you must properly digest and absorb a healthy diet rich in nutrients.

Second, to enhance your detoxification capabilities, this healthy diet should be organic, so as not to overburden your detoxification system. Research studies have shown that children fed an organic diet have less accumulation of toxic chemicals in their tissues than children eating a "normal" Standard American Diet, or SAD. This is critical information, for diet delivers the bulk of children's exposure to pesticides, according to a report of the National Research Council.[219] Furthermore, they point out that this toxic exposure poses a greater health risk to children as compared to adults, primarily because children consume more food on a per-weight basis than adults do. Therefore, it does pay to feed you and your family organic foods. If you cannot eat a strictly organic diet, try to reduce the presence of chemicals by avoiding foods that contain hormones, antibiotics, fumigants, or tend to be grown with a heavy use of pesticides and herbicides. It is also helpful not to purchase foods grown in certain countries outside the United States, where restrictions on pesticides and herbicides are not as stringent. There are a variety of resources to help you find foods with a less toxic burden. One excellent site for this information and other topics on chemical exposure is found at www.ewg.org.[220]

Step 2: Filter Your Water and Air

Along with eating foods that are organic or at least less burdened with toxic chemicals, it is highly recommended that you remove the pollutants from your water through a whole-house reverse osmosis filter system. This is an ideal way to remove the pollutants in your water, from the kitchen tap to the bathtub. If this is cost-prohibitive, at minimum you should get a quality carbon filtering system designed for your kitchen tap to at least remove most of the pollutants from your water for drinking and cooking purposes. The importance of this cannot be overemphasized, for water pollution has been shown to have significant health implications, ranging from gastrointestinal

219 C. Lu, K. Toepel, et al., "Organic diets significantly lower children's dietary exposure to organophosphorus pesticides," Environmental Health Perspectus 114 (2), February 2006. National Research Council, "Pesticides in the diets of infants and children," (1993): 412.

220 You will find all the tools and resources you need to start living a more toxin-free life at www.ewg.org, including shopper's guides for produce, cosmetics, cleaning products, and more.

ailments to neurological damage.[221] It also would be beneficial to install a HEPA/ULPA air filter system in your home to reduce molds, volatile organic compounds, and other sources of indoor pollution. The importance of this becomes apparent when we realize that we modern humans can spend as much as 80 to 90% of our time indoors. Make sure you clean and monitor your heating system; the most common death by poisoning within the United States is from carbon monoxide.

Step 3: "Green Up" Your Personal Environment

A major culprit in the creation of a toxic home environment is the use of chemical-laden household cleaners and personal care products. These products emit volatile organic compounds (VOCs) that are recognized carcinogens, suspected hormone disrupters, and are toxic to respiratory and reproductive/developmental systems. VOCs from household and personal care products contaminate surfaces and dust throughout the home, and come from many different sources; for example, parabens, a suspected carcinogen, comes from deodorants, and phthalates are emitted into the air with fragrances and can disrupt hormones. Diethanolamine (DEA), a common additive to personal care products, is generally used as a foaming agent—it even can be found in children's bubble bath products. It is a suspected carcinogen and is toxic to the respiratory and nervous systems.

Through various studies, these toxic chemicals have been found to be ubiquitous within the home environment. In one study, they tested for the presence of toxic chemicals in the carpet dust of eight Columbus homes and nine Seattle homes and found concentrated levels of carcinogenic PAHs and PCBs. The authors of this study went on to point out that these chemical pollutants in indoor dust and air have been associated with cancer, allergy, asthma, and damage to the nervous system. The study points out that the presence of these toxic chemicals in our homes comes from our use of household and personal care products, as well as being tracked in from the outside.[222] It is therefore vital for you to stop using products in your home containing toxic

221 J. Webb, "Use of the ecosystem approach to population health: the case of mercury contamination in aquatic environments and riparian populations, Andean Amazon, Napo River Valley, Ecuador," *Can J Public Health* 96, no. 1 (Jan–Feb 2005): 44–46.

222 J. W. Roberts and P. Dickey, "Exposure of children to pollutants in house dust and indoor air," *Rev Environ Contam Toxicol* 143 (1995): 59–78.

chemicals, chemicals now known to damage your respiratory, nervous, reproductive, and hormonal systems.

There are good books and websites to assist you in creating a home and community environment that is more "green" and safe for you and your family. For an excellent resource to help you understand indoor pollution and hints on how to overcome it, go to www.checnet.org and click on *HealtheHouse*. To understand exactly what kind of pollution you face in your immediate community, go to www.scorecard.org and type in your ZIP code at the top of the page for a wealth of information. This website will then give you tips on how to use this information to clean up your community. A good book is *Home Safe Home: Protecting Yourself and Your Family from Everyday Toxics and Harmful Household Products* by Debra Lynn Dadd (Putnam Publishing, 1997). *Home Safe Home* offers over 400 tips, such as do-it-yourself formulas for inexpensive, safe products to replace harmful chemicals you expose yourself to every day in your home.

You also want to make sure that you are reducing your exposure to environmental petrochemicals by properly disposing of garden chemicals and utilizing more environmentally friendly products on your lawn, flowers, and vegetables. Lawn and gardening chemicals can be a major source of toxic exposure in your life and must be eliminated if you hope to heal your pain and promote real wellness. Also make sure that you are not exposing your household to car exhaust if you have an attached garage. Seal any leaks in your house, and always turn your car off immediately—never let it idle in your garage. Also, remove any exposure to second-hand smoke; recent research shows that this can be as damaging as being a smoker yourself. And for those who want to look marvelous without poisoning themselves or their family, check out *Drop-Dead Gorgeous: Protecting Yourself from the Hidden Dangers of Cosmetics* by Kim Erickson (Contemporary Books, 2002). This book shows you the many dangers of common over-the-counter products and teaches you how to interpret misleading product labels so you can identify the most hazardous ingredients. It also provides natural alternatives and easy-to-follow recipes for safely creating your own cosmetics at home.

An excellent book that I highly recommend is *Our Stolen Future: Are We Threatening Our Fertility, Intelligence, and Survival?—A Scientific Detective Story* by Theo Colborn, Dianne Dumanoski, and John Peterson Myers (Penguin Group, 1997). This book does an excellent job in explaining to the nonprofessional the tremendous impact that these toxic chemicals can have on human health. This book reads more like a "whodunit" by tracing birth defects, sexual abnormalities, and reproductive failures in wildlife back to their sources: synthetic chemicals that mimic hormones, causing disturbances in normal reproductive and developmental processes. This book then goes on to show why humans are not immune to the effects of these chemical toxins that mimic our hormones.

Nutritional Strategies to Improve Detoxification and Energy Production

After you have started this three-step program to clean up your environment for yourself and your loved ones, you may want to improve your odds by adding certain nutritional and botanical supplements to enhance detoxification pathways and revitalize energy production at the cellular level. You are well on your way to this goal if you are already supplementing omega-3 fatty acids, magnesium malate with B complex, and standardized extracts of ginger and curcumin, as described in chapters 14 and 15. These nutritional supplements will assist your cellular energy production and detoxification capability.

Toxic overload and nutritionally impaired detoxification pathways, though, can extract a real toll on the proper functioning of your body, primarily through oxidative stress and chronic inflammation. The good news is that poor detoxification, oxidative stress, chronic inflammation, and insulin resistance are all so inextricably tied together that much of their challenge can be overcome with the same nutritional program. One primary reason that these factors are so connected is that they all affect the power generators of your cells, the mitochondria. If the factors reduce your mitochondrial function, it can lead to lowered cellular energy production. What tissues or organs this mitochondrial dysfunction most affects depends upon many variables, such as types of chemicals you are exposed to, your diet, and your own personal genetics.

To better understand this connection between oxidative stress, chronic inflammation, insulin resistance, and exposure to chemical toxins, please review chapters 6 through 9 for greater detail. Recall from those chapters, though, that chemical toxins can act as or generate free radicals, causing oxidative stress in tissues exposed to them. This oxidative stress is a mild chronic injury to the tissues involved, causing the production of inflammatory cellular chemicals, leading to chronic low-grade inflammation and possibly chronic pain, if the signals reach all the way to your sensory cortex. Also, some environmental toxic chemicals have been shown to inhibit your cells' ability to utilize insulin in bringing glucose into your cells for energy production, causing insulin resistance.

In chapter 8, it was described how this insulin resistance can turn on specific genes in your cells, leading to states of chronic low-grade inflammation. Therefore, in our modern society, toxic chemical exposure and/or poor detoxification capabilities can eventually lead to oxidative stress, and low-grade inflammation in your tissues leads to more chronic pain. This vicious cycle of oxidative stress and chronic inflammation eventually will damage the mitochondria's ability to produce adequate energy. Damaged mitochondria leak more free radicals, causing more oxidative stress and increasing chronic inflammation, creating more chronic pain. This feed-forward cycle is outlined for you in the flow-chart below.

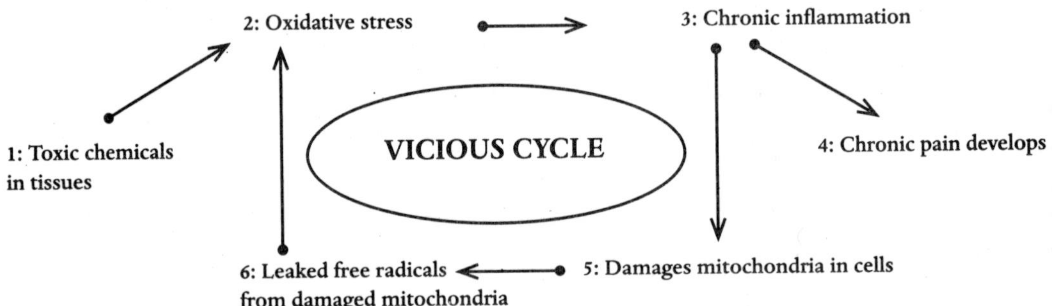

The more your myofascial tissues go around on this feed-forward cycle, the greater and more constant is your pain. Without healthy mitochondria and proper levels of ATP, your cellular function suffers and eventually leads to cell death. This vicious cycle of toxic chemical exposure leading to oxidative stress, chronic inflammation, and mitochondrial dysfunction has been connected to a long list of symptoms and conditions common to our modern society.

Muscle and joint pains, fatigue, dizziness, headaches, irritability, anxiety, depression, poor mental function, digestive problems, chronic infections, and allergies are all commonly reported symptoms. Associated specific disorders include fibromyalgia, chronic fatigue syndrome, multiple chemical sensitivity, asthma, diabetes, cancer, cardiovascular disease, arthritis, and neurodegenerative disorders, such as Alzheimer's disease, Parkinson's disease, and MS. Upon examination, these common symptoms and disease conditions read like a laundry list of our modern health problems. This is why I have painstakingly attempted to explain what exactly oxidative stress, chronic inflammation, and mitochondrial dysfunction are, what their causes are, and most importantly what you can do about them.

By addressing the components of this vicious cycle with the previously described program and the more specific nutritional program that follows, you will be putting yourself on the road to healing your pain and promoting real wellness in your life. Again, this program to heal your chronic muscle and joint pain problems starts with a strong base: a healthy Mediterranean diet, along with supplements of omega-3 fatty acids, magnesium malate, ginger, and curcumin extracts, and the removal of toxic substances from your diet and environment. To this very strong program, you can add specific nutraceuticals to help enhance your detoxification pathways and mitochondrial function; please see the table below for details.

Five-Step Clean-Up	Five-Step Intake Plan	Enhanced Support
1. Eat organic foods as much as possible: reduce pesticides, herbicides	1. Eat a Mediterranean diet, add high-potency multivitamin/mineral formula	Silymarin from milk thistle extract (400 to 600 mg daily) and green tea extract (300 to 600 mg daily)
2. At home, filter your water (carbon filter or reverse osmosis) and air (HEPA/ULPA filters)	2. Do an oil change: supplement omega-3 EPA/DHA fatty acids (3 to 6 g daily)	NAC (N-acetylcysteine) 500 to 1,000 mg per day
3. Clean up your personal environment; buy green household cleaners and personal care products	3. Tune up cellular engines: supplement 600 mg of magnesium with malate (2,400 mg) and high B-vitamin complex	Alpha-lipoic acid (500 to 800 mg per day) with 1 to 2 g acetyl-L-carnitine per day
4. Maintain excellent excretory functions with one to two bowel movements a day	4. Spice up your health supplement with at least 2 g ginger root extract and 1 g curcumin root extract	CoQ10 (50 to 1,000 mg per day) with mixed Vit. E (400 to 1200 IU)
5. Heating systems: clean and monitor regularly; #1 death by poisoning in U.S.	5. Overcome any dysbiosis: remove "bad bugs" and replace with probiotics	Selenium (200 mcg), zinc (30 to 50 mg), and Vit. C (1,000 to 2,000 mg)

NUTRACEUTICALS TO ENHANCE DETOXIFICATION AND MITOCHONDRIAL FUNCTION

Ginger and Curcumin Root Extracts

Probably the most important supplements you can take to improve detoxification and counter oxidative stress are standardized extracts of ginger and curcumin, as already discussed. If you wish to protect your liver and enhance its ability to remove chemical toxins from your body, now is the time to add these impressive herbs to your wellness regime. Recall the study designed to determine how protective curcumin can be: animals were exposed to the severely toxic carbon tetrachloride, along with supplementation of this herbal extract. It was found that the curcumin extract gave significant protection to the liver from this chemical exposure.[223] As discussed in chapter 15, for detoxification and wellness matters, supplementation of 1 gram of curcumin extract and up to 2 grams of ginger extract are usually sufficient, though a higher dosage may be necessary for pain relief.

Silymarin

Silymarin is an extract from the milk thistle plant (*Silybum marianum*) that has been used as a remedy for almost 2,000 years and remains today as a medicine for many types of acute and chronic liver diseases. In recent research, silymarin extract has been shown to prevent liver damage by acting as a strong antioxidant. It does this by enhancing the synthesis of glutathione and by actually increasing the rate that your liver tissue can regenerate itself! Silymarin extract has been shown to increase the level of glutathione in the liver by up to 35% even in "normal" individuals, therefore this supplement may protect and benefit even "healthy" people.

More importantly, recent research has shown silymarin extract to actually increase phase 2 detoxification enzymes in your liver, lung, stomach, skin, and small bowel. In this research, silymarin extract was found to increase two extremely important detoxification enzymes in these multiple tissues: glutathione S-transferase and quinone reductase.[224] Recall earlier in this chapter the tremendous impact that glutathione has

---

223 Deshpande, Gadre, Raste, Pillai, Bhide, and Samuel, "Protective effect," 573–77.

224 J. Zhao and R. Agarwal, "Tissue distribution of silibinin, the major active constituent of silymarin, in mice and its association with enhancement of phase II enzymes: implications in cancer chemoprevention," *Carcinogenesis* 20, no. 11 (November 1999): 2101–8.

on protecting your liver and enhancing detoxification. Some researchers have said that glutathione is a good marker of your actual biological age: the higher the activity, the younger you actually are inside, and the slower you will age! Therefore, this herb is a very good botanical for its anti-aging affects, liver protection, enhancement of detoxification enzymes, and its cancer-prevention capabilities. For detoxification purposes, you need to take between 400 to 600 milligrams of silymarin extract per day. Check out your supplement or formula to make sure that the actual silymarin content is high enough.

Green Tea

The next herb that has shown great success in enhancing your ability to detoxify toxic chemicals is the well-known green tea (*Camellia sinensis*). The use of this herb as a drink and medicine goes back approximately 5,000 years. Traditionally it was used as a digestive aid, but recent research shows it has the ability to protect your liver from chemical assaults. It provides anti-carcinogenic and strong antioxidant activity, as well as enhancement of phase 2 detoxification capabilities. Research has shown that, like silymarin, standardized green tea extracts increase glutathione peroxidase activity in the liver, lungs, and small intestine, which accounts for its ability to enhance the detoxification process throughout your body.[225] Just as glutathione is used in phase 2 of liver detoxification, so is glucuronic acid combined with toxins to allow your body to safely remove them in your bile excretion. This process, glucuronidation, is a predominant detoxification pathway of your body, and standardized green tea extract has been shown to enhance it by as much as 100%. It is suggested by researchers that this ability to increase glucuronidation may be the way that green tea can protect you from cancer.[226] The primary active constituents of green tea are found in the polyphenols, specifically its six catechin compounds. Your green tea supplement should be standardized to at least 60% polyphenols containing the various catechin compounds. Generally, I suggest that detoxification formulas should supply around 300 to 600 milligrams daily

225 S. G. Khan, S. K. Katiyar, R. Agarwal, and H. Mukhtar, "Enhancement of antioxidant and phase II enzymes by oral feeding of green tea polyphenols in drinking water to SKH–1 hairless mice: possible role in cancer chemoprevention," *Cancer Res* 52, no. 14 (July 15, 1992): 4050–52.

226 A. Bu-Abbas, M. N. Clifford, C. Ioannides, and R. Walker, "Stimulation of rat hepatic UDP-glucuronosyl transferase activity following treatment with green tea," *Food Chem Toxicol* 33, no. 1 (January 1995): 27–30.

of green tea standardized to 60% polyphenols containing catechins, depending on your personal needs.

N-acetylcysteine

A nutrient that has been shown to directly raise your tissue levels of the all-important glutathione is the modified amino acid N-acetylcysteine, commonly referred to as NAC. N-acetylcysteine is used by your cells to manufacture glutathione, and research studies have shown that NAC does increase your tissue glutathione levels and boost your cellular immunity.[227] Research has shown N-acetylcysteine to successfully treat liver and kidney failure caused by glutathione depletion, secondary to acetaminophen overdose.[228] Because of NAC's proven ability to successively treat even drug overdose from acetaminophen, it is used extensively to support glutathione detoxification capabilities. NAC is now available as a nutrition supplement. I suggest that detoxification formulas supply about 500 to 1,000 milligrams of NAC per day. It is usually unnecessary to go over 1,000 milligrams of NAC unless you are suffering from a chronic infection, such as chronic fatigue syndrome.

Alpha-lipoic acid and acetyl-L-carnitine

The fourth supplement in this comprehensive program to enhance detoxification and energy production is the combination of the nutrients alpha-lipoic acid and acetyl-L-carnitine. This "dynamic duo" can bolster mitochondrial energy production in your tissues. Acetyl-L-carnitine benefits you by boosting the conversion of fats into energy by your mitochondria. This important nutrient can help to ensure plentiful energy supply in all the tissues of your body; this is especially helpful in allowing muscles to stay relaxed and pain-free. Also, acetyl-L-carnitine has the ability to neutralize damaging free radicals in your tissues. An added bonus to all this is that studies at Stanford University concluded that "acetyl-L-carnitine slows the progression of Alzheimer's disease in younger subjects."[229]

---

227 R. Kinscherf, T. Fischbach, S. Mihm, S. Roth, E. Hohenhaus-Sievert, C. Weiss, L. Edler, P. Bartsch, and W. Droge, "Effect of glutathione depletion and oral N-acetylcysteine treatment on CD4+ and CD8+ cells," *FASEB J* 8, no. 6 (April 1, 1994): 448–51.

228 M. J. Smilkstein, G. L. Knapp, K. W. Kulig, and B. H. Rumack, "Efficacy of oral N-acetylcysteine in the treatment of acetaminophen overdose. Analysis of the national multicenter study (1976 to 1985)," *NEJM* 319, no. 24 (December 15, 1988): 1557–62.

229 J. O. Brooks III, J. A. Yesavage, A. Carta, and D. Bravi, "Acetyl-L-carnitine slows decline in younger patients with Alzheimer's disease: a reanalysis of a double-blind, placebo-controlled study using the trilinear approach," *Int Psychogeriatr* 10, no. 2 (June 1998): 193–203.

When this nutrient is supplemented with alpha-lipoic acid, it provides a metabolic tune-up to your energy-producing mitochondria by reducing oxidative stress and enhancing ATP production. The Bruce Ames research group found, amazingly, that sufficient levels of supplemented lipoic acid and acetyl-L-carnitine had the ability to make older animals young again. These nutrients achieved this by measurably improving the cognitive and physical capabilities of the animals through metabolically tuning up the mitochondria of their muscles and neurons.[230] So if you have chronic pain that may be related to toxicity and mitochondrial dysfunction, or if you would just like to feel younger and not age as quickly, you will want your metabolic tune-up to include alpha- lipoic acid and acetyl-L-carnitine!

What makes alpha-lipoic acid (ALA) such an effective supplement is that it can protect your mitochondria inside and out. Alpha-lipoic acid is rather magical in that it is one of the most potent antioxidants you can take, and it works in water or fats! This ability allows ALA to protect your mitochondrial water-soluble "insides" *and* the fatty mitochondrial membranes that produce your ATP. Alpha-lipoic acid can also replenish other antioxidants, such as vitamins C and E. In addition, it boosts levels of the all-important glutathione within mitochondria. To achieve these benefits, it's important to receive daily about 500 to 800 milligrams of lipoic acid, along with 1.5 to 3 grams of acetyl-L-carnitine, depending on your specific needs. The only drawback is that acetyl-L-carnitine can be somewhat expensive as a supplement. If you find a quality formula that can guarantee you get at least 1.5 grams of acetyl-L-carnitine along with a minimum 500 milligrams of lipoic acid, you should find benefits with your chronic pain and fatigue symptoms. However, if you have a full-blown fibromyalgia and chronic fatigue syndrome with severe symptomatology, you may need to raise the levels of these nutrients, especially that of acetyl-L-carnitine.

Coenzyme Q10

Another extremely important nutrient for individuals with severe chronic pain and fatigue, especially in full-blown fibromyalgia syndrome, is coenzyme Q10. This nutrient was first introduced into the United States in 1983, and since then there has been an explosion of research into its many benefits. Coenzyme Q10, also called CoQ10, is

230 T. M. Hagen, J. Liu, J. Lykkesfeldt, C. M. Wehr, R. T. Ingersoll, V. Vinarsky, J. C. Bartholomew, and B. N. Ames, "Feeding acetyl-L-carnitine and lipoic acid to old rats significantly improves metabolic function while decreasing oxidative stress," *Proc Natl Acad Sci USA* 99, no. 4 (February 19, 2002): 1870–75.

highly concentrated in energy-demanding tissues, such as that of the heart, muscles, and brain. Because these tissues are so energy demanding, they are prone to deficiencies, which explains why they are benefited by CoQ10 supplementation. Sufficient levels of CoQ10 within each and every mitochondrion are necessary for the production of ATP. When the mitochondria of your muscle cells do not have sufficient CoQ10, and therefore do not produce adequate levels of ATP, they become chronically contracted and painful. Clinically and personally, I have found CoQ10 to be extremely important in reversing the symptoms of chronic myofascial disorders, such as fibromyalgia syndrome. In a 2002 study, when fibromyalgia patients were supplemented daily with 200 milligrams of CoQ10, 2 out of 3 reported improved symptoms and quality of life.[231]

If you shop around, you may be able to find nutritional companies that have combined many of these nutraceuticals into one tablet, making detoxification and mitochondrial recovery easier for you. However, make sure these combination formulas have put in adequate levels of each of these nutraceuticals in the tablet to make it effective. Also, a quality concentrated formula can be costly simply because some of these individual nutraceuticals are expensive. To give you some idea, I formulated a combination called Mito-Detox for BIOSPEC Nutritionals with the previously discussed nutraceuticals. Two tablets twice daily of Mito-Detox will provide most of the nutraceuticals at the levels discussed for about $1.40 per day. It is an investment, but one that may be necessary for a while to recover your vitality.

How We Got Here

This chapter represents the culmination of the work we started together in chapters 5 through 8, which explored the underlying metabolic problems that set us up for chronic pain and degenerative disease. As outlined in those earlier chapters, our modern diet, lifestyle, and our addiction to "better living through chemistry" has created a challenge to human health that has never been experienced before. We now have over 4,000 chemical additives dumped into our foods and more than 4 million synthetic compounds awash in our personal environments. The five most toxic industrial chemicals known to humanity are now found stored in the tissues of every human sampled and 287 chemicals that have serious health ramifications have been found within the

231 R. E. Lister, "An open pilot study to evaluate the potential benefits of coenzyme Q10 combined with ginkgo biloba extract in fibromyalgia syndrome," *Int Med Res* 30, no. 2 (March–April 2002): 195–99.

blood of newborns. This exposure is real and affects everyone's well-being, some more than others because of our genetic differences.

What I have tried to demonstrate here is that all these various chemicals have a final common pathway of cellular destruction: that of oxidative stress creating chronic inflammation, leading to more free radicals and thus more systemic inflammation. This vicious cycle eventually harms the mitochondria of your tissues. Stressed mitochondria no longer produce adequate levels of energy (ATP) at the cellular level, causing you to lose vitality, leading to chronic pain and fatigue, and eventually degenerative disease. The important point of this chapter is that there are things you can do right now to defend yourself and your loved ones from this real danger to your health. This comprehensive detoxification and energy enhancement program can help you to regain your vitality to overcome your chronic myofascial pain disorder, whether it's a severely chronic low-back disorder or the all-over pain of fibromyalgia.

If you have suffered with a regional pain disorder, such as years of low-back pain or neck pain and headaches, you can benefit by only applying the basic steps outlined in this comprehensive program. By starting a self-care trigger point therapy program, cleaning up your diet, and adding some magnesium malate to relax muscle tissue and then ginger and curcumin root extracts to lower inflammation, you may quickly heal that regional pain disorder.

However, if you are one of the "canaries in the mine" of our modern culture and suffer with a complex pain disorder, such as widespread pain syndrome, fibromyalgia, or chronic fatigue syndrome, this chapter and the next are ones that you will need to take to heart and apply with the discipline of a warrior. It is your life: take charge and heal your pain, then take that newfound vitality and find something to do for others to complete your healing. And please remember to take advantage of the variety of resources available to help you on your journey (please refer to the website resources section, beginning on page 379).

18

From Chronic Regional Pain to Fibromyalgia Syndrome

Fibromyalgia is not a distinct disease but is actually a syndrome with a complex set of symptoms, the primary ones being "sore all over" and fatigued. Fibromyalgia is estimated to now affect more than 10 million Americans. Fibromyalgia syndrome is 10 to 20 times more likely to affect women of child-bearing age; however, it can occur in men and affects all age groups. Besides widespread musculoskeletal pain, 90% of fibromyalgia patients report symptoms of chronic fatigue, disturbed sleep, and general morning stiffness. Research is only now showing that fibromyalgia is not simply a sleep disorder, therefore sleep medications have not proven to be the answer.

Besides global myofascial pain and fatigue, fibromyalgia sufferers also commonly experience headaches, irritable bowel syndrome (IBS), numbness or tingling of the extremities, restless leg syndrome, painful menstrual periods, depression, anxiety, memory and cognitive problems, and a variety of other symptoms. Since fibromyalgia syndrome can mimic other more dangerous diseases, any individual with this symptom pattern must have a proper diagnostic workup by a competent doctor before accepting the diagnosis of fibromyalgia syndrome. Due to this disabling menagerie of symptoms, nearly one-third of fibromyalgia syndrome patients report that they are unable to hold down a steady job.

Despite poor response to standard fibromyalgia treatment, direct and indirect health-care costs have been documented at more than $5,945/year per fibromyalgia patient. [232]It has also been estimated that fibromyalgia puts an $80 billion drain on the U.S. economy and a tremendous personal burden on those affected by fibromyalgia syndrome.

If you do not suffer from fibromyalgia, the best way to imagine what it is like is to remember a time when you had a flu that "settled" in your muscles, making you ache all over and feel tired and listless. Or recall a time when you physically and emotionally worked yourself to exhaustion, causing you to ache uncomfortably all over. Then imagine this ache and exhaustion is never going to let up, and on top of that you just can't think straight. This is not a perfect example, but it will give someone who has never experienced fibromyalgia or some other chronic widespread myofascial pain syndrome some concept of what these individuals go through each and every day.

How to Assess if You Have Fibromyalgia Syndrome

Many individuals have been diagnosed as having fibromyalgia syndrome (FMS) or think they have fibromyalgia, when in actuality they have a chronic multiregional pain syndrome (MRPS). If you suffer with any form of chronic myofascial pain, the exact diagnostic category you fall into really is not that important. As we will see in this chapter, the mechanisms of pain in fibromyalgia syndrome are the same mechanisms involved in a "simple" chronic regional pain syndrome (CRPS). More importantly, the correction of a chronic regional pain syndrome or that of a full-blown fibromyalgia syndrome primarily involves the same natural approach, as outlined in this book. The only differences in treatment relate to how involved your chronic myofascial disorder is, how long you've had it, and how severe your symptoms are.

For example, there is a difference between full-blown fibromyalgia syndrome with chronic fatigue complicated by irritable bowel syndrome of ten years' duration and chronic regional pain of the low back of two years' duration. If you do suffer with fibromyalgia, you will need to apply the complete recovery program outlined in this book with great discipline if you hope to once and for all actually heal your pain and promote real wellness in your life. If, however, you suffer with disabling back pain, you may find that doing self-administered trigger point therapy, improving your diet, and

232 R. L. Robinson, et al., "Economic cost and epidemiological characteristics of patients with fibromyalgia claims," *J Rheumatol* 30, no. 6 (2003): 1318–25.

taking a month's supply of concentrated ginger and curcumin root extract, along with some magnesium malate, will be enough to heal your pain.

All too often, the problem in the West is that we want to simplify, separate, and categorize anything we must confront. We seem to believe that when we have *It* defined, whatever *It* may be, we now understand and can somehow control *It*! When it comes to illness, we separate the body from the mind and then go on to compile symptoms into discrete diseases. Doctors feel more comfortable once they have a name they can label the patient with that matches a diagnostic code that insurance companies reimburse. As patients, once our doctors have given a name to our suffering, we tend to feel some sense of comfort, even if it brings us no closer to real healing. An example used previously in this book is the diagnosis of dermatitis, which really tells us nothing more about our skin condition than what we already knew: it's inflamed. Or the diagnosis of clinical depression only tells us that we have reached a threshold in modern medicine indicating that our sadness now warrants prescription drugs. The problem with all this is that it gets in the way of our fully understanding and healing the problem before us. With that said, below is the established criteria for receiving the diagnosis of fibromyalgia syndrome.

Fibromyalgia Classification Criteria

To qualify for the diagnosis of fibromyalgia syndrome, according to the American College of Rheumatology 1990 classification, an individual must fulfill the following two criteria (also, there must be no other disease that would explain your symptoms; for example, rheumatic arthritis, systemic lupus, gout hypothyroidism, etc.):

First, a history of widespread pain for at least three months in all four quadrants of your body: pain is on both sides of the body *and* pain is also above and below the waist *and* pain is present in the axial skeleton (neck, mid-back, low-back pain).

Second, you must also have pain on digital pressure in at least 11 of 18 designated fibromyalgia tender points sites: these points must have marked tenderness and possibly refer pain to other areas, on palpation and not just be "tender." Also, pain is elicited with approximately 4 kilograms of pressure.

Your Nervous System and Myofascial Pain from CRPs to FMS

The poorly understood reality is that fibromyalgia syndrome is part of a continuum of chronic myofascial pain and dysfunction disorders. This does not make your diagnosed fibromyalgia any less important or painful, but comprehending this fact will assist you in healing your pain once and for all. For over a decade now, respected researchers have been proving that fibromyalgia is not a discrete disorder or disease but is best understood and treated as part of a range of rheumatological disorders. Research is now showing that fibromyalgia and other chronic myofascial disorders are a consequence of nociceptor sensitization and subsequent central nervous system dysfunction.[233]

To better comprehend this, please recall from earlier chapters the uniqueness of the free nerve endings in your tissues called nociceptors. As previously explained, what is special about the nociceptors of your myofascial tissue is that they do not adapt to stimulation but can actually become increasingly more sensitive to stimulation, a process called peripheral sensitization. This is the process that makes myofascial trigger points so painful, and it plays a major role in the development of chronic myofascial pain syndromes, especially in fibromyalgia syndrome.

It also turns out that once nociceptors become hypersensitive in the muscles, tendons, and ligaments of your joints, they will chronically fire into your spinal cord. This eventually makes the neurons of your spinal cord hypersensitive to any further stimulation, a process called central sensitization. For example, if peripheral sensitization is taking place in the muscles and joints of your low back, it will cause a hypersensitivity of the neurons in the spinal cord in your low back. This creates a recurring painful situation, in which any stimulation of your myofascial tissues from bending or lifting with your low back can cause you mild back pain at times to disabling pain all the time. Your degree of symptoms depends on the number and severity of myofascial trigger points in your low back that are firing into your spinal cord, causing this central sensitization.

The severity of your symptoms also depends on the duration and severity of central sensitization going on in your spinal cord. If this process of central sensitization of your lumbar spinal cord goes on for months, it can make the pain-processing areas in your brain also hypersensitive to any stimulation from your lower body. This evolving process of central sensitization of your brain's pain-processing centers can cause

233 F. Wolfe, "The relation between tender points and fibromyalgia symptom variables: evidence that fibromyalgia is not a discrete disorder in the clinic," *Ann Rheum Dis* 56, no. 4 (April 1997): 268–71.

your chronic myofascial pain to spread neurologically to other areas of your body. This means that your chronic regional pain of the low back has now spread to your upper back and neck, creating a multiregional pain syndrome. This is the neurological dysfunction that is involved in the development of fibromyalgia.

The process just described can go on, ignored or repressed with drugs, for months or years until it hits a certain threshold, causing that individual to be diagnosed with fibromyalgia. It is the underlying pro-inflammatory metabolic problem, as described throughout this book (e.g., toxic chemicals, dysbiosis, insulin resistance, and oxidative stress), that can eventually cause this central sensitization of your nervous system to take off on you, creating the all-over agony of fibromyalgia syndrome.

Some of the areas of your brain that become sensitized are the source of many of the confusing and complex symptoms of fibromyalgia syndrome. Research can now utilize functional magnetic resonance imaging (fMRI) to create actual pictures of these areas of the brain becoming sensitized in fibromyalgia syndrome patients. For a more detailed explanation of central sensitization of your nervous system and the role it plays in your chronic myofascial disorders, please review chapter 8.

Research reported in the medical journal *Pain* found that this dysfunction of nociceptors (pain receptors) in the myofascial tissues of fibromyalgia patients is the same dysfunction present in patients with chronic regional pain syndromes. This research study demonstrated that individuals with chronic regional pain (e.g., shoulder girdle/neck pain or low-back/hip pain) have multiple tender points, just like fibromyalgia patients. They also found that the number and intensity of positive tender points increased as more regions of pain became involved. The group, however, with the most dysfunctional nociceptors in number and severity was found in the patients designated as having fibromyalgia syndrome. This important study found that there is a continuum of chronic musculoskeletal pain disorders that runs from chronic regional pain syndrome (CRPS) to multiregional pain syndrome (MRPS) through widespread pain syndrome (WPS) up to the full-blown fibromyalgia syndrome (FMS). Interestingly, the further along these individuals were on the continuum towards full-blown fibromyalgia, the greater their nociceptor dysfunction and nervous system involvement, which resulted in greater intensity of overall pain, stiffness, fatigue, and sleep disruption (see figure 18.1).[234]

234 G. Carli, A. L. Suman, G. Biasi, and R. Marcolongo, "Reactivity to superficial and deep stimuli in patients with chronic musculoskeletal pain," *Pain* 100, no. 3 (December 2002): 259–69.

Figure 18.1

Increasing nociceptor and central hypersensitization

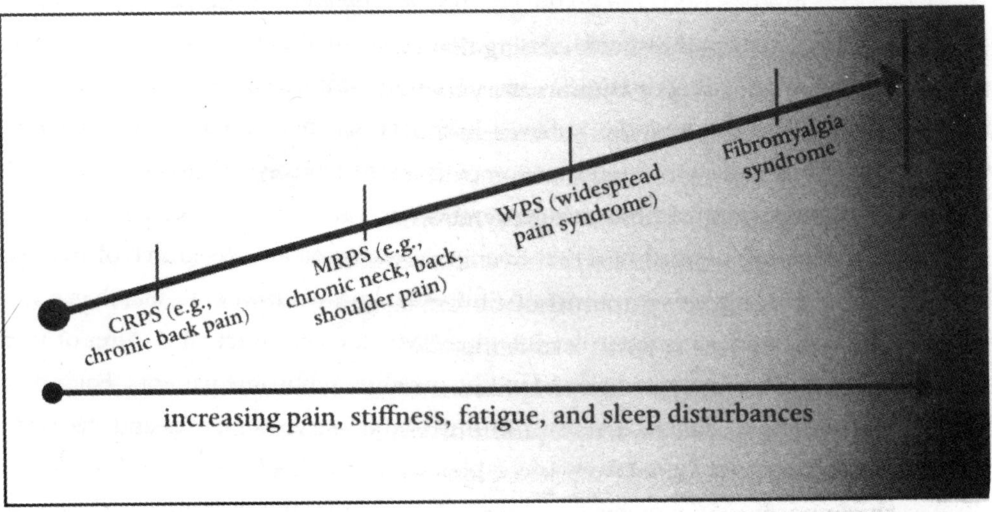

For clarification, CRPS is "chronic regional pain syndrome," which denotes chronic pain and dysfunction limited to one region, or quadrant. The four quadrants are formed by dividing the body at the waist into upper and lower halves, and then dividing the body again down the middle into right and left upper and lower quadrants. Examples of CRPS would be low-back pain into the hip and leg affecting the right lower quadrant, or left shoulder girdle pain causing arm pain and neck stiffness in the left upper quadrant. The next step up in myofascial pain disorders is "multiregional pain syndrome" (MRPS), which is chronic pain and dysfunction in different quadrants of your body, but not fulfilling the criteria of all-four-quadrant pain found in fibromyalgia syndrome. For example, in MRPS, someone may suffer with neck pain, pain in both shoulders, and right hip pain, but no pain in the left lower quadrant, therefore not fulfilling all the criteria for a fibromyalgia syndrome diagnosis. Going up the continuum, the next chronic myofascial pain disorder is "widespread pain syndrome" (WPS). WPS is very similar to fibromyalgia, with chronic pain and tenderness into all four quadrants of the body, but it does not fulfill all the criteria of FMS. This sensitization of your nervous system can then go all the way, with pain developing in all four quadrants of your body and along your spine, with at least 11 of the 18 typical tender points, along with fatigue and other associated symptoms; now you have earned the diagnosis "fibromyalgia syndrome" (FMS).

My point is this: if you suffer with CRPS, MRPS, or WPS, your myofascial pain can be just as severe as someone with the diagnosis of fibromyalgia syndrome. Research studies are now objectively demonstrating that the same hypersensitization process of the nociceptors, spinal cord, and brain is taking place in individuals with "just" chronic low-back pain (CRPS) as well as those with WPS and fibromyalgia syndrome.

Of course, the individuals with fibromyalgia, because of a greater metabolic and nervous system involvement, are also plagued with a long list of associated disabling symptoms when compared to the chronic low-back pain patient. However, the underlying causes of peripheral and central sensitization, caused by numerous NMLs, are the same in all four chronic myofascial disorders. Furthermore, to actually heal the pain of all four syndromes, you need to apply the same program of physically removing the myofascial trigger points with myofascial therapy and address the metabolic dysfunction with the nutritional recovery program outlined in this book. Those with a more complicated disorder, such as WPS or FMS, will need to apply the complete program for a longer period of time to heal their pain.

A recent study compared individuals with chronic regional pain of the low back persisting for more than twelve months to individuals diagnosed with fibromyalgia syndrome. The individuals with the chronic regional pain had multiple tender points in the low back that were nearly as painful as those found in the fibromyalgia group. Even more interesting in this study was the evidence that central sensitization of five pain-processing areas in the brain was present on functional MRI pictures in both the regional low-back pain group as well as those suffering with the global pain of fibromyalgia. Furthermore, this sensitization of areas of the brain relating to pain processing was not found in any of the healthy subjects examined. The conclusion of the study was that at equal levels of pressure, individuals with chronic low-back pain (CRPS) and fibromyalgia (FMS) experience significantly more pain and show activation of central pain-processing areas of the brain, whereas healthy subjects did not.[235] Therefore, this is not a psychological disorder but a physiological one that must be addressed as a physical and metabolic problem.

---

235 T. Giesecke, R. H. Gracely, M. A. Grant, A. Nachemson, F. Petzke, D. A. Williams, and D. J. Clauw, "Evidence of augmented central pain processing in idiopathic chronic low back pain," *Arthritis Rheum* 50, no. 2 (February 2004): 613–23.

Figure 18.2

Many ways up the mountain of chronic myofascial pain

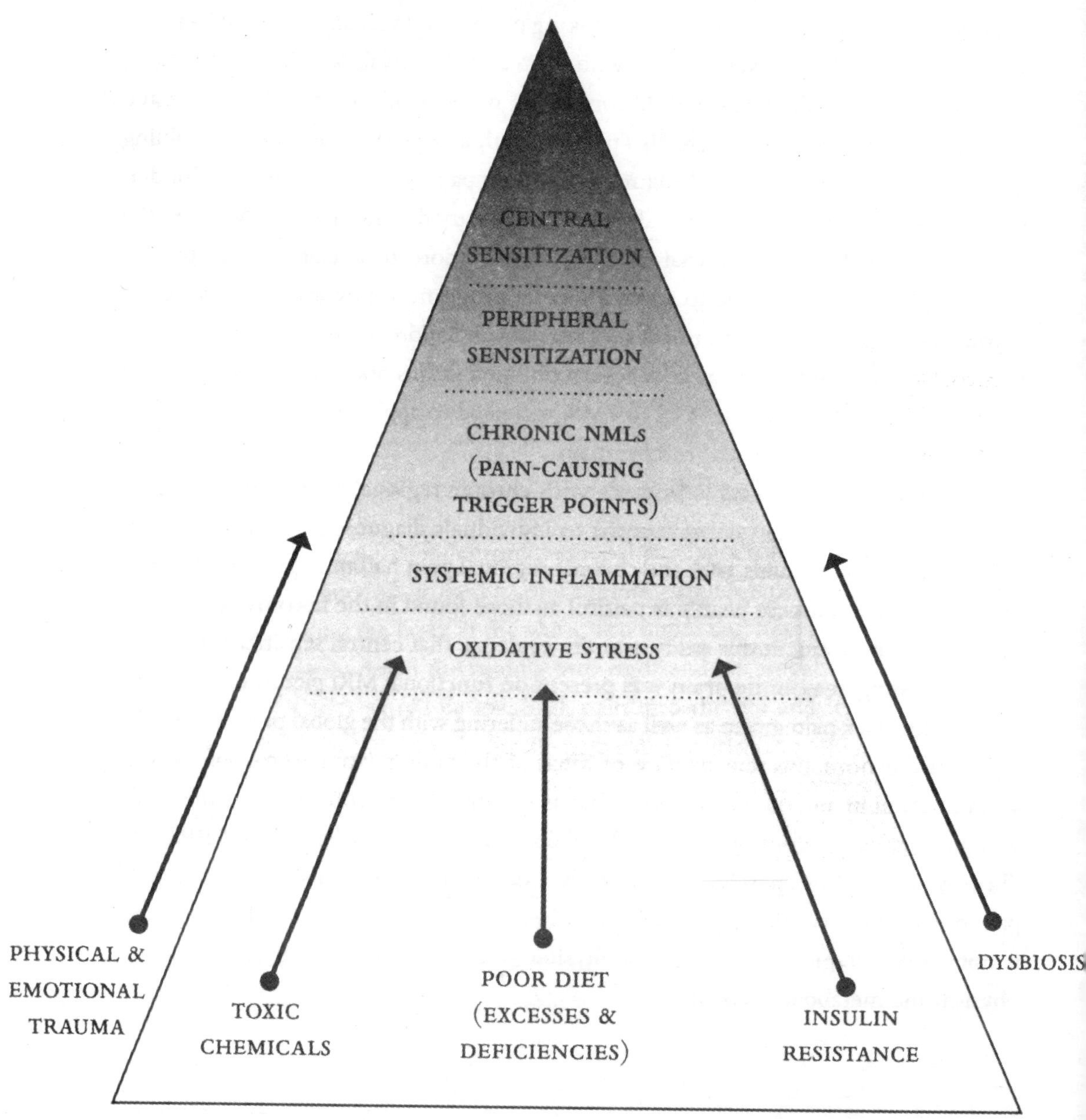

Fibromyalgia: It's Not All in Your Head, It's in Your Spinal Cord and Brain!

For the last five years, Roland Staud at the University of Florida College of Medicine has been a leader in the research on the peripheral and central sensitization involved in fibromyalgia syndrome. I highly recommend that all health-care providers treating fibromyalgia review his work. In a research article titled "Neurobiology of fibromyalgia syndrome," Staud stated that "accumulating evidence suggests that fibromyalgia syndrome (FMS) pain is maintained by tonic impulse input from deep tissues, such as muscle and joints, in combination with central sensitization mechanisms."[236] In simple terms, chronic trigger points or muscle knots in combination with central sensitization, as previously described in this book, *maintain* the pain of fibromyalgia.

Therefore, if you apply gentle trigger point therapy with a self-care tool to physically remove your neuromyofascial lesions, over time you remove the tonic impulse maintaining your fibromyalgic pain. This process of self-care trigger point therapy is described in chapters 9 through 13 of this book. Of course, it is absolutely imperative that you also treat the underlying metabolic dysfunction of the neuromyofascial lesions in your deep tissues, as described in chapters 14 through 17 of this book. Therefore, if you have the misfortune of suffering from multiregional pain syndrome (MRPS), widespread pain syndrome (WPS), or the especially disabling fibromyalgia syndrome (FMS), you will need to apply with great discipline my comprehensive recovery program detailed in chapters 9 through 17 to heal your pain.

At the time of writing this book, the most recent studies published in 2006 and 2007 by the Staud research group had come to the conclusion that these changes in the spinal cord and areas of the brain resulting in central sensitization represent the hallmark of fibromyalgia. They went on to point out that this mechanism of sensitization of the spinal cord and brain is also a hallmark in "many other chronic pain syndromes, including irritable bowel syndrome, temporomandibular disorder, migraine, and low-back pain." In this important study, they point out that once this central sensitization is established in your spinal cord and brain, all you need is *minimal stimulation* to activate and maintain your chronic pain![237] Simply stated, these changes involve sensitization of your central nervous system (spinal cord and brain). Fibromyalgia patients develop

---

236 D. D. Price and R. Staud, "Neurobiology of fibromyalgia syndrome," *J Rheumatol Suppl* 75 (August 2005): 22–28.

237 R. Staud and M. E. Rodriguez, "Mechanisms of disease: pain in fibromyalgia syndrome," *Nat Clin Pract Rheumatol* 2, no. 2 (February 2006): 90–98.

a condition in which severe pain and tenderness is easily maintained throughout their body *without any tissue damage or injury.*

No one questions or tells an amputee with the horrible agony of phantom limb pain that it's "all in your head" or "you're just crazy." With the amputee, just because you cannot see damaged tissue (or any tissue at all), it does not mean the amputee's brain is not experiencing the reality of horrendous, unbearable pain. So why would anyone question the suffering of an individual with WPS or fibromyalgia syndrome just because they cannot see any damaged or inflamed tissue? Without any outward signs of damage, injury, or inflammation, individuals with WPS or fibromyalgia can maintain horrific levels of pain in their muscles, subcutaneous tissues, and even the skin itself, through this process of central sensitization.

This "wind-up" process of central sensitization in fibromyalgia syndrome is a snowballing of the pain response to even the most minor exertion or physical contact. Central sensitization creates a reality in which even repeated touches, such as handshakes or pats on your back, can generate a pain that lingers and increases with each new contact. The development of this diffuse, severe surface tenderness in fibromyalgia patients makes it difficult, if not impossible, to palpate deep myofascial tissues for the NMLs actually causing or maintaining the central sensitization. Research has found that these deep, tender points in muscles and tendons of fibromyalgia patients, are myofascial trigger points that must be removed to end this process of central sensitization.

Comprehensive Wellness Strategies

As a fibromyalgia patient, if you work through your surface tenderness at your own pace with a self-care trigger point tool, eventually you can begin to deactivate the underlying myofascial trigger points deep in your muscles. Research and my own clinical experience have shown that when this is accomplished, your central sensitization begins to lessen. With this, you may begin to experience a great deal of pain relief. If you are too exquisitely tender to apply even very light trigger point therapy, you need to first work very diligently on removing the metabolic factors aggravating your nociceptors.

The four simplest and quickest things you can do for yourself to metabolically lessen your tenderness are: (1) clean up your diet and eat healthier foods, (2) do an "oil change" and take 3 to 6 grams of omega-3 EPA/DHA daily, (3) take 600 to 800 milligrams of magnesium with about 2,400 milligrams of malate, and (4) supplement about 4,000 milligrams of standardized ginger root extract with 2,000 milligrams of standardized curcumin root extract. The exact dosage level depends on your own personal tolerance and severity of symptoms. Once you have implemented these three aspects of my comprehensive program, you may notice some of your tenderness lessening, allowing you to begin to physically remove the myofascial trigger points that are causing your central sensitization. However, to fully heal your pain, there may be other metabolic complications that must be fully addressed to restore your vitality, such as dysbiosis, insulin resistance, enhancement of your detoxification pathways, and improved function of your mitochondria.

Restore Your Vitality!

The greater the role that chronic fatigue, whether physical or mental exhaustion, plays in your fibromyalgia syndrome, the lower your vitality is. Many times, natural health-care practitioners relate this to low adrenal function. Low adrenal function can be a factor in lowered vitality, but what is missed by this approach is your body's ultimate powerhouse and battery, the hundreds to thousands of mitochondria located in each cell of your body. It is their job to produce and store the energy (ATP) you use for any task to be done by any cell. As described in detail in chapter 5, for various reasons your mitochondria can lose their efficiency. When this takes place throughout your tissues, muscles especially, you lose the vitality you need to live a healthy and active life.

Most important to our discussion, with decreased energy production in your myofascial tissues, your muscles will more readily form pain-causing knots. These knots or myofascial trigger points contain sensitized nociceptors within them, which is the peripheral sensitization previously described. This peripheral sensitization eventually begins the process of central sensitization, leading to the chronic pain and associated symptoms you experience with WPS and fibromyalgia. Through this short synopsis, you can see how important it is to restore your vitality in your goal to finally heal your pain and overcome the challenge of fibromyalgia.

To restore your vitality, it's also important to slow down and take care of yourself in this busy, hectic modern lifestyle that we lead. If you do not take care of yourself and are overwhelmed by your fibromyalgia, you will be of no use to yourself or your loved ones. Now is the time, with the knowledge and tools available to you, to heal your pain and overcome the challenge of your fibromyalgia syndrome. First and foremost, it's vital to get good, restorative, restful sleep. However, I have grave concerns about treating fibromyalgia as just a sleep disorder and about the common use of prescription drugs to induce sleep that follows from that approach. To naturally improve your sleep, first you need to create a dark, quiet place to sleep, which can be a real challenge in this postmodern urban world. With artificial light and noise stimulating you, it is no wonder that it may be difficult to fall into a natural, deep sleep.

There are also natural supplements you can utilize. Magnesium has been shown to be very beneficial in naturally inducing a deeper, more restful sleep. So take a good share of your daily 600 to 800 milligrams of magnesium before you retire—say about 300 milligrams one hour before bedtime. You can also utilize combinations of nutraceuticals, such as the amino acid 5-hydroxytryptophan (5-HTP) and theanine, both at 100 milligrams each, one hour before bed. To these formulas, you can add the beneficial botanicals passionflower flowers (*Passiflora incarnate*), hops flower (*Humulus lupulus*), and valerian root. The added benefit of these herbs is that they have been shown to relieve minor muscle pain, improve relaxation, and reduce stress, so you can use them during the day at lighter doses. This dosage depends on your size, weight, gender, and reactivity to these herbs, so start out using half dosage.

The next thing you can do to restore vitality and take care of yourself is to take brisk walks outdoors in the fresh air and sunshine every other day for fifteen minutes. As you begin to feel better, increase your aerobic conditioning by speedwalking for about thirty minutes, five days a week. Speedwalking differs from jogging in that no matter how fast you move, one of your feet is always in contact with the ground. This way, there is no jarring stress to your muscles and joints, while you still get an excellent aerobic workout. To this exercise program, you can eventually add resistance training two to three times a week to build up your muscle tone. Start off with light weights and go easy. And remember to add stretching at the beginning of your program to work on a lengthening your muscles. In fibromyalgia, with the multitude of myofascial trigger points in your muscles that have a tendency to shorten them, it's vital that you gently stretch before speedwalking or resistance training to avoid aggravating your pain.

One of the most important things you can do for yourself is to eat a healthy diet that is primarily vegetarian and organic. If you choose to eat animal products, I advise eating stir-fries with small amounts of fish and fowl added; also, cultured low-fat dairy products can be beneficial. But remember that animal products are high in the pro-inflammatory arachidonic fatty acids, and they tend to contain more pesticides, herbicides, hormones, antibiotics, and industrial chemicals that then are passed on to you. For a complete and comprehensive discussion on the importance of diet and how best to plan your meals, please refer to chapter 14.

Once you are eating healthy foods that help to restore your vitality, it is important to make sure that you are properly digesting and absorbing your food's nutrients. There is an old saying that "you are what you eat," but a more accurate statement would be "you are what you digest and absorb" because that is what will become you! For a complete and comprehensive discussion on digestion, food allergies, absorption, and dysbiosis problems, please see chapter 16. And please don't forget the two vital experiments that are described in that chapter. They proved that 100% of all individuals tested with fibromyalgia syndrome had bacteria overgrowth in their small intestine, "bad bugs" spilling out pain-causing endotoxins! So if you have fibromyalgia, you need to be tested for dysbiosis and then properly treat it!

Once you begin the basics of taking care of yourself and restoring your vitality, you'll want to begin a self-care program of trigger point therapy. You can begin to experiment with this therapy by using a golf ball, tennis ball, or possibly your spouse's thumb. But whatever means you use, you need to find a way to apply very light, sustained therapeutic pressure for one to two minutes to your myofascial trigger points in order to "convince" them to release. This entire physical self-care program is described in full detail in chapters 9 through 13. Please review these sections, giving special focus to your primary areas of pain.

Once you see the benefit of a self-care trigger point therapy program, you may want to invest in a quality trigger point tool. These tools can make it much more convenient and effective to apply specific therapeutic pressure to the trigger points that you need to release, even in difficult-to-reach areas of your body.[238]

Trigger point therapy will be effective, especially when combined with a comprehensive nutritional approach, but it doesn't work overnight or even within weeks. Because

---

238 A product that I designed specifically for this purpose, primarily because of my own daughter's fibromyalgia, is the FENIX Rehab System. This self-care trigger point tool allows you to apply myofascial therapies virtually anywhere on your body while you rest and relax.

of the severe peripheral and central sensitization that is taking place within your nervous system with fibromyalgia, you must go slow, be patient, and give it time. With trigger point therapy, I suggest that you begin with treating specific areas every other day, or concentrate on different areas of the body each day. You must find out, though, what personally works best for you; is it best for you to use very light pressure or firm pressure, can you benefit from long therapy sessions or only short sessions, should you self-treat every day or every other day, and so on.

Everyone's physiology is different, so ultimately you must determine what's best for you. Through the research I've presented, I hope to have convinced you that it is important to develop a self-care trigger point therapy program. It is helpful to find a doctor or therapist who can help you with your myofascial therapy. You may begin to see some progress almost immediately, but full recovery from fibromyalgia will probably be slow. By having your own trigger point therapy tool, you can save yourself the tremendous cost of months of therapy at two to three visits per week, and you will speed up your recovery.

Just one last reminder: as you begin your trigger point therapy program, it's vital that you start on a comprehensive nutritional program to overcome the metabolic challenges found in fibromyalgia syndrome. Details of this part of your comprehensive recovery program can be in found in chapters 14 through 17, in which nutraceutical supplementation is described for dysbiosis, enhancement of detoxification, improved mitochondrial function, insulin resistance, oxidative stress, and systemic inflammation. An overview of this program is provided in table format on the next page.

Good luck, and best wishes for a complete recovery and the ability to take back your life!

Comprehensive Recovery Program for Fibromyalgia		
Seven-Step Clean-up Program	**Six-Step Basic Intake Plan**	**Advanced Metabolic Support**
1. Remove pain-causing muscle-knots with trigger point therapy	1. Eat a healthy Mediterranean diet (see chapter 14)	For an explanation of the metabolic support below, see chapter 17
2. Eat organic foods to reduce antibiotics, hormones, pesticides, and herbicides, and remove all unhealthy foods: HFCS, transfats, etc.	2. Add a high-potency multivitamin and a multi-mineral formula (do not get a one-a-day—generally too low a potency)	1. Silymarin from milk thistle standardized extract (400–600 mg) and green tea standardized extract (250–600 mg) daily
3. At home, filter your water (carbon filter or reverse osmosis) and air (HEPA/ULPA filters), and use a highly filtered vacuum to lower dust exposure	3. Do an oil change: supplement omega-3 fatty acids with at least 6 g of actual EPA/DHA daily, and make sure you remove all "bad fats" (see chapter 14)	2. NAC (N-acetylcysteine; 1,000–1,500 mg daily)
4. Clean up your personal environment: buy green household cleaners and personal care products	4. Tune up cellular engines with a total of 600–800 mg of magnesium with 2,400 mg of malate and high B_1 of 100 to 200 mg (see chapter 14)	3. Alpha-lipoic acid (500–800 mg) with 1–2 g acetyl-L-carnitine taken together daily
5. Maintain excellent excretory functions with 1–2 bowel movements daily	5. Spice up your health supplement with 2–4 g ginger root extract and 1–3 g curcumin root extract (see chapter 15)	4. CoQ10 (50–1,000 mg) with up to 1,000 mg of niacinamide
6. Stop poisoning yourself with smoking (or exposure to second-hand smoke) and excess drinking	6. Overcome dysbiosis: remove "bad bugs" with berberine, and replace with probiotics, or "good bacteria" (see chapter 16)	5. Mixed vitamin E (400–1,200 IU) and vitamin C (2,000–4,000 mg) daily
7. Heating systems: clean and monitor regularly (#1 death by poisoning in U.S.)		6. Selenium (200 mcg), zinc (30–50 mg), and copper (2 mg) daily

SECTION 5

Spiritually Healing Your Pain

For the individual who really wants to take a comprehensive and holistic approach to healing their pain, this section on spiritually healing your pain is a necessity. Modern society, especially in the West, tends to divide the body, mind, and spirit into separate entities. In doing so, we create a situation where real health and happiness is unattainable. As we shall see, there is no such separation, and treating someone as if body, mind, and spirit were separate is a great unwellness in and of itself.

In chapter 19, we examine the neurological basis of our interconnected wholeness. We discover that, to maximize our survival, we are actually hard-wired for fear and anger. We must learn how to circumvent this hard-wiring with our higher brain centers if we wish to find true peace, health, and happiness. Here is where we begin to touch upon the spiritual aspect of healing.

To accomplish this, I borrow from the perennial wisdom of the Axial Age to present my five-step program for spiritually healing your pain. These two realizations and three daily practices are described in detail in chapters 20 and 21. In these final chapters of this comprehensive guide, I hope you find the way to live in greater harmony and peace with yourself, your family and friends, and your world.

19

The Body/Mind Connection to Pain and Suffering

In this final section, let's examine some of the most important but misunderstood factors in your recovery from chronic pain and the restoration of your health. On many levels, our modern approach to healing is somewhat schizophrenic. At one end of the spectrum, you have scientistic[239] modern medicine with its emphasis on the physical reality, which must be physically altered through drugs or surgery. This form of health care works extremely well in trauma and disease care. On the other end of the spectrum, you have the burgeoning growth of holistic, or energetic, medicine. The emphasis here becomes inordinately focused on the role that energy and the mind play in healing, as if the food you take in has only an insignificant part to play.

The problem with this dichotomy is that the body/mind and spirit are still disconnected. Where is the middle way, where the body/mind and spirit dissolves into the truth of everything as One? When you look into a mirror, it is very obvious that you are separate from everything else surrounding you in your environment. It defies reason and logic to come to any other conclusion! But what exists before your eyes is an illusion, an image like the one in the mirror that you call "you." It is the same for the illusion that is reflected within your senses, the image of a world of separate objects

239 I use the word *scientistic* to designate worldviews that masquerade as science, when in actuality they are driven by profit and philosophical prejudices rather than true, open-minded scientific inquiry.

within the reality of an inseparable, whole uni-verse.[240] If there is someone in the room with you, you are sharing bits of each other through each breath you take. If you reach out to hold a hand, at the interface of your palms the boundary between melts away as atoms of each other are exchanged.

But the unity of all goes much deeper than this. You, others in the room, a chair, the wall, everything reflected in the mirror, and even the mirror itself—at one time, it all was the ancient crust of our earth. Rock mixed with water, atmosphere, sunlight, and eons of time evolved into all that has existed, does exist, and will exist on this earth. The rock, water, atmosphere, and sun were all constructed from basic elements forged in the original fireball of creation. These basic elements of existence—hydrogen and helium that burn in the cores of primary stars—were eventually forged into carbon, and the carbon burned into oxygen, nitrogen, calcium, and magnesium. This process continued on in the heart of primary stars throughout the unfolding universe until the ninety-two elements were formed. These sacred primary stars miraculously gave birth to the carbon and nitrogen that would one day form the basis of life, fashioned phosphorus that would be the basis of plant photosynthesis to capture the energy of the sun, invented the iron at the center of your hemoglobin, which carries oxygen to all your tissues, and the calcium that now builds the bones of your body.

Looking deeper into these elements of existence, we find the subatomic particles of their atoms, composed of neutrons and protons at the center and charged electrons whizzing about them in a cloud. This seemingly solid atom at the floor of existence, from which everything is built, is actually empty space. If you could visualize the nucleus of a carbon atom in your body being four inches in diameter, the electron cloud of that atom would be four miles away, and the electrons would be smaller than this period. Everything in between the nucleus and the electrons four miles away would be empty space; the atom is actually 99.9999999999999% nothingness, or emptiness. Then the seemingly solid protons and neutrons are composed of subatomic quarks, which physicists break down into exotic subparticles. However, it is really improper to term them as particles, because in actuality they exhibit wavelike energy behaviors. And as Einstein so eloquently pointed out, $E = mc^2$; energy (E) and mass, or matter (M), are convertible into one another because they arise from the same primeval, sacred ground of being; they are One.

---

240 Our word *universe* comes from the Latin *unus*, meaning "one," and *vertere*, meaning "to turn." Therefore, when we use the word *universe*, we recognize that all is one. To signify this recognition, I will hyphenate the word *uni-verse*, " to turn into one."

Ultimately, the elements of existence that make up you as well as everything about you share the underlying reality of being energy fields in the universe of Nothingness, or "no one thing-ness." In my view, this makes all of reality spirit-in-action, no matter how we choose to define it. With this awareness, whatever you do is realized as spirit dancing with spirit, making you and everything in your life a spiritual act. With this awareness, every real healing action taken by you truly becomes an act of spiritual healing, for no longer does a split of the body/mind and spirit exist. So, when you take the time to relax and breathe deeply, you are aware of spirit taking in spirit. In this awareness, food is no longer crass matter to simply "fill up" with. Devitalized junk food, in a sense, is like bringing in "bad vibrations" or even "evil spirits." When you choose whole, natural foods to nourish yourself, you realize it is a choice that brings real spiritual healing into your life.

When your food is viewed correctly as condensed patterns of energy, you can begin to understand that the quality of all types of energy you bring into your body has a dramatic effect on the outcome of your life. As you bring into your body these various forms of energies from the environment—air, water, food—these energies communicate with your genes. Your genes are the energetic encoding, in molecular form, of instructions from your ancestors on how to live. As energetic beings, we live in a sea of "energies," and so it is crucial we pay attention to the quality of the energies we bring in. It is these energies and how we interact with our genetic instructions that determine if we produce healthy tissues or tissues susceptible to disease and degeneration.

Real, sustainable health cannot be found in blocking vital metabolic pathways with drugs or the intake of "subtle energies" from a healer, but rather by you taking the initiative to create for yourself a more balanced life. If you take in a drug that relieves your symptoms, but nothing is changed in how you live, eat, and think, how long will your drug-induced "health" last? Same thing if you see a natural healer who energetically heals you—how long will the new, healthy balance remain without changing the factors that created the imbalance in the first place? Throughout the chapters in this book, we have seen that the way to healing our pain comes through living a balanced life, eating a balanced diet, and following a more balanced lifestyle.

We have explored how balance is vital, right down to the metabolic pathways of our cells. For example, we found that inflammation is vital for life, but if not kept in proper balance, it can lead to out-of-control acute inflammation or chronic low-grade systemic inflammation, both leading to pain and disease. The same with the vital process of oxidation that our cells utilize to produce ATP—if it is not kept in proper balance, it can lead to oxidative stress and all kinds of health problems. As we shall see in this section, healing our pain and maintaining our health comes from a more balanced emotional and spiritual outlook. This balance can be found in the application of my five-step program, outlined in chapters 20 and 21. But to better grasp the importance and application of my five-step program, it is helpful to first understand a little bit about how our nervous system is hard-wired.

The Source of Our Suffering

Throughout this book, I have often repeated the theme that there is no end to our suffering until we find the courage to take on the warrior spirit and find our own paths to healing our pain. In healing our pain, it may be helpful to understand what we actually mean by the word "healing." Our word *heal* comes from the ancient Indo-European root *hal* (pronounced "hail"), meaning "to make whole." But this haleness (wholeness) that brings true health does not come from focusing on "making me whole again," which is so often the focus of healing today.

The road to real recovery fundamentally lies in recognizing our wholeness through remembering the interconnectedness of our existence. Remembering who you truly are is ultimately a spiritual task. I place this step at the end of the book because I've found it easier for individuals to unveil this awareness once they have improved their diets, lifestyles, and have begun a program of removing their pain-causing muscle knots. Once your pain has begun to subside, it is much easier to focus on the deeper levels of healing.

We are blessed to live at a time when we have access to the teachings of the world's great spiritual traditions, giving us the opportunity to explore our healing at deeper levels. From their inception, these great spiritual traditions have recognized the universality of pain in human existence, but they have also gone on to point the way to healing this pain. These spiritual traditions teach that our suffering is a product of our ignorance; our pain arises from our forgetting the totality of who we truly are. More precisely, we suffer when we fail to recognize who we all are; in Judaic and Christian terminology, we are all Children of God; in Hinduism, we are all Atman; in Buddhism, we all have Buddha Nature; and in Taoism, we are all One with the Tao. Interestingly, even modern science teaches that we and all life forms are composed of the same elements—carbon, hydrogen, oxygen, nitrogen, phosphorus, sulfur, and various minerals—so at our core DNA building blocks, we are all the same.

The spiritual traditions teach that we suffer because of our focus on the small self instead of tuning in to our true identity and the Oneness we are all part of. In other words, to borrow from a well-used phrase, "it's the ego, stupid!" As we shall see in this section, through our identification with the illusion of this small, separate self, we end up living semi-consciously through our most primal base emotions, fear and anger. These great spiritual traditions go on to teach that there is a way to awaken from this attachment to our small self, an awakening that is known by various names in different traditions—salvation, enlightenment, liberation, satori.

Hard-Wired for Fear and Anger

As we have discovered throughout this book, we are hard-wired for pain, which plays a vital role in our survival. All sentient life has the ability to sense a threatening environment, from the simplest one-cell animal sitting alone in a laboratory petri dish to the Nobel-prize-winning scientist standing on a street in crowded New York City. For example, if we put a simple one-cell animal in an unhealthy environment on one side of a petri dish, it will become "irritated" and move out, seeking a healthier life-sustaining environment. With all our complexity, we are no different in our constant quest for life-sustaining physical and psychological environments, no matter how misguided our seeking may become.

Just as we are hard-wired for pain, we are also hard-wired for our base emotions, fear and anger. Like the sensation of pain, these two emotions are vital for our continued survival, and because fear and anger are so necessary to our survival, our central nervous systems can become hypersensitized to these emotions. This can create drastic overreactions emotionally and/or pervading moods of anxiety, hostility, and sadness.

Our word *emotion* comes from the ancient Latin prefix *e-*, "out of," and the root word *movere,* "to move."[241] Therefore, an emotion is the impetus that "moves us out of," or motivates us, within any given moment. The emotion of fear is the feeling that "moves us out of" threatening or unhealthy environments or situations. The benefit to survival is that fear helps the individual organism move away from any real threat. It is a catalyst to remove oneself quickly from danger, or if there is no escape, fear can

241 Throughout this book, I explore the original meanings of words, based on my research and writings. The primary sources for the etymological roots of my work are an original printing (1890) by Rev. Walter Skeat, professor of Anglo-Saxon at the University of Cambridge, U.K., of a book titled *A Concise Etymological Dictionary of the English Language* and a 1995 Oxford printing of his *An Etymological Dictionary of the English Language*. I believe him to be one of the giants of etymology. As a secondary resource and to verify Rev. Skeat's research, I utilize the modern work of Robert K. Barnhart in his 1995 book *The Barnhart Concise Dictionary of Etymology—The Origins of American English Words*.

then be the catalyst that moves us on to a state of anger and aggression so that we may defend ourselves. Fear and anger are beneficial physiological responses, but only when they are short-lived and in response to actual life-threatening situations.

The wiring of your brain directing your behavior and reactions to environmental events is quite complex; a simple explanation follows. Except for your sense of smell, in general every sensation enters your brain through the brain stem at the base of your brain. This sensory experience then goes on up to your thalamus. Your thalamus is the crucial relay station that sorts and then sends incoming signals to centers of vision, sound, emotion, movement, sensation, and reason in your cerebral cortex, the outer grey matter. But before the logic or rational centers of the cerebral cortex can act on any sensory information, your thalamus has sent the data to your emotional brain centers.

Therefore, before you can even think about this sensory information (whether vision, sound, touch, taste), you have already emotionally responded to it. This is why you startle and jump at something in your peripheral vision before your visual and reasoning cortex can fully determine that it is a stick and not a snake. This has a very important survival component; you are hard-wired to respond emotionally ("moving out of") before taking the time to figure out what it is you are reacting to.

This ability to feel fear and to move out of an unhealthy or threatening situation comes about by the activation of a small area in your brain called the amygdala. These paired deep, small, brain centers, located in the right and left temporal lobes of your brain (approximately right above your ears), are each about the size of your thumbnail. They are a primary part of your emotional brain, known as the limbic system. When your amygdalas are activated, they, in turn, activate other areas of your brain that create the fear and anger—psychological and physiological—responses throughout your body. And as you may have already guessed, as with other aspects of your central nervous system, the amygdala-activating pathways can become sensitized, or hypersensitive.

A primary area stimulated by your amygdala is the hypothalamus, which neurologically and hormonally, through the pituitary and adrenal glands, turns on your fight-or-flight response (see figure 19.1). You may have heard of the fight-or-flight stress response of your sympathetic nervous system. In the last few decades, it has become quite popular because of our focus on the detrimental effects of stress on our health. Today, everybody has "stress," but very few of us really understand its origins. What if stress is not so much the external situation but more your *internal reaction* to the event or situation?

Figure 19.1

Pathway of fear and anger through the brain via the sympathetic nervous system stress response

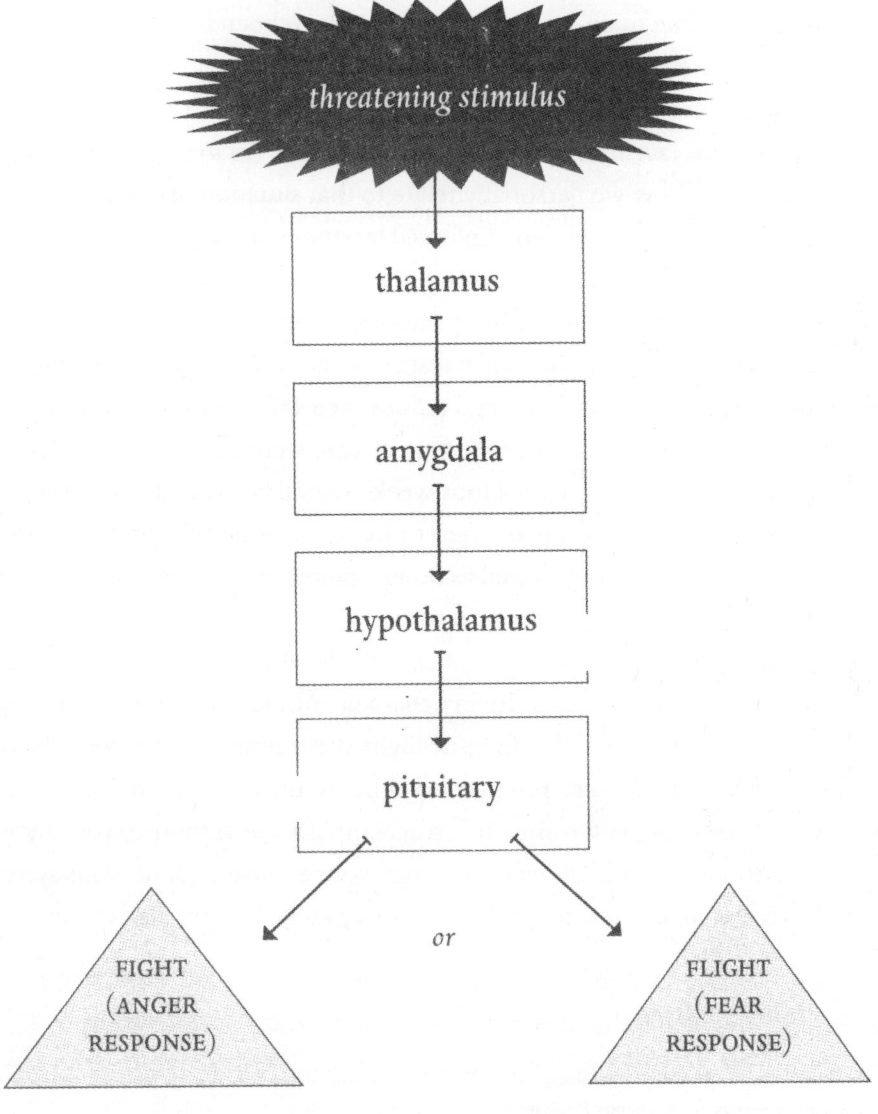

In 1999, a comprehensive scientific review was completed on the research from the previous two decades that had explored the stress response in healthy humans. These studies included both laboratory stress tests and studies that measured the stress response to common stressors such as everyday work, as well as unusual stressors like parachute jumping. The conclusion of the review was that the individuals' perception of the situation was the main determinant of their psychoendocrine (mind and body) stress response. Furthermore, they went on to state that every given stress event has a strictly personal meaning to the individual involved in that event.[242] These reviewed studies establish the fact that it isn't the situation that creates the damaging stress response; rather, it is how we personally relate to that situation or event.

This understanding has also been reinforced by studies demonstrating that the stress response of the amygdala / hypothalamus to the pituitary and adrenals, known simply as the HPA axis (hypothalamic / pituitary / adredal), can actually adapt to a repetitive stressful situation. This means that when test subjects were exposed to the same stressful event, over time they could adapt and reduce their HPA axis stress response. In one recent study, 65 healthy adults, 19 to 45 years of age, were exposed to the Trier Social Stress Test (TSST) three times, with a four-week interval between stress sessions. They found that the HPA axis response and heart rate to stress significantly decreased over the three sessions.[243] This study, as well as others, points out that we can adapt to situations that we originally thought of as stressful.

It is our emotional brain, or limbic system, specifically involving the amygdala and hypothalamus, which turns on this highly charged emotional response, creating what we call the "stress response." This fight-or-flight stress response is extremely vital for your survival, for it is the power you need to either remove or defend yourself from an unhealthy or threatening environment. To accomplish this response, your hypothalamus sets in motion a cascade of events through your sympathetic nervous system and adrenal glands that allows you to either run like a gazelle or fight like a bear.

---

242 M. Biondi and A. Picardi, "Psychological stress and neuroendrocrine function in humans: the last two decades of research," *Psychother Psychosom* 68, no. 3 (1999): 114–50.

243 N. C. Schommer, D. H. Hellhammer, and C. Kirschbaum, "Dissociation between reactivity of the hypothalamus-pituitary-adrenal axis and the sympathetic-adrenal-medullary system to repeated psychosocial stress," *Psychosom Med* 65, no. 3 (May–June 2003): 450–60.

Turning Up Our Emotional "Set Point"

Through this fight-or-flight response, our nervous system is programmed for our survival, and with this programming we have very little choice when our physical and/or psychological existence is truly challenged. When we interpret something as challenging our existence, our amygdala-to-hypothalamic activation gives us two choices. We are told that we can either take flight from or fight with the cause of our fright. The important aspect of all this is the truly challenged part, for like a thermostat on our wall, this emotional "set point" can be set so low that almost everything is perceived as a challenge to our psychological or even physical survival. This lowering of the set point of our "emotional thermostats" is very similar to what happens in the spinal cord and brain when they become hypersensitive to the stimulation of our nociceptors, creating a chronic pain state in the body. In fact, as we shall see, these two mechanisms are highly connected, which is why it is so vital to appreciate the oneness of the body/mind/spirit and its connection to our chronic physical and emotional pain.

When we feel fear and choose to fight, our bodies must then move to an emotional state of readiness for defense and attack. It is the creation of the internal state of anger that gives us the justification, as well as the ability, to defend ourselves and attack another physically or verbally. Once we step into aggression, our higher brain centers of reason tend to take a back seat to our lower "animal" brain. This allows our primitive brain stem, sometimes called the reptilian brain, to ready our entire neuromuscular skeletal system for battle. Generally, social constraint does not allow us to physically attack another, but our bodies still respond to the fear or anger with our muscles tensing in preparation to run or do battle. Moreover, if this stress state of the HPA axis, caused by our fear and anger, becomes repetitive or continuous in our lives, it will naturally cause damage to the body/mind and deteriorate our health over time. This normal, healthy physiological response of fear to aggression is available to us for any actual immediately life-threatening event, but the truth is that in our modern society we rarely experience such actual events.

However, in our ego-driven modern world in which everything revolves around *I*, *me*, and *mine*, the perception of an immediate ego-threatening event may happen numerous times each day, ramping up our stress response. With our modern scientistic view of the ego as being the only self there is, our amygdalas, hypothalamus, and sympathetic nervous system hard-wires us into a painful cycle of fear and anger, constantly defending our small selves, or egos, from attacks. The travesty is that we utilize our anger daily out of our perceived fear that our fragile organism is under physical or psychological attack. This perceived attack can be a look, a word, a gesture—anything that symbolizes to our emotional brain that our small self is being pushed into the nothingness of the unknown, physically or psychologically. Often we come to see our interpersonal relationship problems as threatening to our well-being, and we kick our fight-or-flight response into high gear—frequently attacking those we love.

Humans, of course, share this fight-or-flight autonomic response with other animals. But unlike other animals, we humans have the intellectual capacity to imagine our own deaths. Our keen sense of morbidity and mortality gives rise, in turn, to our heightened sense of a separate self. With this awareness, we are emotionally vulnerable not only to the finality of death for this "skin-encapsulated ego," but also to a host of other possible calamities we are capable of conceptualizing. Therefore, in modern-day humans, the animal fear response that is designed to be triggered by a real and immediate threat to the survival of the organism leaps daily into action in response to our existential dilemmas and interpersonal relationship challenges—but rarely for the physical threat that this hard-wiring of our brain was originally meant for.

Making Our Matter Matter

Furthermore, as animals with an intellect, we have a "consciousness of self," and with a consciousness of self we can have a crisis of consciousness. With this crisis, we can even become lost in the fear of "Who am I?" and "Do I matter?" Our fears spring from two aspects of our identifying with our separate small organism as our entire self. First, we fear for this fragile organism's daily physical safety—or, more specifically, we fear pain and death. Secondly, we fear that our small, separate organism is not enough, that it may not matter; we fear a "psychological death." When we limit ourselves to identifying with this "skin-encapsulated ego" as the only self there is, we become consumed with trying to make it safe from death and strive to somehow make it matter to the outside world. We fear the psychological death of becoming nobody in life and entering the nothingness of death.

In this modern culture, we try to insulate ourselves from these deaths through the "miracles" of medicine: antidepressants and anti-anxiety drugs, transplants, nanotechnology, cloning, bionic parts. In our consumer culture, we try to collect the newest fashions and technological toys, both in quantity and quality. As in other cultures and other times, we do this through clothing, jewelry, cars, homes, jobs, money, and our mates, desperately trying to prove to others that we are somebody. In other words, we create immortality projects. We do this because we need to be loved, and we fear being abandoned; we want to feel we matter, especially to others. By identifying with this separate ego as being "all there is," we can make the end of this organism in physical or psychological death our all-consuming fear. This can lead to the chronic activation of the amygdalas and hypothalamus. We try to make our autonomic fight-or-flight response do what it cannot, in fact, do—save our beleaguered egos from whatever we feel is threatening it.

The Connection That Can Control Our Fear, Anger, and Pain

At this point, you may be wondering what all of this has to do with your chronic low-back pain, shoulder-neck pain, tension headaches, or fibromyalgia. Recent research has now established that while this small area of your brain is "in charge" of your emotions of fear and anger, the amygdalas also highly influence and are influenced by pain in your body. It has been known for some time that there is a reciprocal relationship between persistent, or chronic, pain and the emotions of fear, anxiety, and depression. This, of course, makes total sense to anyone who suffers with chronic pain; you naturally feel more anxious, fearful, and depressed.

The evidence now points to the connection between the prefrontal cortex of your brain and the amygdala as the all-important site of this relationship. This begins to put to rest the debate on the supposed body / mind split. If you were to slap your forehead with your hand in the expression of, "oh my gosh, what was I thinking," your hand would be roughly covering the frontal cortex of your brain, and on the outer frontal edge of this is the prefrontal cortex. This area is your executive decision-maker, and it's also your moral compass. The ability to exert control over your limbic emotional brain, including the amygdala, generally arises from areas within this prefrontal cortex. Different areas within the prefrontal cortex are in constant discussions with our fear- and anger-activating amygdala.

In a comprehensive study, researchers reviewed the available data from neuroimaging, behavior, and biochemical data, and established that the amygdala plays a major role in controlling your pain and your emotional response to pain. These studies went on to identify an area within the amygdala that performs this task, and it is fittingly called the "nociceptive amygdala."[244] Recall our discussions on nociceptors and our nociceptive system throughout this book to understand the extreme significance of this finding in relation to your chronic pain.

In a study reported in the journal *Pain*, researchers were able to establish the fact that nerve receptors in the amygdala went through physical and physiological changes in patients with chronic pain. They also showed that the amygdala had constant influence over the pain response by sending messages downwards to the tissues of the body.[245] These are significant findings: they suggest that if there is a way to change the "emotional dialog" in the limbic portion of your brain, then your experience of your chronic pain can change!

There is even greater significance to this. Remember that the amygdala is wired directly to your hypothalamus, which has influence and control over the healing response throughout the body via multiple neurologic and hormonal pathways. To a neurologist such as myself, this work is extremely exciting, but more important to you is its practical application to promote the healing of your chronic pain. To fully understand this, though, we need to examine the function of your amygdala, which is interesting and exciting because of its ability to improve your well-being. One thing to remember, too, is that your prefrontal cortex, amygdala, and hypothalamus of your brain are connected not only to chronic pain but also to the depression and anxiety that are so prevalent in our society today.

Controlling Our Fear and Anger with Inner Dialog

As humans, we share with other animals this primitive neurohormonal system for processing the powerful emotions of fear and anger. The difference that makes the difference? We humans have the ability to carefully control these powerful, instinctive emotional responses through a progression of intellectual processes such as labeling, rationalization, and ultimately reason. The effect of these intellectual processes on the amygdala and its activation of fear or anger has been demonstrated in various research studies.

244 V. Neugebauer, W. Li, et al., "The amygdala and persistent pain," *The Neuroscientist* 10, no. 3 (2004): 221–34.

245 L. H. Pedersen, J. Scheel-Kruger, and G. Blackburn-Munro, "Amygdala GABA-A receptor involvement in mediating sensory-discriminative and affective-motivational pain responses in a rat model of peripheral nerve injury," *Pain* 127, no. 1–2 (January 2007): 17–26.

Utilizing functional MRI research, scientists can actually show pictures of which areas of the brain are activated during specific emotional and/or intellectual processes. In one study, scientists reported that the right and left amygdala were activated when individuals were shown facial expressions of fear or anger. Interestingly, when the individuals were given the intellectual task of giving a label to their emotions simultaneously with the presentation of the facial expressions, activation of their amygdala was diminished.[246] Giving a label immediately to the facial expression, a dialoguing process of the prefrontal cortex with the amygdala, utilized reason to override the fear or anger response generated by viewing the facial expression. This basic research study suggests how we humans can actually exercise advanced influence on our powerful emotional brains through our inner dialog. But this labeling process can also have a very negative effect on our emotional well-being.

Our unconscious to semiconscious and even sometimes fully conscious internal dialog can be "Don't worry, be happy, that's only (whatever disarms the situation)," or it could be saying "Oh my God, this is terrible, they don't (value, want, need, love) me!" The latter statement can easily generate a painful fear response, which can also create an increased physical pain response in our body through the nociceptive amygdala. This dialog of fear can then easily progress to an inner dialog of anger; from a "Oh my God, he/she doesn't really (want, care, love, fill in the blank) me!" to "Who the hell are they to (speak to me that way, treat me that way, fill in the blank); I'll get back at them, you just watch." This will then generate an inner conversation of anger that you may not be fully aware of, which sets off a physiological response in the amygdala, activating the hypothalamus, generating a "fight" response. You may notice the use of *I*'s and *me*'s in these inner dialogs quite a bit, because the labels of the self-focused ego produce the greatest emotional response.

In other words, the way our rational prefrontal cortex talks to our emotional brain (limbic system) containing the powerful amygdala will determine how we react to our world. We can excite our amygdala with frightening or fighting words, or we can relax it with words of peace. Research has shown that if we excite the amygdala with our inner dialog, we can create greater activation of emotional and physical pain for ourselves. Another way I like to describe this to my patients is, "Your life is in your inner

---

246 A. R. Hariri, S. Y. Bookheimer, and J. C. Mazziotta, "Modulating emotional responses: effects of a neocortical network on the limbic system," *NeuroReport* 11, no. 1 (January 17, 2000): 43–48.

running commentary, your inner narrative." Whether you realize it or not, you have an internal running dialog on life going on inside your brain; some of it is conscious and some of it unconscious, but much of it floats in and out of a semiconscious reality. If we practice, we can begin to hear this semiconscious running commentary that constantly flows through our consciousness, creating the paints we use to color our lives. If we listen closely, we may be surprised to find that this dialog is filled with words that paint a world of fear, anger, and greed.

Building Emotional Strength and Intelligence

Research has shown that my simplistic explanation of a very complex neurological process is not just theory but fact. In the journal *NeuroReport*, they published a study that verified with functional MRI that healthy individuals were able to self-regulate their sadness with dialog from their prefrontal cortex better than depressed individuals. In this study, when healthy individuals were shown sad situations, they were better able to overcome limbic system activation of the amygdala and hypothalamus with "voluntary self-regulation" (dialog) from areas of the prefrontal cortex. In this study, depressed individuals had more difficulty with voluntary regulation of sad feelings, as indicated by their functional MRI and self-rating of their emotional state.[247]

Studies such as these give objective evidence to the belief that we do indeed have some control over our emotional experience. However, just as in skeletal muscle, the brain's ability to moderate or control our negative emotional reactions can weaken or atrophy; in other words, "use it or lose it." Your genetics, of course, do play a role in how big and strong your muscles are, but proper exercises can build them up and make them more efficient, no matter where you start from. This is similar to the ability of the prefrontal cortex to exert influence on your powerful emotional limbic system, especially the amygdala. With your musculoskeletal system, certain specific exercises can be more effective at building your strength, flexibility, and agility than others. The same thing applies to the prefrontal cortex's ability to influence the limbic system of your brain; certain practices can focus on creating more strength, flexibility, agility, and improving your emotional response to life. This, in turn, opens the door to deeper levels of healing your pain!

247 M. Beauregard, V. Paquette, and J. Levesque, "Dysfunction in the neural circuitry of emotional self-regulation in major depressive disorder," *NeuroReport* 17 (2006): 843–46.

If we do not utilize specific practices to strengthen our inner peace and wellness, we end up being driven by our selfish egos, from fear to anger to sadness in an ever-deeper dive to the bottom of pain and despair. It all starts so easily by a simple look or word that activates our powerful amygdala, which turns on our hypothalamus-pituitary-adrenal response, commonly known as the fight-or-flight stress response. We all have experienced the fear, anxiety, tension, and anger that come with this physiological stress response—for example, when your boss calls you on the carpet or a police officer pulls you over. As vital as this is to our survival, reason from the prefrontal cortex and other areas of our brain is needed to keep it in control. When the activation of the amygdala begins, it can create a fear response—many times creating a madness that eventually ends up in sadness.

In our modern life, there are numerous things that trigger this stress response—events that we have little external control over. For example, you're late for an extremely important appointment, such as a job interview, that could mean your very physical survival. Then, unbeknownst to you, there is road construction ahead or a traffic accident that snarls traffic for miles and creates gridlock. Your amygdala will activate your hypothalamus, which will then signal your pituitary gland, which causes the release of stress hormones from your adrenal gland. This, along with the hypothalamus also stimulating your sympathetic nervous system, causes your heart rate to increase, blood pressure to go up, muscles to tense, and your breathing rate to increase. You have adrenaline flowing through your system, urging you to run or do battle.

But you can't get out of your car and physically fight the individuals stopped in front of you, nor can you really run away and abandon your vehicle. Therefore, the ancient, primitive physiological response of fight-or-flight that is pulsating through every vessel and fiber of your body must be ignored or dealt with. If we ignore these responses or act them out on our loved ones, they will have seriously detrimental effects on our health and lives.

We now have some understanding of the horrendous effects that stress places on our physical health and mental well-being, and how it can add to our chronic pain. Therefore, we need to find a way to address these strong physiological urges that are easily triggered the more we identify with the small self, our ego. The perennial wisdom of humanity's great spiritual traditions offers us a very practical way out of this trap. Through specific practices that have been taught throughout the ages, we can begin to find real healing of our physical and mental pain.

In the last two chapters of this book, we will delve into the depths of our spiritual heritage to find the teachings that can help us eloquently dialog with our emotional brain to truly heal. In chapter 20, we will explore two realizations that will teach us how to move beyond the fear and danger of our defensive ego and its primitive fight-or-flight response. Then, in chapter 21, we will use the wisdom gained through those two realizations to implement three daily practices that can bring true and lasting wellness into our lives.

20

Perennial Wisdom's Path to Healing

Earth experienced an age in which humanity received unparalleled spiritual instruction from incomparable teachers. The teachings of this era have been referred to as the perennial philosophy. This significant epoch of great spiritual teachers was centered around 500 BCE, which philosophers now refer to as the Axial Age. It was a time when, inexplicably, great spiritual leaders simultaneously arose from four areas of the world: India, China, the Near East, and Greece. This perennial wisdom was reflected in the teachings of Lao Tsu and Confucius in China; the philosophers of Greece, including Socrates, Parmenides, and Plato; the Hebrew prophets in the Near East; and in India, the Hindu Upanishads and the teachings of the Buddha. It is intriguing that much of the spiritual wisdom that we moderns have been searching for had come pouring out of humanity at this singular point in time, and that now, two and a half millennia later, this wisdom still remains as some of the world's greatest spiritual discourse. I have personally spent my life in study of the perennial philosophy of the Axial Age, as well as other spiritual teachings, and it is from this background that I write these chapters.

As previously discussed, these great spiritual traditions recognized the suffering found in the human condition, but they also pointed to the way of healing this pain and suffering. Within these spiritual traditions are great truths that, when realized and practiced on a daily basis, can free us from our own self-destructive behaviors and the pain that they cause. Utilizing these wisdom traditions as a touchstone, I have created a five-step program for the spiritual healing of your pain and suffering. These five steps and the wisdom contained within them are straightforward and simple, but as with many things of value, they are not always easy to practice.

You may find that the first two steps are the most challenging to understand and apply, but if grasped they make the rest of the practices so much easier to achieve. These practical steps are based on our previous discussion on neurology, that there is a constant running commentary going on in your mind about your life. This is what I call your "life's meditation," and if it is a neurotic narrative, your life will be filled with fear and anger, creating stress and pain. If, however, this is an ongoing *healing* meditation, it can create peace, love, and understanding.

Five-Step Program to Spiritually Heal Your Pain

Realizations:

1. Awaken to "I am nothing; I am everything."
2. Cling to nothing; push nothing away.

Daily Practices (see chapter 21):

3. Give yourself the gift of forgiveness.
4. Open to the happiness in what's happening.
5. Gratefully bless what there is for being.

Step I: Awaken to "I Am Nothing; I Am Everything"

Within the ancient wisdom of these world traditions are universal precepts or principles practiced by humanity throughout the ages. There are obviously many differences between these various spiritual world traditions, based on the local culture where they developed. However, when rendered down, these different traditions convey universal notions that are reflected in these perennial teachings. One of these basic precepts of the perennial philosophy is that at the heart of existence, all is spirit. This is a mysterious, unfathomable spirit found universally within the depths of everything, everywhere.

According to the perennial philosophy, in our taking birth we forget or fall asleep to the actuality of spirit-in-action within everything. In the writings of the sacred Upanishads of ancient India, it is said that "an invisible and subtle essence is the spirit of the whole Universe, that is the true, that is the Self, and thou, thou art that." Or as Jesus said, "The Kingdom of Heaven is within you," and Buddha said, "Look within, thou art the Buddha." To not recognize that "thou art that"—Spirit—is to lose sight of your true nature, of who you truly are. In this, you come to believe that you are that separate, small self, the individual "I," the ego, that no longer finds transcendent union with the Divine-in-All.

The amazing thing is that we don't have to do anything for this "fall" to occur, for it happens naturally when we "fall to earth" and come into flesh as seemingly separate beings of matter. Fear is easily generated when we perceive our True Self as a separate, small self. To protect ourselves, and to prove that this small bit of matter called "I" matters, we can either elevate our egos through greed and grasping or degrade others through anger and attack.

Within the perennial philosophy, this great riddle of the True Self being mistaken for the separate, smaller self has been expressed in different ways through the ages. I believe it has been clearly expressed by the Hindu yogi Nisargadatta Maharaj: "When I see that I am nothing, that is wisdom; when I see that I am everything, that is love." To understand the first part of this riddle, we need to explore what is actually meant by this word *nothing*. Today, the word *nothing* tends to conjure up the sense of lack, deficiency, deprivation, inferiority, and annihilation. But within its ancient origins are two roots, *nan-*, meaning "not one," and *-thyng*, meaning "an entity or being." Therefore, this ancient word *nanthyng* actually meant "no one thing," and if *nothing* is by definition "no one thing," then being nothing allows you to hold the potential for everything, for you cannot be limited to any one thing. Within the answer to this riddle is the awareness of the True Self as being no-thing, and in being no one thing, it holds the potential of being everything.

Being Nothing and Everything

A simple meditation exercise to illustrate this concept is to concentrate upon a simple living thing, such as a plant or flower. As we stare upon this living plant, we might say, "I know what this is; it is a flower." But if we were to point out where the actual self of the flower resides, we would have great difficulty. As we begin to peer deeply into the beingness of the flower, we may be surprised to find many things, in fact *everything but* a separate flower self. For example, we could see clouds, because if the clouds were removed from the flower, there would be no rain or moisture and the flower would never have existed.

If we look more deeply, we may see the sun—for if the sun were removed from the flower, it would be unable to produce the energy it needs through photosynthesis to exist. Peering more deeply into the flower, we could see the minerals and nutrients pulled up from the earth, and therefore we would find elements of the earth in the flower. All these non-flower elements flow through the flower like an ever-changing river. As it's been said, one cannot put one's foot in the same river twice. In other words, there is no permanent, separate self of the flower, only non-flower elements that are connected to everything else in the universe.

With great concentration, we may glimpse deeper into the interconnectedness of this flower (and everything else) by continuing within until we find its DNA and even the atoms of the elements that are also found within us. For example, we would find the complex molecules that form carbohydrates, proteins, and fats, and the very same DNA found within all life. Going deeper within, eventually we would find atoms of the elements that form these molecules, such as carbon, hydrogen, oxygen, nitrogen, phosphorus, and sulfur—elements that were forged in the furnace of ancient stars. Therefore, this plant, ourselves and everything else of this planet really are billion-year-old stardust, and we are not that different or special than anything else. This is something the ego never wants to hear or believe. Going in further, if we had the persistence and patience, our perception could pierce right down through to the subatomic particles that make up the plant's atoms.

Beyond that, we could perceive the actual energy that makes up these supposedly solid particles. This energy is the same primal energy found within the fireball at the very beginning of our universe, an energy that is still present and imbues all that exists. Traveling back out, we can again gaze upon the flower and this time see that it is "nothing," for it is "everything." Through this simple exercise, we can begin to see that, like the flower, we have no permanent self; rather, you and I are a part of, not apart from, an interconnected dance of everything. This is not gibberish from some ancient, uneducated monks, it is a fact that is now known by scientists today. This knowledge has been described by present-day biologists, quantum physicists, and cosmologists, but this knowledge is ultimately useless to the analytical scientist or ourselves unless it is transformed into a way of everyday "spiritual seeing." It is only when it becomes the way of our everyday perception that it actually affects our daily life and promotes healing.

Our Longing to Belong

If you can begin to see the *nanthyng*, the "no one thing" of your True Self, this wisdom will be the first step of letting go of your fearful and defensive death grip on your small self. By letting go of the concrete identity you have created for your ego, you can begin to embrace the fluid interconnectedness of your True Self. You can then find the real love you seek, which is found in the realization that you are everything. This love is something all human beings desire above all else. Much of our ego-driven grasping and greed is about accumulating enough measurable worth so that people will care for us, need us, want us, and ultimately love us, or so we believe. Actually, when we come in to matter and "take birth," the first thing we want to know from our mother is that we *matter*, that she nourishes us and protects us; we long to belong.

By belonging, I mean that experience in life where we feel reciprocally bonded to and nurtured by someone else. Of course, our first sense of belonging is to our mothers. As infants, we are so bonded to our mothers as they nurture us that we have difficulty differentiating ourselves from them, even after birth. But what makes this actually work is that the mother also feels bonded to and nurtured by her relationship with her child. Later, as our sense of self develops, it is the loving father and siblings who come into our awareness and introduce us to the possibility of bonding to a larger sense of belonging. This is further aided by aunts, uncles, cousins, and grandparents, and eventually by friends and neighbors who help nurture our sense of belonging to the larger community. This sense of belonging, or being bonded to and nurtured by, can grow and mature until it even becomes global in its perspective, filled with a healthy egalitarian and ecological compassion for the entire world community. It is an awakening to our true nature, to the interconnectedness of our universe, and to the interdependence of all life.

We experience this profound wisdom within our mother's womb and at her breast. In our mother's womb, we are bathed in total nourishment, floating in an amniotic sea of unconditional love. Here, carried at our mother's core, we become entrained to the rhythm of her heart. This resonance with our mother's heart is where we first come to know the song of belonging. If this glorious birthright is somehow lost to us, if we are not bonded to and nurtured by our mother, father, and family, it will generate a deep fear and anxiety within the core of who we are. As we saw in chapter 19, fears that are not resolved neurologically evolve into anger, and this unresolved madness will become sadness deep within us. This madness and sadness can haunt us for the rest of our lives. Why do we become so mad and sad? This occurs because deep within our heart of hearts, we know that we are made for belonging, not alienation.

This is often the source of the original wound that sensitized our amygdala, setting us up for a heightened, cyclic response of fear and anger to everything in our life; as we have seen, research studies using functional MRIs have proven this. Again, this is exactly what happens in our central nervous system when it becomes sensitized by the continual firing of our myofascial nociceptors, creating a chronic pain disorder.

The good news is that you can actually make positive changes in your central nervous system so that you do not react painfully, physically or emotionally, to your environment. As you will see later in this chapter, *gratitude* and *forgiveness* are keys to creating these positive changes in your nervous system, changes that can open the doors to healing your pain and becoming whole again. If you are an individual who has experienced an early wound from your mother, father, or family that now plagues your life with emotional and physical pain, please remember this: *forgiveness is finally giving up all hope of a better past to build a bridge to a better future.*

Realize That Everything Is Love

When you begin to glimpse the truth—that your true nature is the interconnectedness of everything—you understand that to protect and nourish yourself, you have to protect life all around you. Like the flower meditation, a simple mantra to repeat every day is, "I am connected to everything everywhere, I am loved and I love, this love is the Love that loved me into being." If one's life is created by the running commentary in one's mind, why not play a healing tape? However, to make this little daily meditation more effective, it would be helpful to know what we mean by the word "love."

Our word *love* is probably one of the most overused, misused, and misunderstood words in our language today. Simply stated, love is the ability to perceive the interconnectedness that gives you the capacity to nourish and protect. When you love another, there is no longer an "other"; the other is a part of you. With this awareness of the interconnectedness of life, you realize if those you love are not nourished and protected, they may fail to thrive, and ultimately so will you. "Love is all we have; the only way that each can help the other" (Euripides, *Orestes,* 408 BCE).

The little-known secret here that you now understand from our earlier flower meditation is that each and every one of us is interconnected to each other and to everything in this entire universe, and the gravity, or glue, that binds this all together, is Love. This is not an immature love of self-centeredness or possessiveness; this Love is beyond all boundaries. This mature Love is a perfect circle "whose center is to be found everywhere, and whose circumference can be found nowhere," as a Christian mystic once said. The center of this circle is an awareness that we can become at the core of our being, which breaks us open so all of life pours in unconditionally. This Love is neither small nor selfish but can become so large that it is no longer within us; instead, we rest within it. William Blake's poetry says it best: "Love seeketh not itself to please, nor for itself hath any care, but for another gives its ease and builds a Heaven in Hell's despair" (*Songs of Experience*, 1794).

Nourishing and Protecting Yourself

However, to be truly capable of this loving, you must first begin by nourishing and protecting yourself. If you're not capable of properly caring for yourself, how effective will you be at caring for those you love? What does it mean to "love yourself," and how do you know if you are accomplishing this properly? This is an important question, because so much "stuff" that passes for "taking care of yourself" is selfish, self-centered pandering to the ego. Truly loving yourself many times involves the way of the warrior, through walking the challenging path of self-discipline. No monk is able to reach any level of spiritual awareness without the loving application of discipline.

To truly love yourself is the ability to pick up a product you are about to buy that will go into or on your body, and actually read the label to know if you are nourishing yourself or poisoning yourself. From this book, you are now well aware of the dangerous nonfoods within our packaged products and the toxic chemicals now found within our foods and many self-care products. Therefore, a quick check on whether or not you are truly caring for yourself is to notice if you have the discipline to read all labels on food and personal care products. Also, taking a moment to buckle your seat belt and drive safely is an act of loving yourself and those inside and outside your vehicle. We know that smoking cigarettes destroys vital tissues within our bodies with every puff; to know this and still smoke is to love oneself that much less. To properly care for your self is to do things that not only make you feel better but truly benefit you and the world. You can take drugs to "feel better," but they will not provide real benefit to your overall health and wellness.

To really love yourself, take time out of your busy day to care for yourself. For example, find a quiet peaceful space, put on some relaxing music, then lay down flat on the carpeted floor, stretched out on your back, in the yoga position known as "corpse pose." Then totally ground yourself to the earth through your back as if you were growing roots, and open your heart to the heavens above. Now breathe slowly, deeply, and easily through your abdomen, following your breath. Slowly allow your mind to become more spacious, releasing all troubling thoughts for just this moment (don't worry, they will be there for you, if you want, when you get up). Let all the tension flow out of you through your feet, hands, and head. Lay there for ten minutes, following your breath and letting your tense muscles melt off your weary bones.

After you have completely relaxed for about ten minutes, then utilize a quality self-care trigger point tool to remove your pain-causing muscle knots, as described in chapters 9 through 13. Once you get proficient at this, it should only take about another 5 to 10 minutes to treat your trigger points. This, along with eating a good, wholesome diet and taking specific nutraceuticals, will go a long way in healing your pain and bringing you true wellness.

Probably the most important demonstration of real self-love is to change the destructive narrative in your head to a meditation of healing thoughts. It is that ongoing running commentary quietly blogging on inside your head that creates the very unfolding of your life. If you take this warrior's path of self-discipline, you are on the road to real self-love and real healing. One of the best ways to begin to change your inner narrative to a healing dialog is to apply the following daily meditation from Hindu yogi Nisargadatta Maharaj:

Daily Meditation

"When I see that I am nothing, that is wisdom;
when I see that I am everything, that is love."

Step 2:
Cling to Nothing; Push Nothing Away

The five-step program to spiritually heal your pain contains two primary realizations and three daily practices. The first realization—"I am nothing; I am everything"—is the most central of all the five steps. It is this awareness that begins the process of loosening your death grip on the belief that the small self is all there is; this step opens the door for greater healing. If the wisdom of step one is realized and applied to one's life, then the healing power found in step two—"cling to nothing; push nothing away"—is much easier to achieve. You will then find that steps three, four, and five (in chapter 21) are much easier to practice. To better facilitate comprehension of this second realization, it is easier to examine in it two parts, the first aspect being "cling to nothing."

The Inherent Unsatisfactoriness of Our Wants

The perennial philosophy acknowledged that our world is filled with glorious beauty and sensuality to be experienced and enjoyed. It also recognized that these wondrous, worldly delights awakened within us desires that can easily turn into selfish cravings. It taught that these selfish cravings are driven by our attachment to the small self, or ego. These great spiritual traditions, especially of the East, went on to teach that our suffering and pain is caused by self-centeredness, or selfish cravings—not desire itself but our attachment to our desires. Through our selfish cravings, we imprison ourselves by the walls of *I*, *me*, and *mine*, and we try to stuff all of our infinite True Self into this minute prison cell. The more we crave and cling to things to inflate our small selves, the more we block the healing of our pain.

Within the perennial wisdom of the East, however, there is the awareness that there is a basic, underlying unsatisfactoriness to all worldly gains and successes, right from the beginning. For example, if you crave something you feel you must have and you do not achieve it, this will immediately be unsatisfactory to you and cause you to suffer. On the other hand, if you do finally achieve your pursuit of pleasure or success, you will then live in fear that it or they may be taken from you. Furthermore, when you do achieve the very object of your desires, you eventually find it not as you imagined. In our interpersonal relationships, this reality always demands our growth and maturity to move beyond our preconceived notions if the relationship is to survive.

We live in a painful reality of unsatisfactoriness because:

1. We cannot attain our desires;
2. Our desires do not live up to our expectations, and we want something else;
3. We attained what we wanted, but now we live in fear of losing it.

In the ancient teachings of India, it was taught that, through many lifetimes on this earthly realm, one will eventually realize the truth that existence holds much more than just sensual pleasures and material success. It was taught that we will eventually turn from the selfish cravings of our small self and open our hearts to the desires of the True Self. What are the desires of the True Self? As a modern sage of India once said, "It is not that you Westerners desire too much, it is that you desire too little." Therefore, desire in of itself is not wrong, sinful, or evil; rather, it is one of our greatest strengths. It is our desire for another's happiness that brings compassion into this world, and it is our desire for real healing that brings us liberation. It is not desire that brings us so much pain and suffering, but our clinging to things that we believe will be the source of our happiness. As Mary Wollstonecraft so eloquently stated, "No man chooses evil because it is evil; he only mistakes it for happiness, which is the good he seeks."

The Source of Our Unhappiness

If we crave or cling to something, it has power over us, and we are no longer free. And if we push things away and worry constantly about keeping them out of our lives, they also have a hold on us. Pain and suffering in life arises when we live under the illusion that "If I can only have (fill in the blank), I will then be happy, my life will be complete; I will finally have made it!" On the other hand, we also create pain and suffering for ourselves with the misconception that "If I can only be free of or get rid of (fill in the blank), then I will finally be happy, at peace, and free." It is the human condition to live through these two crippling illusions, assuring ourselves that real happiness, peace, and health is right around the corner once we attain or get rid of (fill in the blank). In fact, all forms of mayhem, murder, and even war itself can be laid at the doorstep of these two illusions, either as individuals or societies. The problem with this belief is that true peace, real health, and actual happiness is an inside job, and nothing we can cling to or push away can bring us the fulfillment we desire.

A central teaching within the perennial wisdom that illustrates the importance of this realization is "the only constant in the universe is change, for everything changes." Another way this teaching is phrased: "anything in this universe that has a beginning has an end; everything is impermanent." Constant change is at every level of existence, from the quantum subparticles to the galaxies of our cosmos, so why do we suffer under the illusion that in our minute life we can hold on to anything? No amount of wealth or fame can shield us from this reality.

To ignore this truth of existence and try to cling to the shifting sands of transient reality is to invite with open arms our own pain and suffering. Change is found in each moment of our life that arises, abides, and then ceases. The truth is, for the next moment of our existence to arise, the present moment must die. We cannot hang on to a pleasant experience or keep our children from growing up or our parents from dying. This is what creates all forms of suffering: the inability to incorporate into our moment-to-moment consciousness that the only constant in the universe is change; that all things tarnish, rust, age, and die. No matter how powerful we become, no matter how grand our "immortality projects" are, they will not protect us from the impermanence of life.

The Destructive Nature of Our Selfish Cravings

Earth will soon no longer sustain our self-cravings. Our present pursuit of prosperity and wealth is causing the irreversible destruction of delicate ecosystems around the world. The human being is but one species of life out of the thirty million or more that share this planet. Noted scientist Peter Vitousek has calculated that the human species greedily appropriates about 40% of Earth's potential productivity and grossly affects the other 60%, while the other thirty million plus species must make do on the remainder.[248] It is vital for us to remember that our survival is dependent on the healthy diversity of a multitude of vibrant ecosystems on this planet. We cannot survive without the multitude of millions of species, but they surely could survive without us.

248 P. M. Vitousek, P. R. Erlich, A. H. Erlich, and P. N. Matson, "Human appropriation of the products of photosynthesis," *BioScience* 36, no. 6 (June 1986): 368–373.

Less than four-tenths of one percent of the planet's water is fresh and free-flowing, and much of this is now poisoned and undrinkable. When we chemically poison an aquifer, it is unusable to us basically forever, for it takes more than 100,000 years for an aquifer to cleanse itself. The topsoil of our planet is the life-giving flesh of our Earth, without which we and most life would die. It has been estimated that over the last 5,000 years, humans have eliminated over 65% of Earth's topsoil.[249] It has been estimated that more than 30% of the world's cropland has been lost in the last 60 years.[250] Of course, this loss of topsoil compounds the problems of human starvation.

It is estimated that each year 60,000,000 people died of starvation; that's about 164,000 every twenty-four hours, and 40,000 of them are children.[251] This is happening while the Western world suffers from diseases linked with overconsumption and obesity, with overweight individuals comprising slightly over 50% of the total population. The United States has the highest rate of overweight people in the world, currently running at about 65% of adults. In fact, if Americans reduced their meat intake by a mere 10%, the grain saved would adequately feed 60,000,000 people each year, saving them from starvation![252]

A study by the Global Footprint Network, reported by the BBC, found that it would take 5.3 Earths for everyone on Earth to live an American lifestyle. As a nation, we are selfishly living way beyond our means. Europe is doing a little better: it would take around 3 Earths to allow everyone on Earth to live a European lifestyle. Our selfish cravings will be our—and everyone's—undoing.[253]

Our gluttony is now the leading cause in the destruction of more species on this planet than has occurred at any other time over the last 65 million years. All species of this planet are now living for the first time within the human habitat, for now whatever we do affects their survival. When someone is murdered, we are instinctively horrified, and it attracts media attention. Yet our pursuit of wealth and riches leads to the extinction of 120 species each and every day, with little awareness by humanity. By the

---

249 Sara J. Scherr, "Soil degradation: a threat to developing-country food security by 2020," *International Food Policy Research Institute*, 1999.

250 D. Pimental and M. Giampietro, "Food, land, population and the U.S. economy," *Carrying Capacity Network*, Washington, D.C., 1994.

251 www.duke.edu/web/planv/realities.html.

252 Ibid.

253 www.fooprintnetwork.org/overshoot/.

year 2000, human greed was pouring over 10 million tons of toxic waste into the environment each and every day. All of this is done in the name of "better living through chemistry," but as we have learned in earlier chapters, these chemicals do enter the biosphere of our planet and eventually our bodies. As this intentional and unnecessary destruction of our planet continues, affecting future generations, we never seem to ask the obvious question: how could modern Homo sapiens live sustainably on this Earth for more than 300,000 years, and then in the last few hundred years bring about a toxicity that now threatens all life?

Teachings within the perennial philosophy eloquently express the problem with selfish craving. The *Tao Te Ching* states:

> The five colors can blind,
> The five tones deafen,
> The five tastes cloy.
> The race, the hunt, can drive people mad
> and their booty leaves them no peace.[254]

And a passage from the Buddha in the Dhammapada is even more to the point:

> It is not iron that imprisons you ...
> But the pleasure you take in gold and jewels.
> The rain could turn to gold
> and still your thirst would not be slaked.
> The fool is his own enemy;
> Seeking riches, he destroys himself.[255]

As we race to package up the earth into commercial products to buy and sell to one another, this unbridled greed becomes a mad chase to our own destruction. Our pursuit of prosperity, wealth, and fame is a desperate drive to show, somehow, to others that *we matter*. We attempt to pile up around our small selves as many products and schemes as possible, to insulate ourselves from our suffering and our fear that we might be nobody. We attempt to entertain and distract ourselves from our deepest

254 *Tao Te Ching* by Lao Tsu (Gai-fu Feng and Jane English, translators; Vintage Books, 1972), chapter 12.

255 *Dhammapada: The Path of Perfection* by Juan Mascaro (Penguin, 1973), chapter 24.

fear: with cell phones, televisions, computers, the Internet, money, jewels, land, fame, and power. It is an immortality project designed to insulate us against our seeming meaninglessness and inevitable death. But there is neither immortality nor peace to be found here, only the opposite: the destruction of our health and our children and grandchildren's future.

Making Enough Simply Enough

It is our desire to attain satisfaction that motivates us and keeps us exploring life! For example, the desire for our continued survival is satisfied by the attainment of enough food and adequate shelter. With whatever it is we desire, within that desire itself is the hope of attaining enough to achieve satisfaction. The question, then, is what is enough in life? The answer may be found in the ancient origins of the word itself. Our word *enough* evolved from its ancient roots *nak,* meaning "to attain," and *ge-*, "together." Possibly, then, the concept signified by the primal origin of our word *enough* (*ge-nak*) was that enough was achieved whenever we attain anything with the common good in mind. We have all probably met people for whom enough is never enough, and for them life always seems miserable. As Epicurus said, "Nothing is enough to the man for whom enough is too little."

There is nowhere we can go, nothing that we can pursue residing *outside* of our self that can give us true satisfaction, happiness, and health. A common metaphor that Hinduism uses to illustrate this vital teaching is that we are like royalty wandering through our domain in abject poverty, not knowing who we truly are because of spiritual amnesia. Satisfaction is instantly at hand if we learn the process of making enough, enough *inside* ourselves, through gratitude. Again, Epicurus states it well: "Whoever does not regard what he has as ample wealth is unhappy, though he be master of the world." Or as Hindu yogi Nisargadatta Maharaj once said of the human condition, "You always want what you don't have and don't want what you do have. Why not be happy by wanting what you have and not wanting what you don't have?"

The Way to Begin Healing

This evolution of consciousness out of selfish craving is the journey to the Love that says "I am everything." Here we begin to realize our belonging to the interwoven web of humanity, our Earth, and the universe itself. We no longer struggle to possess just a part of the whole, for we are now becoming aware that health and happiness is discovered in knowing our "self" as the whole. This wisdom is contained within an ancient story, told by many different cultures and religious traditions, about a village that was allowed to see the difference between heaven and hell. It was given this unusual opportunity because its own horrific selfishness was causing suffering all around it. When the people went to visit hell, they found it filled with multitudes of different people seated around glorious banquet tables filled with a variety of delicious foods. Yet all the people were starving, angry, and in conflict. On close examination, the villagers noticed that all the people in hell were forced to use four-foot-long utensils, which made it impossible to feed themselves.

The villagers were then shown heaven, and they were surprised to find that the people there also sat at large tables laden with delectable foods and were forced to eat with four-foot-long utensils. It was exactly the same as hell, yet all of the community was well-nourished and happy. Extremely perplexed, the villagers begged to know what the difference was. They were told that here in heaven, "we understand the importance of serving one another." In the perennial philosophy, the True Self was found through renouncing the small, selfish self, or the ego. At this juncture of awareness, selfish cravings to "get more" become the awakened desire to give, the cravings for success become the awakened desire to serve, and finally we are awakened to a greater sense of self. The best place to begin this is with our spouse, children, parents, significant others, family members, and friends, for it is their presence and love that most sustains us in this world. They are the most effective doorway out of our wasteland of selfish cravings and into real healing found within the realization of the True Self.

Embraced in the Loving Arms of Compassion

We have seen that much of our pain and suffering is born out of a vicious cycle of fear, anger, and greed that arises from our identification with our ego. Much of the time, these primal emotions of fear and anger are activated by our amygdala because of our defensive ego creating conflicts for us. Once in conflict, we then feel compelled to attack others outside the boundaries of our ever-changing circle of "special love." Special love is an immature love, a love with specific parameters we can put people outside or inside, a love of "us" and "them," where "others" are *outside* of our compassion. We have also seen how the perennial philosophy has described a spiritual peace that can be discovered when we come to transcend our identification with the fearful, small self of our ego. Unfortunately, most of us are all to willing to grant legitimacy to our fears that generate anger and conflict, further solidifying our concepts of *us* and *them*, *good* and *bad*, *right* and *wrong*. It is suggested by the perennial philosophy that the healing and peace we long for does not come from this moral judgment and conflict but from compassion.

So far, we have utilized the realization "I am nothing" to help us begin the process of opening our self to the Self, of moving beyond the battleground of the defensive ego. Then, by utilizing the meditation of the flower, we opened our awareness to the love found in the realization that "I am everything." Through this newfound awareness, we will come to see the power contained within viewing our world with compassion. Of all the teachings found in the perennial philosophy of humanity's Axial Age, the primary one is that of compassion. Why? Because I believe that these great spiritual teachers were aware that compassion is how we find our true nature. In fact, the oldest origin of our word for what we call ourselves—*human*—comes from the ancient Latin word *humanus*, which not only signified a "being of earth" but was also used to mean "kindness, gentleness, courtesy, and compassion"! Possibly when we choose to live not through our primitive brain's fight-or-flight stress response but through compassion, we begin to discover our real nature, our True Self.

Hard-Wired for Compassion

As alluded to in chapter 19, there is a fledgling field in neurology called social neurobiology, or social neuroscience, that is beginning to scientifically demonstrate that we humans, as well as other animals, are hard-wired to connect to and care for one another. This new research establishes that we are neurologically inclined to care for what we feel we belong to. I believe we are therefore hard-wired for compassion. This research is showing that if we wish to truly heal, we must not ignore the importance of belonging to and caring for something beyond our small self.

Developing this compassionate, global perspective is a spiritual awakening that can bring us real healing. For here we evolve beyond the egocentric, small self into the powerful, transpersonal reality where we come to realize that the spirit-in-all is also the divine-in-me. Within this awareness—that all of reality is spirit-in-action manifesting as everything—lies the perennial wisdom that this Earth and all its sentient beings are an expression of our one True Self. In this simple, golden truth is the simple common sense that what I do to others, I ultimately do to myself. Or, as instructed by the *Tao Te Ching*, "When we don't see the Self as self, what do we have to fear? See the world as your Self ... Love the world as your Self." And in Matthew 19:19, Jesus says, "Thou shall love thy neighbor as thy Self." These writings speak directly to the heart of the meaning of compassion.

When we come to this awareness of the Divine-in-All and embrace it as compassion, we begin to awaken to a universe of Love to which we all fully belong. This is an awakening to the passionate inter-beingness of our universe, for all life arises from the intercourse of soil, rain, and sun; without this lovemaking, we would all cease to exist. This is the "love that loved us into being." The heart that beats in your chest pounds out the same rhythm in all humanity, pumping the same ancestral fluid from that primordial sea from which we all arose. And that is true for all life, for all beings of this Earth arose out of that same primal, briny baptism four billion years ago.

But our belonging to this universe is even older than this, for all the building blocks of matter and all the energy that make up us came roaring out of the same primal cosmic egg or big bang at the birth of our universe twenty billion years ago. These elemental particles of creation were the basis for the matter that came to make up our sun, our Earth, and eventually your body. The very hydrogen within our sun and within ourselves was birthed in that first moment of creation, as was the energy we utilize to pick up our children or kiss our loved ones. This is the fabric of our interwoven universe, a seamless tapestry that we, as spirit-in-action, all belong to.

When we lose the possibility of this compassionate perspective with its universal principles, we lose sight of the interconnectedness and interdependence of our cosmos. We never attain a true sense of belonging, where we understand that we are One with our interwoven uni-verse. If we fail to perceive that we are not apart from but a part *of* the world, we then see this world as objects of disparate, crass matter, and we fall under the illusion of separation. This dualism is the birthplace of all conflict in our life created from fear and anger. The dividing or separating our world into subject and object opens the door to manipulating and mistreating our Earth and others from a self-centered, self-serving, destructive perspective. In this dualistic view of "I" as the primary subject in a world of separate objects, the truth of who we are and the real health found in our wholeness is lost to us.

Armed with Compassion by Heaven

This awareness of our belonging to a divine oneness flows out of the perennial philosophy. For example, the Isa Upanishads of India instruct us to "see your self in all beings and all beings in your Self." It also says that it is only when we behold the material and sacred world as One that we find wisdom and freedom. The *Tao Te Ching* is simple and eloquent in its expression of this wisdom; again, it states: "When we don't see the Self as self, what do we have to fear? See the world as your Self. Have faith in the way things are. Love the world as your Self; then you can care for all things."[256]

In this state of belonging to our universe there is no need of moral judgment, for we care for "the other" as we care for ourselves; there is no longer an "other." As Jesus said, "Love thy neighbor as thy Self." And, as stated by the perennial wisdom of Hinduism's Bhagavad Gita, "Even on earth, the world is transformed by those whose minds are established in the vision of Oneness." This transformation in us opens the door for the greatest spiritual practices available to us, genuine gratefulness and forgiveness.

In the *Tao Te Ching*, Lao Tsu stated that "Heaven arms with compassion those whom she would not see destroyed." What is this compassion, that it can be so powerful in our lives? Our word *compassion* is from the Latin roots *com*, "together," and *pati*, "to endure." The Latin root, *pati*, came from the earlier Greek word *pathos,* meaning "of deep emotion." *Compassion* then literally meant "the enduring together of the pathos," or the deep emotion that life brings, whether it comes out of the "10,000 joys or the 10,000 sorrows that living brings," as Buddhism states. When we embrace together the sorrow, the joy, or the suffering of another, we become stronger than we could ever be alone. Compassion is our greatest strength, for it is the surest and best way to bring us into the divine Oneness and help us to heal.

This "enduring together the pathos" does not mean to *become* the pathos, the personal fear and/or anger of the other individual, but to become one without being overcome. *Endure* is from the Latin roots *en,* denoting "in," and *durare,* "to last." In compassion we endure together through the love that brings us together. Armed by heaven with compassion and the love it springs from, we are not destroyed but find peace and endure. Meister Eckhart, a Christian mystic of the twelfth century, said that "love knows no pain." That is, we may feel pain, but when we are living in a spiritually

256 *Tao Te Ching* by Lao Tsu (Stephen Mitchell, translator; Harper & Row Publishers, 1988).

mature relationship to love and compassion, nothing can damage the love; it knows no pain.

With this love one can say yes to life and all its sorrow, for we come to the realization that real pain and sorrow are birthed out of what brings us joy. The truth is we experience real pain and sorrow in this life precisely because life is good and holds great beauty and joy for us. Only the loss of something or someone that brings us joy and beauty, only that which we love, matters enough to cause us real pain and sorrow. Therefore the sources of our greatest joys hold the potential for our greatest sorrows. But it is our ability to love that allows us the courage to face this suffering honestly. Love is the very desire that brought us into life, and it is a mature, unconditional love that can uplift and carry us through life. As the poet Virgil said, "Love conquers all things: Let us too surrender to Love." With this love that conquers all things and armed by heaven's compassion, we will find the ability to heal our pain and find peace.

The Peace That Passes All Understanding

In the egocentric perspective, there is only the passion for the small self; in the sociocentric or ethnocentric perspective, there is passion for the group and compassion within the group or tribe. However, the peace of perfect compassion is without boundaries, for the roots of the word *compassion* tell us that it is the ability to "deeply feel (*pathos*) together (*com-*)." Furthermore, our word *compassion* does not have a prefix or suffix that tells us how to limit this understanding in any way. Again, as Lao Tsu said, "Heaven arms with compassion those whom she would not see destroyed." It is only when heaven arms us with compassion that the truth of who we are is revealed, and in this peace we become one with our humanity. Compassion, therefore, is not only our true nature but our only true salvation and the greatest force for healing our pain.

However, even in this compassionate sense of our belonging to the Divine-in-All, one can still struggle for survival in nature or at the hands of others who attack you for being outside their group, or even at the hands of a microscopic virus. It should go without saying that this compassionate, profound sense of belonging is not some magic that suspends the workings of nature or instantaneously transforms the nature of all your fellow human beings. It does not force the workings of the cosmos or God to conform to our personal plans. Life still lives on life, and in this awareness one is even more alive to the suffering of the interwoven web of life.

What is ultimately available within this sense of our belonging to the Divine-in-All is perfect peace. This is perfect peace because it is a peace that is complete without any conditions. This is "the peace that passes all understanding"—a peace that pervades one's heart as one resides in the compassionate, nondual heart of our universe. This is our heart of hearts that does not contain any *us* and *them*, only the love for the Divine-in-All. Here, in this awareness of truly Belonging, your life moves on, and conflict around you, of course, does arise. However, in the awareness of Belonging, the torment of conflict within oneself can be released, as peace is uncovered in the adversity and happiness is discovered in what's happening, all through the grace of gratitude and the gift of forgiveness.

In the final chapter of this book, we will examine the three daily practices of my five-step program that can help you transform your inner narrative to a healing meditation.

21

The Healing Power of Forgiveness and Gratitude

You will discover a greater ability to heal yourself with the spiritual practices of gratitude and forgiveness than with any pill, potion, or lotion! The ability to apply these practices is made possible through the awareness gained in the previous chapters, the wisdom found in "I am nothing," the love found in "I am everything," and the freedom gained through the awareness of "cling to nothing; push nothing away," which clears away the obstructions of the small self for the application of these spiritual practices. With this advantage, let us now delve into the power of forgiveness and gratitude.

When we become angry and verbally attack another, we must realize somewhere inside of us that we are now vulnerable to retaliation and counterattack. Furthermore, to justify our ongoing anger toward another, we must believe, whether correctly or incorrectly, that personally we are under attack from that person. With this belief, we inevitably live in a world fearing further attacks by them or others. In this fear we must, for our own survival, continue to use past remembered occurrences or slights to continually activate the amygdala of our emotional brain. This generates anger and the "fight response," keeping us physiologically ready for battle. Here we can see the vicious cycle of fear manifesting as anger, anger in turn creating more fear, and then fear necessitating more anger and hostility. In our world of fear and anger, there is very little room for kindness and compassion, except for the allies we can recruit for our battles.

How We Destroy Our Peace

It is through our identifying with and focusing on our separate, fragile ego that we lose touch with our own humanity. We are no longer at peace with our world but face the world in defensive, angered opposition. In creating opposition, we begin the cycle of anger and conflict all over again. Is this the world we want, to live a life dictated to us by our external circumstances? Do we want a world that causes us to enter into a painful cycle of fear and anger, or can we choose to live lives liberated from the dictates of our primitive emotional responses, preferring to live from the heart of our own humanity?

How This Madness Can Go to Sadness

Caught in the primitive responses of fear and anger, our personal world can turn into an oppressive sadness, especially in our youth. The ancient Anglo-Saxon root of our English word *anger* is *ange,* meaning "to be oppressed and sad." The wisdom in our words speaks plainly to the possibility of anger becoming buried deep in sadness. Often, if we look deeply into our sadness, we find buried or suppressed a great madness or hostility. This is especially prevalent in our youth, when anger becomes easily activated and many times buried because no one has taught us how to learn its lessons.

Frequently it begins with a misunderstanding. For example, we may have felt that one of our parents or teachers was somehow telling us we did not matter or that we were not good enough or loved. In our fear of not being good enough, loved, or basically of not mattering, we become defensive and angered. This anger frightens us, and what we come to think of or say to someone we love can sicken us. We now fear our parent or teacher was right; we are "no good," and we become depressed; our fear went to madness, which then became our sadness. When we feel this primal rage rise up against those we care for, we can become frightened of ourselves and our powerful, primitive emotions of anger. This rage can be fed by angry thoughts so mean and bitter that they even begin to disgust us, and so we bury this anger in the shadows. We can subconsciously or even consciously turn on ourselves for being so "bad and rotten" and for having such thoughts or saying or doing such things! With this self-loathing, we become depressed by our own thoughts or actions.

Our anger, as the origins of the words tell us, is not resourceful or helpful buried within ourselves or thrust upon another. Our anger is best utilized as a catalyst to learn more about ourselves and as a catalyst to heal. This is not a moral judgment of anger, for anger is not bad or evil, only very painful for us as well as for others. Our madness can easily become sadness as the original hostility becomes buried within our shadows. In a society where depression is pandemic, it may be beneficial to examine our depths for repressed anger, not so we can express it but more importantly to heal it with our pain.

A Different View of Anger

Today anger seems to be viewed as something vital to our everyday interpersonal life, as beneficial rather than problematic and painful. Psychology today seems to view anger as something advantageous; we almost feel righteous in our individual anger—that it is a beneficial force that keeps us from being someone else's "doormat" and helps us to get our due! This only serves to feed the ego. Even Buddhism has been admonished by modern Western psychologists for seemingly speaking out against anger, which is a part of the basic Buddhist teaching. Not that Buddhism says to bury our anger, only to be mindful of it, to move beyond it, and to learn from it. From the sayings of the Buddha in the Dhammapada:

> See yourself in Others, then whom can you hurt? For your fellow man is like you. They want to be happy. Never harm them. Never speak harsh words, for they will rebound upon you. Angry words hurt, and the hurt rebounds.[257]

> Let go of anger. Let go of pride. When you are bound by nothing, you go beyond sorrow. Anger is like a chariot careering wildly, he who curbs his anger is the true charioteer, others merely hold the reins. With gentleness overcome anger. With generosity overcome meanness, with truth overcome deceit. Speak the truth. Give whatever you can. Never be angry. Beware of the anger of the body. Master the body, let it serve truth. Beware of the anger of the mouth. Master your words, let them serve truth. Beware of the anger of the mind. Master your thoughts, let them serve truth. The wise have mastered anger of the body, word, and mind.[258]

---

257 *Dhammapada,* ch. 10.

258 Ibid., ch. 17.

It is primarily the teachings of Jesus that have come to influence much of the Western world. Jesus says in Matthew 5:43–45 "Ye have heard that it hath been said, thou shall love thy neighbor, and hate thine enemy. But I say unto you, Love your enemies, bless them that curse you, do good to them that hate you, and pray for them which despitefully use you, and persecute you; that ye may be the children of your Father which is in heaven: for he maketh his sun to rise on the evil and on the good, and sendeth rain on the just and on the unjust." Jesus's teachings do not leave much room for us to ever be angry, hateful, or unforgiving of anyone!

When we awaken to the true source and meaning of our anger and its futility, we find that this awareness does not guarantee a change in the world outside of us, for anger, meanness, and attacks will go on around us. But like an eye in the hurricane of hatred swirling about us, we can see the peace at the center of residing in the wisdom of no "us and them." Here, in this awareness, when we begin to feel our anger, it becomes a beacon that signals us to move out of the quagmire of past hurts or misunderstandings and into our power in the present moment. The gift of the awakened present moment is that it is unbounded by past and future, anger and fear, and with this present we can move on to the opportunity of peace and love found in forgiveness and compassion.

Step 3: Give Yourself the Gift of Forgiveness

How do we extricate ourselves from anger? The teachings of Siddhartha Gautama, known as the Buddha, taught complete compassion for self and others as the way out of this suffering. Foremost he taught that the way out of anger was to overcome it before it arose. He taught that through discipline, one could become "a true charioteer" of one's own mind. On the other hand, Jesus's teachings emphasized forgiveness as the way out of this "pain and grief" (*ange*) of anger. Peter once asked Jesus, "Sir, how often should I forgive my brother if he keeps wronging me—up to seven times?" And Jesus said to him, "Not just seven: seventy times seven." This seventy times seven is not an actual number; according to the idiom of that time, it represented infinity. In other words, you must never stop forgiving, even if ultimately you truly must defend yourself.

Why would Jesus instruct us to unconditionally forgive and never cease from forgiving? What power does forgiveness hold for our own lives? To understand its power, again we must go to the primordial root of the word itself. Our word *forgiveness* is from the Anglo-Saxon word *forgifan*. It arose from the ancient root word *gifan*, which literally meant "to hand over without cost," as in our word *gift*, a word that also comes from *gifan*. But what kind of gift is this forgiveness?

It is the other half of the word that instructs us on this matter. In our word *forgiveness*, the prefix *for-* acts as an intensifier, denoting "*to completely* hand over without cost" without any reservations. Therefore, forgiveness is the foremost gift we can give to ourselves, as well as everyone else involved, for it is a gift that is given unconditionally. Therefore, when we forgive according to the wisdom within the words, we are to do it unconditionally, without any strings attached. We hand it over without any cost to the other or our self. Any forgiveness that has any conditions is incomplete and therefore not truly a forgiveness at all.

The Real Gift of Forgiveness

We tend to believe that forgiveness is for the recipient, but the foremost gift of all is received by the one who forgives. Why? When we refuse to forgive or conditionally forgive another, we end up holding on to resentment and bitterness. As long as we do not forgive, we are trapped in resenting the remembered act that we are angry for and ultimately hurt by. With resentment, we are doomed to feel the pain over and over again. This is what the origin of the word *resentment* meant, for it comes from the Latin *sentire,* meaning "to feel," and the prefix *re-*, meaning "again." The Latin suffix *-mentum* denoted "the act or process of," so resentment becomes an act of feeling the pain over and over again. And as we saw in chapter 19, our neurology forms a strong connection between emotional and physical pain.

When we forgive others, they simply receive our heartfelt words, whereas we who forgive receive so much more, for we get our lives back. As much as people want to make forgiveness an issue of morality, it is not; it is an issue of the conservation of your own vitality. Please recall that energy, or vitality, is the most important thing we need to heal our pain! If we choose not to forgive and we do not "completely (*for*) hand over without cost (*gifan*)," we become drained from the strain of holding on unconsciously to the painful memories through resentment. Again, as we have seen in chapter 19, through hanging on to emotional issues, we can "wind up," or sensitize, our amygdala, causing a chronic activation of our HPA axis. Through our neuroendocrine system, this HPA stress response can cause our muscles to tense and our minds to fatigue. With this we begin to actually lose our lives, draining our vitality for living drop by drop.

This physical and mental tension actually uses up great volumes of cellular ATP. Recall the detrimental effect that tissue depletion of ATP has on our health and the role it plays in generating chronic pain. Nutritional deficiencies, endotoxins, and chemical pollutants can poison our ability to produce adequate levels of cellular ATP in certain tissues, leading to pain and fatigue. Through chronic activation of the HPA axis stress response, resentment and the lack of forgiveness can poison our ability to maintain an adequate level of vitality for health. This is not a metaphor, it is an actual place where spiritual healing can make a physical difference in your health and mental well-being. The challenge is to make a truthful inventory of your hidden shadow self and honestly face the unforgiveness buried there.

The gift of our simple, heartfelt words "I forgive you" is the gift of life to us and all others involved, and therefore forgiveness is the foremost gift to give. The absolution of forgiveness is the solution to our suffering and "the pain and grief" of our suppressed fear and anger. Our word *absolution* is from the suffix *-ion*, denoting "the process of," the Latin root *solvere,* meaning "to loosen or untie," and the prefix *ab-*, denoting "from." Therefore, the absolution of forgiveness is the process of setting ourselves and others free from the binding ties of fear, anger, hatred, and bitterness. In this absolution of forgiveness, we find the "gift" of vitality that completely sets us free to truly heal once and for all!

To further the freedom gained by forgiveness, it may be helpful to practice the wisdom of amnesty, which is from the ancient Greek word *amnestia,* literally meaning "to forget a wrong" done to us. If we learn the lessons from actually living Love through the hurtful experiences of life and then forget the perceived or actual wrong done to us, we free up massive amounts of energy. All the energy it takes to hold on to the memory and the anger and resentment it creates is vitality we can now use to heal. The wisdom within forgiveness and amnesty shows us the way out of the pain and grief of anger to greater fulfillment of the Love within our lives. The words "I forgive you" can provide us with tremendous health and wellness by freeing us from draining ourselves of life's sustaining vitality, so do it now with complete honesty. What have you got to lose but some pride and pain? The wisdom within forgiveness can show you the way out of the sadness of madness to find real happiness in each moment of your life now.

Step 4: Open to the Happiness in What's Happening

When we use the word *happiness*, generally we mean the experience of joy that arises from personal conditions being met. With this, happiness becomes only a fleeting condition or circumstance outside our self, something that we must pursue and somehow grasp. Therefore, if we are unable to grasp it, we are doomed to be miserable and unhappy. Even with all the material abundance in our modern society, the dissatisfaction found in our selfish cravings only degenerates into greater pathology. The latest statistics show that 14.4% of Americans aged 12 and older use illicit drugs.[259] In 2006, the UN estimated worldwide illicit drug use to be only about 5% of the global population.[260] This means that the richest nation on Earth has an illegal drug use rate *three times* that of the rest of the world! Furthermore, the Substance Abuse and Mental Health Services Administration (SAMHSA) states that prescription drugs now play a role in one quarter of all overdose deaths in the United States.[261]

Our collective unhappiness seems only to increase as each individual goes on pursuing his or her personal happiness. According to the perennial philosophy, it is the placing of personal conditions, goals, or demands on life that brings us our suffering. Our unhappiness does not arise so much from where we stand, it comes more from not seeing the awe and wonder in where we stand. As expressed by the great Russian author Leo Tolstoy, "Happiness does not depend upon outward things, but on the way we see them."

Buddha stated in the Dhammapada that all beings seek happiness; it is our nature. Sri Ramana Maharshi is said to have been one of the greatest spiritual teachers of modern India. The world-famous psychologist Carl G. Jung, upon meeting Sri Ramana, said that he is "something quite phenomenal. In India he is the whitest spot in a white space." Sri Ramana taught "there is no happiness in any object of the world. Happiness is the very nature of the Self; happiness and Self are not different." Therefore, happiness is the true nature of the Self, which can be found everywhere, in every occasion.

---

259 Substance Abuse and Mental Health Services Administration, U.S. Department of Health and Human Services, 2005 National Survey on Drug Use and Health: Tables (Rockville, MD: Office of Applied Studies, Sept. 2006), tables 1.1a and 1.1b.

260 United Nations Office on Drugs and Crime (UNODC), *World Drug Report 2006*, vol. 1: Analysis (Vienna, Austria: UNODC, June 2006), p. 9.

261 U.S. Department of Health and Human Services, Substance Abuse and Mental Health Services Administration (SMHSA), "Mortality data from drug abuse warning network, 2002" (www.oak.smhsa.gov).

The actual origin of our word *happiness* supports the view of the perennial philosophy that the nature of the True Self is happiness, which cannot be found by setting goals. It comes from the root *hap*, "what comes to pass or occurs"—as in to *hap*-pen; the suffix *-ness*, "the state of being"; and *-y* or *-i*, meaning "full of." The original connotation of our word *happiness* is "the state of being filled with whatever occurs" in life. This would be a state without conditions, for there are no other prefixes or suffixes that modify our word *happiness*. Therefore, happiness is found in being fully present in the moment, without conditions.

Happiness is being truly in the present moment, it is being here now. Happiness is not a condition of joyous outbursts and excitement, though those feelings are many times the outcome of being happy. Happiness is the state of being filled to the brim with the wonder of each moment, with awe of life's awesomeness and awfulness. Happiness is being fully present in the adventure of what's happening. If you have ever met a person who has realized this and lives it, you know what a joy it is to be in such a person's presence.

The Gift of Being Fully Present

Happiness is a state we become, it is not goal we can pursue or possess. The question we need to then ask ourselves is, do we desire to grasp happiness or to *become* happiness? When we desire to pursue happiness, it is a sign of spiritual immaturity that leads to neverending selfish cravings, and therefore to increased pain and suffering. The truth of what happiness is—"the state of being full of what occurs"—is the True Self in its full aliveness without conditions, not clinging or pushing away, but knowing the wisdom that it is nothing and love that is everything. In our happiness uncovered in the adventure of each arriving moment, we discover the "gift" in being fully present. It is interesting to note that both uses of the word *present*, as in "gift" and as in "near at hand," come from the same Latin word *praesens*, which is from the roots *sens*, "being or existence," and *prae*, "in front of or before you." The original notion of present or presence is the "being or existence that is before you."

The greatest gift that we can give to ourselves is to be fully present and honor the "existence that is before us"—our own! It is the gift of vitality that comes neither with living in the remembered past—that is gone forever—nor in the future that never truly arrives. To be in the present is to be here, now, in the moment, where all our power to become the happiness of the True Self resides. Once we are truly present with ourselves, we can give the greatest gift to another, the present of our presence. The questions remain, though, of how we become this happiness in each moment that arises, and how we begin to reveal our true nature of happiness.

Step 5: Gratefully Bless What There Is for Being

Lao Tsu, of the Axial Age 2,600 years ago, stated:

> The sage never tries to store things up.
> The more he does for others, the more he has.
> The more one gives to others, the greater his abundance.[262]

We have probably all heard the spiritual truth expressed in "you reap what you sow." When we do give freely to others from the grace that surrounds us, we receive a harvest that is tenfold. How then do we keep ourselves open to the grace that flows about us? It is through our ability to be grateful in all things. Our word *grateful* literally means "to be full (*ful*) of grace (*gratia*)." So when we are grateful in all things, we become filled with and awaken to the grace that enfolds and supports us.

Plato said it best 2,500 years ago: "A grateful mind is a great mind which eventually attracts to itself great things." Both of our words *grateful* and *gratitude* arose from the same Latin word *gratia*, which means "love, loveliness, mercy, kindness, and thanks." This is reminiscent of the ancient Latin word for human nature or *humanitas*, meaning "loving kindness, mercy, and compassion." Could it be that we find our true human nature when we are grateful (*gratia*) and open ourselves to the grace that surrounds us? Possibly this is how a grateful mind attracts great things and we become happier and wealthier.

The Latin word *gratia* (grace) evolved from the more ancient root *ghar*, "to glow and shine." Therefore, at the primordial root of our words *grateful* and *gratitude,* lies an even deeper spiritual awareness. When we live a life of gratitude, we open our world to grace and we make our lives glow with the kindness and love that gratefulness brings. This pure attitude of gratitude is the constant activity of gift giving. We probably have all experienced the joy of giving someone a much-wanted gift, and our joy was greater than if we were receiving the gift ourselves!

---

262 *Tao Te Ching,* chapter 81.

What do we give when we live in gratitude? We give thanks; we enter into thanksgiving. Here, in unconditional thankfulness for life and all that arises from it, we open ourselves to the plenitude of kindness and love that surrounds us. In Ephesians 5:20, St. Paul said, "Give thanks always for all things," and a Christian mystic of the thirteenth century, Meister Eckhart, said, "If the only prayer you say in your whole life is 'Thank you,' that would suffice." If we are in chronic pain and wish to heal, how do we give thanks for all things always? By being mindful and remembering to notice, for when we forget to notice we slowly dis-member our life. When we are not mindful, we end up taking things for granted, and we will find in life that what we take for granted is generally taken away. But how do we become mindful and remember to notice?

We must become diligent by continually reminding our senses to notice all the blessings that surround us. Listen to W. H. Auden from his poem "Precious Five," in which he admonishes his five senses to take notice and surrender to gratitude:

> Be happy, precious five
> So long as I'm alive
> Nor try to ask me what
> You should be happy for

Auden goes on to say that he wants to roar against creation in anger for all the misery that goes on in the world, but he cannot. In his poem, Auden explains why he cannot complain; because it is useless and we are made for something greater!

> The sky would only wait
> Till all my breath was gone
> And then reiterate
> As if I wasn't there
> That singular command
> I do not understand
> Bless what there is for being
> Which has to be obeyed, for
> What else am I made for,
> Agreeing or disagreeing.[263]

---

263 *W. H. Auden Reading His Poetry* by W. H. Auden (HarperCollins Audio, 1993).

The Grateful Heart of Blessing

Jesus also gave this singular command that is so difficult to understand, for his command was not just for the "blessed events" in life but even for the painful ones. He stated, "But I say unto you, Love your enemies, bless them that curse you, do good to them that hate you, and pray for them which despitefully use you, and persecute you" (Matthew 5: 44–45).

Jesus also said something about gratefulness that has puzzled humanity for 2,000 years. It is recorded in no less than four places in the New Testament, and Jesus said it in conjunction with at least two different parables. He said, "For to him who has will more be given, and he will have abundance; but from him who has not, even what he has will be taken away." This does not seem to be the treatment of a kind and loving God, to take away what little someone has and give abundance to one who already has plenty. A cynic, however, might say that this is how our world does indeed seem to work. But if we examine Jesus's statement carefully, we will find a primary law of our universe within his riddle.

In the last part of the statement, he says "from him who has not, even what he has will be taken away." The question is, if someone has nothing, how can anything be taken away? It would seem that Jesus is saying that if we live and act as if we have nothing, then whatever we do have will be lost to us. What we take for granted will surely be taken away—maybe not always physically taken away, but it will be lost to our hearts. Ignore someone or take something for granted, and we lose all interest and joy in them or it. But when we truly take notice in life, we become nobler in the living of it! And if we recognize all that we have in gratefulness, "more will be given, and [we] will have abundance."

Some theologians have interpreted Jesus's statement as saying that "to those who know the truth, more will be given." But what, then, is this truth, other than how to live in gratitude, "be grateful in all things," and "bless what there is for being"? What, then, is this blessing that is so powerful an agent in our lives, and why would it be so transformative?

Our word *bless* comes from an ancient and fascinating origin that tells us exactly what it means to bless and be blessed. The oldest Indo-European root for our word *bless* is *blo*, "to bloom, blossom, and flourish." Within this primordial origin is the awareness and wisdom that our blessing someone or something is simply our compassionate desire for them to bloom and flourish. When we count our blessings in life and then take time to bless others, what are we actually doing? We are causing our lives and the lives of those around us to bloom, blossom, and flourish, for "him who has will more be given, and he will have abundance."

William Butler Yeats captured this in a poem he wrote about himself sitting in a coffee shop and what he experienced in simply blessing:

> While upon the shop and street I gazed
> My body of a sudden blazed,
> And twenty minutes more or less
> It seemed so great my happiness
> That I was blessed and could bless.[264]

Or, as W. H. Auden said:

> That singular command
> I do not understand
> Bless what there is for being[265]

This unconditional blessing bestowed upon life brings us into the grace of gratefulness. Blessings should not be reserved for places of worship or only for the ordained to bestow upon others. It is a powerful act with which anyone, anytime and in any place, can favor themselves or another.

What are the things in life that we bless and call blessings? When we count our blessings, what do we usually count? If we were to just count how many times someone says "bless you" to us each day, we would generally come up with zero blessings (except possibly when we sneeze). However, when we are asked to count our blessings, we tend to name those aspects or people in our lives that make us feel loved and secure, that which allows us "to bloom and blossom" (*blo*) as people. When we bless people in our lives, it is usually because we love them and wish that they feel loved and safe from harm, that they are happy and prosper.

This sense of blessing, at its root, comes from a noble and grateful heart. To be moved each and every day to bless someone or something in our lives, we must first

---

264 "Vacillation" by William Butler Yeats, on PoemHunter.com.

265 *W. H. Auden Reading His Poetry* by W. H. Auden (HarperCollins Audio, 1993).

take notice of them and not take them for granted. Taking notice is the first step in giving thanks each day for their presence in our lives. In fully giving thanks, we finally stop to think and we become mindful with gratitude. Here we arrive at Plato's law: "A grateful mind is a great mind which eventually attracts to itself great things." By having a grateful heart and giving voice to it by "blessing what there is for being," we ourselves bloom and flourish by attracting great things into our lives. And the primary thing we begin to gather unto ourself is the vitality to heal our pain.

When we are busy blessing "what there is for being," we are filled with thoughts of gratitude, and we have a grateful heart that helps us to flourish and heal; according to Plato, we bring "great things" to our grateful selves. Here we enter a beatific world, which *Webster's Dictionary* defines as "belonging to a state of bliss or happiness." How do we get to this state of bliss? The root of our word *beatific* tells us how, for it comes from the Latin word *beatus,* meaning "to be blessed." As W. H. Auden said, "for what else are we made" but to bless and be blessed, to love and be loved, and to find peace, health, and happiness in our lives? Surely we are not here to grab as many toys and products as we can, destroying our children's future and our own physical and mental well-being. With all the material products we have attained, have we made our lives any happier or our survival any more assured—or only more in question?

So how, day to day, does one begin to live these spiritual practices that can powerfully assist us in our healing? How do we know that we are truly living a spiritual life filled with gratitude and compassion? It is as straightforward as knowing if you are practicing real self-love by reading all the labels of the food you eat. Remember earlier our discussion on the importance of checking labels to see that we are putting into our body/mind nourishing whole foods without poisons—a genuine act of real self-love. It is also simple, straightforward gestures that portray a spiritual life of gratitude and compassion.

Each day I try to stay mindful, to "give thanks always for all things." I begin each day with a morning prayer of gratefulness, giving simple thanks for all my blessings and blessing all that nourishes me physically, emotionally, and spiritually. Every morning before rising, I simply take inventory of my life and give thanks. Starting with my physical ability to get out of bed and move about my world, I give thanks. Taking a moment, imagining what it would be like not to be able to walk away from my bed, I become filled with gratitude. Then, looking at my hands, I give thanks for the ability to use them to work, to create, and to love.

Continuing my prayer, I then go on to mentally journey throughout my body and give thanks for each blessing. After noticing the very wonder of simple physical capabilities, I give thanks for adequate healthy food and my ability to digest, absorb, and assimilate the needed nutrients to maintain my life. At this point, I also give thanks for my ability to detoxify and remove all wastes from my body. Then, using visualization, I imagine nutrients from the earth and oxygen from the sky uniting in my body to build and energize healthy tissues in every region of my body; this fills me with gratitude for this miracle. Sadly, I am aware that for millions of humans throughout the world, this is not possible.

Taking special notice of my "precious five," I give thanks for my eyes, ears, nose, mouth, and touch. I imagine for that moment what it would be like not to see, hear, smell, taste, or touch the exquisite beauty in this world. In that moment, I am very grateful to be able "bless what there is for being" with my "precious five." In this morning ritual, I also recognize my challenges as well as the grace that surrounds me. In the end, I realize that to experience the awe in this living, I must open-heartedly embrace life's awful as well as awesome aspects each and every day.

You can continue throughout your day to make this form of mindfulness a practical part of your life. The practice is made easier by freeing yourself through awakening to the wisdom that you are Nothing, as well as the Love found in being Everything. This letting go of the death grip we hold on our egos can allow us to give our self the greatest gift of all: the gift of forgiveness for all injuries, real and perceived. You can give yourself this gift throughout your day by giving special notice to any thoughts of anger that arise. Anytime anger arises from a past transgression that caused you pain—no matter how distant or recent an event, no matter how slight or immense it may seem—utilize it as an opportunity to practice forgiveness. And remember: if you are reacting to something in the present, it is already in the past.

To begin real healing, it is usually best and most difficult to start with those closest to you: your mother, father, siblings, aunt, uncle, neighbor, friend—anyone who has injured you, real or perceived. Again, this is not a moral imperative, but a way for you to free up massive amounts of energy for your healing. Remember: anger is not wrong, only very painful, and it is best used as a catalyst to make real, substantive change in your life.

With this newfound freedom, open to the happiness that is unfolding in what is happening around you in each present moment. In this happiness, find a beatific world and, most importantly, become "armed by compassion." As the Tao the Ching instructs us, "See the world as your Self. Have faith in the way things are. Love the world as your Self; then you can care for all things." We can accomplish this by becoming aware— aware that our American lifestyle would take more than five Earths to maintain it, if everyone was to live like us.[266] You can learn a great deal more about the impact our Western lifestyle is having on this Earth by going to www.footprintnetwork.org.

We are chewing up this Earth faster than she can renew herself. If we wish to heal on a deeper level by living a more compassionate life, we then must do what we can to relieve the suffering of others caused by how we live. We cannot "save" the Earth—the Earth does not need us to save her, for over a long-enough time, she can overcome anything we dish out. However, we do need her healthy and whole, so we must learn to compassionately share her with all humans, with all sentient beings, by doing whatever we can.

We can choose to drive a smaller, more fuel-efficient car; carpool; use mass transit; bike; or even walk. We can choose to replace the inefficient lights in our homes with efficient, compact fluorescent light bulbs, and turn off all lights when not needed. We can unplug appliances when they are not in use, for they still draw energy. We can purchase energy-efficient appliances. In addition, we can take the time to reuse and recycle everything possible. For more assistance on this, you can go to http://www.greenerchoices.org. These are all compassionate acts of love, similar to when we take the time to read all the labels on the foods we eat and feed our family. There is so much more one can do to help alleviate the suffering of this world; this is just a beginning. However, when you open your heart and become involved with engaged compassion, you open your life to real healing.

Living with a noble and grateful heart, taking the time each and every day to bless others and all that enriches our lives—these mindful acts can move us out of the unbridled greed and grasping that is destroying our children's future and our own health and peace of mind. Blessing is the most creative act we can do, for it awakens the grateful heart of our own humanity and opens us to real healing. As Yeats understood, how great is our happiness that we are blessed and can bless!

Bless you for reading my words; may they set you on the path to healing your pain.

---

266 http://news.bbc.co.uk/2/hi/science/nature/6033407.stm.

Index

BOOKS OF RELATED INTEREST FROM NAB

A COMPLETE GUIDE TO HEALING : Elements of Energy Therapies —*Ted Andrews*

With the help of this book you can take your first step towards developing your innate ability to heal. The straightforward techniques detailed here will serve to pinpoint what you can control in yourself, what you need to learn about yourself, and what you need to change to become healthier on all levels.

ISBN: 978-81-7822-119-9

AYURVEDIC SPA: Treatments for large and small spas as well as home care to help everyone become healthy, happy, and inspired --*Melanie & Robert Sachs*

***Ayurvedic Spa* offers...**

• Ayurvedic assessments to better customize treatments and help anyone select personalized beauty and body care rituals. • Detailed descriptions and photos of spa treatments. • Stress reducing exercises and meditations from the Tibetan tradition. • Guidelines on how to integrate Ayurvedic treatments into your spa and into the life of your clients, friends, or family.

ISBN: 978-81-7822-328-5

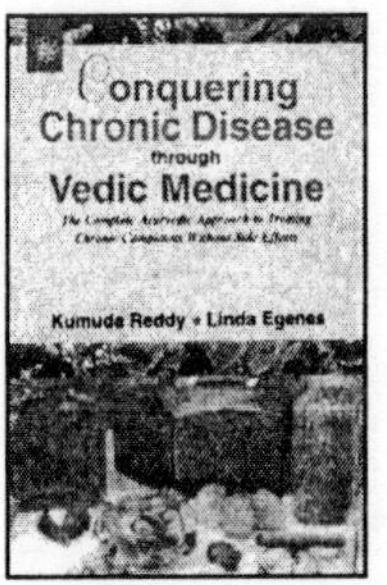

CONQUERING CHRONIC DISEASE THROUGH VEDIC MEDICINE: The Complete Ayurvedic Approach to Treating Chronic Complaints Without Side Effects —*Kumuda Reddy & Linda Egenes*

In this well-organized and thoughtful book, Dr. Kumuda Reddy presents the one current, viable option for those suffering from chronic disease: Vedic Medicine. The text is also a practical guide for health professionals who want to incorporate these principles into conventional medical practices.

ISBN: 978-81-7822-169-4

FOREVER HEALTHY: Preventing and Treating Disease through Timeless Natural Medicine — *Kumuda Reddy & Stan Kendz*

If you've ever looked for a better way, a more fundamental way to improve your health, look no further. Here age-old principles of health and healing from the Ayurveda tradition are described in clear, simple prose. As the authors explain, there is an inner intelligence within each of us that governs and co-ordinates all the life processes of the body.

ISBN: 978-81-7822-171-7

MAGNETIC HEALING: Advanced Techniques for the Application of Magnetic Forces —*Buryl Payne*

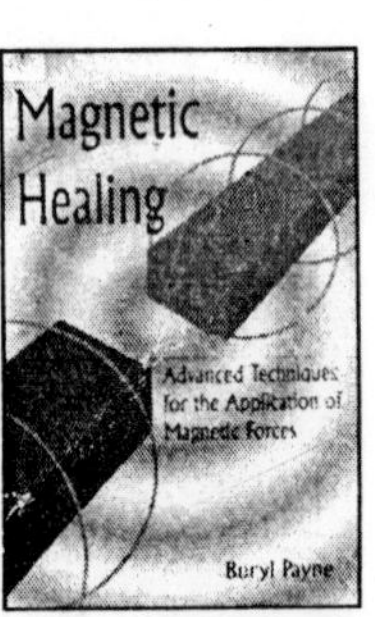

Through this book discover the positive benefits of magnetism for improving your health and well-being. This book will answer all your questions related to magnetic healing. Here you will see, how the magnetic therapy has transformed from a arcane art into a science.

ISBN: 978-81-7822-002-4

VEDIC HEALTH CARE SYSTEM: Clinical Practice of Sushrutokta Marm Chikitsa and Siravedhan —*Ram Lal Sah, Binod Kumar Joshi & Geeta Joshi*

According to Sushrut, an uninterrupted circulation of the living factor Rasa (Chinese call it Qi) is responsible for good health. The disease appears in its true form in that channel where there is an obstruction. The disease is cured if the path or speed of circulation of Rasa is revived. This Rasa is circulated in the Dhamanis. The four types of Siras responsible for the circulation of Vat, Pitta, Kaph and Rakta are almost situated at the Marmas. Stimulation of theseMarmas revives the circulation of Rasa in the Dhamanis.

ISBN: 978-81-7822-041-3